W9-CCZ-461

The Basic Business Library
Library
Core Resources

The Basic Business Library
Core Resources

Fourth Edition

Edited by Rashelle S. Karp
Bernard S. Schlessinger, Associate Editor

An Oryx Book

Greenwood Press
Westport, Connecticut • London

Library of Congress Cataloging-in-Publication Data

The basic business library : core resources.—4th ed. / edited by Rashelle S. Karp ;
Bernard S. Schlessinger, associate editor.
    p. cm.
   Includes bibliographical references and index.
   ISBN 1–57356–512–1 (alk. paper)
   1. Business libraries—United States. 2. Business—Bibliography. 3. Business—Computer
network resources. 4. Business libraries—United States—Bibliography. 5.
Business—Reference books—Bibliography. I. Karp, Rashelle S. II. Schlessinger, Bernard
S., 1930–
Z675.B8B37   2002
016.0276'9—dc21   2002025349

British Library Cataloguing in Publication Data is available.

Library of Congress Catalog Card Number: 2002025349
ISBN: 1–57356–512–1

First published in 2002

Greenwood Press, 88 Post Road West, Westport, CT 06881
An imprint of Greenwood Publishing Group, Inc.
www.greenwood.com

Printed in the United States of America

∞™

The paper used in this book complies with the
Permanent Paper Standard issued by the National
Information Standards Organization (Z39.48–1984).

10 9 8 7 6 5 4 3 2 1

Contents

Preface

Continuing the objectives of the previous three editions, the fourth edition of *The Basic Business Library: Core Resources* serves as a checklist of essential business reference tools that smaller libraries can use to evaluate their business reference collections and services, and as a core list and set of essays for smaller libraries beginning a business reference area. An additional objective, recognized after the third edition began to be used as a text for library science courses, is to serve the needs of library science professors and their students who are learning about the field of business librarianship. Also, comments received after the publication of the third edition indicated that the book was being used by larger libraries than those for which it had been intended, and that the academic library market had become as large as the original public library market. Accordingly, the core list was broadened to better reflect the market.

The fourth edition has been completely revised to reflect the dramatic changes in business reference and resources over the past seven years. When the third edition was published in 1995, the Internet and universal online access to information were just beyond the reach of most small libraries. The most dramatic change since then has been the pervasiveness of affordable Internet and online access to business information, as well as the trend toward making resources available only in digitized formats. Because of these changes, this fourth edition departs from the format of previous editions in the following ways:

- Where available, URLs have been provided for information sources.
- The resources in the core lists provide costs for the print versions and access information for online costs. Costs are not provided for online versions because of the variability in pricing that exists in the current marketplace, based on such criteria as a library's patron base, consortium membership, ability to pay, parallel print subscriptions, and on the librarian's negotiation skills.
- "Continuing Training of the Business Information Professional in the 1990s: The International View," a chapter in previous editions, has been deleted from this edition. Given the fast pace of business in the current environment, it seemed that a chapter encouraging business librarians to engage in continuing professional development was no

longer necessary, and that a listing of types of continuing
education opportunities might be redundant for our audience. Additionally, given our global environment, the
international focus of this chapter in previous editions is, of
necessity, covered in the other chapters of the new edition.

- "The Literature of Business Reference and Business Libraries," another chapter in previous editions, has been replaced
  with a bibliographic essay on business libraries. Although an
  annotated bibliography of business literature might have
  been useful, the chapter did not seem to be as helpful in
  today's age of instant and unlimited access to information
  through electronic venues. Additionally, the changing
  nature of Web sites and the inability to confidently cite the
  source of electronic articles made the editors uneasy about
  the ability of others to access the recommended sources.
- A new chapter, "Marketing the Business Library," has been
  added.

Part 1, "Core List of Printed Reference Sources," has been updated and
revised. Each title in the first three editions was reexamined and reevaluated.
Some did not have a newer edition and were dropped from the current list.
Others were important enough to retain in spite of their old publication date
(e.g., Michael Lavin's *Business Information: How to Find It, How to Use It*). A
number of titles in the current edition did not exist at the time of the last
edition so they are totally new to the list. The reverse also happened—a number of titles ceased to be published and were dropped from the list. The editors
are indebted to Ruthie Brock and Carol Byrne; their selection of titles that
reflect the changes in the economy and business culture since the last edition
resulted in a collection of 210 resources, with a total 2002 cost of $65,204.98.
Knowing that this cost might be prohibitive for smaller libraries, Ruthie and
Carol have, whenever possible, mentioned less costly alternative titles and
suggested purchasing some items biennially or as one-time purchases, in lieu
of subscription or standing order obligations. The total dollar amount for libraries with extremely tight budgets is $34,981.98 (annotations for sources
that are recommended for "budget conscious" libraries are noted with an aster-
isk at the beginning of or within the entry). The original core list, developed
in 1975 by a group of practicing librarians at a business reference workshop at
the Library School at the State University of New York (SUNY), Albany, was
priced at $5,000. By the time of the first edition of this book (1983), the 156
titles in the core list had a total assignable cost of $11,000. The 177 titles in
the core list of the second edition (1989) were priced at $29,000, and the 200
titles in the core list for the third edition (1995) cost a total of $38,000.

The 10 state-of-the-art essays in Part 2, "Business Reference Sources and Services: Essays," were totally revised by expert practitioners, most of whom are new to this edition. The senior authors remained the same for the essays on investment sources (Barbara A. Huett) and the core list of resources (Ruthie Brock). Authors new to this edition are Carol Byrne (core list), Toni P. Olshan and Stephen S. Crandall (acquisitions and collection development), Lucy Heckman (online databases), Eric Forte and Michael R. Oppenheim (government documents), Jerry Bornstein (business reference), Joseph P. Grunenwald (marketing the business library), David Miller (organization of materials), Jane Moore McGinn (business libraries), and Elizabeth C. Clarage (business periodicals). Also new to this edition are three consultants who provided additional input and review for the chapter on online databases: Basil Martin, Peggy Lynn Teich, and Marilyn Harhai. The editors are indebted to all these outstanding experts who have contributed their time and expertise for the benefit of business librarians and patrons.

The editors' combined 60 years of involvement with business librarians and business librarianship have been rewarding at all times. We hope that this fourth edition will prove to be as useful to librarians and students as the previous editions.

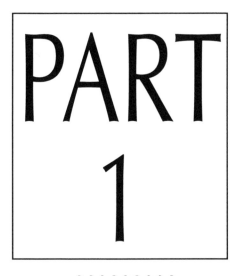

Core List of Printed Business Reference Sources

Core List

Compiled by Ruth Brock and Carol Byrne

The items included in the core list are all published in print. Publisher's Web sites are provided for more information, as well as URLs for Web versions of some of the print sources. The total cost for the list's 210 resources is $65,204.98. Because this cost might be prohibitive for smaller libraries, less costly alternative titles are suggested (when possible), and items that might be purchased biennially or as one-time purchases, in lieu of subscription or standing order obligations, are also identified. Libraries with extremely tight budgets may wish to focus their attention on the resources whose main entries are preceded with an asterisk, denoting a resource that is especially recommended for "budget conscious" libraries. The total dollar amount for the "budget conscious" resources is $34,981.98.

*1.1. **Accounting and Finance for Your Small Business.** E. James Burton and Steven M. Bragg. 2nd ed. New York: John Wiley & Sons, Inc., © 2001. $24.95.

   Authority and scope: Intended as a reference source, much like a manual, this book serves as an update for those who have business degrees and as an introduction to many business concepts for those who have not. Arranged in three sections: Preparing to Operate the Business, Operating the Business, and Evaluating the Operations of the Business, the title provides detailed information about how to run the financial and accounting operations of a company, track cash flows, conduct analyses, analyze key financial information, determine insurance requirements, and compile tax liabilities.

   Evaluation: Peppered throughout this book are examples and illustrations representing the concepts presented. Smaller and more practitioner oriented than a textbook and reasonably priced, the title is recommended for public and academic libraries.

*1.2. **Accounting and Tax Index [2002].** Ann Arbor, MI: UMI, 1992–. Quarterly, with annual cumulations. $460.00. Available on the Web through ProQuest.

   Authority and scope: This continuation, in part, of the *Accountants' Index*, which was published for 70 years (1921–1991) by the American Institute of Certified Public Accountants (AICPA) covers all aspects of accounting and taxation, as well as related subjects of financial management, compensation,

Ruth Brock and Carol Byrne are business librarians at the University of Texas at Arlington.

consulting, and the financial services industry. In addition to 300 core journals, UMI selectively indexes more than 1,000 publications to compile this index. Each entry is listed under an average of three subject headings, based on a controlled vocabulary.

Evaluation: This index fills a gap for many libraries, giving the needed coverage of the accounting literature lacking in other sources. It continues to be timely and relatively inexpensive, enabling most libraries to be able to afford it.

*1.3. Accounting Irregularities and Financial Fraud: A Corporate Governance Guide [2002]. Michael R. Young, ed. 2nd ed. New York: Aspen Law & Business, © 2002. $129.00.

Authority and scope: Previously published by Harcourt Professional Publishing, this guide is now published by a division of Aspen Publishers, a company that has existed for over 40 years and prides itself on offering practical solution-based information keyed to the latest pronouncements, legislative, judicial or regulatory developments. This is a "how-to" book on preventing fraudulent financial reporting and how to deal with the aftermath of accounting irregularities if they happen, including recommendations for restoring corporate credibility after such an event.

Evaluation: When it comes to accounting irregularities, it cannot be overstated: an ounce of prevention is worth a pound of cure. In the wake of the Enron and Arthur Anderson debacles, this book provides outside directors of corporate boards, audit committee members, senior executives, CFOs, CPAs, in-house lawyers, and outside law firms of corporations with information to avoid such crises and at worst, if faced with such a crisis, helps direct them toward the proper course of action. It is recommended for all business-oriented collections.

1.4. Acronyms, Initialisms & Abbreviations Dictionary: A Guide to Alphabetic Designations, Contractions, Acronyms, Initialisms, and Similar Condensed Appellations [2002]. Mary Rose Bonk, ed. 30th ed. Detroit, MI: Gale Group, 1960–. $805.00. Price includes interedition supplement.

Authority and scope: First published in 1960 and recognized in 1985 as one of the 25 most distinguished reference titles published during the past quarter century by the Reference and Adult Services Division of the American Library Association, this dictionary now contains a half million entries which define and clarify a wide variety of acronyms, initialisms, or abbreviations. Business-oriented entries are covered, including many company stock symbols. The acronyms are arranged in alphabetical order in a two-column format. Volume 1 is in three parts, divided alphabetically. An international version is available for $240.00. A *Reverse Acronyms, Initialisms, & Abbreviations Dictionary*, priced separately at $415.00, arranges the terms alphabetically by the meaning of the acronym, initialism, or abbreviation, allowing users to look up the full name or definition and locate the abbreviated form.

Evaluation: This is the most comprehensive resource for acronyms, abbreviations and initialisms and is recommended for all types of libraries. Most libraries would only need the main set, arranged by acronym. The international version may be of interest to selective libraries with specialized needs. The *Reverse Acronyms* set is not recommended for most libraries because the cost would seem to outweigh the benefit.

*1.5. **Advertising Age: Crain's International Newspaper of Marketing.** New York: Crain Communications. 1930–. Weekly. $119.00. Available online from Lexis Nexis and Factiva/Dow Jones Interactive. Web version: http://adage.com/

    Authority and scope: *Advertising Age* covers the current advertising and marketing scene for television, cable, radio, magazines, newspapers, the Internet and other interactive media. This long-established weekly trade publication is noted for special surveys and reports of the industry, including rankings of the most successful advertisers, media companies, agencies, marketing research organizations, and brands. Some of the statistics, rankings, and surveys are also available on the Web site, the daily online news companion to the weekly print magazine. However, stories in one do not always appear in the other.

    Evaluation: This excellent source for students and professionals following trends in advertising and marketing is a mainstay, and is recommended for business libraries and academic libraries serving business users.

*1.6. **All States Tax Handbook [2001].** New York: Research Institute of America, 1977–. Annual. $48.00.

    Authority and scope: Presented in graphic format, using charts, tables, lists, and calendars, this handbook provides comparative information for basic tax rates and structures for all 50 states and the District of Columbia. Key facts and special rules are included for income taxes, sales and use taxes, and other state taxes. Although some information in the book is provided for individual taxation, most is targeted for businesses, especially businesses that have multistate operations. A broader approach to state-by-state laws is Gale Group's **National Survey of State Laws* (4th ed., 2002) for $99.00.

    Evaluation: For businesses operating in more than one state, or for businesses moving or expanding to another state, this guide can aid in making better business decisions in the way that taxes affect the bottom line. It is recommended for medium to large public and academic libraries and for corporate libraries supporting multistate operations.

*1.7. **Almanac of Business and Industrial Financial Ratios [2002 edition].** Leo Troy. 33rd ed. Upper Saddle River, NJ: Prentice Hall, © 2001. Annual. $150.00. Price includes book and CD-ROM. Web site: http://www.phdirect.com.

    Authority and scope: The *Almanac's* data are derived from corporate activity reported to the IRS by all active corporations. The 2002 edition of this book uses financial data from the period 7/98 through 6/99, the most recent information available from the IRS at the time of publication. This edition marks the first use of the North American Industry Classification System (NAICS), replacing the former Standard Industrial Classification (SIC). This change brings with it several important differences from previous editions. It gives special attention to industries producing and furnishing advanced technologies, new and emerging industries, as well as service industries in general. Also, because of the new classification system and the addition of new industries, the 2002 *Almanac* could not match all old and new industrial classifications, and therefore discontinued the trend analysis of past issues. It does continue dividing the data into two main tables: one that includes the entire universe of active reporting companies and one that includes a subset of the universe, companies with net income. Performance results on 192 industries are given for the total industry, as well as with a breakdown by asset size, providing 50 items of data and ratios.

Evaluation: A library can rarely have "too much" information for analyzing companies and industries as evidenced by the demand from accountants, managers, financial analysts, entrepreneurs, investors, and business students in many libraries. Ratios are valuable in that they provide a benchmark for measuring financial and operating performance of competitors in the same industry. The major ratio publications approach the subject differently and derive the raw data from different sources. It is therefore advantageous to acquire all of the major ratio books, if possible, in order to provide users with several options. Titles of additional recommended sources for ratios are: Robert Morris' *Annual Statement Studies*, Dun and Bradstreet *Industry Norms and Key Business Ratios*, and *IRS Corporate Financial Ratios*.

*1.8. **American Demographics: Consumer Trends for Business Leaders.** Stamford, CT: Media Central, 1979–. Monthly. Subscription, $69.00; single copy, $4.99.

Authority and scope: *American Demographics* offers insights on how today's trends affect tomorrow's consumer markets, and brings to its readers implications of changing demographics rather than a focus on statistics per se. The successful use of colorful charts, maps, and illustrations brings statistics to life, making well-written articles based on "numbers" enticing to readers. Each issue has at least two major articles, usually a cover story and a feature article.

Evaluation: This magazine continues to be recognized as a high-quality publication, recently winning six national magazine awards. Marketing statistics become meaningful and interesting in this reader-friendly magazine. Because it reflects cultural changes as well as market trends, it is recommended for all types of general libraries as well as business-oriented libraries.

*1.9. **American Wholesalers and Distributors Directory: A Comprehensive Guide Offering Industry Details on Approximately 27,000 Wholesalers and Distributors in the United States.** Louise Gagne, ed. 11th ed. Detroit, MI: Gale Group, © 2002. $240.00.

Authority and scope: Now in its eleventh edition, this directory includes small businesses as well as large corporations who buy hundreds of thousands of products from manufacturers and then sort, assemble, grade, and store them for resale to retailers and to commercial, agricultural, governmental, and industrial users. The main arrangement is by broad subject/product lines, then alphabetically by company. Key features of each entry include contact information, principal product line information, employee figures, sales figures, e-mail addresses, and URLs (Internet addresses). The volume includes a product-line category thesaurus and also contains three indexes: the Standard Industrial Classification (SIC) index; the geographic index; and the alphabetic index.

Evaluation: Although not very "sexy," wholesalers and distributors play an important role in the United States economy. The information provided in this directory can be vital to small business owners or consumers in a community and might serve to round out a collection of business directories in a public library. Academic libraries would also want to offer it in their collection.

1.10. Annual Guide to Stocks 2002: Directory of Obsolete Securities. Jersey City, NJ: Financial Information Incorporated, 1970–. $695.00. Web site: http://www.fiinet.com.

Authority and scope: Better known as the *Directory of Obsolete Securities*, this publication is designed to identify old stock certificates, with a chronological record including the details of the final action that rendered it obsolete. The directory includes a brief profile for banks and companies whose original identities have been lost as a result of a merger, acquisition, change in name, dissolution, reorganization, bankruptcy, or charter cancellation. Each listing also includes the new name of the company (if any) and the year in which the action occurred. Whenever possible, to further complete each company's history, an indication has been made as to whether its stock has any remaining value, or if any stockholders' equity still exists. With each new edition of the directory, another year's data is added. For this volume, obsolete companies are included from 1926 to 2001.

Evaluation: Whether analyzing old stock certificates found when cleaning out Aunt Mabel's trunk, doing company research, or preparing a tax return, questions regarding the status of a company inevitably come up. The publisher of this volume is an authoritative record keeper of this kind of information and has Wall Street brokerage and investment bankers as customers. It should be purchased approximately every three years by most public and academic libraries, or more frequently if budget allows. An alternative source that can be used to determine the official status of a company that may have gone out of existence is the *Mergent Company Archives Manual* (2001, $295.00).

*1.11. Automotive News. Market Data Book [2001]. Keith E. Crain and Peter Brown, eds. Detroit, MI: Crain Communications, 1976–. $17.00. Web site: http://www.autonews.com/datacenter.cms.

Authority and scope: Available as part of the subscription to *Automotive News* or sold separately, this data book covers statistics related to cars and light trucks, many of which are of likely interest to consumers, such as specification details by make and model and prices of latest model cars, pickup trucks, minivans, vans, and sport-utility vehicles. Dealership data is also given, such as profitability ranking by new vehicle make, sales per dealership by make of car or light truck, and automotive ad spending in the United States. *Automotive News* subscribers have access to the data through the Web site above, with slightly less data available in the print edition of the *Data Book*.

Evaluation: This publication provides good value, giving detailed market information at a very reasonable price. Since coverage does not duplicate most of the content in *Ward's Motor Vehicle Facts and Figures* (Ward's Communications, 2001, $55.00), both titles can easily be justified in public and academic libraries.

*1.12. The Aviation and Aerospace Almanac [2002]. Richard Lampl. Washington, DC: Aviation Week/McGraw-Hill, 1993–. Annual. $129.00.

Authority and scope: Compiled by the editors and staff of *Aviation Daily* and *Aerospace Daily*, this almanac provides more than 1,000 pages of facts, statistics, and forecasts related to the aviation and aerospace industries. However, no narrative analyses of data are provided. Among the myriad of tables included are financial and operations details for major carriers, market share data, aviation "firsts," number of passenger arrivals into the United States country-by-country, transportation accidents by mode, passengers denied boarding (bumped), mishandled baggage reports, air travel consumer reports by complaint categories, fuel cost and consumption, United States airport runway pavement conditions, number of United States airports, average passenger revenue per passenger-mile, historical air traffic data, worldwide space launchings by site (1957–2000), rankings of airports by various categories, rankings of United States foreign trade freight gateways by value of shipments, and United States and world aviation forecasts. In addition, separate chapters for United States government agencies related to the aviation/aerospace industry serve as directories to significant personnel in those agencies. New information in this 2002 edition includes expanded information on the Chinese military and commercial industry, airport on-time analysis, regional and hub analysis, and fare analysis.

Evaluation: Business students and professionals who are analyzing the airlines, consumers who are making travel decisions, or individuals studying about the space program can all reap rewards from the enormous amount of information available in this almanac. Public, academic, and many special corporate libraries should have this title in their collection.

*1.13. Barron's How to Prepare for the Stockbrokers Exam: Series 7. Michael T. Curley and Joseph A. Walker. 2nd ed. Hauppauge, NY: Barron's Educational Series, Inc., © 2000. $16.95.

Authority and scope: This self-study guide includes a full-length test with 250 questions that closely approximate the actual Series 7 examination. Each chapter is followed by a review test, with answers provided to all questions. Detailed chapters cover the following exam subjects: corporate securities, United States government securities, money market instruments, municipal securities, direct participation programs, securities analysis, the new issue market, the over-the-counter market, and securities on margin.

Evaluation: In addition to preparing candidates for questions on the exam, this guide offers additional helpful information including the approximate number of questions in each category and the styles of questions asked. For individuals who plan to become stockbrokers, this guide takes some very complex topics and reduces them into manageable chunks, emphasizing the most important details, and using examples whenever appropriate. This book is about as "user-friendly" as a complex subject like this allows. The authors are well qualified: Michael Curley is a Member of the Board of Arbitrators, National Association of Securities Dealers, and Joseph A. Walker is a former member of the New York Stock Exchange Examination Qualification Committee. This book is recommended for public and academic libraries.

*1.14. Barron's: National Business and Financial Weekly. New York: Dow Jones, 1921–. Weekly. $145.00/yr. Web site: http://www.barrons.com/.

Authority and scope: For more than 75 years, Barron's has provided news of United States and world financial markets and in-depth analysis for investors, both amateur and professional. Articles and market week statistics cover stocks, bonds, indexes, futures, options, real estate, mutual funds, government securities, variable annuities, closed-end funds, money market funds, regulatory policies, and international markets. Interviews with successful investors and prominent corporate figures are often included. Dow Jones averages in half-hourly increments are given for each day of the previous week and stocks comprising the Dow Jones average are listed. Lipper's Mutual Fund Report is included quarterly.

Evaluation: A very detailed weekly investment publication, this tabloid is filled with interesting articles and timely statistics, and is recommended for all business-oriented libraries.

*1.15. Best Customers: Demographics of Consumer Demand. Cheryl Russell and Susan Mitchell. 2nd ed. Ithaca, NY: New Strategist Publications, Inc., © 2001. $89.95. Individual chapters or entire book can now be purchased in PDF format (requires Adobe Acrobat Reader) or Excel format at http://newstrategist.com.

Authority and scope: This second edition of *Best Customers* examines how changing demographics are reshaping the consumer marketplace. Using data from the Bureau of Labor Statistics' Consumer Expenditure Survey, household spending patterns are analyzed. The title looks at spending on 300 products and services by age of householder, household income, household type, and region of residence. It identifies which age levels or income levels, for example, spend the most on a product or service (these are identified as the "best customers") and which control the largest share of the spending (these are identified as the "biggest customers"). The products purchased by these consumers are detailed under the following categories: alcoholic beverages, apparel, computers, education, entertainment, financial products and services, food at home, food away from home, gifts, health care, household furnishings, services and supplies, personal care, reading material, shelter and utilities, tobacco products, transportation, and travel. According to the authors, three major demographic trends are reshaping consumer markets: the middle-aging of the baby-boom generation, the coming-of-age of the Millennial generation, and the growing sophistication of older Americans. Other more specialized demographically oriented titles provided by this publisher are *American Incomes: Demographics of Who Has Money* (4th ed., 2001, $89.95), *American Generations: Who They Are, How They Live, How They Think* (3rd ed., 2000, $89.95), and *Racial and Ethnic Diversity: Asians, Blacks, Hispanics, Native Americans, and Whites* (3rd ed., 2000, $94.95).

Evaluation: The information in *Best Customers* is an excellent way for entrepreneurs or business students to get spending data by specific consumer group for many specific types of products. The title has broader coverage than some of the other titles by this publisher, but the other titles should also be considered for most public and academic libraries. There is always a demand for "snapshots" of how Americans live and spend their money, and these books offer a variety of snapshots. Secondary sources such as these offer an inexpensive way for small libraries to get demographic and market data. Larger libraries should also purchase them to supplement other primary sources in their collections that may not be as user-friendly.

1.16. Best's Insurance Reports: Life-Health, Property-Casualty, and International [2002 edition]. Oldwick, NJ: A.M. Best Company, 1900–. Annual. Life-Health ed., $985.00; Property-Casualty ed., $985.00; International ed., $985.00. Web site: http://www.ambest.com/.

Authority and scope: A.M. Best Company has been providing reports and ratings on insurance companies for the better part of a century. The purpose of Best's rating system is to provide an opinion of an insurer's financial strength and ability to meet ongoing obligations to policyholders. The reports in these three editions include the well-known Best rating, both current and a five-year rating history, as well as a narrative explaining the rating rationale, financial and operating data including key financial indicators, and locations licensed to operate. Web site information for companies is provided when available. Various charts, lists and rankings are also included. For insurance industry performance analysis, large public and academic libraries may want to consider *Best's Aggregates and Averages* (*Life Health* or *Property Casualty*, 2002, $350 each).

Evaluation: The annual editions of *Best's Insurance Reports* provide substantive information to use as the basis for an analysis of an insurance company; however, they should be used in conjunction with other more frequently updated sources when there is a concern about the solvency of an insurance company. The ambest.com Web site provides updates on ratings included in the books and insurance industry news reports. As an added source or as an alternative, a competitor's publication, *Guide to Life, Health & Annuity Insurers* by Weiss Ratings, Inc. can be purchased as a subscription ($438.00 for four quarterly editions or $219.00 for one-time purchase). Larger libraries and special corporate libraries may want to have both; libraries on a smaller budget are advised to purchase the less expensive but reputable Weiss publication.

1.17. Biographical Dictionary of American Business Leaders. John N. Inghram, Westport, CT: Greenwood Press, © 1983. 3 vols. $395.00.

Authority and scope: Over 800 biographies are included in this dictionary. The entries begin with basic biographical data. The main entry section concentrates on the individuals' business achievements. A short bibliography concludes the entry. Appendixes One through Seven group the leaders by industry, company, birthplace, main location of business activity, religion, ethnicity, and year of birth. Appendix Eight lists 53 women leaders. Greenwood has also published two other titles: *Contemporary American Business Leaders* (1990, $105.00), which complements the 1983 edition by adding 150 business leaders who exemplify major American business trends from 1945 forward; and *African-American Business Leaders* (1994, $120.00), which highlights the achievements of over 120 African American business leaders. Both titles are by John N. Inghram and Lynne B. Feldman.

Evaluation: All three titles in the above description are recommended for any academic, public or corporate library, and are a must for any business-oriented library. While these titles do not include most of the business leaders since the rise of the Internet, they do provide useful biographical information on other United States business leaders who have had a significant impact in the business world. An alternative to the Greenwood Press title is a two-volume set containing over 400 biographies, *American Business Leaders: From Colonial Times to the Present*, published by ABC-Clio (1999, $175.00).

*1.18. Black's Law Dictionary. Bryan A. Garner, ed. 7th ed. St. Paul, MN: West Group, © 1999. Deluxe Thumb Index ed., $94.10; regular ed., $55.95; Pocket ed. $24.95.

Authority and scope: The seventh edition of this standard legal resource represents another major revision of the work originally created by Henry Campbell Black in 1891. More than 4,500 entries in the book are entirely new since the sixth edition was published in 1990. According to the editor, the remaining 20,000 entries have been thoroughly revised, sharpened, and tightened. More than 2,000 newly added quotations from some 400 important works of Anglo-American legal scholarship appear throughout the text to help convey the nuances of the legal vocabulary. Pronunciation guidance is provided for difficult words. For the first time, etymologies systematically appear. An appendix lists 400 works cited. Other appendices include: 2,200 legal maxims, the United States Constitution, the Universal Declaration of Human Rights, a Time Chart of the United States Supreme Court, a Federal Circuits map, and British Regnal Years.

Evaluation: An exhaustive and authoritative source, *Black's Law Dictionary* is considered to be the standard legal dictionary and should be in all public and academic libraries, as well as many specialized business libraries. This edition has been modernized to include such legal concepts as cyberstalking, parental kidnapping, and reproductive rights, among others.

*1.19. The Bond Book: Everything Investors Need to Know About Treasuries, Municipals, GNMAs, Corporates, Zeros, Bond Funds, Money Market Funds, and More. Annette Thau. 2nd ed. New York: McGraw-Hill, © 2001. $29.95.

Authority and scope: What is a bond? In the first five chapters of this book, which comprise Part One, answers to that question and other basics are covered, with no prior knowledge assumed. Part Two introduces the various types of bonds. Part Three covers bond funds, and Part Four concludes with portfolio management, which involves asset allocation and being knowledgeable enough to take advantage of changes in the levels of interest rates. The author, a former municipal bond analyst and visiting scholar at Columbia University's Graduate School of Business, saw the need for a practical source for investors to learn how to buy bonds and make them a profitable component of their investment portfolios. In this edition, information has been added to cover the newest securities, such as inflation-indexed bonds, I savings bonds, CMOs, emerging market bonds, and more. Also new to this edition is a section on using the Internet for researching and buying bonds, and a revised and expanded section on bond funds. Because the interest rate environment has changed dramatically since the earlier edition, this update is welcome.

Evaluation: In times of volatile stock markets, the bond market is often seen as a "safe haven." However, many people find bonds to be confusing, especially with the variety of new choices that have become available in recent years. This book will help individuals who are new to the bond market to understand how bonds work, how to buy and sell them, and how to select the instrument that matches their tolerance for risk. As a result, investors will likely be more informed and more comfortable with their decisions in the bond market. The title is recommended for all public and academic libraries.

1.20. Brands and Their Companies: Consumer Products and Their Manufacturers with Addresses and Phone Numbers [2002]. Linda D. Hall, ed. 24th ed. 2 vols. Detroit, MI: Gale Group, © 2002. $880.00. Price includes mid-year supplement.

Authority and scope: A primary source for consumer brand information, *Brands and Their Companies* provides linkages from more than 380,000 brands to the companies that manufacture or distribute the products. Brand names that are no longer being produced as well as those that have become generic are included. Brand listings are in alphabetical order and include the trade name, a brief description of the product, and company name. Company listings include the company name, address, phone number, fax and toll-free numbers, URLs (Internet addresses) and e-mail addresses, when available. Catalogs and directories for many of the products listed in the volumes are given in the resource listing, with contact information and catalog cost.

Evaluation: This compilation provides historical and current information about obscure as well as famous brand names. Although the publisher also produces a counterpart to this set called *Companies and Their Brands*, it is not as useful and is not recommended due to the cost.

In fact, the cost for *Brands and Their Companies* is also prohibitive for many libraries in relation to the benefit. Only libraries with sufficient budgets and demand to justify the expenditure should purchase this set. Purchasing infrequently is another way to economize for this title.

*1.21. **Broadcasting & Cable Yearbook [2002].** New Providence, NJ: R.R. Bowker, 1935–. Annual. $210.00.

Authority and scope: Useful market statistics as well as historical information are included in 10 sections: Industry Overview; Television; Cable; Radio; Satellites and Other Carriers; Programming Services; Technological Services; Brokers & Professional Services; Associations, Events, Education & Awards; Law and Regulation & Government Agencies. Television and radio stations on the Internet are given with their Web addresses. Listings are provided for low-power TV stations, Spanish-language TV stations, independent stations, digital channel assignments, and college and university stations. Stations are listed in various ways, including by state, by channel, by call letters, and by frequency. Top designated market areas (DMAs) are ranked in various ways. Data for pre-television growth of radio broadcasting, radio station growth since television, and radios sold since 1958 are given. Broadcasting and newspaper cross-owner-ship data are presented, as well as mergers in the industry.

Evaluation: For those directly or indirectly involved in the broadcasting or cable industries, virtually all sources potentially needed to do business are included, whether for equipment purchasing, programming services, law firms specializing in communications law, or talent agents. A wealth of information regarding various rules and regulations affecting the industry are given. Although geared for those active in the industry, this publication also has a generous amount of information for individuals interested in various aspects of broadcasting. It is recommended for most public and academic libraries, as well as special libraries with an interest in broadcasting.

*1.22. **Business 2.0.** San Francisco: **Business 2.0 Media, Inc.,** 1998–. Monthly. $19.99/yr. Web site: http://www.business2.com.

Authority and scope: Started in 1995, with a focus on the Internet and the new economy, this magazine changed from an earlier title to become *Business 2.0* in 1998. It has gradually broadened its content and has managed to survive in spite of a down draft in the economy and the demise of similar publications. In 2001, the magazine was purchased by Time, Inc. and the content merged with *eCompany Now*, a magazine that was not as well known. *Business 2.0* continues to have a bent toward business and technology. With its focus on how technology, and the Internet in particular, are driving changes in business, it strikes an appeal to the new generation of entrepreneurs, without losing sight of mainstream issues. The company recently named Time magazine's technology editor and managing editor of Time.com to be the editor of the *Business 2.0* magazine. *Business 2.0* has a vibrant Web site that allows simultaneous searches to be conducted in *Business 2.0*, *Fortune*, and *Money* magazines, also owned by Time, Inc., an AOL Time Warner company.

Evaluation: In the recent years since many of the dot.coms have failed, many of the magazines that covered them have also collapsed, changed their focus, or have been acquired. With Time, Inc.'s ownership clout behind the magazine now, it should survive. It is recommended for public, academic, and most corporate libraries.

*1.23. Business Information: How to Find It, How to Use It. Michael R. Lavin. 2nd ed. Westport, CT: Oryx Press, © 1992. $42.50

Authority and scope: *Business Information* combines detailed descriptions of business sources with explanations of what the featured information means, so that users who are not experts can effectively use the sources. The book is arranged in five parts with 20 chapters covering topics such as sources and forms of business information, corporate finances for private companies and public companies, basic investment information, introduction to statistical reasoning, general economic statistics, industry statistics, and more.

Evaluation: Until a new edition of this book is published, this edition is still one of the best, if not *the* best guide for business research. Individuals and librarians without business backgrounds who want to learn how to find and use appropriate business sources can benefit from Michael Lavin's expertise. It is recommended for libraries of all sizes with business collections.

*1.24. Business Plans Handbook: A Compilation of Actual Business Plans Developed by Small Businesses Throughout North America. Detroit: MI: Gale Group, 1995–. 9 vols. to date. Vol. 9, © 2002. $140.00 per vol.

Authority and scope: Each volume of this ongoing collection contains approximately 25 business plans completed by entrepreneurs seeking funding for their small businesses. Each plan represents an owner's successful explanation to a bank or funding source of why the business should exist or expand and why a lender should fund the enterprise. Plans in the book illustrate the financial data generally required of loan applicants, including income statements, balance sheets, cash flows, and financial projections. Real business plans (with fictitious names) that have been successfully funded are the criteria for inclusion. Some examples include plans for a kennel, microbrewery, gift store, hair salon, pizzeria, art glass studio, paintball sport company, and cookie and muffin shop, among others. Also included are four appendices with two business plan templates, a directory of organizations, agencies, and consultants of interest to small business owners, a glossary of small business terms, and a bibliography. A cumulative index for all business plans is now available with each new volume.

Evaluation: From business plans that are for run-of-the-mill businesses to business plans for more innovative businesses, this publication hits the mark. It is an example of the publisher listening to customers, the librarians, who wanted a reference source of this kind. When entrepreneurs were struggling to create a business plan to get financing, they did their research in the library. The librarians wanted to help them by having "models" of plans to guide them through the process. Since different types of businesses have slightly different requirements, using business plans from real businesses is a practical and helpful idea. The supplementary material provided in the volumes is also beneficial. Articles in the bibliography vary from general small business topics to articles related to specialized start-up businesses. This growing set is recommended for all public and academic libraries. Another useful and affordable title, **Anatomy of a Business Plan* by Linda Pinson (Dearborn Trade Publishing, 2001, $21.95, guides readers through the process of writing a business plan).

*1.25. Business Rankings Annual: Lists of Companies, Products, Services, and Activities Compiled from a Variety of Published Sources [2003]. Sheila M. Dow, ed. 2 vols. Detroit, MI: Gale Group, 1989–. $315.00. Each edition includes a cumulative index published separately as Volume 2.

Authority and scope: The existence of this published annual is indicative of the number of requests librarians receive about ranked information. The ranked lists are gathered from various periodicals. For each entry, this book typically provides the "top ten" along with pertinent details about the original ranking, units of measurement (such as dollars or percent), number of listees in the ranking source, and bibliographic citation of the source. URLs (Internet addresses) are also given if available. The main index gives the name of each category under which a company, product, or person is ranked. A standard industrial classification index and a conversion guide from SIC (Standard Industrial Classification) to the North American Industry Classification System are provided.

Evaluation: Americans love to know that something is the best or one of the best, hence the popularity of "top ten" lists and rankings of just about anything imaginable. The *Business Rankings Annual* is based on this concept, and reference librarians declared this book an outstanding reference source when it was first published. It is a handy source for quick and immediate answers to some questions, but for those who need the entire list or more detail from the original source, the bibliographic information is provided in order to track it down. Small libraries that cannot afford to subscribe to the wide array of specialized publications from which these rankings originate, can benefit from this compilation. Other libraries can use it as a starting point. It is recommended for all business-oriented libraries.

*1.26. Business Research Sources: A Reference Navigator. F. Patrick Butler. Boston: Irwin/McGraw-Hill, © 1999. $42.60.

Authority and scope: Intended primarily for university business students and people who are paid to make commercial decisions, this guide includes over 100 key business sources. For each chapter, the author's formula is presented in four parts: description of the publication, sample table of contents, sample pages, and recommended supplement. The first three parts are for the main publication discussed in that chapter, and the recommended supplement suggests another quality reference work that offers some excellent supporting information or otherwise unique attributes. Primary arrangement of the book includes the following sections: general business reference sources; directories, almanacs, periodicals, indexes, and encyclopedias; computer databases and vendors; statistics, demographics, and consumerism; governmental affairs and nongovernmental organizations; the organizational functions; and international references.

Evaluation: Written by a business professor, this guide is presented in a practical and friendly style, with inclusion of some basic tips for doing research. His purpose is to reduce the information overload phenomena experienced by many in our information age. This publication is not the high quality of Michael Lavin's *Business Information: How to Find It, How to Use It*, but is in the same vein and is more recent than the Lavin book discussed elsewhere in this compilation. It is recommended for libraries of all sizes with business collections.

*1.27. Business Statistics of the United States [2001]. Cornelia J. Strawser. 7th ed. Lanham, MD: Bernan Press, 1995–. $147.00.

Authority and scope: This edition of *Business Statistics* contains more than 2,000 data series covering the United States economy, including GDP, employment, production, prices, productivity, international trade, money supply, and interest rates, with historical data revisions released by government agencies fully incorporated. New to this edition is the comprehensive revision of the National Income and Product Accounts, along with quarterly and annual data for the GDP and its major components, as well as productivity measures from 1963 through 2000. Also included are data on hourly and weekly earnings for more service industries and measures of household debt-service burden. Familiar features include more than 150 basic data tables, most presenting 30 years of annual data and four years of monthly data, with additional historical data for selected series. Bernan publishes another important title, *Housing Statistics of the United States* (4th ed. 2001, $147.00), which focuses on demographics and the demand, production, and finance data related to the housing market.

Evaluation: Published for many years by the United States Commerce Department's Bureau of Economic Analysis (BEA), *Business Statistics'* last edition appeared in 1992. At that time, the BEA discontinued it, along with the maintenance of the database from which the publication was derived. Since 1995, Bernan Press has taken on the task of gathering the data from various government and private sources and publishing this work under the original title. This important compilation of statistics, which measure our collective business and economic activities, should be a core holding for all libraries.

*1.28. Business Week. New York: McGraw-Hill. 1929–. Weekly. $54.95/yr. Web version: http://www.businessweek.com/.

Authority and scope: This general business magazine has been published for more than 70 years, providing insights for the business executive in a global environment, covering new technologies, and tracking news and trends impacting an industry segment or the economy as a whole. Each issue usually has a lengthy cover story. Special features include the quarterly Mutual Fund Performance Update, the Executive Compensation Scoreboard, R&D Scoreboard, and the Industry Outlook. Periodically, company listings are highlighted, such as Business Week 1000, Business Week Global 1000, Best Small Growth Companies, and Best B-Schools.

Evaluation: Invaluable for keeping current with business trends and developments, *Business Week* is recommended for public, academic, and corporate libraries. Print subscribers get unrestricted access to online content.

*1.29. Cabell's Directory of Publishing Opportunities in [Accounting, Economics and Finance, Management, Marketing]. David W.E. Cabell and Deborah L. English, eds. 8th ed. Beaumont, TX: Cabell Publishing Company, © 2001. 4 vols. College/Library Set, $419.80. Accounting only, $89.95; Economics and

Finance only, $89.95; Management only, $149.95; Marketing only, $89.95. Web site: http://www.cabells.com/.

Authority and scope: In the eighth edition of this directory, contents of the volumes have been grouped differently than in the last edition. Accounting and marketing are now individually published, one volume each; economics and finance are together in a two-volume set; and management is published separately in a four-volume set. Journal titles that are oriented to information systems, technology, or operations research, which are not geared to disciplines covered elsewhere, tend to be included in the management set. The basic organization has remained intact. The table of contents lists the journals alphabetically, and each journal entry provides submission information including a fax number, e-mail address, and Web site; manuscript guidelines; acceptance rate; review type, process, and time; number of reviewers; circulation and price; and type of readership. Separate tables in the back arrange the journals under broad topics and provide information on type of review, number of external reviewers, and acceptance rate. Altogether, over 1,160 journals are listed in the four directories, with some overlap between the volumes for journals that are sufficiently broad in coverage or interdisciplinary. For example, *Harvard Business Review* is listed in all four sets.

Evaluation: This directory continues to be a valuable resource for professors, graduate students, and researchers in academia who are seeking appropriate places to submit journal articles. Public libraries may also have demand from practitioners who are interested in sharing their expertise by publishing an article. Some of the journals included target both academics and business people as their audience; others target one or the other. Glossy business magazines, such as *Business Week*, *Forbes*, and *Fortune* are not the focus of this directory, and are generally omitted. Librarians can also find useful information that may aid them in making decisions regarding their journal collection. Strengths of this directory include the provision of such hard-to-find information as acceptance rate, percentage of invited articles, number of reviewers, circulation information, and the explanatory material related to "refereed" articles, useful for administrators and accrediting committees. Most libraries, especially academic libraries, would want the complete set of all four directories, unless cost is a factor. The management set covers over 530 journals, the largest number in one package, while accounting has 130+, economics and finance has 350+, and marketing has 160+ titles.

1.30. Career Guide [2002]: D&B Employment Opportunities Directory. Bethlehem, PA: Dun & Bradstreet, 1984–. Annual. $510.00 for libraries. Web site: http://www.dnb.com/.

Authority and scope: Jobseekers who are recent college graduates, including those with associate degrees, as well as persons who are contemplating a job change, can use one of six arrangements in *Career Guide* to search for a new employer, with employers arranged alphabetically, geographically, by industry, by branch offices geographically, by discipline hired geographically, and by employers offering work study or internship programs. Career fields most often sought

by the employers listed are sales, marketing, management, engineering, life/physi-
cal sciences, computer science, mathematics, statistics, planning, accounting,
finance, liberal arts, and other technical and professional areas.

Evaluation: Useful information about potential employers, such as training and internal career development opportunities, company benefits, and college disciplines typically hired make up for the somewhat limited number of
employers included in this directory. Another valuable feature is that the *Career
Guide* is not limited to the for-profit sector. Numerous organizations from school
districts, universities, libraries, county government, transit authorities, and hospitals are also included. Because the policy of this publisher is to lease, not sell
its directories, this title is recommended for libraries that can budget for the
ongoing cost of yearly updates. Other libraries may want to consider *The National Job Bank* (18th ed., 2002) as a less expensive alternative that can be periodically purchased (not leased) for $425.00.

*1.31. **Competitive Intelligence: Create an Intelligent Organization and Compete to Win.** Michelle Cook and Curtis Cook. London: Kogan Page, © 2000.
$40.00.

Authority and scope: Directed to the executive or entrepreneur in today's
global economy, this book defines competitive intelligence, debunking a dozen
myths in the first chapter. The authors point out that the intelligence cycle is
the process by which raw information is acquired, gathered, transmitted, evaluated, analyzed, and made available for decision-making. Types of information
needed, sources for finding the information, and three categories of analysis
(market, industry, and company) are given. Benchmarking, technology tools
and techniques, legal and ethical considerations, and global information sources
are also covered. Finally, setting up a competitive intelligence function and pro-
tecting one's company from competitors are explained. The book concludes with
a case study of competitive intelligence at Corel Corporation. The authors are
members of the Society of Competitive Intelligence, publishers of the e-zine,
ciexperts.com, and are founding partners of an international business development and strategy firm based in Ottawa, Canada. Another excellent title with
real companies' case studies is *Proven Strategies in Competitive Intelligence: Lessons from the Trenches* (John Wiley & Sons, 2001, $39.95).

Evaluation: With the plethora of information available today, finding the
right information, and then analyzing, presenting, and using it to make strategic
decisions in a timely manner is no small feat. This book is a useful guide for
companies striving for the competitive edge. Recommended for public, academic,
and corporate libraries.

*1.32. **Complete Book of Business Schools [2002 edition].** Nedda Gilbert. New
York: Random House, Inc., 2000–. $23.00. Web site: http://www.princetonreview.
com/ and http://www.randomhouse.com.

Authority and scope: Admission officers, recruiters, and business school
grads were interviewed to provide "the real scoop" on b-school to potential business students in this *Princeton Review* guide. Included is "how to get in," with
explanations on how admissions criteria are weighted, and advice on "writing

your way into business school with essays that work." The book indicates what top admissions committees are looking for, and gives examples of the best essays submitted to the top schools. Profiles of 246 business schools give basic information regarding degrees offered, facilities available, study abroad options, statistics about students, expenses and financial aid options, admissions information, and employment information. Some universities have supplemented their profiles with their own catalog pages. The book concludes with indexes by university, b-school, and location.

Evaluation: Written in a casual style, this guide provides useful tips for those who need help in the competitive world of business school admissions. It is recommended for both public and academic libraries. Programs described are all accredited by AACSB International—The Association to Advance Collegiate Schools of Business.

*1.33. **The Complete Handbook of Business Meetings.** Eli Mina. New York, NY: AMACOM, American Management Association, © 2000. $29.95. Available electronically through netLibrary.

Authority and scope: The author presents ideas that are intended for meeting chairs, meeting attendees, CEOs, and staff so that meetings held by an organization will be more productive and lead to better decisions. Pros and cons of three collective decision-making models are given: autocratic, majority-based, and consensus. Other specifics offered include facilitating a contentious meeting, taking minutes of meetings, choosing virtual meetings as an alternative to face-to-face meetings, and applying common sense to parliamentary procedure and rules of order. Common meeting ailments are discussed and remedies are presented in the final chapter devoted to "troubleshooting."

Evaluation: In spite of the fact that the author holds the designations of professional registered parliamentarian (PRP) and certified professional parliamentarian (CRP), this handbook offers a user-friendly approach to conducting meetings for all types of organizations. For example, phrases such as "I propose to close debate," instead of "I call the question" and "I propose that we postpone this decision until the next meeting," instead of "I move to table," are advocated. With a commonsense approach such as this, perhaps more individuals would willingly serve as chairs of boards and committees. This title is recommended for all libraries.

1.34. **Consultants & Consulting Organizations Directory [2001].** Julie Mitchell, ed., 24th ed. Detroit, MI: Gale Group, 2001. $810.00.

Authority and scope: Designed to unite businesses, government agencies, institutions, and individuals with the experts who can aid them in some aspect of doing their business, this edition of the directory lists over 25,000 consulting firms and independent consultants throughout the United States and Canada. Arranged in 14 subject sections, entries are numbered and are referenced in three indexes: geographic, consulting activities, and consulting firms. Entries include most of the following information: firm or individual's name, contact information, Web site address(es), and company and/or personal e-mail addresses.

Additionally, the directory includes a description of consulting activities, including areas of expertise and special services offered, with emphasis on unique or proprietary, geographic areas served, recent publications or videos produced, titles of seminars, programs presented by members of the organization, and branch office information. The subjects for consultant organizations fall into the broad categories of business and industry, science and technology, environment and agriculture, or social services and human welfare, with more detailed subdivisions under each.

Evaluation: Following an important and helpful trend, the publisher has increased the number of e-mail and Web site addresses included to aid in contacting consultants and accessing their data. This directory is one of the major directories for consultants and is recommended for all but the smallest academic and public libraries.

*1.35. **Corporate Directory of United States Public Companies** [2002]. San Mateo, CA: Walker's Research, LLC, 1989–. Annual. $360.00. Web site: http://www.walkersresearch.com/.

Authority and scope: The *Corporate Directory* provides company profiles of more than 11,000 publicly traded companies in the United States, including 1,200 foreign companies filing American Depository Receipts (ADRs). In addition to general information and five years of sales/income/earnings per share data, the publication presents balance sheet data, business descriptions, and stock data such as exchange, ticker symbol, recent price, outstanding shares and shareholders, and shares held by officers and directors. Names and titles (and ages and compensation, when available) for officers and directors are given, as are names of individuals, businesses, or family groups that own substantial portions of company stock. Major subsidiaries are also listed. Information has been compiled from corporate documents filed with the United States Securities and Exchange Commission (SEC) and other related company resources. Company Web sites are given whenever possible. A total of eight indexes are available, including company name, subsidiary/parent, geographic (by state, then zip code), Standard Industrial Classification (SIC), officers and directors, owners, stock exchange/ticker, and the Fortune 1000.

Evaluation: This annual publication is ideal for small libraries that cannot subscribe to more expensive services for company information. The content provides more than the minimum directory type of information, and the numerous indexes offer a variety of ways to find what is needed. For the cost, these features enhance the value immensely by addressing the needs of different kinds of users. One drawback is that the January publication date limits most financial information to a whole year prior, since most companies have fiscal year endings in December with a later SEC filing date. Companies with year endings earlier than December, however, have more current financial data in the directory.

*1.36. **Cost of Living Index.** Arlington, VA: ACCRA, 1968–. Quarterly. $140.00/yr. Single copies, $65. Web site: http://www.accra.org/.

Authority and scope: Started in 1968 by ACCRA, a nonprofit organization originally founded as the American Chamber of Commerce Researchers Association, this quarterly reference source compares living costs among urban areas. Each issue includes more than 300 cities. The data are presented in two sections. In the first section, an urban area index shows a composite index and six component indexes (grocery items, housing, utilities, transportation, health care, and miscellaneous goods and services) for each place listed. The composite index for each city is measured against a benchmark of 100. The result indicates a cost of living less than or greater than the average of all participating cities. The *Index* reflects cost differentials among cities for a mid-management standard of living, set by a weighting structure, and is not intended to measure inflation. In the second section, average prices are reported for 59 items for each participating location. The 59 items fall throughout the six categories listed above but include such things as a can of tuna, a gallon of regular unleaded gasoline, the dry-cleaning cost of a man's two-piece suit, and a full-price movie ticket, as well as the cost of a hospital room and a visit to the dentist. After the final listing for average prices of the 59 items for each urban area, the second section presents the median, average, standard deviation, and range for each item.

Evaluation: A handy publication to aid the decision-making process of relocating a family or a business, or for other decisions where comparative locally specific cost-of-living data are needed, this source is recommended for large public and academic libraries, as well as corporate libraries. Budget-conscious libraries can purchase a single issue from time to time. For inflation data, users are also steered to the United States Bureau of Labor Statistics at www.bls.gov. The United States government does include the ACCRA cost of living data in its publication, *Statistical Abstract of the United States*.

*1.37. County and City Extra, 2001: Annual Metro, City and County Data Book. Deirdre A. Gaquin and Katherine A. DeBrandt, eds. 10th ed. Lanham, MD: Bernan Press, 1992–. $120.00. County and City Extra: Special Decennial Census Edition. Lanham, MD: Bernan Press, © 2002. $95.00. Web site: http://www.bernan.com/.

Authority and scope: This annual publication provides up-to-date statistical information for congressional districts, state, county, and metropolitan areas with a population of 25,000 or more. The latest population estimates, as well as current statistics on education, employment and unemployment, vital statistics, health resources, production by industry, crime, city government finances, and distribution of federal funds are included in five main tables. County, city, metropolitan, and congressional district rankings precede the main table sections. Table A presents state data; Table B contains state and county data; Table C covers the metropolitan area; Table D presents city data; and Table E contains the congressional district data. The appendices include geographic concepts and codes, metropolitan statistical areas and components, maps of states and congressional districts, cities by counties, source notes, and explanations.

Evaluation: The publication cycle of the annual version of *County and City Extra* is being changed to a fall release beginning in 2002. The *Decennial Census Edition* covers population and housing statistics only, not the broader coverage of the annual publication. With 80 percent of its content derived from information that is gathered once every ten years, the *Decennial* volume is an important basic resource. These Bernan publications are reliable and authoritative sources for statistical information, and are recommended for all libraries.

1.38. **Craighead's International Business, Travel and Relocation Guide to 84 Countries. [2002].** 11th ed., White Plains, NY: Monstermoving.com, Inc., 4 vols. $750.00. Web site: http://www.monstermoving.com; http://www.galegroup.com.

Authority and scope: Sporting a redesigned single-column layout, this four-volume set is arranged alphabetically by country with each country report including key facts about the country, what to take and what not to take if moving to that country, general geographic and climatological information, history, customs, etiquette and protocols, selecting a school, how to locate housing, and information related to social life. Country reports are approximately 30 to 40 pages in length. Two appendices have been added. One called "Essentials of Relocation," covers health issues, housing, insurance, and motor vehicles. The other offers close to 200 Internet addresses with useful information for the international business person.

Evaluation: This comprehensive travel and relocation guide provides a practical resource for information for living abroad. Individuals planning to relocate, take a business trip, or vacation in a foreign country will find the information in Craighead's set extremely valuable, as it addresses differences in day-to-day matters that any newcomers, but Americans in particular, would prefer to know in advance. Using Craighead's prior to foreign travel will undoubtedly make for fewer surprises and a more enjoyable experience, regardless of whether the visit is to a developed or developing location. This is an excellent tool for any library to own, however small libraries may find the cost prohibitive. The *World Cost of Living Survey* (1999, $265.00) is a possible substitute for small libraries.

*1.39. **CRB Commodity Yearbook [2002].** Bridge Information Systems. New York: John Wiley & Sons, 1939–. Annual. $99.95. CD-ROM $195.00.

Authority and scope: Drawn from a variety of sources, this annual volume compiles data related to over 100 commodities. Each commodity entry begins with a narrative overview, describing the origin of the commodity in the United States and other countries, followed typically by a description of supply and demand, production and consumption, and other facts, including comparative year-to-year statistics. Factors which have influenced prices of some commodities, such as droughts, wars, diseases, or politics are included, as they may do so again in the future. Several pages of tables and charts with data on 10-year price, production, shipment, volume, contracts, exports, and/or imports follow the narrative section, depending on the commodity.

Evaluation: A long-standing and reliable source of data on commodities such as grain, metals, heating oil, eggs, pork bellies, diamonds, interest rates, and stock index futures, this is now copyrighted by Bridge Commodity Research Bureau, a division of Bridge Information Systems and published by John Wiley & Sons. The responsibility for the publication has evolved, but it has remained a consistent and informative specialized guide, and belongs in all business-oriented libraries except the smallest public libraries.

*1.40. **D&B Regional Business Directory [2002].** Bethlehem, PA: Dun & Bradstreet, 1989–. Annual. 3 vols. $540.00. Web site: http://www.dnb.com/.

Authority and scope: The information for D&B's 54 regional directories has been developed by combining Standard Metropolitan Statistical Areas (SMSAs) with additional surrounding counties that have been determined to have a related economic impact (Economic Area Indicators or EAIs). The result is intended to be a more inclusive and accurate representation of a local economy. Establishments to be included are then limited by the publisher to those with the largest number of employees. Retail establishments have been limited to the top 3,000 stores. Each business description includes address, telephone number, description of primary line of business, primary and secondary four-digit SIC codes, number of employees at the location, total employees, annual sales (except for branch locations), status (headquarters, branch or single-location), parent company name, up to 10 key officers, year founded, and indication of public ownership with stock exchange and stock symbol. The main section is arranged geographically by city and by zip code within each city. An alphabetically arranged cross-reference index and an SIC code section contain brief records with page references to the main entry. Top 1,000 business rankings, both by sales and by employee size, are included in volume one.

Evaluation: Dun & Bradstreet practices directory "leasing" rather than ownership, which is problematic for some libraries, either philosophically or financially. Nevertheless, business-oriented libraries in the regions covered will want to have this important information, as it is useful for business-to-business marketing, job seekers, fundraisers, and those assessing the local business community. As of the 2002 edition, Dun & Bradstreet had not switched to the North American Industry Classification System (NAICS) to replace SIC codes.

*1.41. **Datapedia of the United States 1790-2005.** George Thomas Kurian, ed. 2nd ed. Lanham, MD: Bernan, © 2001. $125.00. Web site: http://www.bernan. com.

Authority and scope: *Datapedia* collates historical data from a selection of social, economic, political indicators and cultural developments nationwide. It updates the *Historical Statistics of the United States, Colonial Times to 1970*. The book's 23 subject areas are patterned after the *Historical Statistics* volume for convenient comparison and cross-referencing. Table numbers were also coordinated for easier comparisons. Each subject chapter begins with a brief narrative documenting some of the major events and pattern shifts that have occurred. Graphs and charts demonstrate some of the most important changes visually. The remaining chapter contains numerical time series data relevant to the subject area. Every table cites the source publication at the base of the table. Some of the selected subjects include population, energy, government, health, housing, and transportation. Projections to 2010 are included whenever possible. For example the 2000 census indicates there are 34.7 million senior citizens in the United States. That number is expected to be 39.4 million by 2010, an increase of 4.7 million senior citizens. The source list and index complete the volume.

Evaluation: Students and researchers alike will want to use *Datapedia* for its expansive time series data and the convenience it offers by having an immense amount of data together in one place. When considered as a companion to the earlier *Historical* volume, the researcher will appreciate the continuity of table numbers for data continuity between the two sources. *Datapedia* is recommended for academic and public libraries.

*1.42. **Dictionary of Business Terms.** Jack P. Friedman, ed. 3rd ed. Hauppauge, NY: Barron's Educational Series, Inc., © 2000. $13.95. Web site: http://www. barronseduc.com/.

Authority and scope: This compact, general-purpose business dictionary includes definitions of more than 7,500 terms, including examples of how the terms are used and multiple definitions in some cases. Definitions are brief and include cross-references to terms defined elsewhere in the book, identified by capital letters.

Evaluation: This dictionary is well done and useful for a wide range of business terminology. It should be available in public, academic, and business-oriented libraries. The present edition has been changed to be in tune with changes in the business world. For example, it includes a definition for "at sign" and illustrates the definition with the @ symbol, explaining that it is used in pricing (e.g., 3 items @ $1 each), but is now more common in e-mail addresses. Another unique take is for the word "Word," which is defined as a popular word processing application.

*1.43. **Dictionary of International Business Terms.** John J. Capela and Stephen W. Hartman. 2nd ed. Hauppauge, NY: Barron's Educational Series, Inc., © 2000. $13.95. Web site: http://www.barronseduc.com/.

Authority and scope: Definitions of over 4,200 international business terms and 400 internet terms are included in this dictionary, covering the international dimensions of accounting, business policy and strategy, information systems and technology, marketing, management, finance, and trade. Extensive appendices provide abbreviations and acronyms, United States government trade-related offices, United States and foreign chambers of commerce, international organizations, a multilingual reference table, measurement conversions, and a listing of international business resources available on the Web.

Evaluation: The small size of this book and others like it in the Barron's business guide series make them handy for quick look-ups. Managers, entrepreneurs, and students alike will find this dictionary helpful in understanding terminology used in the international marketplace. It is recommended for public and academic libraries, as well as corporate libraries supporting international and Internet commerce.

*1.44. Dictionary of Marketing Terms. Jane Imber. 3rd ed. Hauppauge, NY: Barron's, © 2000. $12.95. Web site: http://www.barronseduc.com/.

Authority and scope: More than 4,000 marketing terms and definitions are included in this dictionary. Up-to-date definitions for consumer marketing, e-commerce, advertising art, copy, production, radio and TV advertising, media analysis retail, direct mail, relationship marketing, business-to-business promotion, and more are included. Examples give a working knowledge of the terms. Abbreviations and acronyms are included in an appendix.

Evaluation: Published as one of Barron's business guides, this handy dictionary is packed with definitions of marketing terms. Public, academic, and special business libraries should include this book in their collections.

1.45. Directories in Print: A Descriptive Guide to Print and Non-Print Directories, Buyer's Guides, Rosters and Other Address Lists of All Kinds [2002]. Amy L. Darga, ed. 21st ed. Detroit, MI: Gale Group, 1980–. 2 vols. $425.00. With mid-year supplement, $545.00.

Authority and scope: This annotated guide lists approximately 15,500 national and international directories, and has been expanded to include directories of U.S., state, cities, and local scope. Each entry describes up to 29 points of information, such as contact information (e-mail and Web addresses, fax and 800 numbers), brief description, price, frequency, latest edition, editor, whether ads are accepted, circulation, former titles, ISSN, order information, online information, and alternative formats. Entries are grouped into 26 broad categories. *Directories in Print* offers three indexes: an alternate formats index, subject index, and title/keyword index. A supplement is published between main editions.

Evaluation: A very useful feature of this directory of directories is information on the status of defunct and out-of-print directories. Another useful element is inclusion of a few publications that are not true directories, which are listed because users might expect them to be included. That it has previously been selected as an "Outstanding Reference Source" by the Reference and Adult Services Division of the American Library Association is testament to its quality. It is recommended for larger business, academic, and public libraries and can be used for collection development to enhance the reference collection, as well as identifying specialized sources for referral.

*1.46. Directory of American Firms Operating in Foreign Countries [2001]. 16th ed. Uniworld Business Publications, Inc., 1956–. 3 vols. $325.00. CD-ROM $975.00. Web site: http://www.uniworldbp.com/.

Authority and scope: Published for 45 years, this directory has been the authoritative source of information on American firms with foreign affiliates. It lists 2,600 United States parent companies with 34,500 foreign subsidiaries, affiliates or branches in 190 countries. Volume 1 lists American companies alphabetically, providing United States address, principal product or service, number of employees, countries in which affiliates are located, and names of the CEO, person in charge of foreign operations, and human resources director. Volumes 2 and 3 list foreign operations by country, giving the local address, telephone, fax number, and principle products or services. A companion volume, *Directory of Foreign Firms Operating in the United States* (11th ed., © 2002, $250.00), lists approximately 2,800 foreign business firms in 79 countries that own or have substantially invested in business in the United States.

Evaluation: Indicative of the increased globalization of business, the number of subsidiaries and affiliates of United States companies has grown from 18,000 in the fourteenth edition to nearly 35,000 in this edition. Ironically, parent company numbers have remained fairly even, since new companies have emerged, but others have gone out of existence, largely through mergers and acquisitions. The information in this directory is vital for international job seekers as well as for businesses who are looking to expand internationally. The *Directory* would be more useful to job seekers with foreign language skills if it had a geographic index with lists of foreign firms in specific cities. Nevertheless, all but the smallest academic and public libraries should purchase the main set. Larger libraries should consider both sets.

1.47. The Directory of Corporate Affiliations: Who Owns Whom [2002]. New Providence, NJ: LexisNexis Group, 1969–. 6 vols. $1,399.00 CD-ROM, $1,995.00, with quarterly updates. Web Subscription, $1,795.00. Web site: http://corporateaffiliations.com/.

Authority and scope: *The Directory of Corporate Affiliations* is a comprehensive resource listing more than 170,000 major public and private businesses in the United States and throughout the world, showing corporate linkages to affiliates, subsidiaries, and divisions to the eighth level of corporate reportage. General criteria for inclusion are that domestic companies have revenues over $10 million, substantial assets or net worth, or a work force in excess of 300 persons. Non-U.S. based corporations must demonstrate revenues in excess of $50 million. Organization is by location of the parent company, with all subsidiaries of the parent, no matter where they are located, found together under the parent company. Companies headquartered in the United States have been further divided into public and private volumes. Volumes I and II are the master indexes which provide access by company name, brand name, geographic location for U.S., geographic location for non-U.S., SIC (industry), and corporate responsibilities. Volumes III and IV contain the public companies (parent companies, subsidiaries, divisions, and affiliates), Volume V contains private companies, and Volume VI contains international companies. Entries typically include addresses, phone/fax numbers, e-mail addresses and Web sites, year founded, stock exchange with ticker (if public), assets, liabilities, estimate of annual revenue and earnings, number of employees, ownership percentage, key personnel, and a description of the business with SIC codes. Each volume has "new listings" and "mergers, acquisitions, and name changes" sections. The international volume also includes foreign consulates, United States embassies, American and foreign chambers of commerce, major international public holidays, foreign exchange rates, and international telephone information. Contact details for outside service firms, such as auditors, legal firms, or transfer agents are provided and when available, counts of domestic and international offices and plants.

Evaluation: This six-volume set is recommended for major business collections, whether in academic or public libraries. In this ever-changing world of business ownership, it is useful to have a reliable source that will answer most of the questions related to corporate structure. Updated content is added to the Web version weekly. For a smaller or mid-size library, this directory is quite expensive, but it would be a core holding, if the library could afford it. If not, *The Corporate Directory of U.S. Public Companies* is an excellent alternative at roughly one fourth of the cost (Walkers Research, 2002, $360.00).

*1.48. Directory of Executive Recruiters [2002]. 31st ed. Kennedy Information, LLC, compiler. Fitzwilliam, NH: Kennedy Information, 1971–. Annual. $47.95. Web site: http://www.kennedyinformation.com/.

Authority and scope: In the 31tst edition of this directory, more than 5,700 search firms are included and cross-indexed by management function, geography, and industry. Over 14,000 key recruiters and their areas of specialty are also identified. Each listing gives a mailing address for the firm's main office, and phone, fax, and wWeb addresses. Also included is a general description, functional and industry areas covered by the firm, minimum salary for positions handled by the firm, memberships, and branch office contacts and specialties. In addition to United States recruiting firms, the guide also lists Canadian and Mexican executive recruiting firms. An affiliated fee-based Web site, www.ExecutiveAgent.com/, is available for resume submission to targeted recruiters in the Executive Recruiter database.

Evaluation: A useful and unique feature of this directory is its inclusion of both retained and contingency search firms. Both types of search firms charge the client employer a fee, not the prospective employee; however, contingency recruiters are more often used for junior and mid-level executives, typically for positions with salaries below $70,000. This directory is affordable and is recommended for mid-size and large public and academic libraries. An expanded hardbound corporate edition is recommended for business libraries of firms that utilize executive search services.

1.49. Directory of Mail Order Catalogs: A Comprehensive Guide to Consumer Mail Order Catalog Companies [2002]. Richard Gottlieb, ed. 16th ed. Millerton, NY: Grey House Publishing, 1981–. Annual. $250.00. Internet subscription is available. Web site: http://www.greyhouse.com/.

Authority and scope: The sixteenth edition of this directory provides information on close to 12,000 mail order companies and the catalogs they produce. The catalogs produced by these companies are listed in 44 specific industries. In addition, there are four indexes: a catalog and company name index in one alphabetical listing; a geographic index arranged by state; a product index; and a Web sites index arranged by product category. Each entry provides names of executive personnel and buyers; listings of credit cards accepted; cost of the catalog, if any; frequency of mailings; average order size; printing details of the catalog; mailing list information, including whether names may be rented; years in business; and sales estimates, as well as the usual company name and address information, toll-free numbers, fax numbers, and Web addresses. Fifty-five percent of the listings have Web site information. The publisher also offers a *Directory of Business to Business Catalogs*.

Evaluation: Despite competition from online shopping on the Web, the catalog industry has continued to grow. This directory reflects an addition of 1,500 new catalog companies. Business collections in major public libraries and business libraries supporting marketing and direct mail activities should own this directory, and perhaps the *Business to Business* version.

1.50. Directory of U.S. Importers. Newark, NJ: Commonwealth Business Media, Inc. © 2002. $475.00 with free e-index. Purchased with the Directory of U.S. Exporters the cost is $675.00 with free e-index. Web site: http://www.pierspub.com/.

Authority and scope: This comprehensive directory lists all U.S. importers, imported products classified by Harmonized Commodity codes, and information from the U.S. Commerce Department on customs regulations and procedures governing imports. Arranged alphabetically by company with each state, the entries include the address, officers, number of employees, date of establishment, bank reference, ports of entry and products imported. Supplemental sections list both U.S. and foreign consulates and embassies, banks that provide import assistance, associations, trade commissions, foreign trade zones, and world ports. With its companion volume, the Directory of United States Exporters provides parallel information for export companies.

Evaluation: With increased internationalization of trade, both directories are recommend for large academic and public libraries whose community is actively engaged in the import/export operations.

*1.51. Doing Business Guides: [Country]. New York: PricewaterhouseCoopers, 1961–. $34.95. (single issue) Web site: http://www.pwcglobal.com/.

Authority and scope: These country-specific guides are published for more than 80 countries in which PricewaterhouseCoopers firms operate or have established offices. The popular guide series is updated periodically. Each guide focuses on the investment climate of a particular country. Important facts are given about the country, including local customs, living standards, cultural and economic information, business environment, and opportunities for trade and foreign investment. The structure of the banking system is covered as well as labor relations information. In addition, information about accounting, audit requirements and practices, the tax system, and tax treaties are provided. Appendixes vary by country and may cover tax rebates, accounting and legal advisors, checklists, or other pertinent information. This and Pricewaterhouse Coopers' *Guide for Businessmen and Investors* are guides designed to expedite planning and investment decisions.

Evaluation: The information provided in the *Doing Business Guides* is important for any business that is considering operating or trading with one of the foreign countries covered in this series. The series is recommended for business-oriented, public, and academic libraries that have patrons interested in international business information.

*1.52. Doing Business in Mexico: A Practical Guide. Gus Gordon and Thurmon Williams. New York: Haworth Press, Inc., © 2002. $49.95.

Authority and scope: One author, Gus Gordon, is a CPA and a professor who has provided consulting services to companies, including small businesses and maquiladoras. The other author, Thurman Williams, is a former CEO and Chairman of Sears de Mexico and also works as a consultant for large companies. The information they have compiled is designed for entrepreneurs, managers, and investors who are considering doing business in Mexico. They point out important technical differences between doing business in the United States and Mexico regarding legal, accounting, and tax issues. They also discuss differences in business and social protocol between our two countries. One chapter includes a primer on foreign currency risk. Also, a glossary of financial terms is included, with both English-Spanish and Spanish-English versions.

Evaluation: This small book is less than 150 pages, and should be considered a starting place for someone considering an international business venture in Mexico. The book includes basic information needed to start a business, or to import or export, but its primary value comes with the knowledge these authors have gained and the practical advice given. Drawing from their own experiences, they share what they've learned, so that others may benefit and be fully cognizant of both the opportunities and the risks. This book is recommended for libraries with international business clientele.

*1.53. Economic Census. U.S. Bureau of the Census. Washington, DC: Government Printing Office, 1929–. Quinquennial. Some reports are free, others are print-on-demand in the $25–50 range on the Census Web site. Census Web site: http://www.census.gov/epcd/www/econ97.html; Government Printing Office Bookstore Web site: http://gpo.bookstore.gov.

Authority and scope: The economic census is taken every five years during years ending in two or seven to determine how many business establishments there are in different industries, and to ascertain trends from the national to the local level. Major changes have taken place with the Economic Census for 1997. For the first time, most data were collected using the North American Industry Classification System, with only limited reports using the Standard Industrial Classification. The new classification is used by Canada and Mexico as part of the NAFTA Agreement and serves to update the SIC system to include new industries that didn't exist when the previous system was developed. Distribution of the Economic Census has also changed. For the first time, most reports were issued only in an electronic format. Summary reports were the only reports issued in a print format for the 1997 economic census.

Evaluation: This snapshot of the United States economy is eagerly anticipated every five years and many commercial publications derive their data from these United States government sources. Some published reports can be purchased through the U.S. Government Printing Office online bookstore.

*1.54. Economic Indicators Handbook: Time Series, Conversions, Documentation. Arsen J. Darnay, ed. and compiler. 6th ed. Detroit, MI: Gale Group, © 2002. $195.00. Web site: http://www.galegroup.com/.

Authority and scope: Now in its sixth edition, this handbook presents key statistical series commonly used to measure the economy of the United States. Statistics are shown for the earliest date available: 1869 for the GNP, 1913 for CPI, and the 1940s for most business cycle indicators. Each major category is introduced with brief explanations, including an indication of significance. Recent changes by the Bureau of Labor Statistics for the Consumer Price Index (CPI) metro area series, included dropping the entertainment category in favor of the education and communication category, and dropping one metro area. National Income and Product Account (NIPA) data reflect the most recent benchmark changes. A relatively new measurement of national accounts involves the calculation of chain-type indexes. An explanation of what these are and how they work is presented in the introduction, as well as information on other statistical conventions. A keyword index to the topics covered in the text and tables is provided.

Evaluation: Economic indicators selected for this handbook are those most widely reported in the press, and thus thought to be most in demand. The CPI data for 26 metro areas continues to make up the dominant portion of the book. Budget-conscious librarians in smaller libraries may want to consider *Guide to Economic Indicators* by Norman Frumkin (3rd ed. M.E. Sharpe, 2000) for $25.95. The breadth and depth of the data in the Gale book are lacking, but the basic features of more than 70 statistical measures of the United States economy are explained and presented. Larger libraries may want to have both.

*1.55. Economic Report of the President. Transmitted to the Congress together with the Annual Report of the Council of Economic Advisers. February 2002. U.S. Council of Economic Advisers. Washington, DC: Government Printing Office, 1947–. Annual. $29.00. Web site: http://www.access.gpo.gov/eop/index.html.

Authority and scope: This publication of the Council of Economic Advisers presents the administration's domestic and international economic policies, from the administration's point of view. This edition is the first Economic Report of the George W. Bush presidency. The publication traditionally pulls together a variety of facts and statistics related to the state of the nation, which are normally published in a variety of sources, and uses tables, charts, and graphs to illustrate much of the data. Two appendices are included: a Report to the President on the Activities of the Council of Economic Advisers During 2001, and statistical tables relating to income, employment, and production, which include a variety of tables relating to GDP (e.g., 1959–2001 and GDP by industry 1959–2000). The Council also has primary responsibility for compiling the monthly Economic Indicators, issued by the Joint Economic Committee of the Congress (see Web site http://www.access.gpo.gov/congress/cong002.html).

Evaluation: The narrative and statistics in this report are presented in a way that makes a complex subject less intimidating than in most tomes dealing with economics. The data throughout, and especially in appendix B, is extensive and most tables can also be downloaded in spreadsheet format from the web. This report is of interest to students of business and political science, economists, historians, and to citizens interested in an overview of the nation's economy; the source is recommended for all public and academic libraries.

*1.56. Economist. London: The Economist. 1843–. Weekly. Combined print and Web subscription, $125.00; Web subscription only, $59.00; Web site: http://www.economist.com/.

Authority and scope: Published for more than one-and-a-half centuries, this news magazine reports on and analyzes various aspects of the world economic and political scene with both brief and feature-length articles, often focusing on political leaders who are newsmakers of the week. In addition to the emphasis on events in specific countries or regions, regular sections cover science and technology, books and arts, and business. Some articles poke fun or are tongue-in-cheek. The last few pages of each issue are devoted to economic indicators and financial indicators for 15 industrial countries, and emerging market indicators for 25 countries. The Web edition of the *Economist* includes additional countries.

Evaluation: Considered an essential and respected source for international news, the *Economist* is recommended for all business, academic, and larger public libraries. Print subscribers get added value through access to the Web version, which includes all premium content and archived material back to 1997.

*1.57. Editor and Publisher Market Guide [2002]. David Maddux, ed. 78th ed. New York: Editor & Publisher, 1924–. Annual. $145.00. $495.00 includes book and CD-ROM. Web site: http://www.editorandpublisher.com.

Authority and scope: Published as a guide to newspaper markets, this publication includes a significant amount of demographic data. Facts and figures are provided for over 1,600 cities, which describe the local area in regard to highways, distances to other major population centers, vital local industries, freight carriers, rail and bus and air service, population, number of households, banking information, passenger autos registered, electric meters, gas meters, employees by industry, paydays, average weekly salary, minimum and maximum temperatures for all four seasons, tap water ph data, mineral content and fluoridation, principal shopping centers, retail outlet discount stores, chain stores, auto dealerships, military installations, colleges and universities (with enrollment data), and newspapers published, including contact information. This edition of the guide includes tables that show state-by-state, MSA-by-MSA and county/city census and 2001/2006 forecast data for various demographic and economic data, such as age and ethnicity. A "better living index" provides ranking tables that compare cost-of-living information, crime data, and education statistics by city. A special section with retail sales and forecasts by retail category is provided, as is a section with Canadian market data. Also included are maps with MSAs, CMSAs, county boundaries, county seats, and locations of cities publishing a daily newspaper.

Evaluation: Whether sizing up a potential market or choosing a place to relocate, this publication has good information to compare the possibilities. Its ease of use, moderate price, and valuable demographic data warrant purchase by public and academic libraries.

*1.58. Emerson's Directory of Leading United States Accounting Firms [2000-2001]. 6th ed. Bellevue, WA: The Emerson Company, 1988–. Biennial. $195.00. Web site: http://www.emersoncompany.com/.

Authority and scope: As its title implies, the coverage in this directory focuses on the largest accounting firms in the nation. Profiles of selected firms highlight such facts as the founding date, firm leaders by functional area, primary industry segment served, consulting services offered, and a narrative of the firm's history. The directory offers a variety of other ways to learn about the top 500 accounting firms: an alphabetical listing; a ranked list by number of employees; a geographical arrangement by state and city; firms with multiple offices by state by primary industry segments served and by primary consulting services offered; firm leaders by functional area; top 500 firm leaders alphabetically; and selected firm Internet addresses.

Evaluation: This directory provides a much-needed service for information about accounting firms, since information about them is more difficult to find than that for publicly traded companies. The publisher has responded to feedback from purchasers of the directory who have indicated a preference for more information about fewer firms than what the earlier versions of the directory provided. Access is free, but somewhat limited at the Web site. The directory is recommended for all libraries that serve business users.

*1.59. Encyclopedia of American Industries [2001]. Rebecca Marlow-Ferguson, ed. 3rd ed. Detroit, MI: Gale Group, © 2001. $560.00.

Authority and scope: In two volumes, the third edition of this encyclopedia covers every industry recognized by the United States Standardized Industrial Classification (SIC) system, including 459 manufacturing industries and 545 service and non-manufacturing industries. Each entry also includes the corresponding North American Industry Classification System (NAICS). Conversion tables between SIC and NAICS are provided. Sections of coverage in an essay include some of the following: an industry snapshot, organization and structure, background and development, current conditions, industry leaders, workforce, the global marketplace, research and technology, and further reading.

Evaluation: As an alternative to the Standard and Poor's subscription-based product, *Industry Surveys*, the Gale Group's publication can be purchased each time a new edition comes out, rather than on a subscription basis, which may be an advantage to some smaller libraries. The consequence of publishing updates less frequently is that the information in the *Encyclopedia of American Industries* is not as timely. Nevertheless, the reference tool is filled with detailed background and development information concerning the industry, as well as interesting facts and trends, identification of the key players in the industry, labor issues, and market production and demand information. Many libraries will want to have both publishers' products, because of the demand for industry information, but the decision would be based on budgetary concerns.

1.60. Encyclopedia of Associations: National Organizations of the United States [2002]. Tara E. Sheets, ed. 38th ed. Detroit, MI: Gale Group, 1956–. Annual. Volume 1 (in three parts): National Organizations of the U.S., $560.00. Volume 2: Geographic and Executive Indexes, $440.00. Volume 3: Supplement, $470.00. Also available on CD-ROM, and GaleNet. Web site: http://www.galegroup.com/.

Authority and scope: This comprehensive reference source is a classified directory of more than 23,000 trade and professional associations; social welfare, religious, and public affairs organizations; labor unions; fraternal and patriotic organizations; hobby groups; and fan clubs. Details provided for each group include name, address, e-mail, phone number, fax, Web site, founding date, acronyms, chief officer, membership total, purpose and activities of the group, staff size, special committees, budget, computerized services, former names, dates of meetings, and publications issued. Editions for regional and international organizations are also published.

Evaluation: This is an indispensable reference tool for all public and academic libraries. Annual purchase of volume one is recommended. Purchase of both volumes one and two are recommended for large libraries only. Libraries should only purchase volume three when semiannual updates are important; otherwise, it can be excluded. Budget-conscious libraries may want to consider *National Trade and Professional Associations of the United States* (2002, $149.00) as an alternative.

*1.61. Encyclopedia of Busine$$ and Finance. Burton S. Kaliski, ed. New York: Macmillan Reference USA, © 2001. 2 vols. $250.00. Web site: http://www.galegroup.com/macmillan/.

Authority and scope: This two-volume set contains more than 300 entries covering major business areas such as accounting, finance, information systems, and management. Articles vary in length, depth, and quality, with bibliographic information included at the end of the article entry. Articles are alphabetically arranged, with in-depth cross-referencing available for many entries. The career entries provide job descriptions, responsibilities, educational requirements, career opportunities, and organizational contact information.

Evaluation: *Encyclopedia of Business and Finance* is an excellent resource for individuals whether writing a research paper on inventory control or seeking career-related information. Recommended for public and academic libraries.

*1.62. **Encyclopedia of Business Letters, Fax Memos and E-mail.** Robert W. Bly. Franklin Lakes, NJ: Career Press, © 1999. $18.99. Web site: http://www. careerpress.com/.

Authority and scope: In today's business world, communication is as important as ever; there are just more choices than there used to be. The author of this book operates on the premise that readers of correspondence don't have time to read long letters. This handbook provides guidance on when to use each form of communication, provides rules to do it most effectively, and suggests 12 quick tips for better business writing. In addition, several hundred model letters are included to cover a wide range of situations, including employment-related letters, letters to colleagues, sales letters, letters to customers, direct marketing letters, and credit and collection letters.

Evaluation: The author provides on-the-mark material, gives excellent examples, offers models for all sides of issues in more than one style or tone, and gives a list of pointers to include when customizing a letter for each situation. Recommended for all libraries.

*1.63. **Encyclopedia of Careers and Vocational Guidance.** Holli R. Cosgrove, ed., 11th ed. Chicago, IL: Ferguson Publishing Company, © 2000. 4 vols. $159.95. CD-ROM single edition: $159.95; Networked edition: $269.95. Web site: http://www.fergpubco.com/.

Authority and scope: This encyclopedia has been in print for more than 25 years, bringing together information gathered from companies, associations, organizations, individuals and government sources about various careers and occupations. In volume one, there are 91 articles related to career fields (formerly the industry profiles section). Career articles, now totaling 684, are found in volumes two, three, and four, where individual job descriptions are fully defined. Volume one includes other features, such as career guidance related to preparing for a career, finding a job, applying for a job, and being hired, with subtopics ranging from assessment tests to information interviewing and Web sites related to salary and job offer negotiation. In addition, volume one includes an appendix for career resources and associations for individuals with disabilities, and an appendix for information on internships, apprenticeships, and training programs. Volume one concludes with four classification schemes that refer to specific chapters and pages where the career field or job title is covered, and a master list of job titles. The four classification schemes included are: Dictionary of Occupational Titles (DOT), Guide for Occupational Exploration (GOE), National Occupational Classification System (NOC—Canadian), and O*Net (U.S. Department of Labor).

Evaluation: This career guide will assist a range of people from high school students to adults changing careers. Some of the new features, such as inclusion of cross-references throughout the text, quick reference articles for topics which don't fit elsewhere, inclusion of sidebars which have interesting or valuable factual information, and the addition of hundreds of e-mail and Web addresses have increased the usability and value of the resource. Because the career fields included have a wide range of minimum requirements, the guide is recommended for public and academic libraries of all sizes.

*1.64. **Encyclopedia of Emerging Industries.** Susan J. Cindric, ed. 4th ed. Detroit, MI: Gale Group, © 2000. $305.00. Web site: http://www.galegroup.com/.

Authority and scope: The fourth edition describes the formation, growth, and current status of 118 up-and-coming industries and industry segments in the United States. Graphs, charts, and tables are included to illustrate sales figures, market share, industry growth rates, and historical trends. Some photos are also included. Each essay begins with an industry snapshot, and includes the organization and structure, background and development, pioneers in the field, current conditions, industry leaders, America and the world, and further reading.

Evaluation: This publication fills a void, reflecting the many changes going on in the economy. In some cases, featured industries are offshoots of older, well-established industries, but are a faster growing segment. Examples of some of the industries covered are computer security, cryonics, digital mapping, health spas, extreme sports, and XML (extensible markup language). The *Encyclopedia* is recommended for public as well as academic libraries. Budget conscious librarians may need to choose between this title and the *Encyclopedia of American Industries*, also published by Gale Group.

*1.65. **Encyclopedia of Major Marketing Campaigns.** Thomas Riggs, ed. Detroit, MI: Gale Group, © 2000. $275.00. Web site: http://www.galegroup.com/.

Authority and scope: Profiles of 500 marketing campaigns of the twentieth century are provided. Each entry includes a campaign overview and the historical context needed to understand it, the target market, the competitors and frequently even the competitors' campaigns, the strategy used, the outcome, and any awards won. A list of sources for further reading is given at the end of each entry. Sidebars discuss related topics to help in understanding the campaign, brand, product, or company. Four hundred photographs illustrate campaigns and products. Indexes provide access by subject (using phrases and concepts of the advertising/marketing industry), and by general terms, which name specific brands, products, people, awards, and agencies. The main arrangement is alphabetical by the name of the company for which the ad campaign was carried out.

Evaluation: This book can take the reader down memory lane, or can provide the reader with entertainment and a marketing education that will in itself be memorable. It partially depends on the age of the reader. Most of the campaigns covered occurred after the 1950s, with some earlier. Some campaigns are contemporary, such as the "Got Milk?" campaign. One of the best books in the field to come along, it should be in all libraries, because of easy reading and because its value is not limited to business clientele.

*1.66. Encyclopedia of Management. Marilyn M. Helms, ed. 4th ed. Detroit, MI: Gale Group, © 2000. $250.00. Web site: http://www.galegroup.com/.

   Authority and scope: *Encyclopedia of Management* is a collection of approximately 350 signed essays by recognized authorities in the field of business. The alphabetical arrangement allows for a quick response to a reference query. Each essay entry includes a definition, background information, current practices, and future trends, plus a selection of further reading suggestions. Tables, charts, graphs, and formulas are included with many of the essays. The encyclopedia provides a section entitled "Guide to Functional-Area Readings" in which the essay subjects are arranged into 16 functional categories, including general management, marketing management and marketing research, production and operations management, and performance measures and assessment. The category arrangement provides the user with a preselected reading program.

   Evaluation: This single-volume encyclopedia contains a wealth of current business terminology, valuable for individuals interested in business management. Business students will find the "Guide to Functional-Area Readings" most beneficial. *Encyclopedia of Management* is recommended for medium to large academic or public libraries with business specializations. Small libraries may find the cost prohibitive.

*1.67. *Encyclopedia of Small Business.* 2nd ed. Detroit, MI: Gale Group, © 2002. 2 vols. $425.00. Web site: http://www.galegroup.com.

   Authority and scope: This two-volume set contains more than 575 essays on a variety of business topics of interest to the small business owner or entrepreneur. The topical essays arranged alphabetically discuss such topics as business start-up, employee compensation, financial planning, Internet commerce, tax planning and more. Cross-references direct the reader to related topics and bibliographic citations provide additional resource information. The master index at the end of volume two adds to the accessibility of the set.

   Evaluation: *Encyclopedia of Small Business* contains a wealth of valuable information for anyone interested in starting, owning or operating a small business. Gale indicates "updates are planned for every four years." This could be problematic with the current economic environment. The *Encyclopedia* is recommended for academic and public libraries.

*1.68. Encyclopedia of the US Census. Margo J. Anderson, ed. Washington, DC: CQ Press, 2000. $140.00. Web site: http://www.cqpress.com/.

   Authority and scope: The *Encyclopedia of the US Census* is a compilation of essays alphabetically arranged by topic. Census-taking techniques and concepts are discussed, along with the historical and political aspects of the census. The volume includes over 120 essays written by census experts, scholars, and professionals on such topics as census mechanics, questionnaire preparations, census-taking process, and return of the census questionnaire. Other essays discuss demographic information retrieval, how to get access to census data, snapshots of the decennial censuses starting with the 1790 census, and legal and privacy issues of the census. Cross-references and bibliographies accompany the signed essays. Charts, maps, tables, and figures accompany many of the essays. The appendix includes a chronology, growth and cost figures, a glossary, and census Web site addresses. A detailed index directs the researcher to the needed information quickly.

Evaluation: *Encyclopedia of the US Census* was developed as a reference source for illuminating the process and history of gathering census information. Public and academic libraries should include this informative book in their reference collections.

*1.69. **Ernst & Young's Personal Financial Planning Guide.** Robert J. Garner, Robert B. Coplan, Martin Nissenbaum, Barbara J. Raasch, and Charles L. Ratner. Special Tax Edition. New York: John Wiley & Sons, © 2001. $19.95. Web site: http://www.wiley.com/.

Authority and scope: Using the expertise of the Ernst & Young personal financial and tax planning specialists, this book has been published as a guide for individuals to assess their own personal financial situation, to determine their financial strengths and weaknesses, and to take control of planning for their future. To accomplish this, the book has been divided into two parts. Part I concentrates on the fundamentals of financial planning and Part II focuses on financial planning as it pertains to specific life events, such as getting married, being a single parent, buying and selling a home, funding a college education, losing a spouse or life partner, and starting your own business. This edition incorporates tax law changes from the Economic Growth and Tax Relief Reconciliation Act of 2001.

Evaluation: Getting started on a financial plan is an important but difficult thing for many people to do. This book is organized to make it as painless as possible, with the key advice being "just do it!" The source is useful either for individuals who want to do their own financial planning or for those who want to prepare before meeting with a professional financial planner. Recommended for public libraries.

*1.70. **The Etiquette Advantage in Business: Personal Skills for Professional Success.** Peggy Post and Peter Post. New York, NY: HarperCollins Publishers, Inc., © 1999. $35.00.

Authority and scope: Written by members of the current generation of etiquette experts from the Emily Post family, this book covers a gambit of etiquette information for the home office worker to the overseas traveler. Chapter topics include employment preparations, office protocol, business attire (formal and informal), executive etiquette, external etiquette (proper forms of address and business travel), introductions (conversation and telephone), business meetings, correspondence (electronic and paper), business entertainment (formal and informal), and social life and customs for the international traveller.

Evaluation: The *Etiquette Advantage* provides a basic course in manners for individuals who have never had the chance or opportunity to learn the fundamentals of good behavior or who simply need to brush up on what is expected in situations that are more formal than typically experienced in the day-to-day work environment. Recommended for all business-oriented libraries.

1.71. Eurojargon. Anne Ramsay. Chicago, IL: Fitzroy Dearborn Publishers, © 2000. 6th ed. $45.00.

Authority and scope: *Eurojargon* is a dictionary filled with over 4,000 abbreviations, acronyms and sobriquests (special names). The terms are those used throughout the European Union (EU) to identify projects, schemes, and agencies as a way to prevent translation issues. The terms are filed in a letter-by-letter alphabetical system. "See" references, addresses, and internet addresses are provided when appropriate. For more in-depth treatment of issues related to the European Union, Fitzroy Dearborn has published *The European Handbook*, Jackie Gower, ed. (2nd ed., 2002, $55.00).

Evaluation: Business professionals partnering with European companies or countries needing to understand the specialized terminology in order to have the most productive projects and meetings will benefit from this book. For academic and public libraries whose business community is engaged in international business, this dictionary should fill that need.

*1.72. Europa World Year Book [2001]. 42nd ed. London: Europa Publications Limited, 1926–. Annual. 2 vols. $815.00.

Authority and scope: Published annually since 1926, this directory of politics, economics, commerce, and social conditions for nations of the world contains information arranged by country within four categories: an overview of recent history, government, defense, economic affairs, social welfare, and education; statistics, including national accounts, external trade, currency and exchange rates, and social indicators; constitution and form of government; and a directory of key government officials, political organizations, diplomatic representatives, judges of major courts, churches, major newspapers, magazines, radio and television stations (sometimes with their editorial slant), publishers, banks, stock exchanges, trade associations, utilities, tourism, and transportation agencies. Space is given to a country as is necessary for coverage (e.g., the entry for Chad is 16 pages long while the one for Germany is 42 pages). The first 360+ pages of the first volume are devoted to extensive coverage of the United Nations, its related agencies and bodies and 60 other major international and regional organizations, as well as 1,000 brief entries describing other international organizations in various subject areas providing pertinent details and contact information.

Evaluation: Updated annually, this title provides relatively current, authoritative, and useful information. *Europa World Year Book* is recommended for all but the smallest public and academic libraries.

1.73. F & S Index, United States [2002]. Detroit, MI: Gale Group, 1960–. Monthly with quarterly and annual cumulations. 4 vols. Annual. $1350.00. Web site: http://www.galegroup.com/.

Authority and scope: *F & S Index* (formerly known as *Predicasts F & S Index, United States.*) provides a compilation of company, product, and industry information from more than 750 financial publications, business-oriented newspapers, special reports, and trade magazines. Each entry provides a brief one-line description of the article contents, a standardized abbreviation for cited publications, and the date and page numbers for the article. Volume one, Industries & Products, uses a modified seven-digit SIC product code to organize, by industry, articles on new products, market data, plant capacities, equipment expenditures and technologies. Within product codes, articles are further classified under subheadings such as Government and Society, Management Procedures, Market Information, Organizations and Institutions, and People. General economic information is also included. Volume two provides articles accessed by company name. Companies are arranged alphabetically and topics covered include mergers and acquisitions, corporate announcements, profits, and sales information. *F&S Index Europe* and *F&S Index International* are companion services.

Evaluation: *F&S Index, United States* can provide outstanding access to companies, their products, and the industries they comprise and is recommended for business collections in large academic and public libraries. Libraries with international business interests should consider purchasing all three indices.

*1.74. The Facts on File Dictionary of Biotechnology and Genetic Engineering. Mark L. Steinberg and Sharon D. Cosloy. New ed. New York: Checkmark Books, © 2001. $29.95.

Authority and scope: Written by two researchers at the RCMI research facility at the City College of New York, this dictionary includes basic as well as technical terminology in a number of areas. When technical terms are used within a definition, the authors have defined them elsewhere in the book. This new edition takes into account recent discoveries of molecular mechanisms that regulate both normal and abnormal cell growths as well as recent advances, in molecular terms, of the causes and cures of genetically determined diseases. Appendices include acronyms and other abbreviations; The Chemical Elements; The Genetic Code; Purine and Pyrimidine Bases Found in Nucleic Acids; and Side Chains (R Groups) for Individual Amino Acids.

Evaluation: In recent years, much of the research in biotechnology and genetic engineering has moved from the academic world into the industrial setting where the development of new products has proceeded explosively, carrying with it a need to understand the new terminology. This guide can benefit students, lawyers, and physicians, as well as employees and others trying to keep abreast of this rapidly changing field, and is recommended for all libraries with business collections.

*1.75. **Federal Reserve Bulletin.** Washington, DC: Publications Services, United States Board of Governors of the Federal Reserve System, 1915–. Monthly. $25.00/yr. Web site: http://www.federalreserve.gov/pubs/bulletin/default.htm.

Authority and scope: The official publication of the Federal Reserve Board, the *Bulletin* presents the Board's reports and testimony to Congress on monetary and economic issues, announcements, policy actions of the Federal Open Market Committee, legal developments, reports on foreign exchange operations, information on the 12 Federal Reserve Banks, and descriptions of publications that are available. The Financial and Business Statistics section contains current statistics such as money supply, interest rates, reserves, mortgages, and consumer credit. Many statistics are available in more detail in the Statistical Release publications of the Federal Reserve System.

Evaluation: Some articles in the *Bulletin* are technical and geared toward other economists and analysts while others are written for an audience with less financial expertise. Considering its affordable cost and range of readability, all but the smallest public and academic libraries should purchase this title.

*1.76. **Financial and Strategic Management for Nonprofit Organizations.** Herrington J. Bryce. 3rd ed. San Francisco: Jossey-Bass Publishers, © 2000. $60.00. Web site: http://www.josseybass.com.

Authority and scope: *Financial and Strategic Management for Nonprofit Organizations* is an essential handbook for nonprofit leaders. This comprehensive resource covers key accounting, financial, legal, and managerial issues that face the nonprofit manager. The book is organized into five parts with a total of nineteen chapters that cover such topics as the fundamentals of nonprofit laws, fundraising, budgeting, strategic planning, compensation and more. Chapter one covers the "fundamental pillars of nonprofit management," the basic concepts a nonprofit leader must master in order to manage successfully. Chapters are independent of one another with cross-referencing to related topics. A variety of appendixes include sample documents such as a draft letter awarding tax-exempt status and the unified registration statement for charitable organizations and more. The notes section references the resources chapter by chapter.

Evaluation: *Financial and Strategic Management for Nonprofit Organizations* is an essential reference tool for the nonprofit executive. Individuals who are involved in the nonprofit sector for the first time in almost any capacity will also benefit from the breadth of information that is covered. This inexpensive volume is recommended for all academic and public libraries.

*1.77. **Financial Studies of the Small Business [2001–2002].** Karen Goodman, ed., 24th ed. Winter Haven, FL: Financial Research Associates, 1976–. Annual. $104.00. Web site: http://www.frafssb.com/.

Authority and scope: Figures from 30,000 financial statements supplied by 1,500 certified public accounting firms were used to develop financial ratios for the small business (capitalization under $1,000,000). Analysis is provided for 70 types of businesses, including retail firms, wholesalers, service firms, contractors, professional services, and manufacturers. Examples range from gift shops to nursing homes to dental practitioners. Each entry presents a composite balance sheet and income statement followed by 16 ratios. Appendices provide ratios based on sales volume, ratios for the 25 percent most profitable businesses, and the five-year trend for each business.

Evaluation: Because it provides information not easily found for small firms at a reasonable price, this publication is highly recommended for any library in which there is an interest in small business and local economic development.

*1.78. Forbes.** New York: Forbes, Inc., 1917–. Biweekly. $59.95. Web site: http://www.forbes.com/.

Authority and scope: Available since 1917, *Forbes* has articles related to current happenings in the world of business. Geared to executives, managers, and investors, it covers specific companies, industries, the economy, technology, business personalities, and investment news. It also offers a variety of special issues with rankings (such as "Private 500" company rankings), or "best of" stories (such as "Best of the Web"). Two supplements are included: *Forbes FYI* and *Forbes ASAP*.

Evaluation: This magazine draws the reader in with its catchy article titles and colorful look. As one of the best for business news, it is recommended for all libraries with business clientele.

*1.79. Fortune.** New York: Time, Inc., 1930–. Biweekly, $66.87. Web site: http://www.fortune.com/.

Authority and scope: Published since 1930, *Fortune* magazine covers business-related trends and events, including technology, the environment, investing, and international business. Famous for its rankings of companies, domestic and global, the most anticipated of which, the "Fortune 500" list, is usually published each April or May. *Best Companies to Work For*, *Fastest Growing Companies*, and *Most Admired Companies* are some others.

Evaluation: A mainstay and an outstanding general business magazine, *Fortune* is recommended for all libraries.

*1.80. The [2002] Franchise Annual: The Original Franchise Handbook and Directory.** Ted Dixon and Lisa Carpenter, eds. 33rd ed. Lewiston, NY: INFO Press, 1969–. Annual. $39.95. Web site: http://www.infonews.com/.

Authority and scope: The 33rd edition of this directory includes 5,052 franchises, including over 200 that are new. Of the franchises included, 3,175 are American listings, 1,338 are Canadian, and 539 are overseas. The introductory information covers laws and regulations governing franchises, as well as other guidelines for prospective franchisees to follow. Contact information for related associations worldwide is also provided. American franchises are listed in the main directory and are grouped by type of franchise, followed by other countries' listings, also grouped by type of franchise. A master index arranged by franchise name concludes the book. A Web site offers recent excerpts from the *INFO Franchise Newsletter* and the *Franchise Annual Directory*.

Evaluation: This well-established directory, including a large number of franchises, is reasonably priced, and is a recommended purchase for all public and academic libraries.

*1.81. Fraser's Canadian Trade Directory [2002]. Toronto, ON: Rogers Publishing, Ltd., 1913–. Annual. 4 vols. $130.00 (in US$). For both print and CD-ROM, $155.00 (US$). Web site: http://www.frasers.com/.

Authority and scope: Fraser's directory is Canada's equivalent to the U.S.'s *Thomas Register*. It includes more than 40,000 suppliers of industrial products and services, more than 80,000 branch offices, and approximately 30,000 product and service categories. Volumes one through three list products in a classified arrangement and include an index to the classifications. Volume four has sections for reproductions of catalogs, company profiles, trade names, and companies foreign to Canada with representatives or distributors in the country. The print and CD-ROM versions include some information that is not available on the Web site: contact names and titles, full product line descriptions, full trade/brand name descriptions, number of employees, and year established. The Web site, with limited information, is available free with registration.

Evaluation: In light of trade agreements between the United States and Canada, this directory is potentially useful to business clientele in the United States who may be looking for a trading partner. Large public and academic libraries should update this title annually. Smaller libraries may choose to purchase the directory on an alternating year basis.

1.82. Gale Directory of Databases [2002]. Mark Faerber, ed. Detroit, MI: Gale Group, 1993–. Volume 1, Online Databases, $280.00. Volume 2, CD-ROM, Diskette, Magnetic Tape, Handheld and Batch Access Database Products, $185.00. Also available on GaleNet. Web site: http://www.galegroup.com/.

Authority and scope: This directory provides detailed descriptions and contact information for more than 12,500 databases available online throughout the world. Volume one contains profiles of online databases made publicly available from the producer or an online service. Volume two contains profiles of database products offered in various portable formats (such as CD-ROM and diskettes) and through batch processing. Each volume is arranged by three sections of descriptive entries and a geographic index, a subject index, and a master index. Among the data included are rates for online charges, conditions of access, type of database, scope and subject coverage, online availability, alternative formats, language, time span covered, and first year available. Symbols alert the reader when an item is a new listing or when significant changes have been made to an existing listing.

Evaluation: Comprehensive and up to date, this directory is especially recommended for corporate libraries, but is useful for large academic libraries as well.

*1.83. Gale Directory of Publications and Broadcast Media: An Annual Guide to Publications and Broadcasting Stations, Including Newspapers, Magazines, Journals, Radio Stations, Television Stations, and Cable Systems [2002]. Jeff

Sumner, ed. 136th ed. Detroit, MI: Gale Group, 1869–. 5 vols. $745.00, includes a free update midway between editions. Also available on GaleNet. Web site: http://www.galegroup.com/.

    Authority and scope: Published since 1869, this source for media information now has 54,000 entries, covering radio, television, and cable stations and systems, in addition to newspapers, magazines, journals, and other periodicals. The set has expanded to five volumes. The first two volumes include the main entries, which are arranged by state and city, with all media listed for each location. Each publication entry contains a description, founding date, frequency, printing method, key personnel, ISSN, cost, ad rates, e-mail, Web address if available, and circulation figures. Broadcast listings include call letters and frequency/channel or cable company name, operating hours, key personnel, wattage, e-mail addresses, and format, as well as area of dominant influence. Volume three provides a master index by name of publication, station, or system; an array of indexes which lead the user to titles by specialty group such as ethnic publications, college publications, religious publications, women's publications, or trade, technical, and professional publications; radio stations by format; newspapers by type and by newspaper feature editors, for a total of 21 indexes. Media industry statistics are also included in volume three. Volume four features a regional market index and volume five includes entries from Albania to Zimbabwe, international maps, and an international master index. More than 13,400 international television, radio, and print entries are now included.

    Evaluation: One of the best-known and respected directories of its kind, this reference is recommended for libraries serving media practitioners and journalism students, as well as the general public. The inclusion of ad rates, often needed by small business owners or journalism students, is a useful feature.

*1.84. Gale Encyclopedia of United States Economic History. Thomas Carson, ed. Detroit, MI: Gale Group, © 1999. 2 vols. $55.00. Web site: http://www. galegroup.com/.

    Authority and scope: Alphabetically arranged, this encyclopedia offers a variety of types of entries selected by a board of university and high school teachers and librarians. It contains era overviews, which help readers identify the major long-term economic changes within each era; issues, which discuss controversial topics and policies; geographical coverage, which provide economic histories of states as well as the original colonies; key events and movements, which delve into the causes and effects of major developments; biographies, which emphasize the importance of humans; historic business and industry profiles, which hone in on the influence of corporations or industries in shaping the economy over time; and economic concepts and terms, which provide background information for people with little or no formal education in economics. In addition to the expected articles on inventors and robber barons, readers will also find information on successful women, minority leaders, and early histories of the Aztec, Maya, Inca, and Native Americans. A table of contents is arranged chronologically by 10 "eras," followed by a chronology section that includes brief narratives for significant dates within each era. Sources for further reading are provided on the longer essays. Although the content includes some articles of early history, essays focusing on the nineteenth and twentieth centuries are most prevalent. Many topics of contemporary interest are included, such as the "graying of America" and the Internet. An index is included.

Evaluation: The *Encyclopedia's* level of interest is intentionally geared toward high school and first- and second-year college students, which makes this a recommended source for most public and academic libraries, especially those serving high schools and community colleges.

*1.85. The Global Competitiveness Report [2001–2002]. World Economic Forum and the Center for International Development at Harvard University. New York: Oxford University Press, © 2002. $65.00. Web site: http://www.oup-usa.org/.

Authority and scope: Focusing on countries or economic areas for which statistical data are maintained on a separate and independent basis, this report includes essays and analyses reflecting the state of the global economy and competition between economies of the world. The report attempts to identify impediments to economic growth and serve as a tool to help in the design of policies to improve a nation's competitive position in the world economy. Individual profiles of each country, with data from survey responses and seventeen additional countries have been added, a reflection of the rising integration of developing countries into the global economy. Two major indices used to rank each country are the growth competitiveness index, which aims to measure factors contributing to future growth of an economy (rate of change of GDP per person); and the current competitiveness index, which aims to identify the factors that underpin high current productivity (economic performance measured by the level of GDP per person). Each country profile also includes the National Competitiveness Balance Sheet, which lists competitive advantages and disadvantages. Among the contributors to this report are well-known experts in international development and competitive strategy, such as Michael E. Porter and Jeffrey D. Sachs of Harvard University and Klaus Schwab, President of the World Economic Forum.

Evaluation: Because of its affordability and useful data on the role of corporations and governments in determining economic vitality, this is recommended for all libraries.

*1.86. GMAT for Dummies. Suzee Vlk. 4th ed. Foster City, CA: IDG Books Worldwide, Inc., © 2000. $16.99. Web site: http://www.hungryminds.com/.

Authority and scope: *GMAT for Dummies* is part of the popular "Dummies" series of books that are geared to make learning easier and more fun, whether it's learning new application software skills or preparing for the Graduate Management Admission Test, now only given in electronic format. The author, Suzee Vlk, has been a test-prep specialist since 1975.

Evaluation: Created with humor in an "Us versus Them" style, the resource is filled with useful tips and shortcuts that will help test-takers improve their scores, and is recommended for public and academic libraries. Many other "Dummies" books are available and suitable for filling gaps in business collections at a reasonable price. These include *Business Etiquette for Dummies*, *Home-Based Businesses for Dummies*, *Business Plans for Dummies*, and *Negotiating for Dummies*.

*1.87. Guide to Everyday Economic Statistics. Gary E. Clayton and Martin Gerhard Giesbrecht. 5th ed. Boston, MA: McGraw-Hill, © 2001. $17.40. Web site: http://www.EconSources.com/.

> **Authority and scope:** Written by a professor and a professor emeritus of economics at Northern Kentucky University, this tiny paperback guide is geared to helping students and citizens understand the important indicators that measure our economy. The authors focus on indicators that are widely reported.

> **Evaluation:** Complex information is converted into manageable bite-size pieces and explained in ordinary language. The statistic is placed in context so that the reader can better understand how the individual statistic relates to the larger picture. Because of its potential uses as a reference source for every citizen who is interested in having a better understanding of our nation's economy, this is recommended for all libraries.

1.88. Guide to U.S. Government Publications [2001]. Donna Batten, ed. Detroit, MI: Gale Group, 1973–. $360.00. Web site: http://www.galegroup.com/.

> **Authority and scope:** Originated by John Andriot, a librarian, in the 1950s as the *Guide to United States Government Serials and Periodicals*, this later became the *Guide to United States Government Publications*. Published by the Gale Group since 1999, the *Guide* continues to provide a comprehensive guide to the important series, periodicals, and reference tools published by United States government agencies. A useful feature is the agency class chronology which gives the complete history of current Superintendent of Documents class number assignments and traces them back, allowing the user to track the many changes of older serials. The index now has more than 36,000 entries, with agencies indexed first, then titles, followed by a keyword in title index. A practical guide to the SuDocs (Superintendent of Documents) classification system is provided preceding of the table of contents. Entries are arranged throughout the book by classification number and include such information as title, starting dates, frequency, earlier and later references, item number, Dewey number, LC classification number, LC card number, and annotations.

> **Evaluation:** Although printed government publications are decreasing in number as electronic sources replace them, there is still a need for an authoritative source to aid in tracing publications. This guide serves that need, and is recommended for larger libraries with significant government publication collections.

*1.89. Handbook of Common Stocks. New York: Mergent, FIS, Inc., 1955–. Quarterly. $54.95. Web site: http://www.fisonline.com/.

> **Authority and scope:** Mergent's *Handbook* provides a basic one page business and financial analysis for over 950 stocks listed on the New York Stock Exchange. A similar handbook is available for Nasdaq companies. Companies are listed in alphabetical order, the stock symbol, exchange, recent price,

a chart of long-term prices, dividends, brief company background, recent developments, prospects, and 10 years of comparative statistics and ratios.

Evaluation: Beginning investors will want to use this handbook for basic stock research since it serves as an excellent resource for current and historical data on major companies. It is especially recommended for small academic and public libraries due to the amount of data and reasonable price. Larger libraries may want to use the *Handbook of Common Stocks* as a quick or ready reference tool.

*1.90. **Handbook of U.S. Labor Statistics: Employment, Earnings, Prices, Productivity, and Other Labor Data.** Eva E. Jacobs, ed. 4th ed. Lanham, MD: Bernan Press, © 2001. $89.00. Web site: http://www.bernanpress.com/.

Authority and scope: Following the demise of the *Handbook of Labor Statistics*, which was last published by the Bureau of Labor Statistics in 1989, Bernan Press began to publish its *Handbook of United States Labor Statistics*. The editor, Eva E. Jacobs, worked at the Bureau of Labor Statistics for over 20 years and has been editor of this Bernan publication since its first edition. The privately published edition maintains and updates the statistical information about labor market conditions, prices, and productivity, and continues to add data and new features. New in this edition are projections of employment to 2008, new tables of changes in productivity by industry, data on employees earning wages at or below the federal minimum, data on employee absences, labor force status of the foreign born population, and additional tables on contingent workers and on consumer expenditures.

Evaluation: Bernan Press has received well-deserved recognition for this publication by the Reference and User Services Association of the American Library Association, which named it as an "Outstanding Reference Source" and by its selection by *Choice* magazine as an "Outstanding Academic Book." It is reasonably priced and is regarded as essential for all libraries.

*1.91. **Handbook of North American Industry [1999].** John E. Cremens, 2nd ed. Washington, DC: Bernan Press, 1998–. $175.00. Web site: http://www.bernan.com/.

Authority and scope: The *Handbook of North American Industry* provides detailed economic data for the United States, Mexico, and Canada, and is divided into two parts: "The North American Economy" and "Industries in North America." Part one includes essays concerning the progress of NAFTA, employment, wages and benefits, and labor unions in North America. A variety of tables list industry rankings, exchange rates and rate indexes, and purchasing power parities. Part two provides an industry-by-industry comparison based on the two-digit industry SIC code. Individual industries are grouped under three major industry categories: agricultural, mining, and construction; manufacturing; and trade and services. Industry information covers products and services, what's new (trends, laws, and regulations), growth, investment, prices, employment, earnings and productivity, finance, Canada and Mexico components, and international trade. Three appendices contain information on the North American Industry Classification System, Governmental Structure—Canada, Mexico and the United States, and the Maquilador-9802 program.

Evaluation: This handbook provides comprehensive, unbiased economic statistics. The tables are easy to read and interpret. One drawback is the absence of an index. *Handbook of North American Industry* is a basic reference book and is recommended for all business-oriented academic and public libraries.

*1.92. Headquarters USA: A Directory of Contact Information for Headquarters and Other Central Offices of Major Businesses & Organizations Worldwide [2002]. Jennifer C. Perkins, ed. 24th ed. Detroit, MI: Omnigraphics, 1997–. 2 vols. $175.00. Web site: http://www.omnigraphics.com/.

Authority and scope: Previously known as *Business Phone Book USA*, the title of the 2001 edition was changed to *Headquarters USA* to better fit the scope of the publication. Over time, the number of "non-business" listings has grown steadily. More than 35 percent of the directory's content is now focused on associations, other organizations, agencies, institutions, as well as a "People" category, which includes noteworthy authors, journalists, celebrities, politicians, scientists, and others. Web sites have grown to be an important part of the book's make-up as well (more than 50 percent of listings include them) and approximately 25 percent of the listings have e-mail addresses. This edition contains 123,000 unique listings. Most include fax numbers and about one-third have toll-free telephone numbers. A useful section profiling the 50 largest United States cities is intended to assist business travelers, and includes important phone numbers (e.g., time and temperature, medical referral); information on convention and visitors bureaus and chambers of commerce; Web sites offering information about the city; and listings for accommodations, restaurants, transportation, banks, shopping, business services, media, colleges and universities, hospitals, attractions, sports teams and facilities, and events. Some other unique sections include "conglomerates," with contact information for a parent company as well as many of its diversified subsidiaries or divisions; an index to United States offices of foreign companies; and a listing of major companies' stock symbols identified with the appropriate company name.

Evaluation: This ready reference tool packs a wide range of useful information into two volumes. Many charts and tables provide information that is often scattered in many places, such as mileage charts between major cities, airport codes, telephone area codes, and zip codes. A page is even provided for telephone area code changes, both recent and upcoming, for areas of the country with the fastest population growth. This practical resource is recommended for all libraries.

*1.93. Hoover's Handbook of American Business [2002]. Austin, TX: Hoover's Inc., © 1991–. Annual. 2 vols. $159.95. Web site: http://www.hoovers.com/.

Authority and scope: This two-volume set profiles 750 of America's largest companies. Hoover's "List Lover's Compendium" section, some 50 pages, ranks the largest, smallest, fastest-growing, and best companies using a variety of criteria. The profile section, which follows the compendium, is arranged alphabetically by company name. Each profile is two pages in length and contains a brief company overview, history, officers, company locations, stock exchange and ticker symbol, products and operations, competitors, historical financials and employees, stock price history, and fiscal year-end data. The indexes list companies by industry, headquarters location, brands, company names, and people named in the profiles.

Evaluation: *Hoover's Handbook of American Business* is an excellent ready reference tool for company information. The profiles offer interesting narratives about the start-up and landmark events in the history of the company, written in a style that is not intimidating. This resource is recommended for academic, public, and corporate libraries.

*1.94. **Hoover's Handbook of Emerging Companies [2002].** 9th ed. Austin, TX: Hoovers, Inc., 1993/1994–. Annual. $99.95. Web site: http://hoovers.com/.

Authority and scope: This *Emerging Companies* handbook features 500 small-growth companies, and is divided into two sections. The main section covers full-page profiles for 125 companies. Each entry includes an overview (brief company description, history, industry position, and growth plans); a listing of officers with ages and pay; headquarters locations and contact information; products, services; top competitors; a six-year table for financial performance; stock exchange and ticker symbol; employment trends; and various ratios for the latest fiscal year. The remaining 400 brief company profiles contain summary information, including company headquarters, contact information, main officers, company type (public or private), latest sales figures, number of employees, fiscal-year end date, and competitors. The List Lover's Compendium ranks the top companies by various measures. Indexes list companies by industry, headquarter location, company names, and people.

Evaluation: In previous years, the editors used growth of sales and market value as the main criteria for inclusion. In this edition, more attention was paid to profitability. *Hoover's Handbook on Emerging Companies* does an excellent job of providing quality information at an affordable cost and is recommended for all public and academic libraries. Jobseekers and investors will find the Hoover's *Handbooks* valuable resources for interview and investment information.

*1.95. **Hoover's Handbook of Private Companies [2002]** Austin, TX: Hoover's Inc., © 1997–. Annual. $139.95. Web site: http://hoovers.com/.

Authority and scope: Over 750 nonpublic companies are profiled in this edition of *Private Companies,* including 250 companies profiled in the two-page format. Each two-page profile contains a brief company overview, history, officers, company locations, stock exchange and ticker symbol, products and operations, competitors, historical financial and employee figures, stock price history, and fiscal year-end data. Charitable organizations such as the Salvation Army USA, hospitals and healthcare organizations such as Blue Cross; major university systems such as the State University of New York, and research organizations such as Sematech, Inc. are included. Brief summaries are given for the remaining companies, noting company headquarters, contact information, main officers, company type (public or private), latest sales figures, number of employees, fiscal year-end data, and three key competitors, followed by a brief paragraph detailing who they are, what they do, and where they are trying to go. Hoover's once again includes the List Lover's Compendium rankings. The indexes list companies by headquarter location, brands, company names and people.

Evaluation: The beauty of this book is that for 250 enterprises, it devotes one whole page of each entry, telling an interesting story of how it came into being, and the major events that have impacted it to the present. The shorter entries for the remaining 500 companies include a mini version written in the same interesting style. This style and format has become part of Hoover's identity, and is especially noteworthy with this volume because publishers of private company information typically provide only the bare facts. Private company information, like emerging companies' information, is not easily attained, so this handbook fills a void for many collections, and is recommended for business-oriented, academic and public libraries.

*1.96. Hoover's Handbook of World Business [2002]. Austin, TX: Hoover's Inc., © 1992–. Annual. $129.95. Web site: http://www.hoovers.com/.

Authority and scope: The *World Business* handbook contains 300 profiles of private, public, and state-owned companies located throughout Europe, Asia, and Central America. One full page of each two-page entry tells the company story with background information, and whenever possible, information regarding the company's strategy and reputation. Throughout *Hoover's Handbooks*, information on the company's products with the percent of total sales for each is usually given. Percentages are also given for sales by geographic region whenever possible. Rankings for top companies in various countries and the world are included in the List Lover's Compendium. Also included are lists of companies that comprise various stock indexes in other countries, top companies in various industries, and top trading partners and foreign investors in the U.S. Indexes list companies by industry, headquarter location, brands, company names and people. Another product, sold separately for $39.95, is *Hoover's MasterList of International Companies* published in 2001, which provides basic information for more than 3,000 public and private companies from around the world.

Evaluation: *Hoover's Handbook of World Business* is one of the most complete sources for information on large, non-U.S.–based enterprises, and should be a standard reference tool on any reference desk. This handbook, like the previous three above, is recommended for all academic and public libraries.

*1.97. How to Form Your Own [Texas] Corporation. Anthony Mancuso. 5th ed. Berkeley, CA: Nolo Press, © 2000. $39.95, book with CD-ROM. Web site: http://www.nolo.com/.

Authority and scope: The champion of self-help law for the general public, Nolo has published *How to Form Your Own Corporation* books for the states of California, New York, and Texas. With the information and forms in the book, costs of incorporating can be minimized by filling in standardized "boilerplates." The book is also intended to help the reader ask specific, informed questions when it becomes necessary to seek a lawyer's advice.

Evaluation: This is a legal guide written in plain English, which also provides pro and con information regarding various types of business establishments such as sole proprietorships, partnerships, or limited liability companies. The guide states that an attorney may need to be consulted for advice geared to a specific situation, since the book provides only general advice about the law. Because organizing and operating a corporation involves a significant amount of financial and tax work, this book also recommends a list of questions to ask an accountant or tax advisor. For states not covered by this guide, another Nolo title is recommended: *Legal Guide for Starting and Running a Small Business* by Fred. S. Steingold (6th ed. 2000) for $29.95. These guides are affordable for small libraries and can help entrepreneurs get started. For larger libraries, the individual state's statutes, which would provide state-specific information regarding the forming of a corporation, albeit in language that is more legalese, might be preferred.

*1.98. The Human Resources Glossary: The Complete Desk Reference for HR Executives, Managers, and Practitioners. William R. Tracey. 2nd ed. Boca Raton, FL: St. Lucie Press, © 1998. $69.95.

Authority and scope: Tracey's *Human Resources Glossary* provides over 8,500 definitions, abbreviations, phrases, and acronyms that apply to human resources functions in government, business, and industry, explaining each term in context. In situations where the definition has legal ramifications, legislation is cited. Tracey's glossary cites more than 100 federal laws and court decisions, and is divided into two parts: the main portion, which contains the glossary, and the other, which contains the Index of Key Terms. A listing of associations, organizations, and research institutions, with contact information for human resources (HR) practitioners, is included.

Evaluation: *Human Resources Glossary* provides the human resource professional with key HR terminology for more effective communication on human resource issues, and is recommended for academic and public libraries.

*1.99. Industrial Costs in Mexico 2001: A Guide for Foreign Investors. [Mexico City]: BANCOMEXT, 2000. $11.10. (100 Pesos) English edition. Web sites: http://www.bancomext.com; http://www.bancomextdallas.com.

Authority and scope: To assist foreign investors, this guide presents information on industrial parks in Mexico. Of 6,385 companies already operating in 193 industrial parks, 54 percent are foreign companies. Information about the industrial parks within Mexico is divided into five zones: North, Central, South, East, and West. Economic data, weather, and transportation infrastructure information are given for each zone. Average costs per square foot for land and industrial bays are provided in United States dollars. Services and infrastructure offered by the industrial parks; average labor costs (including skilled, unskilled, executive and administrative); rates for water and utilities; indicators on housing costs; and health and country club membership fees are included. Information is derived from a variety of sources, including the parks themselves, Telefonos de Mexico, Avantel, Pemex, the Federal Electricity Commission, and the local water and sewage commissions. The information is also available at BANCOMEXT's Web site, with the most recent updates.

Evaluation: As a neighbor and second largest trading partner, Mexico continues to grow in importance to the United States. For anyone interested in business opportunities in Mexico, the source offers hard-to-find information, and is recommended for public, academic, and corporate libraries.

*1.100. Industry Norms and Key Business Ratios [2000–2001]. Desktop ed. New York: Dun & Bradstreet, Inc., 2001. Annual. 1983–. $380.00. Web site: http://www.dnb.com/.

Authority and scope: Industry Norms and Key Business Ratios provides key financial measures and business ratios, based on efficiency, profitability, and solvency, and can be used to compare the financial performance of a company against its industry's financial average. Dun and Bradstreet continues to identify industries by the four-digit Standard Industrial Classification (SIC) code, starting with SIC 0100 and ending at SIC 8999, rather than the newer North American Industry Classification. The categories cover agriculture, mining, construction, transportation, communication, utilities, manufacturing, wholesaling, retailing, financial, real estate, and services. Data is presented in a tabular arrangement with the SIC codes across the top of the page, and solvency, efficiency, and profitability information cascading down the left side of the page.

Evaluation: The desktop edition of Industry Norms and Key Business Ratios is recommended for business-oriented academic and public libraries. Hopefully, the publisher will make the transition to NAICS codes soon. In the meantime, business professionals and student researchers should welcome Industry Norms and Key Business Ratios as a valuable benchmarking tool.

*1.101. International Business Etiquette, Asia and the Pacific Rim: What You Need to Know to Conduct Business Abroad with Charm and Savvy. Ann Marie Sabath. Franklin Lakes, NJ: Career Press, © 1999. $14.99.

Authority and scope: This international etiquette book addresses the business do's and don'ts in 13 countries, including Australia, China, Hong Kong, Indonesia, Japan, Malaysia, New Zealand, The Philippines, Singapore, South Korea, Taiwan, Thailand, and Vietnam. Similar books for countries in Latin America and Europe are available by this author. Each chapter begins with an overview of the country and some facts and statistics, followed by points of etiquette. Tips under the heading of "whatever you do . . ." are intended to raise awareness of how the customs and manners of the country are different from those to which the user may be accustomed. Topics of etiquette covered are business attire, entertaining/dining, conversation, gestures and public manners, gift-giving, greetings and introductions, meeting manners, punctuality, seating, tipping, invitations to a home, and women in business. Several chapters include sections that are culture-specific, such as business card etiquette, or the proper use of chopsticks. The author has founded a company specializing in business etiquette, and has trained individuals in etiquette at major companies.

Evaluation: In the expanding world of trade and business transactions, proper etiquette is crucial to successful business relationships. These helpful guides should be in most public and academic libraries and in business-oriented libraries with international operations.

*1.102. International Business Information: How To Find It, How to Use It. Ruth A. Pagell and Michael Halperin. 2nd ed. Westport, CT: Oryx Press, © 1998. $65.00.

Authority and scope: Among other credentials, the authors both hold an MBA and MS in library science. They have modeled the concept of this book and its title after Michael Lavin's book, *Business Information: How to Find It, How to Use It*. They not only attempt to make researchers aware of various international sources, they include visual excerpts of a source, along with an explanation of the source's content, arrangement, and special features.

Evaluation: Until a new edition of this book is published, this edition is still one of the best, if not the best guides for international business research. Individuals and librarians without business backgrounds who want to learn how to find and use appropriate business sources can benefit from Pagell's and Halperin's expertise. It is recommended for libraries of all sizes with business collections. Another publication that can be used in conjunction with the Pagell and Halperin book is *International Business Information on the Web: Searcher Magazine's Guide to Sites and Strategies for Global Business Research*, published by Info Today (2001, $29.95).

1.103. International Directory of Company Histories. Detroit, MI: St. James Press, 1988–. 44 vols. to date, approximately 4–6 vols. published per year. $197.00 per volume.

Authority and scope: *International Directory of Company Histories* covers more than 5,300 multinational companies. Most companies selected for the series have achieved a minimum annual sales figure of $25 million U.S. dollars and are leading influences in their respective industries or geographic locations. Public and private companies, as well as nonprofit entities are included. Entry information includes the company's legal name, headquarter information, Web address, incorporation date, sales figures, ticker symbol, and stock exchange, plus the primary NAICS code. Each company entry is approximately three to four pages in length and provides a short summary of the company's mission, goals, and ideals, followed by company milestones, principle subsidiaries, and competitors. A further reading section concludes the entry profile.

Evaluation: Since the original volumes were published in this continuously growing set, criteria for inclusion has evolved from including very large multinational companies (with over two billion dollars in sales) to including smaller companies (with $25 million dollars in sales), often located in a single country. The volumes are filled with fascinating facts and key business strategies for each company listed in this continuously growing set. *International Directory of Company Histories* is highly recommended for business-oriented, academic and public libraries. Except for the earliest volumes of the set, each volume is priced separately and is self-contained (with a cumulative index to the entire set), so libraries that are unable to purchase the whole set may purchase as many volumes as affordable. This outstanding resource is valuable for both novice and advanced researchers doing company research.

*1.104. **International Encyclopedia of the Stock Market [1999].** Michael Sheimo, ed. Chicago, IL: Fitzroy Dearborn Publishers, © 1999. 2 vols. $275.00. Web site: http://www.fitzroydearborn.com/.

   Authority and scope: This two-volume encyclopedia is arranged alphabetically by topic, for the most part. A major exception is entries related to stock exchanges, which are listed under the country name where they are located. This enables multiple stock exchanges in one country to be grouped together, along with other related economic and financial information of that country. Entries include definitions of terms, including slang of historic and contemporary world stock markets. Also included are entries for people, countries, institutions, and events. If a term is specific to a country, the country name is given in parentheses after the entry heading. Cross-references are provided as needed. A brief explanation of the growth of emerging stock markets, a list of world currencies, and a list of finance, trade, and banking organizations are appended. An annotated bibliography and an index conclude the set.

   Evaluation: The globalization of business and the trends of stock markets to consolidate and reorganize were factors that helped to determine that the scope of this stock market encyclopedia should be international. Much of the information was derived from the various individual stock exchanges and regulatory agencies directly. Additional information came from the International Finance Corporation, an arm of the World Bank, as well as numerous individuals. The outcome is a valuable work, recommended for public, academic, and corporate research libraries serving students, investors, and investment professionals.

1.105. **International Financial Statistics [2001].** International Monetary Fund. Washington, DC: International Monetary Fund, 1948–. 12 monthly issues and yearbook. Subscription, $286.00; Yearbook only, $72.00. Also available on CD-ROM. Web site: http://www.imf.org.

   Authority and scope: This International Monetary Fund publication is the primary statistical resource for all aspects of domestic and international finance for the 178 member countries. *International Financial Statistics (IFS)* monthly issues report current data on money and banking, international banking and liquidity, exchange rates, interest rates, wages, employment, government finance, national accounts, and population. The European Union member country entries also include a time series for the European currency unit prior to January 1999. The *IFS Yearbook* provides annual data in a table format for a 29-year time span, and is alphabetically arranged by country and territory. The entries are generally two to four pages in length. Previous yearbooks provide historical coverage back to 1948. The *International Financial Statistics* monthly issues update the yearbook in quarterly units for a three-year time period.

Evaluation: *International Financial Statistics* provides researchers with many years of data for a large number of countries in one volume, making it convenient in analyzing trends of one country or in comparing the data of several countries. The monthly edition of this valuable resource is recommended for all but the smallest business library. Annual purchase of the *International Financial Statistics Yearbook* should be adequate for smaller libraries. Some libraries will need both, where budget permits.

*1.106. **International Jobs Directory: 1001 Employers and Great Tips for Success!** Ronald L. Krannich and Caryl Rae Krannich. 3rd ed. Manassas Park, VA: Impact Publications, © 1999. $19.95. Web site: http://www.impactpublications.com/.

Authority and scope: The *International Jobs Directory* performs a unique function in that it identifies organizations that are involved in the international arena that are noted for hiring individuals for international positions. Contact information for these international organizations is given, as well as addresses of Web sites. As a follow-up to the *Directory*, the authors have compiled an updated and expanded collection of URLs in a *Directory of Websites for International Jobs (2002, $19.95).

Evaluation: The Internet, cable television, and international trade have all contributed to a world that is "shrinking." In this environment, we are able to know much more about other places than ever before. For many people this piques an interest in working and living in another country, and for individuals with that interest, this book and the newer *Directory of Websites for International Jobs,* fill a niche by providing appropriate leads to help them find the right opportunity. It is recommended for public and academic libraries.

1.107. **International Marketing Forecasts [2001].** London: Euromonitor, © 2001. Annual. $1,090.00. European Marketing Forecasts, $1,190.00 Both in World Marketing Forecasts on the Internet, $3,700.00.

Authority and scope: Focusing on non-European countries, such as Australia, Canada, Israel, Saudi Arabia, South Africa, South Korea, and the United States, the *International Marketing Forecasts* edition serves as a companion volume to the European edition. Statistical data for consumer markets are given for 320 different products in 52 countries, including forecasts for alcoholic and non-alcoholic drinks, over-the-counter drugs, cosmetics and toiletries, household cleaning products, toys and games, tobacco, clothing and footwear, and consumer electronics. Further breakdowns within each of these categories are provided for the statistical tables showing volume consumption and retail expenditures. For example, the section related to "drinks" includes 15 major drinks categories, including various types of bottled water. A general section covers demographic forecasts, economic forecasts, retailing forecasts, and forecasts related to possession of various modern appliances or high tech items. Although forecasting is not an exact science, Euromonitor has many years of experience putting together actual and predictive data related to consumer markets.

   Evaluation: In a global economy, it is important to understand consumer demand beyond our own national borders. This edition and its counterpart for European countries provide the kind of information useful to small businesses and large corporations alike for exporting products abroad. It is recommended for large public and academic libraries.

1.108. International Trade Statistics Yearbook [1998]. United Nations, Department of Economic and Social Affairs. New York: United Nations, 1950–. Annual. 2 vols. $135.00. Web site: http://www.un.org/.

   Authority and scope: Basic trade statistics for 170 countries are provided. The statistics detail external trade performance in terms of the overall trends in current value, volume and price, significance of trading partners, and the importance of individual commodities imported and exported. Volume one, *Trade by Country*, provides import and export commodity figures according to the Standard International Trade Classification Revisions (SITC) 1, 2, or 3. The data is arranged in 10 key series (five for imports and five for exports) based on the SITC revisions started in 1953. The other data included in this volume summarize various aspects of world trade, such as imports and exports totals by region and country, and the structure of world exports by commodity class and region. Volume two, *Commodities*, arranges data first by commodity then by country. Commodity tables illustrate five years of data for up to 50 countries, in order of magnitude of import or export trade in the commodity. Total trade values for particular commodities are analyzed by region and country for a 10-year period.

   Evaluation: The *International Trade Statistics Yearbook* provides comprehensive import and export trade data and is recommended for academic, special business, and large public libraries supporting clientele extensively involved in international business. Although data lags behind due to the compilation and publication processes, it is still an important information resource.

*1.109. It's Getting Better All the Time: 100 Greatest Trends of the Last 100 Years. Stephen Moore and Julian L. Simon. Washington, DC: Cato Institute, © 2000. $14.95. Web site: http://www.catoinstitute.com/.

   Authority and scope: The title of this book captures its essence well; this book does not simply document trends, but rather takes a "big picture" look at the quality of life in the United States and even in developing countries, and points to significant progress made during the last century. Besides expected topics, such as lower infant mortality rates, there are topics related to long-term trends for consumption of animal protein, light bulb life, music units sold, and much more. The 100 trends fall into 21 broad categories such as diets and nutrition; the American worker; the state of children and teens; the information age; social and cultural indicators; and invention, innovation, and scientific progress. Each section has an introductory overview of one page or less followed by a double-page spread for each trend in that section with narrative on one side and one or two colorful graphs depicting the trends. Almost every indicator of health, safety, the environment, and living conditions trend in a positive direction. Sources for the data are documented.

Evaluation: Simple in presentation, this book is valuable for business people who need to quote a few facts for a speech, for students who want statistics explained in a way that is easy to understand, or for those who appreciate good graphics. This small, affordable book is packed with interesting facts, and reflects in real trends how our lives have changed since 1900. It is a book that should find an appreciative audience in any library.

*1.110. **J.K. Lasser's Your Income Tax [2002].** J.K. Lasser Institute. New York: John Wiley & Sons, 1937–. Annual. $16.95 Web site: http://jklasser.com.

Authority and scope: This well-known tax guide simplifies complex tax questions into layman's language and is filled with examples illustrating how to work through the different tax forms. A professional edition is also available. An excellent alternative to *Lasser's Your Income Tax* volume is the *Ernst & Young Tax Guide* [2002, $16.95].

Evaluation: This 800-page book provides comprehensive information about a complex and sometimes confusing topic, and is an excellent resource for individuals who prepare their own income tax returns. *Your Income Tax* is recommended for all academic and public libraries.

*1.111. **Journal of Accountancy.** New York: American Institute of Certified Public Accountants, 1906–. Monthly. $50.00. Web site: http://www.aicpa.org/pubs/jofa/joahome.htm.

Authority and scope: Published by the American Institute of Certified Public Accountants (AICPA), the journal not only provides articles on issues facing the accounting profession but also serves as the vehicle for dissemination of selected AICPA, Government Accounting Standards Board (GASB), and Financial Accounting Standards Board (FASB) pronouncements. Article topics include professional issues, taxation, international accounting, governmental accounting, practice management, and technical analysis. Issues routinely include the text of recent official releases and a list of exposure drafts outstanding. A feature that has appeal beyond the accounting profession is a section for technology-related questions and answers. Various tips pertaining to common application software or Windows operating system are explained. The journal articles are indexed by various periodical indexing services that cover business.

Evaluation: The *Journal of Accountancy* is recommended for business-oriented academic and public libraries as a way of keeping abreast of accounting issues. Selected releases issued by the standards-making bodies are published in full-text, providing some access to official pronouncements for libraries that do not have full subscriptions to them.

*1.112. **The Legal Guide for Starting and Running a Small Business.** Fred S. Steingold. 6th ed. Berkeley, CA: Nolo Press, © 2000. $34.95. Web site: http://www.nolo.com/.

Authority and scope: Attorney Steingold's book provides information every business owner needs to know to establish and run a small business. Subjects

covered include legal structures (sole proprietorship, partnership, or corporation), hiring and firing employees, creating good contracts, buying a business or
franchise, negotiating a favorable lease, working with independent contractors,
resolving business disputes, buying insurance, and keeping records for tax purposes.

Evaluation: In this excellent book, which fills the need for a user-friendly
approach to a complex topic, Steingold explains the basics of starting and running a business in simple everyday terminology. He leaves specialized topics,
such a public stock offerings, to other publications. *The Legal Guide for Starting
and Running a Small Business* is recommended for all libraries serving small business clientele.

1.113. Legal Information: How to Find It, How to Use It. Kent C. Olson.
Westport, CT: Oryx Press, © 1999. $39.40. Web site: http://www.oryxpress.com/.

Authority and scope: This legal resource not only looks at the law, but at
other aspects of the legal system such as the history, politics, and structure of
lawmaking institutions. The main arrangement is in four parts: part one is an
introduction to the legal system, part two focuses on sources that explain and
discuss legal matters, part three looks at federal law, and part four looks at state
law, albeit in a more general way, due to variations in state laws. Each part
consists of two to four chapters. The author acknowledges the value of the
Internet for legal research as one of several search options, along with library
books and other electronic resources. Rather than focusing only on the resources
available on the Internet, consideration of all of these approaches is integrated
throughout the book, with special recognition of resources available in general
libraries or at free Internet sites.

Evaluation: The organization of this book helps provide a basic understanding of the legal system necessary to approach legal research in a logical and
knowledgeable manner. With the background knowledge gained, researchers
will be prepared to delve into the statutes and case law. The user-friendly style
would also help librarians gain a better understanding of the United States legal
system for legal research, and for better purchasing decisions regarding law materials. Recommended for libraries with law collections.

*1.114. Legal Research: How to Find and Understand the Law. Stephen Elias
and Susan Levinkind. 8th ed. Berkeley, CA: Nolo Press, © 2000. $34.95. Web
site: http://www.nolo.com/.

Authority and scope: This guide is organized in a way that accommodates
legal researchers of varying degrees of expertise. The beginner can begin with
chapter 2, which is an introduction to a strategy or method for approaching
almost any legal research, and proceed through the book to chapter 12, which
puts all the steps together, using a case-study example. More advanced researchers can refer to any chapter that is appropriate, if they need a refresher or a
detailed explanation relevant to their research project. The final chapter covers
legal research online, with information about what is "out there" and what is
not. Considerable detail is given about internet search engines, Boolean logic,

and search strategies on the Web. Additional information about legal research using the internet is integrated into various chapters throughout the book. Nolo's *Legal Encyclopedia* on the Web site listed above is suggested as a good starting place for many legal topics.

Evaluation: Nolo books are well known for their user-friendly style and this title is no exception. It is especially recommended for libraries with significant legal resources, but should also be available in libraries of all kinds, as understanding basic legal research can be important for any citizen or employee. The inclusion of legal research tips using the Internet, enhances the value of the guide.

1.115. Lesly's Handbook of Public Relations and Communications. Philip Lesly, ed. 5th ed. Lincolnwood, IL: Contemporary Books, © 1998. $100.00. Web site: http://www.contbooks.com/.

Authority and scope: The fifth edition of Lesly's handbook contains 49 chapters that are divided into six major sections: What Public Relations Is and Does; What Public Relations Includes; Analysis, Research, and Planning; Techniques of Communication; How an Organization Utilizes Public Relations; and The Practice of Public Relations. The appendixes include sources information for media directors, domestic and international public relations organizations, code of professional standards, an updated glossary, and a bibliography of sources.

Evaluation: Lesly's handbook is standard for the public relations field because of its comprehensiveness. Large public, academic, and business libraries that serve a marketing and public relations community will find *Lesly's Handbook of Public Relations and Communication* to be a valuable resource. A slightly newer title that is an alternative to this standby is *The Practice of Public Relations* by Fraser P. Seitel (Prentice-Hall, 2000, $105.33).

*1.116. Lifestyle Market Analyst: The Essential Source for Demographic and Lifestyle Activities [2002]. Des Plaines, IL: SRDS and Equifax, 1989–. Annual. $429.00. Web site: http://www.srds.com/.

Authority and scope: The *Lifestyle Market Analyst* provides information about the American population, beyond geographic and demographic breakdowns. It includes extensive lifestyle information on the interests, hobbies, and activities popular in each geographic and demographic breakdown. The volume is arranged in four sections: market profiles, lifestyle profiles, consumer segment profiles, and consumer magazine and direct marketing lists (targeted to each lifestyle profile). In the 2002 edition, two new consumer lifestyles have been added: subscribers to online services, and CD-ROM owners.

Evaluation: For libraries serving patrons who are doing preliminary market analysis at the local, regional, or national level, this volume provides hard-to-get data at a reasonable price. The special value of this publication is that it indicates which demographic market (i.e., age, income level, or geographic area) favors various products or lifestyle choices, making it possible to identify where potential customers live and how they spend their time and money. Designated market area and national-level profiles in each edition are very current. For example, the 2002 edition, surveys were conducted on a sample of 7.1 million households between December 2000 and December 2001. Small business owners and business students should benefit from finding this source in their local public or academic library. A less expensive consumer demographic source for the smallest libraries is *Best Customers: Demographics of Consumer Demand* (New Strategist Publications, Inc., 2001, $89.95).

1.117. Market Share Reporter: Annual Compilation of Reported Market Share Data on Companies, Products and Services [2002]. Robert S. Lazich, ed. 12th ed. Detroit, MI: Gale Research Inc., 1991–. $275.00. Available on CD-ROM and online through LexisNexis Group. Web site: http://www.galegroup.com/.

Authority and scope: *Market Share Reporter (MSR)* presents comparative business statistics from published market shares for the geographic areas of North America, Canada and Mexico. Entries fall into four broad market share categories: corporate; institutional, including state, provinces, and not-for-profits; brand; and product, commodity, service, and facility shares. Coverage includes nearly 3,300 companies, 1,600 brands, and approximately 1,800 product, commodity, service, and facility categories. Miscellaneous areas such as governmental expenditure and environmental issues fall into an "other shares" category. Pie charts and bar graphs appear frequently in the various entries, with sources cited at the base of each entry. Index and appendix sections are included to facilitate use. The index section comprises five indexes: source; place names; products, services, names, and issues; company; and brands. The appendix section provides an annotated source list, plus SIC/NAICS and NAICS/SIC conversion charts. *Market Share Reporter* data continues to be organized by SIC (Standard Industrial Classification) system. The companion volume, *World Market Share Reporter*, covers global market share information.

Evaluation: The business world is continually interested in market share data. While *MSR* data lags behind, due to its reliance on content that is derived from other published sources, it is still an important information resource and is recommended for academic and large public libraries.

1.118. Mergent Company Archives Manual [2001]. New York: Mergent FIS, Inc., © 2000. Annual. $ 295.00. Available online from Mergent, FIS, Inc. Web site: http://www.fisonline.com.

Authority and scope: The *Company Archives* is an alphabetical record of over 2,700 U.S. public companies that merged, were acquired, went bankrupt or ceased business since 1996. Each entry includes a company name, address, merger information, short business narrative, officers and directors, property holdings, auditors, shareholder and employee figures, final two balance sheets, last three income statements, long-term debt, capital stock, and the cessation date the company ended its public existence. Information is gleaned from the corporation, stockholder reports, and Securities Exchange Commission reports among others.

Evaluation: The *Company Archives* provides a concise financial picture on companies that are no longer in business. Business students can use the final balance sheet or income statement information in *Company Archives* to analyze a company's bottom line prior to its end. Mergent's *Company Archives* is recommended for academic and public libraries. Individuals who are trying to determine the value of old stock certificates will want to consult the *Annual Guide to Stocks: Directory of Obsolete Securities* ($655.00) for this type of information.

*1.119. Mergent Industrial Manual [2001]. New York: Mergent FIS, Inc., 1909–. Annual. $1,750.00. Web site: http://www.fisonline.com/.

Authority and scope: *Mergent Industrial Manual*, a two-volume set, publishes company information for the top 2,000 companies listed on the American and New York Stock exchanges. Entry information is obtained from Securities and Exchange Commission, corporate or stockholder reports, and includes company history, business description, product and properties, subsidiaries, company officers and directors, financial statements, cash flow, financial and income statements, balance sheets, debt ratings, and stocks and bond activity. A special features section located in the center of volume one includes a geographical index, companies listed by SIC code, as well as interim earnings and dividends, stock splits, various composite averages, preferred stock yields averages, and other market-related index data. *Mergent Industrial Manual* is one in a series of seven manuals. Other titles issued separately include: *Bank & Finance*, *International*, *Municipal & Government*, *OTC Industrial*, *OTC Unlisted*, *Public Utility*, and *Transportation*.

Evaluation: Owning the complete set of *Mergent Manuals* provides exceptional access to detailed company information. Libraries with limited budgets should consider purchasing the *Industrial Manual* and only adding other manuals based on the needs of their community. *Standard and Poor's Corporation Records* is a comparable resource for corporate information. Both services provide excellent company information. At least one of these services, Mergent or Standard and Poor's, is recommended for business-oriented, academic, and public libraries.

1.120. Mexico: A Comprehensive Development Agenda for the New Era. Marcelo M. Giugale, Olivier Lafourcade, and Vinh H. Nguyen, eds. [2001]. Washington, DC: World Bank, $65.00. Web site: http://www.worldbank.org.

Authority and scope: With this book, the World Bank provides a "state of the country" analysis of the fastest growing economy in Latin America. It presents a scholarly account of the conditions in Mexico with facts and data, strategic options for the future, and recommendations. It is arranged along five broad themes: fiscal sustainability, growth and competitiveness, poverty and inequality, sustainable future and good government. These themes are brought together and summarized in an opening synthesis chapter, which is repeated in Spanish. The synthesis and the first 5 chapters are available as pdf files that can be downloaded from the World Bank Web site.

Evaluation: For companies with a serious interest in doing business in or with Mexico, this book gives the unvarnished facts regarding the challenges facing the country. The authors believe that the historic political changes brought by the 2000 elections bode well for reform. Recommended for academic libraries and large public libraries, and for researchers who want an in-depth analysis of the country and its economic and social infrastructure. An alternative source with a succinct description of the business climate and issues for foreign investors is *Doing Business in Mexico*, published by Haworth Press (2002, $49.95)

*1.121. [2002] Miller GAAP Guide: Restatement and Analysis of Current FASB Standards. Jan R. Williams. San Diego, CA: Harcourt Professional Publishing, 1978–. Annual. $99.00. Web site: http://www.elsevier-international.com.

Authority and scope: The meaning of the term "generally accepted accounting principles" (GAAP) has varied over time, but was officially clarified with Statement of Auditing Standards 69, which outlined four hierarchical categories of established accounting principles. This edition of the *GAAP Guide* explains and analyzes promulgated accounting principles in the highest level of the four levels of GAAP hierarchy in use today. For non-accountants in particular, a helpful guide to the four levels and their corresponding Miller coverage is provided. A comprehensive cross-reference system developed by the publisher to specific chapters of other Miller publications functions as a topical table of contents to facilitate research related to the Generally Accepted Accounting Principles. Another cross-reference table is arranged by a chronological list of original pronouncements, which references the chapter in this guide where they appear or references succeeding pronouncements if it has been superseded.

Evaluation: A widely respected publisher in the professional accounting arena, the Miller "Library" provides portable and affordable guides to accounting pronouncements and related resources. While academic libraries with strong accounting programs should subscribe to the Library as well as the official pronouncements from the Financial Accounting Standards Board, Government Accounting Standards Board, American Institute of Certified Public Accountants, and the Securities Exchange Commission, smaller libraries with less intense accounting demand can purchase appropriate volumes from the Miller Library as an alternative. For the most recent activities of the FASB and the AICPA, larger libraries may want to subscribe to the Miller GAAP Update Service.

*1.122. Million Dollar Directory [2002]. New York: Dun & Bradstreet, 1964–. Annual. 5 vols. $2,200.00. Web site: http://www.dnb.com/.

Authority and scope: This well-known Dun & Bradstreet directory provides detailed information for more than 160,000 of America's largest companies including 136,000 private firms. To qualify for inclusion, a company must have 180 or more employees at the headquarters or main site and over nine million in sales volume. Industrial firms, as well as utilities, banks and trust companies, transportation and insurance companies, wholesalers and retailers, and domestic subsidiaries of foreign corporations are included. In volumes one to three, alphabetical company listings provide headquarter address, annual sales, number of employees, stock exchange and ticker symbol, SIC code, key personnel, and principle product. Public and private companies are identified by a small symbol in front of the company name. Volumes four and five are cross-reference tools for access by geographical area and SIC Code. The geographic and SIC volumes can be used to identify and target new companies for marketing or sales promotions.

Evaluation: D&B's *Million Dollar Directory* is a popular directory for company information. The *Million Dollar Directory* is a lease product recommended for large business-orientated academic or public libraries with an active business community. *D & B Regional Business Directory* at $540.00 is a reasonable selection for smaller libraries with limited funds.

*1.123. The Mission Statement Book: 301 Corporate Mission Statements from America's Top Companies. Jeffrey Abrahams. Revised and Updated. Berkeley, CA: Ten Speed Press, © 1999. $21.95. Web site: http://www.tenspeedpress.com/.

Authority and scope: Since the first edition of the *Mission Statement Book* in 1995, numerous mergers, acquisitions, and company name changes have taken place, causing some companies to be dropped from the book. Also, some companies who didn't have mission statements then, do so now. The number of mission statements has remained the same, but there is a different mix of companies including 40 new entries. Initially, and for this updated edition, most companies were selected from *Fortune* or *Forbes* lists of top companies, or were listed in the book, *The 100 Best Companies to Work for in America*. In part one, the author defines what a mission statement is and how it is used; why it is important for companies and organizations to have one; what the elements of a mission statement are; how mission statements differ; and how to write a mission statement. Part two includes profiles for 301 companies, along with their mission statements. Part three provides two indexes: the companies listed within industry categories, so that employees who are writing mission statements can easily determine what competitors' mission statements look like; and an index arranged by state.

Evaluation: This book fills a niche. Companies that are writing or rewriting a mission statement will find the book helpful, as will business students, investors, and other communication professionals. It should be in all public and academic libraries serving such a clientele.

1.124. Monthly Bulletin of Statistics. New York: United Nations, 1947–. Monthly. $295.00. Web site: http://www.un.org/Pubs/whatsnew/mbsonlin.htm.

Authority and scope: Published by the Department of International Economic and Social Affairs of the United Nations, this comprehensive bulletin provides economic and social statistical data for more than 200 countries and territories. Each issue covers over 74 subjects, including industrial production, trade, transportation, national accounts, wage and price indexes, population, human resources, forestry, mining, manufacturing, construction, electricity and gas, and finance. Special monthly features cover such topics as fuel imports, industrial output, world ship building, and civil aviation traffic. Where possible, statistical figures cover at least five different years, plus the most recent 18 months. The bulletin provides monthly updates to many of the series reported in the annual *Statistical Yearbook* of the United Nations.

Evaluation: Large and medium academic or business-oriented libraries needing comprehensive and up-to-date economic and social statistics on foreign countries will find the *Monthly Bulletin of Statistics* a valuable reference resource for their collections.

*1.125. **Monthly Labor Review.** U.S. Bureau of Labor Statistics. Washington, DC: Government Printing Office, 1915–. Monthly. $31.00. Web version: http://stats.bls.gov/opub/mlr/mlrhome.htm.

Authority and scope: *Monthly Labor Review* is the foremost journal for statistical data, analysis, and research from the Bureau of Labor Statistics, an agency within the United States Department of Labor. Experts from the private sector along with bureau professionals present a plethora of research in a variety of fields. Each issue contains reports and articles on employment, unemployment, prices, living conditions, compensation, working conditions, employment projections, occupational injuries and illnesses, inflation, and productivity. The print edition includes an extensive section of tables with current labor statistics. Additional statistical information on employment, unemployment, and labor force can be located in *Employment and Earnings* (http://stats.bls.gov/cpseeq.htm). *Compensation and Working Conditions: CSC* (http://stats.bls.gov/opub/cwc/cwcwelc.htm) includes data on collective bargaining and compensation issues. The *Handbook of United States Labor Statistics* provides detailed historical data on United States employment, earnings, prices, productivity, and living conditions, as well as other topics such as data on training, alternative work arrangements, union affiliation, and occupational injuries.

Evaluation: *Monthly Labor Review* is highly recommended for all business-oriented libraries, especially for any library whose clientele is tracking local and national employment issues.

*1.126. **Morningstar Funds [2002].** Chicago, IL: Morningstar, Inc., 1993–. Annual. $39.95. Web site: http://morningstar.com/.

Authority and scope: Morningstar, one of the leaders in mutual funds analysis, has selected their choice of the top 500 mutual funds and provides a brief one-page report for each mutual fund selected. Each fund report includes a brief narrative statement; a 10-year historical profile; performance analysis; risk analysis for one-, three-, five- and 10-year time periods; portfolio analysis; expenses and fees charts; contact information; Web address; and investment style. The introductory pages discuss the advantages and pitfalls of purchasing mutual funds and the habits of tax efficient investors. Following this, a group of tables and charts give the top and bottom performers, benchmark average, and a variety of high/low ratios.

Evaluation: *Funds* provides investors with valuable fund data for a subset of the funds in the Morningstar database. It is inexpensive and is recommended for libraries on a tight budget. *Morningstar Mutual Funds*, a biweekly service, provides more current data for a larger number of mutual funds. Large academic and public libraries that have clientele who are actively investing in mutual funds should consider the more expensive service.

*1.127. Music Business Handbook and Career Guide. David Baskerville. 7th ed. Thousand Oaks, CA: Sage Publications, © 2001. $42.95. Web site: http://www.sagepublications.com/.

   Authority and scope: The unique world of the music business is covered in this handbook and career guide through the following chapters: Overview; The Music Business System; Professional Songwriting; Music Publishing; Music Copyright; Music Licensing; Unions and Guilds; Agents, Managers, and Attorneys; Artist Management; Concert Promotion; Music and Theater; Music Product Merchandising; Arts Administration; Scope of the Recording Industry; Record Markets; Artists' Recording Contracts; Record Production; Record Promotion; Distribution; and Retailing; Studios and Engineers; Business Music; Music in Radio; Music in Television; Music in Advertising; Dramatic Scoring for Motion Pictures and TV; Career Options; Career Development; Canadian Music Industry and International Copyright. Appendixes include publishing rights forms, copyright forms, selected readings, and a list of professional organizations. The book concludes with a glossary and an index.

   Evaluation: The music industry is complex and not well represented in many career sources. For those interested in learning more about the business of music, this handbook should fit the bill, and is recommended for most public and academic libraries, and special libraries in the music or entertainment industry.

*1.128. Mutual Funds Update. Rockville, MD: Wiesenberger—A Thomson Financial Company, 1940–. Monthly. $329/yr.; $449 with Yearbook. Web site: http://www.wiesenberger.com/.

   Authority and scope: The Wiesenberger name has been a source of published information on investment companies for more than 60 years, continuously issuing a yearbook with data on mutual funds, money market funds, closed-end funds, and insurance company variable annuities. The *Mutual Funds Update* covers 9,500 funds and has been issued in its current form since 1992. Each issue begins with the Mutual Fund Report, including a brief review of the previous month's financial market scene and other summary and ranking information. The bulk of each issue is devoted to individual fund performance details, grouped together by type of fund. At the start of each fund category, Wiesenberger provides the benchmark data as a comparative measure for the individual funds. Data included are total return for current month, year-to-date, latest 12 months, and annualized return for 3, 5, and 10 years as well as the fund's rank relative to other funds. Indicators on how the fund performed in recent up and down market cycles, the beta rating, and Wiesenberger's score are also given. The footnote section at the end lists funds added, funds liquidated, name changes, and other fund attributes.

Evaluation: This publisher continues to provide the "big picture" as well as the minutiae for the mutual fund industry and does it well. Morningstar, a competing mutual fund publisher, is also well-known and offers similar information. The subscription to the Mutual Funds Updates includes a yearbook, *Wiesenberger's Investment Companies Yearbook*, which consolidates pertinent current and historical data and graphs for each fund and is extremely useful for analyzing and reevaluating personal investments in mutual funds on an annual basis. It is recommended for business, public, and academic libraries.

*1.129. The National Construction Estimator [2001]. Dave Ogershok. 50th ed. Carlsbad, CA: Craftsman Book Co., © 2001. Annual. $47.50. Web site: http://www.craftsman-book.com/.

Authority and scope: *The National Construction Estimator* is a reference resource for estimating residential, commercial, and industrial construction costs around the United States. A variety of associations, organizations, and architects provide the necessary information. *The Estimator* is divided into two main parts, residential, and industrial and commercial. The first several pages cover craft codes and crews, and labor adjustment costs. An area modification table is provided to help account for local wage productivity and material cost differences. The residential section includes information on home and apartment construction estimates for masonry, wood, and steel framing, decking, roofing, and other construction topics. The section is arranged alphabetically by construction trade and material type. The industrial and commercial pages deal with costs not covered in the residential pages such as site, special construction (ADA issues), and unique electrical costs. A comprehensive index concludes the volume. A CD-ROM provides electronic access to the book plus an "easy-to-use" estimating program, which lets the user create construction cost estimates.

Evaluation: The *National Construction Estimator* is an excellent resource for builders, engineers, architects, or individuals interested in the costs for building or remodeling projects. The *Estimator* is recommended for any library whose community is actively engaged in construction.

*1.130. National Five-Digit Zip Code & Post Office Directory [2002]. Washington, DC: U.S. Postal Service, Superintendent of Documents, 1981–. Annual. 2 vols. $31.50. Web site: http://www.usps.com/.

Authority and scope: This two-volume directory contains postal service information and zip codes by state, city, and street for all United States addresses, government offices, military installations, and universities. The directory provides an alphabetical list of post offices, a numerical list of post offices by zip code, state postal abbreviations, and delivery service statistics. Volume one covers Alabama to Montana and volume two covers Nebraska to Wyoming. Information for nonstandard mail, classes of mail, and ZIP +4 is also included in volume two.

Evaluation: The *National Five-Digit Code & Post Office Directory* is recommended for any academic and public library as an essential reference resource. A majority of the directory information is available at the United States Postal Services Web site, including ZIP +4 searching, locating post offices, and postage calculations.

*1.131. **The National JobBank** [2002]. Michelle Roy Kelly and Heather L. Vinhateiro, eds. Holbrook, MA: Adams Media Corporation, 1983–. Annual. $425.00. Web site: http://www.nationaljobbank.com/.

Authority and scope: The latest edition of *National JobBank,* in three sections, provides over 21,000 company profiles. Section one alphabetically arranges each company by state. Each entry includes company name, address and phone number; e-mail and Web site contact information; brief business description; common positions in the firm; general benefit information; educational background; corporate headquarter location; number of branch locations; number of employees locally and nationwide; and stock exchange and ticker symbol information. Section two, devoted to job search advice and interviewing tips, details the basics of good resumes, cover letters, thank you letters, networking strategies, interview preparation, attire, and interview strategies. The third section is an alphabetical index of companies by industry. Within the industry unit, the companies are listed alphabetically by state.

Evaluation: The *National JobBank* directory is jam-packed with practical information for individuals seeking employment. It might be considered as an alternative to the Dun & Bradstreet publication, *Career Guide,* which is more expensive at $510 and is a leased product. Although some entry information is inconsistent, the advantage of purchase rather than lease is considerable. *National JobBank* is recommended for both public and academic libraries.

*1.132. **National Trade and Professional Associations of the United States.** [2002]. 37th ed. Washington, DC: Columbia Books, Inc., 1982–. Annual. $149.00. Web site: http://www.columbiabooks.com/ntpa.cfm.

Authority and scope: Over 7,600 labor unions, and professional and trade organizations are listed in the *National Trade and Professional Associations* (NTPA) directory. The *Directory* comprises six unique indexes. The association index provides an alphabetical listing of the organizations with entry information including address, telephone, fax and toll-free numbers, e-mail and/or Web address; membership figures; staff; annual budget; executive officials; very brief background information; publications; and conference/meetings dates and locations. Other indexes include subject, geographic, budget size (14 categories, from under $10,000 to over $100,000 dollars), executive names, and association acronym. The *State & Regional Associations (SRA),* a companion directory that sells separately for $79.00, is a selective collection of state and regional trade associations in the country.

Evaluation: These moderately priced directories are an excellent alternative to the *Encyclopedia of Associations* for any public or academic library with a limited budget.

*1.133. The New Palgrave: A Dictionary of Economics. John Eatwell, Murray Milgate, and Pete Newman, eds. New York: Stockton Press, 1987. 4 vols. $750.00. Web site: http://www.palgrave.com/reference/.

Authority and scope: The *Dictionary* contains nearly 2,000 articles written by more than 900 economists, historians, and statisticians. This edition encompasses both theoretical and applied economics, with essay topics ranging from absentee to zero-sum games. Articles are signed, and cross-references provide access to related articles. The more than 700 biographical entries include a bibliography of selected works by and about the individual. A bibliography of works cited follows the cross-reference section. Appendices list biographical subjects by country, and subject articles are listed under 53 fields of study.

Evaluation: *The New Palgrave: A Dictionary of Economics* is a major tool for economic research. *The New Palgrave Dictionary of Economics and the Law* and *The New Palgrave Dictionary of Money and Finance* are companion volumes, which can be used in conjunction to extend the understanding of economics, finance, and law for both the novice and expert researcher. The three works are recommended for academic and large public libraries with an active business community. Libraries with budget constraints should purchase only the volumes that support their library community.

1.134. The New Palgrave Dictionary of Economics and the Law. Peter Newman, ed. New York: Stockton Press, © 1998. 3 vols. $690.00. Web site: http://www.palgrave.com/reference/.

Authority and scope: The essays in *The New Palgrave Dictionary of Economics and the Law* explore the intersections of economics and law. Nobel laureates in economics and distinguished legal scholars are the authors of the 339 essays included in the three volumes. Essays average about 5,000 words, excluding the bibliographies, with topics ranging from airline deregulation to wildlife law. The subject classification section lists each essay under seven categories: society, economy, polity, law in general, common law systems, regulation, and biographies. Essays are signed, and cross-references provide access to related entries. Subject classification and bibliographical information follow the cross-reference section. Biographical entries include a bibliography of selected works by and about the individual.

Evaluation: Students and scholars researching the relationship between economics and law will find the Dictionary of Economics and the Law an excellent resource. There is some essay overlap with the *Dictionary of Economics*. The *Dictionary of Economics and the Law* is recommended for large academic and public libraries catering to a substantial business audience. The *Dictionary of Money and Finance* and the *Dictionary of Economics*, when used with the *Dictionary of Economics and the Law*, extend the knowledge of economics, finance, and law for both the novice and expert researcher. Libraries with limited budgets should select according to their library clientele.

1.135. The New Palgrave Dictionary of Money and Finance. Peter Newman, Murray Milgate and John Eatwell, eds. London: Macmillan Press Limited, © 1992. 3 vols. $595.00. Web site: http://www.palgrave.com/reference/.

Authority and scope: The *Dictionary of Money and Finance* format is identical to that of the *Dictionary of Economics* and the *Dictionary of Economics and the Law*. This three-volume set includes over 1,000 essays, written by more than 800 academic and professional authorities, on the domestic and international aspects of money, banking, and finance. The essay topics range from absorption approach to zero-coupon bonds. Each essay is signed and includes cross-references to related articles and a bibliography, which provides a list of works cited in the essay and other publications for further research. Biographical information is not included. The *Dictionary* also contains a comprehensive subject index and a list of contributing authors. *Dictionary's* subject coverage makes it a leading resource for individuals needing in-depth reliable references for any aspect of money and finance issues.

Evaluation: As stated previously, the *Dictionary of Economics* and the *Dictionary of Economics and the Law* are excellent companion volumes. Large academic and public libraries should consider owning all three. Smaller libraries with limited budgets may want purchase the *Encyclopedia of Business and Finance* ($250.00), a less expensive title, as an alternative.

*1.136. North American Industry Classification System—United States, 1997. Washington, DC: Executive Office of the President, Office of Management and Budget, U.S. Government Printing Office, © 1997. $32.50. Available on CD-ROM. Web version: http://www.census.gov/.

Authority and scope: The *North American Industry Classification System* (NAICS) is a six-digit classification system created by the United States, Canada, and Mexico in 1997, to gather comparable statistics on business activity across North America. NAICS includes industry definitions, and corresponding tables between the 1987 Standard Industrial Classification (SIC) codes and the 1997 NAICS codes. The system divides U.S., Canadian, and Mexican industries by type of activity, and assigns an industry code that is determined by the product or service rendered. All fields of economic activity (agriculture, forestry, construction, manufacturing, wholesale and retail trade, finance, real estate, and technology) are covered. The new system more accurately reflects the growing service-based economies and changes in technologies, which have occurred since the last classification update, but further revisions are planned. *NAICS*, like the SIC manual, is divided into two indexes: numerical by industry and alphabetical by subject. NAICS data is slowly replacing SIC data in many business resources.

Evaluation: Researchers who analyze industries over a period of years will have to deal with both the NAICS and the older SIC codes and the inconsistencies between them. The *North American Industry Classification System* is an essential reference resource for researching industry information, and is recommended for all business, academic, and public libraries.

*1.137. **Notable Corporate Chronologies.** Julie A. Mitchell, ed. Detroit, MI: Gale Group, Inc., © 2001. 3rd ed. $450.00. Web site: http://www.galegroup.com/.

Authority and scope: This two-volume set provides chronologies for over 1,800 corporations that operate in the United States and abroad. Each company entry includes the company address, phone and fax numbers, a timeline, and a further reading selection. The timeline explains the major events that affected the company's history. Mergers and acquisitions, product introductions, financial milestones, and major stock offerings dates are also included in the chronologies. The Chronology Highlights in volume two provide a historical snapshot of major events for the companies listed. Starting in 1700–1799, the timeline proceeds in 10-year increments until the present date, listing major noteworthy events. The Anniversary pages list major anniversary dates for the various corporations. Geographic and master indexes follow the anniversary listings.

Evaluation: By gathering information about significant events of so many companies, *Notable Corporate Chronologies* saves researchers a great deal of time. It is recommended for academic and public libraries. Libraries with limited funds may want to purchase *Notable Corporate Chronologies* instead of the more expensive *International Directory of Company Histories* volumes.

*1.138. **Occupational Outlook Handbook [2002/2003].** U.S. Bureau of Labor Statistics. Washington, DC: Government Printing Office, 1949–. Hardcover, $51.00; paper, $49.00, CD-ROM, $23.00. Web version: http://www.bls.gov/oco/home.htm.

Authority and scope: The *Occupational Outlook Handbook* is the United States government's primary publication on career information, providing detailed descriptions for various occupations and careers. Revised every two years, the handbook lists essential information on career preparation, salary expectation, prospective changes in the workplace, skill levels, and required job qualifications. It describes 250 occupations in detail, covering about 114 million jobs, or 86 percent of all jobs in the nation. Emphasis is on occupations that require extensive education or training. Job entries present the nature of the work, working conditions, education and training requirements, advancement possibilities, earnings, the outlook to the year 2006, and sources of additional information. Brief summaries for another 73 occupations include the number of employees and forecast employment changes. A companion publication, *Career Guide to Industries*, surveys occupations from an industry perspective, reporting the number of jobs, geographic areas that have the most jobs, and size of the establishments.

Evaluation: The popular *Occupational Outlook Handbook* is recommended for all academic and public libraries as a first purchase, while *Career Guide to Industries* (http://stats.bls.gov/cghome.htm) is suggested as supplemental purchase. Electronic access is available for both resources. A knock-off book, *America's Top 300 Jobs*, credits the U.S. Department of Labor and *Occupational Outlook Handbook* for its content, so libraries that have purchased one do not need the other.

*1.139. 100 Best Nonprofits to Work For. Leslie Hamilton and Robert Tragert. 2nd ed. Stamford, CT: Thomson Learning Inc., © 2000. $16.95. Web site: http://www.thomsonlearning.com/.

Authority and Scope: Over 10 million people are employed by the nonprofit organizations listed in this book. Selection was based on employee figures (100+), operation budget ($1 million), years of operation (minimum of three years), and internal mission orientation (purpose and goals). Each entry includes an overview of the nonprofit's operation, staff and budget issues, mission statement, goals and objectives, relevant information for identifying a job within the organization, a forecast of the future for both the employees and the nonprofit, and a verbatim quote by or about the organization. Jobseekers should find the information very useful for the interview process. Appendix A offers advice on job searching in the private sector and on how to customize the cover letter and resume. Appendix B lists employment resources. Appendix C lists the 100 nonprofits by field of operation.

Evaluation: *100 Best Nonprofits to Work For* is recommended for all public and academic libraries, especially considering its reasonable price. Individuals seeking employment in the nonprofit sector should find this book an excellent resource in matching their personal philosophy with a target organization.

*1.140. 101 Best Businesses to Start. The Philip Lief Group, Inc., and Russell Roberts. NY: Broadway Books, © 2000. $19.95. Web site: http://philipliefgroup.com/.

Authority and scope: This small book provides a plethora of information for starting a small business. Entrepreneurs impart real-life experiences, highlighting the challenges and rewards of starting such businesses as a gourmet shop, dating service, adult day care center, bed and breakfast inn, or a food take-out. The different businesses are listed under 11 industry categories such as business services, computers, food and drink, healthcare and fitness, and travel and entertainment. Entry information includes a complete business description, startup and operating cost guidelines, profit projections, work strategies, and staff needs. The computer section provides information for Internet business opportunities.

Evaluation: Small to medium public libraries will want to purchase this book for their collections. Large business-oriented academic and public libraries should consider the *Small Business Sourcebook* as the alternative source for startup information.

*1.141. Opportunities in Biotechnology Careers. Sheldon S. Brown. Chicago, IL: NTC/Contemporary Publishing Group, © 2000. $15.95. Web site: http://www.ntc-cb.com/.

Authority and scope: Biotechnology is an area and a career field that was once dominated by research, but which now offers opportunities for real-life applications that impact people's lives. From preventing or treating diseases to improving agricultural products, advancements in biotechnology have become more commonplace. The biotechnology field as presented in this source, now includes a demand for people such as managers, marketing personnel, salespeople, lawyers, regulatory specialists, and financial analysts.

Evaluation: Traditional career sources may not adequately cover this new burgeoning field. This title should address the need and is recommended for all types of libraries with a demand for career information.

1.142. Organization Charts: Structures of 230 Businesses, Government Agencies and Non-profit Organizations. Nick Sternberg and Scott Heil eds. 3rd ed. Detroit, MI: Gale Group, © 2000. $218.00. Web site: http://www.galegroup.com/.

Authority and scope: The organizational charts included in this edition are collected from more than 30 countries and span over 95 industry sectors. Twenty-nine of the companies appeared on the Fortune 500 list in 1999, and a number of them have revenues of $1 billion or more. The preface provides a brief discussion about organizational models and the significance of different structures. A special section discusses nine companies that underwent major structural changes. A summary box provides a brief description of the organization, company address, telephone and fax numbers, Web address, and primary SIC and NAICS codes. Charts are alphabetically organized by company name, with each chart including a source note with reference source and revision information. The volume also indexes companies by Standard Industrial Classification (SIC), North American Industry Classification System (NAICS), and country.

Evaluation: Organizational charts are not easily found, making this a unique and essential source to round out a business collection. The charts provide valuable information for business and psychology researchers. *Organization Charts* is recommended for business-oriented academic, corporate, and medium to large public libraries.

1.143. Oxbridge Directory of Newsletters [2001]. Deborah Striplin, ed. New York: Oxbridge Communications, Inc., 1979–. Annual. $745.00. Available on CD-ROM, $795.00. Web site: http://www.mediafinder.com/.

Authority and scope: This directory includes over 20,000 newsletters, loose-leaf publications, bulletins, and fax letters. Entries are alphabetically listed under 265 categories with entry information including publisher name, address, telephone and fax numbers, editor, editorial description, history, subscription, advertising, circulation information, printing method, online availability, and primary readership. The Multi-Publisher index provides an alphabetical list of publishers who publish more than one title. Also included are indexes to publisher by state, to title/ISSN, and to title changes.

Evaluation: Oxbridge's coverage spans a wide range of associations, businesses, and other consumer type papers that are difficult to locate. It is recommended for libraries whose community includes patrons interested in this type of publication information.

1.144. Personnel Management Abstracts. Chelsea, MI: Personnel Management Abstracts, 1955–. Quarterly with annual cumulations. $180.00.

Authority and scope: *Personnel Management Abstracts* indexes more than 100 academic and trade journals publishing articles on topics such as the management of people and labor economic issues. Noted for its substantial abstracts, this easy-to-use index is divided into broad subject categories (e.g., arbitration, employee benefits, motivation) with individual abstracts posted to as many categories as are appropriate. There is a separate author name index and a selective list of recently published titles in the personnel management category.

Evaluation: Researchers seeking information on personnel or labor relations should find this index a valuable resource. *Personnel Management Abstracts* is recommended for corporate collections supporting personnel functions and business collections in all but the smallest academic and public libraries.

*1.145. Peterson's Job Opportunities in Business. Princeton, NJ: Peterson's, 1984–. Annual. $18.95. Web site: http://www.petersons.com/.

Authority and scope: *Peterson's Job Opportunities in Business* (formerly known as *Peterson's Job Opportunities for Business Majors*) provides an excellent list of over 2,000 companies hiring business and liberal arts majors. The entries are alphabetically arranged by state, then by company. Company profile information includes a brief business description, general address information, Web address, personnel officer, the number of current and previous year employees, sales, industry designation, top competitors, and company type (public or private). Additional information includes job hunting, and resume and interview suggestions plus several indexes that provide company, primary industry, and metropolitan area information.

Evaluation: As a source of basic company information for job seekers, *Peterson's* is recommended for all public and academic libraries.

*1.146. Places Rated Almanac. David Savageau and Ralph D'Agostino. 6th ed. Foster City, CA: IDG Books Worldwide, Inc., © 2000. $24.95. Web site: http://www.frommers.com/.

Authority and scope: *Places Rated Almanac* provides answers to often-asked questions about 354 metropolitan areas from the United States and Canada in this revised edition. The metro areas are rated in nine categories: costs of living, job outlook, transportation, education, health care, crime, the arts, recreation, and climate. A metropolitan area is defined as any city or urbanized population of at least 50,000, located in a county or counties with a total population of at least 100,000. The almanac includes a preference inventory to help determine what category elements are most important to the user. The book is filled with maps and charts to illustrate the "best small towns" or list "fading industries." Appendix A lists the metropolitan areas alphabetically; Appendix B charts population diversity by age and income for the metro areas; Appendix C provides contact information for the various metropolitan areas.

Evaluation: Because of its hundreds of interesting facts about places rated, and its reasonable cost, this book is recommended for all libraries.

*1.147. Plunkett's Energy Industry Almanac [2002–2003]. Jack W. Plunkett. Houston, TX: Plunkett Research, Ltd., © 2001. Biennial. $199.00. The CD-

ROM company profile database accompanies either the print or e-book edition. Web site: http://www.plunkettresearch.com/.

Authority and scope: Plunkett's guide to the energy industry begins with a discussion of major trends affecting the energy industry, such as deregulation of the electric utilities industry, rapid advance of technology leading to reduced operating costs and new efficiencies, mergers and consolidation, and reliance on oil imports. It also covers the outlook for petroleum and natural gas, energy industry contacts, and careers in energy, followed by a focus on the individual company profiles of the "energy 400," including those that make equipment or provide services to the industry. A list of companies, grouped by categories using the North American Industry Classification System, is provided, as well as a table of comparative data, with companies grouped by industry segment. The standard Plunkett format for the individual company entries is used, including some unique categories such as "salaries/benefits," "competitive advantage," and indicators for advancement potential for women and minorities.

Evaluation: The *Energy Industry Almanac* provides basic company information. Originally developed as a biennial publication, Plunkett's Web site provides access to the ever changing energy environment. There is increased interest in this industry and this title should be updated annually to make it more relevant. Nevertheless, it has been included because it takes a slightly different approach than other energy related sources. For smaller libraries that cannot afford some of the more expensive sources for public company information, this would provide basic information for companies in the energy and related fields. Because of the biennial update, the choice of edition to be purchased is critical.

*1.148. **Plunkett's Health Care Industry Almanac.** Jack W. Plunkett. Houston, TX: Plunkett Research, Ltd., © 2001. $199.99. The CD-ROM company profile database accompanies either the print or e-book edition. Web site: http://www.plunkettresearch.com/.

Authority and scope: *Plunkett's Health Care Industry Almanac* profiles over major 500 companies, with chapters treating trends currently affecting the health care industry; an overview of the nation's health care; a list of industry contacts; graphics of Medicare, Medicaid, and drug statistics; the use and cost of technology in the health care industry; and information for more than 30 health care careers and 500 health care companies. Each career entry includes significant points about the career, nature of the work, working conditions, employment issues, job outlook, earnings, related occupations, and a selection of additional information sources. The individual company information provides the company name, type of business, brand/division/affiliation data, contact information, top executive names and titles, annual financial sales, salary and benefits, competitive advantage information, number of women and minority officers or directors, growth plans, and primary location information. Special indexes include firms noted for advancing women and minorities, annual R & D budgets, and subsidiary, brands, and selected affiliations. Plunkett Research, Ltd. also publishes *Plunkett's E-Commerce & Internet Business Almanac* and *Plunkett's InfoTech Industry Almanac*.

Evaluation: *Plunkett's Health Care Industry Almanac* is recommended for academic and public libraries, especially where the community includes individuals interested in pursuing a career or job in the health care industry.

*1.149. Plunkett's Telecommunications Industry Almanac. Jack W. Plunkett. Houston, TX: Plunkett Research, Ltd., © 2001. $249.99. CD-ROM company profile database accompanies either the print or e-book edition. Web site: http://www.plunkettresearch.com/.

Authority and scope: Over 400 company profiles on the telecommunications industry are included in two main sections. The first section contains information related to trends, service and equipment outlooks, industry contacts, and career opportunities. The second section provides an alphabetical list of companies. Individual company information includes company name; type of business; brand name; division or affiliations; contact numbers; top executive names and titles; annual financial sales; salaries and benefits; competitive advantage information; numbers of women and minority officers or directors; growth plan; and primary location information. State and regional indexes are also included. Plunkett Research, Ltd. also publishes *Plunkett's E-Commerce & Internet Business Almanac* and *InfoTech Industry Almanac*.

Evaluation: *Plunkett's Telecommunications Industry Almanac* is recommended for academic and public libraries, especially where the community includes individuals interested in pursuing a career or job in the telecommunications industry.

*1.150. Portrait of Health in the United States: Major Statistical Trends and Guide to Resources [First Edition, 2001]. Daniel Melnick and Beatrice Rouse, eds. Lanham, MD: Bernan, © 2001. $147.00. Web site: http://www.bernan.com/.

Authority and scope: With the publication of this guide, Bernan has added another important statistical title to its Data Book series. However, as the title of the book implies, it is more than a compilation of statistics. Rather, it portrays the health status of the nation with narrative material that explains various health-related trends, followed by the data and other graphics. Chapters are divided into behavioral, environmental, and regulatory factors (health correlates); indicators of wellness and disease (conditions); access to health care; and the effects of health on people and society (consequences). Included are the estimated costs to society from premature death and lost productivity of almost 40 health conditions. The "portrait" estimates that health expenditures have risen from 5.1 percent to 13.5 percent of the gross domestic product (GDP) between 1960 and 1998, yet over the past six decades, rates of diseases, injuries, and deaths have declined. The final chapter is a narrative guide to additional resources for health statistics, including both print materials and Web sites.

Evaluation: The guide provides a broad array of health data in one convenient source, accompanied by interpretation of the data as it pertains to major trends. Of potential interest to researchers, caregivers, and employers, this title is recommended for public and academic libraries.

*1.151. Prentice Hall Office Administrator's Deskbook. Mary A. Devries. Upper Saddle River, NJ: Prentice Hall, © 2000. $42.00. Web site: http://www.phdirect.com/business/.

Authority and scope: Office professionals need to be knowledgeable about the latest technology and up-to-date office procedures. This book addresses new and traditional challenges faced by those who work as office professionals. Topics such as videoconferencing, e-tickets, HTML, telecommuting, and wireless communications, as well as correspondence, budgeting, filing systems, purchasing, and time management are covered. Other subject matter includes management theories and forms of corporate organization, business law, accounting and taxes, investment and finance, insurance, and real estate. Tips on spelling, grammar, and usage are presented, as are pointers for writing letters and memos.

Evaluation: With more than 1,200 entries, this book anticipates almost every conceivable question or situation an office professional might encounter, and is recommended for public libraries and business-oriented collections.

*1.152. Professional Careers Sourcebook: Where to Find Help Planning Careers That Require College or Technical Degrees. Christine Maurer, Kathleen E. Maki, and Kathleen M. Savage, eds. 7th ed. Farmington Hills, MI: Gale Group, Inc., © 1999. $125.00. Web site: http://www.galegroup.com/.

Authority and scope: *Professional Careers Sourcebook* profiles over 120 professional and technical careers requiring either a college degree or specialized education. Profile information covers job descriptions, including salary and employment outlook; career guides; professional associations; standard and certification agencies; test guides and certification examination; awards, scholarships, grants, and fellowships; educational programs and directories; basic handbooks and reference guides; professional and trade journals; and professional conventions and meetings. The entry information includes the name of the organization, association, or publication; address; telephone, fax, and toll-free numbers; e-mail or Web address; and a brief description of the service. Online and Internet resources for career planning and development are listed in appendix one; appendix two lists state occupational and professional licensing agencies; appendix three covers occupational information extracted from the Bureau of Labor Statistics. A resource bibliography is also provided in the appendix area. A master career list is located in the front portion of the book.

Evaluation: The *Professional Careers Sourcebook* is an excellent reference book for any type of library. Even libraries with a limited budget should consider investing in the sourcebook.

*1.153. Public Venture Capital: Government Funding Sources for Technology Entrepreneurs [2001]. Henry Etzkowitz, Magnus Gulbrandsen, and Janet Levitt. San Diego, CA: Harcourt Professional Publishing, © 2001. $155.00 includes CD-ROM. Web site: http://www.elsevier-international.com/.

Authority and scope: The purpose of public venture capital is to generate jobs, to assist the growth of the economy, and to increase tax revenues in the long term. This resource exposes entrepreneurs to the concept of public venture capital. One example, the Small Business Innovation Research (SBIR) program, has given out more than 40,000 awards since its inception; another, the Advanced Technology Program (ATP), has awarded more than 500. The book identifies sources that can provide both initial and later-stage venture capital for technology and innovative companies, covers practical tips and techniques to win awards, and offers a user's guide to government programs for technology entrepreneurs and innovative firms.

Evaluation: The authors, a professor, a Ph.D. student, and a consultant, have various kinds of expertise related to university–industry–government relations and have experience analyzing proposals or receiving research grants. Capital for start-ups is always difficult to get, so another source of money for entrepreneurs is undoubtedly welcome. Public and academic libraries serving technology entrepreneurs and innovative firms should consider adding this title to their collections.

1.154. Rand McNally Commercial Atlas and Marketing Guide [2002]. 133rd ed. Skokie, IL: Rand McNally, 1976–. Annual. $395.00. Web site: http://www.randmcnally.com/.

Authority and scope: Combining current economic and geographic information using maps, tables, and charts, this atlas provides visual analyses and interpretive information for population, income, and sales data variously aggregated by state, county, city, trading area, and Metropolitan Statistical Areas (MSAs). Examples include U.S. maps and data listings identifying trading areas, manufacturing areas, retail sales areas, and principle business centers with population, income, and sales data. State maps are also included with a variety of symbols identifying such information as county seat, population, elevation, zip code, post office, presence of hospital, numbers of college students or prison inmates, and identification of commercial activities such as banking town, principal business center, and airlines or railroads serving the place. Transportation data include a map of the interstate highway system with mileage and driving time between cities, a map of main line railroad service between leading cities with a chart of rail mileage between cities, and a map of Amtrak routes. Communications information includes listings and maps of telephone area codes, postal rates and regulations, and zip codes. Detailed Metropolitan Statistical Area maps are provided for 12 United States MSAs and two Canadian MSAs, with entire urban areas designated, including names of suburbs and many neighborhoods within the main city.

Evaluation: The *Commercial Atlas and Marketing Guide* provides graphic information for business planners, whether large corporations or small businesses. For public and academic libraries, in particular those that do not expect to purchase the considerably more complex and expensive Geographical Information Systems (GIS) equipment and software, this source continues to offer high value for the dollar. It is recommended for libraries serving businesses that are making decisions to locate or relocate as well as any that are expanding their target markets.

*1.155. Resumes in Cyberspace: Your Complete Guide to a Computerized Job Search. Pat Criscito. 2nd ed. Hauppauge, NY: Barron's Educational Series, © 2000. $14.95. Web site: http://barronseduc.com.

Authority and scope: The author, a Certified Professional Resume Writer with more than 25 years of experience and 10,000 resumes to her credit, organized this resource to assist job searchers in creating scannable paper resumes that can be turned into electronic versions for e-mail or posting on the Internet. Numerous lists are included, such as "power verbs" for resumes; companies known to use computerized applicant tracking systems; Web addresses for companies that accept resumes online; the "big ten" career Web sites; and "all the rest," including career sites grouped by industry, international jobs, jobs in the United States, professional associations, college and university career centers, and sites which provide value-added information (e.g., salaries, hiring trends). Suggestions are given for researching potential employers, using the Internet to "network," participating in newsgroups, subscribing to job-related mailing lists, and creating a home page for one's resume.

Evaluation: According to the author, the number of employers who use the Internet to fill job openings has grown significantly in recent years, from 12 percent in 1997 to 48 percent in 1999. Accordingly, it is important for job seekers to know how to take advantage of the technology to distribute their resumes electronically and to use the Internet to discover job opportunities. The basic approach, with helpful background explanations provided by this author, is valuable to someone just starting to become familiar with the Internet and resume writing, while the comprehensive lists of Web sites will satisfy the sophisticated surfer who is job hunting. This well-written and reasonably priced book is recommended for all types of libraries.

*1.156. RMA Annual Statement Studies [2001–2002]. Philadelphia, PA: Robert Morris Associates, 1923–. $145.00. Also available on CD-ROM. Web site: http://www.rmahq.org/.

Authority and scope: The financial data in *RMA Annual Statement Studies* comes from the financial statements of member bank customers of Robert Morris Associates (RMA). *RMA Annual Statement Studies* contains composite financial data for more than 350 industries, compiled from over 150,000 statements. Twenty-two broad categories help organize the information. Industries that fall within the broader category are arranged by Standard Industrial Classification (SIC) code as a double-page format. Corresponding North American Industrial Classification System codes (NAICS) are also provided. Industry data appears on both the left- and right-hand pages. Columns on the far left of the double-page spread provide comparative current data by asset size categories; columns on the far right provide comparative current data by categories of annual sales. The center section, which overlaps both pages, provides comparative historical data for all assets or sales for the current and four previous years. Sixteen widely used financial and operating ratios are covered. Total sales and assets are provided for each category and can be used to recalculate the common size figures from a percentage to a dollar amount. RMA also presents an extensive discussion of ratios with definitions and examples. Indexes by industry descriptions, SIC, and NAICS codes are available, as well as a bibliography of industry-specific sources of published information. *Almanac of Business and Industrial Financial Ratios* is another good resource for ratio information.

Evaluation: *RMA Annual Statement Studies* is one of the most widely used sources for financial and operating ratios for a large number of industries. Dun & Bradstreet's *Industry Norms and Key Business Ratios* is a competing publication, which covers more industries, but in a more concise form without historical data. The *Annual Statement Studies* is recommended for all libraries with a strong business clientele. Libraries with a significant business clientele will want to purchase both titles.

*1.157. **Sales and Marketing Management (S&MM).** New York: Bill Communications, 1981–. $48.00. Web site: http://www.salesandmarketing.com/.

Authority and scope: *Sales and Marketing Management* is a primary resource for executives managing sales and marketing functions. Journal articles cover such topics as strategies, tactics, research and evaluation, with columns included on computers, telemarketing, and sales force management. *Survey of Buying Power*, which is a supplement to *S&MM* released in September, covers current population, income, media market rankings, retail sales and buying power, and market projections. Statistics in the source are reported by state, metropolitan area, county, and city, with totals for each area and the nation as a whole for population, income, and sales as follows: population and percentage of United States total; median age, by age groups; number of households and percentage of United States total; effective buying income (EBI, or disposable income) and percentage of United States total; per capita EBI; average household EBI; median household EBI; households by five income groups; retail sales and percentage of United States total; per household retail sales; retail sales by store groups; and a sales/advertising ratio. The same indices are ranked for metropolitan areas. The *Survey of Buying Power* also contains media market statistics.

Evaluation: *Sales and Marketing Management* covers all phases of marketing. The special supplement, *Survey of Buying Power*, which provides current and projected statistics on United States metropolitan areas, adds justification for all business-oriented libraries to include a subscription to this important periodical.

*1.158. **Sexual Harassment on the Job: What It Is and How to Stop It.** William Petrocelli and Barbara Kate Repa. 4th ed. Berkeley, CA: Nolo, © 1999. $19.95. Web site: http://www.nolo.com/.

Authority and scope: Attorneys Petrocelli and Repa explain what sexual harassment is and what can be done to prevent it. The authors explain the laws that make sexual harassment illegal in the workplace in a book comprised of nine chapters, an appendix and index. The chapters include treatments of the definition, causes, effects, history of sexual harassment laws and alternatives to ending sexual harassment; the various conducts of sexual harassment (sexual-nature, unreasonable, severe, unwelcome) from a legal standpoint, with a discussion of the employer's liability; the beginning steps to stopping sexual harassment; workplace policies and programs; legal remedies; EEOC, the U.S. Civil Rights Act and state fair employment laws; and tort actions, lawyers, and legal research issues. The appendix provides a list of organizations that can be consulted for information or assistance with sexual harassment issues. Petrocelli and Repa include sample sexual harassment policies, and complaint and survey forms.

Evaluation: *Sexual Harassment on the Job* is recommended for all academic and public libraries as a basic tool on sexual harassment. Employers and employees alike should benefit from having access to this step-by-step guide to prevent sexual harassment in the workplace.

*1.159. Shopping Center Directory. 42nd ed. Chicago, IL: National Research Bureau, © 2001. 4 vols. $685.00. Web site: http://www.nrbonline.com/.

Authority and scope: This comprehensive directory provides a wealth of information on more than 39,000 shopping centers in the United States, gathered from owners, developers, managers, or leasing agents. The shopping centers listed in the directory are generally 100,000 square feet or larger. A star to the left of the center's name indicates it is a new listing. Each volume covers a specific region of the United States with shopping centers alphabetically arranged by state and metropolitan area. The in-depth listing includes the center's name, address and location information, major owner/s, and leasing or management agencies. Space availability, square footage cost, and construction or renovation plans are also provided. Tables and maps are used for visual reference to the physical location of a center. Metropolitan area, county, and city indexes help the researcher locate specific listings.

Evaluation: The *Shopping Center Directory* is recommended for business-oriented academic and public libraries. It would be especially useful for individuals interested in opening a business in a shopping center.

*1.160. Small Business Sourcebook: The Entrepreneur's Resource [2002]. 15th ed. Sonya D. Hill, ed. Detroit, MI: Gale Research Co., 1983–. Annual. 2 vols. $350.00. Web site: http://www.galegroup.com/.

Authority and scope: Gale Group, a veteran publisher, has compiled this resource guide for 338 specific small businesses. An individual interested in opening a coffee shop, for example, would use the sourcebook to locate startup guides, primary trade associations, education directories or programs, reference and statistical sources, supply sources, trade periodicals, shows and conventions, business and franchise opportunities, audio/videocassettes, consultants, computer software/systems, Internet resources, handbooks, and other business-related services. A general small business section provides similar information for 97 related topics such as accounting, marketing, franchising, electronic commerce, and e-business. The state-by-state section provides a variety of business assistance information such as new business incubators, legislative assistance offices, consultants, trade and professional organizations, small business development organizations, and venture capital firms. The federal assistance portion lists a variety of federal, regional, and local agencies, which focus on assisting the small business entrepreneur. A master index to both volumes is included. The small and general business sections are alphabetically arranged by business type. The state and federal sections are alphabetical by state.

Evaluation: The *Small Business Sourcebook* is a comprehensive set which belongs in all business-oriented public and academic libraries and is an excellent starting point for the budding entrepreneur.

1.161. The Software Encyclopedia: A Guide for Personal, Professional and Business Users [2001]. New York: R.R. Bowker Company, 1985–. 2 vols. $285.00. Web site: http://www.bowker.com/.

Authority and scope: *The Software Encyclopedia* provides comprehensive information on more than 32,400 software titles from over 3,400 publishers and distributors. Software programs are classified under 670 subject categories with the software entries indexed by title and publisher in volume one, and by system compatibility and application in volume two. Both volumes contain a list of the top software applications for 1998 through 2001. Title, publisher, and distributor listings in volume one are alphabetically arranged with each entry including the title, version number, publication date, system requirements, cost, availability of customer support, ISBN or publisher's identification number, brief product annotation, publisher, and package extracts. A Publisher and Distributor index includes company/distributor name, standard contact information, and e-mail and Web address. Volume two indexes the software products by system compatibility, then alphabetically by title under specific application subjects.

Evaluation: *The Software Encyclopedia* covers a variety of formats from CD-ROM to disk, and should help individuals or organizations identify, compare, and select software products for purchasing decisions. The source is recommended for business-oriented, large academic, and public libraries.

*1.162. The Sourcebook of ZIP Code Demographics [2002]. 16th ed. Arlington, VA: CACI, Inc., 1984–. Annual. $495.00. *Sourcebook of County Demographics*, $395.00. Both books are available on CD-ROM as *Sourcebook America*, $995.00. Web site: http://www.escribis.com/.

Authority and scope: The *Sourcebook of ZIP Code Demographics* is a major research tool for gathering key socioeconomic and demographic data for every U.S. zip code. The sixteenth edition provides updated population, households, income, families, age, race, and spending potentials for particular products based on the 2002 census. Over 80 demographic variables are profiled, with information based on the latest census figures. The source is partitioned into several sections with demographic variables presented in a tabular format. Section one contains four profiles for each residential zip code: population change, population composition, income, and spending potential. Table A details population, households, and family figures; Table B covers race and age distribution figures; Table C reports household income distribution and disposable income by age of household; and Table D provides financial services, home, entertainment, and personal spending figures. The detail provided by the *Sourcebook* is illustrated in the population statistics. For each zip code, the sourcebook gives figures for 1992, estimates for 2001, projections to 2006, and the annual percentage of change from 1992 to 2001. State and national summaries available at the bottom of each page allow for quick comparison of zip code totals. State summary figures are compiled for all tables appearing in section one. The ACORN (A Classification of Residential Neighborhoods) section lists consumer type by zip code. The business data pages list the predominant industry by zip code, total number of businesses, and employment figures. Appendix I lists the nonresidential zip codes by state; Appendix II provides a list of two-digit SIC codes; Appendix III lists the County FIPS codes. *The Sourcebook of County Demographics*, provides aggregate data at the county level.

Evaluation: *The Sourcebook of ZIP Code Demographics* is recommended for academic and public libraries as the first choice for socioeconomic demographics. Well-organized and easy to use, it is an excellent tool for marketing research data. Libraries on a limited budget may want to purchase the sourcebook biannually.

1.163. Standard & Poor's Industry Surveys. New York: Standard & Poor's, 1973–. 3 vols. per quarter. $1,500/yr. Web site: http://www.standardpoor.com/.

Authority and scope: *S&P's Industry Surveys* provides an overview of 52 U.S. industries. Each industry report includes a table of contents, narrative description, history, trends, financial and company information, glossary of terms, and a section on how to perform an analysis of the industry. Industry References (associations, periodicals, and Web sites), Composite Industry Data (industry norms and ratios), and Comparative Company Analysis (comparison of 50 major companies) complete the industry report section. All charts and graphs cite the information source.

Evaluation: Standard & Poor's, one of the most respected names in providing business information, publishes this excellent resource for both the advanced and novice business researcher. Despite the almost prohibitive cost, *S&P Industry Surveys* is recommended for very large academic and public libraries with a strong business clientele.

*1.164. Standard & Poor's Register of Corporations, Directors and Executives [2002]. New York: McGraw-Hill Co, Inc., 1928–. 3 vols. Annual. $675.00. Web site: http://www.standardpoor.com/.

Authority and scope: This comprehensive directory provides company information for more than 75,000 corporations, including U.S and Canadian businesses plus a selection of key international corporations. Volume one contains an alphabetical listing of the companies. Entry information includes the address; contact information (telephone, fax, and e-mail); Web address; company officials; accounting, primary bank, and law firm; employee figures; and stock exchange, ticker symbol, and sales figures when available. NAICS codes are provided, with the primary number given first. Subsidiary entries are listed separately, with references to the parent company. Volume two provides an alphabetical listing for more than 71,000 individuals serving as officers, directors, trustees, partners, or business affiliates. Entry information includes contact information (business and residence), birthplace and year, college affiliation, and organization memberships. Volume three is divided into seven color-coded sections: Standard Industrial Classification (SIC) numbers with explanations, companies listed by SIC code, geographic index, corporate family indexes (subsidiaries, divisions, and affiliates), obituary records, and new listings for individuals and companies.

Evaluation: The *Register* provides basic information on public, private, subsidiary, and foreign companies, with biographical information on top executives, and access points through a variety of specialized indexes. For libraries with restricted budgets and limited demand for company and industry information, this directory is recommended over others. Large academic and public libraries with more comprehensive business collections should consider purchasing this title in addition to other directories such as *Ward's Business Directory of United States Private and Public Companies* or *The Directory of Corporate Affiliations*.

*1.165. Standard & Poor's Statistical Service. New York: Standard & Poor's. Monthly with cumulations. $1,142.00. Web site: http://www.standardpoor.com/.

Authority and scope: *S&P's Statistical Service* is issued in two parts, Current Statistics for updated information, and Basic Statistics, which provides historical data. The statistical information is compiled from a variety of United States government sources, Dun & Bradstreet, the United Nations, trade associations, and S&P proprietary databases. The current issue contains monthly data for the previous three years with totals and annual averages for those years. The current monthly issue supersedes the previous month and updates the Basic Statistics pages which are grouped into categories including banking and finance; production and labor; price indexes; income and trade; building; electric power and fuels; metals; transportation; textiles, chemicals, and paper; and agriculture products. Interest rates, labor statistics, and production and consumption figures used to track the U.S. economy are also included in the Basic Statistics section. At least 20 years of historical data is provided in the Basic Statistics unit. Another publication issued annually as part of the subscription, the *Security Price Index Record*, provides daily statistics on the stock indexes comprising the S&P 500 for 50 years. For individual industry groups of the S&P 500 and other market measures, statistics are given either weekly, monthly, quarterly, or annually for different time spans, depending on the item.

Evaluation: *S&P's Statistical Service* sacrifices supplemental explanation and interpretation of the complex data to provide instead better access and convenience. The arrangement of the data and the clarity of the headings make this source easier to use than many of the government data sources. *S&P's Statistical Service* is recommended for large public and academic libraries, as well as smaller libraries with business clientele.

*1.166. Standard & Poor's The Outlook. New York: Standard & Poor's, 1937–. Weekly. $298.00. Web site: http://www.standardpoor.com/.

Authority and scope: Each weekly issue of this well-known investment advisory service is usually 12 pages in length and begins with a lead article about the economy and major investment news. Feature articles, rankings, and recommendations on stocks of individual companies, stocks of certain industries, or stocks with specific qualities comprise the rest of the issue. Articles give advice for investors with varying degrees of risk tolerance, experience, and investment goals. Features often included are the Master List of Recommended Issues, the Stock Appreciation Ranking System (STARS), In the Limelight, STARS Status, Master List Closeup, Managing Your Portfolio, and the Midyear/Annual Forecasts. Bonds and mutual funds are also covered, but to a lesser degree. Every two weeks the newsletter publishes a recommended "buy" list based on the STARS rating system. Once a month *The Outlook* publishes a "sell" list. The stock performances of industry groups within the S&P 500 are presented in a monthly table, and a cumulative index is issued periodically. Indexing is by company name, subject, and special feature.

Evaluation: The newsletter format, with use of color, graphics, and bold heading, makes this publication easy to read and study. It should be in all academic and public libraries.

*1.167. The Standard Code of Parliamentary Procedure. Alice Sturgis. 4th ed. American Institute of Parliamentarians, New York, NY: McGraw-Hill, © 2001. $14.95.

Authority and scope: The *Standard Code of Parliamentary Procedure*, a more commonsense approach to parliamentary procedures, is a response to the complexity of Robert's Rules of Order. The book covers a wide range of procedural topics starting with the significance and fundamentals of parliamentary law. Chapters 3 through 10 concentrate on presentation; classification; precedence; governing rules; and main, subsidiary, privileged, and incidental motions. Chapters 11 and 12 deal with meeting notices and proposals; quorums, order of business, and debates are covered in chapters 13 through 15. Voting actions and methods are discussed in chapters 16 and 17. Chapters 18 to 21 cover nominations, officers, and committee member issues. Chapters 22 through 28 concern conventions, minutes, charters, bylaws, rules, finances, legal classification, right of members, right of the organization, and staff and consultant topics. Chapter 29 offers a discussion of the differences between Robert's Rules of Order and the Standard Code. Chapter 30 presents a list of frequently asked questions and answers. The appendixes include examples of bylaw provisions, model minutes, definitions of parliamentary terms, and chart of principal rules and chief purpose motions.

Evaluation: *The Standard Code of Parliamentary Procedure* is a comprehensive practical guide for interpreting parliamentary procedures, especially for individuals with limited experience in parliamentary procedures. *The Standard Code* is an excellent alternative or companion to *Robert's Rules of Order*, and is recommended for all libraries.

1.168. Standard Directory of Advertisers [2002]. New Providence, NJ: Lexis Nexis Group, 1915–. 2 vols. with January and October supplements. $799.00. Also available on CD-ROM as *Advertiser and Agency Red Books.* $1,495.00. *Standard Directory of International Advertisers & Agencies.* $629.00. Web site: http://www.nationalregisterpub.com/.

Authority and scope: The *Standard Directory of Advertisers,* also known as the *Red Book,* covers over 25,000 United States and Canadian companies that spend a minimum of $200,000 on advertising. The business classification volume divides the companies by their primary service or product into one of 55 areas. The company index lists United States companies by state and city and Canadian companies by province and city. Entry information includes company name, address and telecommunication data, business description, personnel, statistics and SIC codes, as well as approximate advertising expenditures, the advertising agency or firm employed, type of media, and a list of brands handled by the agency with the executive responsible for the company's account. A Service & Suppliers index completes volume one. The *Red Book* also lists the top 25 advertisers in newspapers, magazines, television (networked, cable, spot and syndication), and radio (spot, and network). Another section of the source provides a list of mergers, acquisitions, name changes and new listings that occurred during the previous year. An association index and abbreviations list complete the volume. Volume two contains indexes that list products by state, brand name, SIC code, and personnel. The Internet/Online category is new to the product by state index. Brief entry information includes a reference to the main company listings in volume one. The *Standard Directory of International Advertisers and Agencies* provides similar information on over 3,500 advertisers and advertising agencies in over 120 countries.

Evaluation: The *Red Book* continues to provide quality information for advertising research and information. Both the *Standard Directory of Advertisers* and the *Standard Directory of International Advertisers & Agencies* are recommended for large academic, public, and special libraries whose communities are actively engaged in the marketing and advertising arenas.

1.169. Standard Directory of Advertising Agencies [2002]. New Providence, NJ: LexisNexis Group, 1917–. Editions are published in January and July with supplements published in April and October. $799.00. Also available on CD-ROM as *Advertiser and Agency Red Books: Standard Directory of International Advertisers,* $629.00. Web site: http://www.nationalregisterpub.com/.

Authority and scope: *Standard Directory of Advertising Agencies,* also known as the *Agency Red Book,* profiles over 10,000 agencies in the United States, and is divided into indexes that list advertising agencies, media services, sales promotion agencies, and public relations firms, plus a list of services and suppliers. The advertising agencies section provides a complete agency profile. Other index sections provide brief entry information, with references to the main agency listing. Each profile includes the name, address, telephone, fax, e-mail, and Web site information, as well as the top executives and media personnel, number of employees, year founded, agency's specialization, annual billings with a breakdown by media, current and new accounts, and branch agency information. The directory also lists agency brands ranked by gross income, top 10 United States media billings, world's top 50 advertising groups, number of agencies per state, who owns whom, and the recent industry winners for the International Andy, Effie, and Clio awards.

Evaluation: The *Agency Red Book* continues to provide a wealth of information needed by marketing and advertising researchers, and is recommended for large business-oriented public and academic libraries whose clientele can use marketing and advertising information.

*1.170. **Standard Industrial Classification Manual 1987.** U.S. Office of Management and Budget. Washington, DC: Government Printing Office, © 1987. Web sites: http://www.census.gov/; http://www.osha.gov/oshstats/sicser.html (searchable version).

Authority and scope: The *Standard Industrial Classification* (SIC) is a four-digit classification system previously used by the United States to gather a variety of industry statistics. The classification system divided United States industries by type of activity and assigned an industry code that was determined by the product or service rendered. The entire field of economic activity was covered by this system. This *SIC* Manual is divided into two indexes, numerical by industry and alphabetical by subject. In 1997, the Standard Industrial Classification system was replaced by the North American Industry Classification System (NAICS). NAICS data is slowly replacing the SIC information in many of the business resources. Researchers will need to use both the SIC and NAICS codes for industry research for years, even after all the resources are converted to NAICS.

Evaluation: *Standard Industrial Classification Manual* remains an essential reference resource for researching industry information and should be in all business-oriented libraries. Since a major change from one classification system to another will affect data collection and interpretation for many years, especially for researchers who are trying to analyze an industry over a period of years, this manual should not be discarded.

1.171. **Standard Rate and Data Service: Business Publication Advertising Source.** Des Plaines, IL: Standard Rate and Data Service, 1919–. 3 parts. Monthly (parts one & two) Quarterly (part three). $712.00. Web site: http://www.srds.com/.

Authority and scope: *Business Publication Advertising Source* lists more than 9,700 trade publications by industry category, and is issued in three parts, with part one being the most important. Part one covers domestic publications except for health care, part two covers domestic health care publications, and part three covers international publications (including health care). Publications are listed by title within the classified subject sections. Information provided for each title includes publisher, address, telephone, fax, e-mail, Web address, frequency, contact personnel, publisher's editorial statement of the target audiences, advertising rates, contract and copy regulations, special features, and circulation data. The title index and cross-references are located in the front of each part. Classified advertising media are covered in parts two and three, with card decks in the latter part. SRDS publishes advertising rates and data for other major media in the parallel publications *Newspaper Advertising Source* ($692.00), *Consumer Magazine Advertising* ($691.00), *Radio Advertising* ($510.00), *TV and Cable Source* ($464.00), *Interactive Advertising Source* ($486.00) and other publications and services.

Evaluation: The SRDS publications, designed to provide advertising data, also identify trade publications by industry, national regional editions and special issue buying guides. The *Business Publication Advertising Source* is important for all business-oriented libraries. Major business libraries should consider purchasing the additional SRDS publications to support the advertising and marketing needs of their business clientele.

*1.172. **The State of Working America. [2000-2001].** Armonk, NY: M.E. Sharpe, Inc., © 2000. $24.95. Web site: http://www.EPINET.ORG/.

Authority and scope: This edition of *Working America* reviews the economic impact of living standards on American workers. The authors have compiled an abundance of information covering wealth, poverty, family incomes, jobs, wages, and taxes. Regional and international comparisons are also presented. Tables and graphs are used to document the data presented in the book, with each table and graph citing the original publication resource. The EPINET.ORG (Economic Policy Institute) Web site provides updates with current analysis for issues addressed in the book. DataZone presents up-to-date historical series information on income, wages, employment, poverty, and other topics. The information can be viewed online and downloaded to spreadsheets.

Evaluation: The *State of Working America* presents a wide range of issues with up-to-date analysis provided via the EPI Web site. It is recommended for both public and academic libraries.

*1.173. *State Profiles: The Population and Economy of Each U.S. State.* Helmut Wendel and Sohair Abu-Aish, eds. 2nd ed. Lanham, MD: Bernan, © 2002. $147.00. Web site: http://www.bernan.com.

Authority and scope: *State Profiles* gathers economic and demographic data from a number of government resources in addition to the U.S. Census Bureau and Bureau of Economic Analysis. Data in this edition is based on the 2000 census. The book begins with an overview of national trends for the United States plus the data for which each state will be compared. State profiles are alphabetically arranged. Each profile begins with an overview of the state's key economic and demographic structure plus a summary of important trends with charts comparing the states population growth to the national and regional averages. The balance of the profile covers the population and labor force, income and poverty, housing, economic structure, education, health and government finances. This standard format allows for clear-cut comparisons between the states, regional and national figures. The book concludes with the Notes and Definitions pages listing the consulted statistical sources followed by a geographic index.

Evaluation: Individuals needing basic state-level information will discover an array of valuable data in *State Profiles*. *State Profiles* is recommended for academic and public libraries. Small libraries with limited funds will find *State Rankings 2002: A Statistical View of the 50 United States at $54.95 a valuable compromise.

*1.174. Statesman's Yearbook: The Politics, Cultures and Economies of the World [2002]. Barry Turner, ed. 138th ed. New York: Grove's Dictionaries Inc., 1864–. Annual. $140.00. Web site: http://www.palgrove.com/reference/#yearbook.

Authority and scope: The *Statesman's Yearbook* has a long history of reliable publication providing a variety of information on economic, political, and cultural standings of the nations of the world. Country information includes key historical events, territory and population data, social statistics, climate, constitution and government, recent elections and current administration information, defense, international relations, economy, industry and international trade, communications, social institutions, culture, diplomatic representatives, and a list for further readings. The first pages of the yearbook provide a list of United Nations' member states with admittance year and percentage of budget contributions. The yearbook includes the Universal Declaration of Human Rights, a list of specialized agencies, and European Union information, plus an array of other issues dealing with the United Nations organization.

Evaluation: The *Statesman's Yearbook* provides recent, authoritative information. It is relatively inexpensive and is recommended for all libraries.

*1.175. Statistical Abstract of the United States [2001]. The National Data Book. 121st ed. U.S. Bureau of the Census. Washington, DC: Government Printing Office, 1878–. Annual. Hardcover, $46.00; paper, $39.00. Web site: http://www.census.gov/statab/www/.

Authority and scope: The U.S. Census Bureau has published the *Statistical Abstract* since 1878. The *Statistical Abstract* gathers data from both private and government entities to provide a "summary of statistics on the social, political, and economic organization of the United States." National statistics are featured; however, data for regions, states, metropolitan areas, and cities are occasionally provided. Tables include data for populations, vital statistics, health and nutrition, education, immigration statistics, domestic and foreign trade, law enforcement, geography and environment, elections, science, social insurance, defense, labor, income, prices, banking and finance, manufacturers, government finances, and employment statistics. A majority of the tables cover several years, with a few going back to the 1800s. Every table cites the source publication, where additional detail is often available. The *State and Metropolitan Area Data Book* and *City and County Area Data Book* are supplements to the *Statistical Abstract*. Numerous tables are cumulated in *Historical Statistics of the United States, Colonial Times to 1970* and the *Historical Statistics of the States of the United States: Two Centuries of the Census 1790-1990*.

Evaluation: *Statistical Abstracts of the United States* remains the first place to look for statistical information, and is recommended for all libraries as an essential ready reference source.

1.176. Statistical Reference Index: A Selective Guide to American Statistical Publications from Private Organizations and State Governments Sources. Washington, DC: LexisNexis Academic & Library Solutions (formerly Congressional Information Service), 1980–. Monthly with annual cumulations. The microfiche document collection is sold separately. Price varies for Public & Academic Libraries. *Statistical Universe*, includes SRI data. Web site: http://www.lexisnexis.com/academic/.

Authority and scope: The *Statistical Reference Index (SRI)* which consists of a printed index and abstract, plus a microfiche collection of data resources, provides access to more than 1,900 publications that contain statistical information. Information is gathered from an extensive body of business, financial, and social statistical data published by national trade and professional associations, state governments, research centers, universities, institutions, businesses, and commercial publishers. Typically, data that is indexed is multiperiod, comparative information on a wide range of industries, rankings, indicators, and demographics. Publication types covered include periodicals, one-time publications, annuals, and other serials. *SRI* is compiled in two parts: the index and the abstracts. The index provides access by category, subjects and names, publication title, and issuing source. The abstracts contain a bibliographic citation, description, and each publication's availability. Cumulative indexes are issued in four-year intervals.

Evaluation: *Statistical Reference Index*, one of the most comprehensive indexes available for accessing privately published statistics, is now also available electronically as part of the *Statistical Universe* database. *SRI*'s cost is prohibitive for many small libraries that could benefit by its availability. It is recommended that large academic and public libraries whose communities are heavy users of statistical data subscribe to the Web version. Purchasing the microfiche collection or the *Statistical Universe* database on the Web would significantly enhance any library's holdings, even though it is expensive. Academic and public libraries would benefit by a consortial arrangement for *Statistical Universe*.

*1.177. Statistical Yearbook [2001]. 45th ed. Paris, France: UNESCO Institute for Statistics, 1948–. $125.00. Both print and CD-ROM, $259.00. Web site: http://www.un.org/depts/unsd/.

Authority and scope: In July of 1999, the UNESCO Institute for Statistics was charged with the responsibility for publishing the *Statistical Yearbook*, and a decision to include longer time series data from 1970 to the latest date, whenever possible, was instituted at that time. The *Statistical Yearbook* provides statistics for 200 countries on the global economy and other major trends. Education, population, and social statistics; international economic relations; and economic activity are covered. The *Yearbook* is divided into four chapters. Chapter 1 summarizes graphically world literacy and education rates by age, gender, and race. Chapter 2 details the education statistics on regional and country levels, including data on educational attainment, students, graduates, teaching staff, and education expenditures. Chapter 3 presents research and development issues, such as number of persons involved in research and development, R&D expenditures, types of personnel engaged in R&D (researcher, technician, support staff), and expenditures on R&D by source (business, government, education, nonprofit, and funds from abroad). Chapter 4 provides culture and communications statistics for book production, newspapers, films and cinemas, and radio and television. The CD-ROM version provides data from 1980 to 1997/98, with over 80 full image tables. Searching and downloading capabilities allow the researcher to manipulate the data for more comprehensive analysis.

Evaluation: The *Statistical Yearbook* in print or CD-ROM is a valuable resource for country-to-country research. The *Yearbook* is recommended particularly for large public and academic libraries; small libraries may elect to purchase the yearbook in alternating years, depending on their demand for this type of information.

*1.178. Statistics Sources: A Subject Guide to Data on Industrial, Business, Social, Education, Financial, and Other Topics for the United States and Internationally. Jacqueline Wasserman O'Brien and Steven R. Wasserman, eds. 25th ed. Detroit, MI: Gale Group, © 2001. 2 vols. $495.00. Web site: http://www.galegroup.com/.

Authority and scope: Completely revised, this comprehensive subject guide to statistics on business, social, educational and other topics for the United States lists statistical information sources for more than 20,000 topics from over 2,000 sources. The subject categories (alphabetically arranged) list published or unpublished, print or nonprint, government or private sector, and United States or international statistical sources. In addition, offices of compilers of statistics are cited as sources in recognition of their access to unpublished statistics. State and individual country geographic headings are interfiled within the subject categories. Two key sources of statistics are listed at the beginning of a geographic heading: for a state, they are the primary statistics source, followed by the state data center agency; for a country, they are the national statistical office (with address), followed by primary statistics sources(s). "A Selected Bibliography of Key Statistical Sources," "Federal Statistical Telephone Contacts," and the "Federal Statistical Database" sections precede the main statistical section. Appendix A alphabetically lists source publications, giving title, publisher, address, and telephone number; Appendix B provides a list of institutions, organizations, and agencies responsible for nonpublished statistical data.

Evaluation: *Statistics Sources* is recommended for large business, academic, and public libraries as an identification tool for a wide range of statistical resources. It is a particularly important reference tool for libraries that do not subscribe to the LexisNexis Group (formerly Congressional Information Service) products, *American Statistics Index, Statistical Reference Index, Index to International Statistics*, or the electronic edition of *Statistical Universe*. Small libraries may elect to purchase the *Statistics Sources* set in alternating years, especially if on a limited budget.

*1.179. Stock Market Rules: 70 of the Most Widely Held Investment Axioms Explained, Examined and Exposed. Michael D. Sheimo. 2nd ed. New York: McGraw-Hill, © 1999. $18.95.

Authority and scope: "Buy on the rumor, sell on the news" and "never get married to the stock" are two of 70 axioms covered in *Stock Market Rules*. Using facts and figures, as well as charts and graphs, each "rule" is analyzed for its validity. Some hold up under scrutiny, while others are debunked. Although many of the axioms or rules are said to be helpful, investors need to understand the meaning behind the saying. The axioms are used to explain the concepts in more depth. The author, who is also editor of *International Encyclopedia of the Stock Market* has more than 25 years of experience in business as a stockbroker and consultant.

Evaluation: This book examines which popular and long-held investment mantras still hold true in today's investment environment. By using this captivating approach to the topic of investing, readers are able to digest the information in palatable "chunks." Axiom topics can be read in any order. Beginners, who aren't interested in or ready for hedging, for example, can skip "the perfect hedge is short against the box" axiom. There are axioms for all levels of investors, and the book would be a good addition to collections of public and academic libraries.

*1.180. Tapping the Government Grapevine: The User-Friendly Guide to United States Government Information Sources. Judith Schiek Robinson. 3rd ed. Westport, CT: Oryx Press, © 1998. $45.50. Web site: http:// www.oryxpress.com/.

Authority and scope: Over 85 percent of this edition is new because of the changing technology environment. Since the previous edition, many government publications are now only available electronically. *Tapping the Government Grapevine* covers both the electronic and traditional government information resources. Chapters 1 through 4 provide a general introduction to government resources, access issues, and depository resources. Chapters 5 through 15 cover bibliographies and indexes; scientific information; copyright, patents and trademarks; legislative, executive, and judicial resources; regulations; statistics; primary and nonprint sources; and foreign and international resources. The six appendices include publisher addresses, Web sites, citation signposts, exercise answers, abbreviations and popular names, and Web addresses. Each chapter includes a list of readings. Chapter 14 contains a document tool kit for nondepository libraries.

Evaluation: *Tapping the Government Grapevine* is a user's guide for locating government information. The illustrations, quotes, charts, and graphics scattered throughout the book add value to the text. A particularly outstanding illustration is the "How a bill becomes a law" chart. The book is recommended for all public, corporate and academic libraries. Another publication which can be used as an alternative in *U.S. Government Information on the Web: Getting the*

Information You Need, by Peter Hernon et al. (Libraries Unlimited, 2001, $45.00). A related book by Peter Hernon et al., *United States Government Information: Policies and Sources* will also be published by Libraries Unlimited (2002, $70.00).

*1.181. Telecom & Networking Glossary: Understanding Communications Technology. Robert Mastin, ed. Newport, RI: Aegis Publishing Group, © 2001. $14.95. Web site: http://www.aegisbooks.com/.

Authority and scope: Published by an organization that specializes in books related to telecommunications and data networking that are intended for people with nontechnical backgrounds, this small book includes definitions of communications technology terms and related acronyms. It not only gives the meaning of a term, but also explains how it fits into the overall scheme of things and how it compares with other related technologies. Diagrams and figures illustrating some concepts are included.

Evaluation: This handy book should help anyone who is unfamiliar with telecommunications jargon, and is affordable for even the smallest of libraries. There is an online version of the glossary available at the Web address above.

* 1.182. Terrorism and Business: The Impact of September 11, 2001. Dean C. Alexander and Yonah Alexander. Ardsley, NY: Transnational Publishers, Inc., © 2002. $18.95.

Authority and scope: Dean C. Alexander is a lawyer and co-author Yonah Alexander is a professor and co-director of the Inter-University Center for legal studies at the International Law Institute. The authors have written numerous books and articles on business, international affairs, law and terrorism. With a brief historical backdrop of international terrorism back to ancient times, this book begins by chronicling the events of 9/11 along with the anthrax-laced letters, which were sent in the following months. In chapter 2, the authors present the immediate and near-term economic costs of the terrorist incidents, primarily to the United States, but its global impact as well. Chapter 3 analyzes the impact of terrorism on selected sectors of corporate America, such as airlines and insurance. Chapter 4 focuses on the demand for certain defense and security-related products and services as businesses are mobilized help fight the war on terrorism. In chapter 5, the consequences of the acts of terrorism on labor are discussed, including the number of employee deaths suffered by specific firms and the broader aftermath with subsequent layoffs. In the final chapter, the authors relate the multifaceted responses to terrorism made by the United States government. A 50-page chapter-by-chapter bibliography concludes the book.

Evaluation: While the total human toll and financial ramifications of the September 11th terrorist attacks and the ensuing distribution of anthrax through our postal system may never be tallied completely, the authors of this book have put together an impressive package of facts on the impact to families, corporations, nonprofit organizations, financial markets, and economies of the nation, some states, and local communities. Throughout the book, lessons learned are given, with examples of how these events have caused companies and government officials to change the way they operate regarding security issues for em-

ployees and citizens of the United States. The book does not get into philosophical or political issues, but offers readers a concise overview of the event
and its aftermath, with a primary focus on the financial impact. It is recommended for all library collections. Libraries serving businesses may also want to
purchase Transnational Publishers' other books on terrorism, such as *Cyber
Terrorism and Information Warfare: Threats and Responses (2001, $25.00).

*1.183. **Thomson Bank Directory [2001].** 249th ed. Skokie, IL: Thomson Financial Publishing, 1876–. 5 vols. $535.00, one-time purchase. Web site: http://
www.tfp.com/.

Authority and scope: Published by a reputable financial publisher, Thomson
Financial Publishing, this five-volume set provides information on banks of the
world. Two volumes are devoted to banks of the United States and two to banks
outside of the United States. The fifth volume, *The Worldwide Correspondents
Guide* has information used by banks to perform interbank communications and
funds transfers. In the main volumes, entry lengths vary, but head office listings
usually include two years of comparative condensed financial statements. Listings for larger banks also usually include the type of charter, relationship with
other banks, location of branches, up to 30 key officers, branch deposits, asset
rank, funds transfer/processing information, and public credit ratings from
Thomson BankWatch, Capital Intelligence, Fitch IBCA, Moody's, and/or Standard and Poor's. Bank name changes, mergers, and other structural changes are
described, with brief explanations and dates. Arrangement for the directory is
geographical, with population, county name, and federal district number inserted as a divider between each city, and with a summary page for each country
section and for each state of the United States. Special sections containing statistics, rankings, and important regulatory agency contact information, as well
as additional information of interest primarily to banking professionals, round
out the directory. Some banks' logos, marketing names, and slogans are given.

Evaluation: This directory has a wealth of important information related
to the conduct of business for banks in the United States as well as valuable
information for those who need to contact or transact business with any bank in
the world. Of special value are the credit ratings and *The Thomson BankWatch*
reports that focus on banks in trouble. Most business-oriented libraries will want
to purchase the five-volume set with global coverage. For a one-time purchase
of $431, smaller libraries can purchase the one-volume *North American Financial
Institutions Directory* (published every six months), which covers the United
States, Canada, Mexico, Caribbean, and Central America. Formerly competing
directories, the Polk directories are now published by Thomson Financial.

*1.184. **Thorndike Encyclopedia of Banking and Financial Tables 2001 Yearbook.** David Thorndike. 3rd ed. Arlington, VA: A.S. Pratt, © 2000. $195.00.
Web site: http://www.aspratt.com/.

Authority and scope: The *2001 Yearbook* supplements *Thorndike Encyclopedia of Banking and Financial Tables* (3rd ed., 1987). Together, these volumes
create a comprehensive collection of tables of banking, mortgage, investment,

and financial computations. The basic volume is revised occasionally, and completely new tables are added to each yearbook to reflect the changing monetary arena. The *2001 Yearbook* contains three new categories (investments, after tax yields, and IRA) with 16 new tables, including some which illustrate total returns, growth rates, current worth of future payments, after-tax yields from capital gains, and IRA distribution schedules. Individuals concerned about saving for or financing their retirement will find the financial tables a valuable aid in the financial planning process.

Evaluation: Libraries that currently own the 1987 edition *of Thorndike Encyclopedia of Banking and Financial Tables* will want to purchase the Yearbook for continued timeliness. Both the *Encyclopedia* and the *Yearbook* are recommended for all business-oriented libraries and all but the smallest public libraries.

1.185. Trade Shows Worldwide: An International Directory of Events, Facilities and Suppliers [2002]. 17th ed. Tyra Y. Phillips, ed. Detroit, MI: Gale Group, 1990–. $335.00. Web site: http://www.galegroup.com/.

Authority and scope: *Trade Shows Worldwide* provides contact information for more than 12,500 trade shows and professional exhibits from over 75 countries. Complete event descriptions, locations, and exhibit fees are included. The directory also contains descriptions of more than 1,900 conference and convention centers, including space availability and services provided within the center; lists of exhibit builders, transportation firms, and other industry suppliers; hotel and motel systems; visitor and convention centers with address, telephone, e-mail, and Web address information; and lists of professional associations and consultants for trade show planning. The rankings index lists shows by amount of space and number of hotel rooms needed as well as rankings of conference and convention centers by space availability. Entries are indexed by date, location, and subject; with a master index which lists all events, facilities, and service providers.

Evaluation: *Trade Shows Worldwide* provides comprehensive and easy access to national and international trade show information, valuable for individuals, organizations, or associations responsible for planning a conference, event, or trade show. It is recommended for large public and academic libraries.

*1.186. ULI Market Profiles [2000]. Washington, DC: Urban Land Institute, 1986–. 3 vols. North America ($150.00), Europe ($25.00), and Pacific Rim ($25.00) $200.00 set. Web site: http://www.uli.org/.

Authority and scope: The *ULI Market Profiles* provides in-depth analysis for 117 metropolitan areas around the globe. The North America volume profiles 74 markets; the European volume covers 27; and the Pacific Rim volume covers 16. Profiles vary in length from four to 12 pages, and consist of a descriptive account of the area's real estate markets (retail, residential, office, and industrial), a map showing development patterns, and tables providing details on the markets' various development sectors. Profiles on international markets are less consistent, but utilize the same format and provide as much detail as available. Some of the international metropolitan areas covered are Barcelona, Berlin, Delhi, Paris, Sydney, and Warsaw. Individual authors are credited with each report, and contact information is provided in the appendix of each volume.

Evaluation: *ULI Market Profiles* includes concise economic and real estate market data for metropolitan areas not widely available, and would be of benefit to individuals or businesses planning a visit or relocation. It is recommended for medium to large academic and public libraries, and business libraries with clients interested in urban locations and development issues.

*1.187. **Ulrich's International Periodicals Directory [2002].** 40th ed. New Providence, NJ: R.R. Bowker, 1932–. Annual. 5 vols. $649.00. Web site: http://www.ulrichsweb.com/.

Authority and scope: R.R. Bowker, a respected reference publisher, produces this directory of more than 164,000 serials published worldwide and more than 6,700 United States newspapers. This edition includes over 6,300 new serial titles with a publication start date from January 1, 1998. Entries, arranged under 887 subject headings, contain some 45 entry elements, including main entry title, former titles, publisher name and contact information, ISBN, LC classification, Dewey Decimal classification number, language, frequency, cost, indexing and abstracting information, journal description, advertising rates and contact personnel, document suppliers, Copyright Clearance Center, rights and permission contact, and URL information. The latter part of volume four contains the list of serial cessations, ISSN, and the title index. Volume five provides the United States newspaper index and a variety of special indexes which list refereed or peer-review serials, serials available on CD-ROM, CD-ROM producers, serials online, online vendors, and publications of international organizations. The newspaper section lists daily, weekly, and specialized newspapers published in the United States. Entry elements include title, frequency, publication start date, city, state, ISSN, contact information, cost, publisher, editor, advertising rates and contact personnel, special features, circulation, wire services, e-mail and URL information. The newspaper cessation title list completes the newspaper volume.

Evaluation: *Ulrich's* reputation for reliability and comprehensiveness leads veteran librarians to regard it as a basic part of any reference collection. Its subject arrangement provides easy access to large amounts of information. The online and CD-ROM products and vendor listings provide valuable information for those libraries moving into the digital environment. A competitor for this publication, *Standard Periodical Directory*, is considerably more expensive at $1195.00. Ulrich's is recommended for academic and public libraries.

*1.188. **United States Government Manual 2001–2002.** Washington, DC: Office of the Federal Register, National Archives and Records Service, General Services Administration, 1935–. Annual. $40.00. Available electronically. Web site: http://www.access.gpo.gov/nara/nara001.html.

Authority and scope: This official handbook of the United States government provides comprehensive information on the agencies of the legislative, judicial, and executive branches, including information on quasi-official agencies, commissions, boards, and other organizations in which the United States government participates. A typical agency entry includes principal officials, a brief history and summary of the agency's role and purpose, an organizational chart along with a description of programs and activities, and contract and grant information. The appendices provide information concerning agency termination, transfers, or name changes, plus a list of commonly used abbreviations and acronyms.

Evaluation: The *Government Manual*, an inexpensive and cost-effective resource tool, is recommended for all libraries. Small and medium-sized public libraries that provide service to entrepreneurs or small businesses should find this tool particularly useful.

*1.189. USA Electric Utility Industry Directory.** 8th ed. Durango, CO: PennWell, © 2000. $195.00. Web site: http://www.pennwell.com/.

Authority and scope: This directory provides detailed information about the changing electric utility industry, including material on holding companies, investor-owned electric utilities, municipal and other publicly owned utilities, rural electric cooperatives, federal, state and district systems, and Canadian utilities. The amount of information varies with the size of the operation. In addition to company addresses, phone numbers, and Web sites, information for large utilities includes key personnel, total assets, total long-term debt, ownership, number of employees, size of territory, services provided, annual net generation, peak demand, system heat rate, makeup of load, kwh sales, average annual residential usage, residential customer rate, number of customers for each category, percent of generation by fuel type, and major interconnections. In addition, contact information is given for regulatory agencies. Indexes provide access by company name, geographic location, and named personnel. The book concludes with an article summarizing utilities' recent divestitures, and an industry report on the top 91 investor-owned utilities.

Evaluation: This title provides company descriptions as well as other information about an industry that is undergoing dramatic change. It is recommended for public, academic, and special libraries that serve users in this arena.

1.190. USA Today.** Daily. Arlington, VA: Gannett, 1982–. $156.00. Web site: http://www.usatoday.com/.

Authority and scope: Launched in 1982, this Gannett paper has changed very little through the years. The paper continues to use color and graphics in its four sections: news, money, sports, and life stories. Articles are generally without regional or local emphasis and usually include some type of color graphic or photograph. Brief news items from all 50 states are presented on a state-by-state basis and the editorial page gives opinions on both sides of an issue. Weather is presented in a colorful full-page layout on the last page of the news section.

Evaluation: Originally targeted for a mobile audience, *USA Today* provides busy people with a quick read on the day's news. The graphical representations of survey results, company or industry comparisons, or facts about the country's culture are impressive. Although not strictly a business newspaper, it does a good job of tracking trends and technology, as well as presenting information of importance to business. *USA Today* is recommended for all but the smallest of libraries.

*1.191. U.S. Industry & Trade Outlook [2000].** London: McGraw-Hill, 1998–2000. $69.95. Also available on CD-ROM. $125.00. Web site: http://www.ita.doc.gov/td/industry/otea/outlook/.

Authority and scope: U.S. *Industry & Trade Outlook* (formerly *U.S. Industrial Outlook*) provides an industry-by-industry overview of the United States economy in this final print edition. Coverage includes a forecast for United States industries, highlighting trends and top industry performers, plus a new section on e-commerce. Fifty-four chapters cover manufacturing, services, construction, tourism, and natural resources industries. Each chapter includes historical data, industry trends, technology, international competition, forecasts (for one, two, and five years), graphs highlighting international and domestic trends, and references for further research. As a joint project of the International Trade Administration and Stat-USA, this resource will now be moving to the Web. Updates for industries will be added to the Web site gradually. When the Web edition of the *Outlook* reaches its target of 50-some industries, yearly subscriptions will be offered at a reasonable rate. The first ten chapters originally scheduled for Web access in fall 2001 are currently on hold as of January 2002.

Evaluation: The *Industry & Trade Outlook* is written by a variety of independent analysts and professionals and provides reliable summary data on trends and forecasts for United States industries. This valuable resource is recommended for all public and academic libraries.

*1.192. Value Line Investment Survey.** New York: Arnold Bernhard, 1931–. Weekly. $570.00. Also available in electronic formats. Web site: http://valueline.com/.

Authority and scope: *Value Line Investment Survey* provides up-to-date information on more than 1,700 stocks in more than 90 industries. Every week, about 125 stocks from six to eight industries are reviewed and analyzed. Part one, "Summary Index," issued weekly, serves as the finding aid in locating the latest quarterly and supplemental reports, providing a selection of stock screens that help investors identify prospective stock investments. Part two, "Ratings & Reports," provides a full-page report on each of the 1,700 individual stocks. Each report includes a summary of the company's past performance, current status, 15-year statistical history, and three- to five-year outlook, plus an industry review. Part three "Selection & Opinion," is Value Line's weekly newsletter in which individual stocks are highlighted, current market conditions are analyzed, and investor advice is provided. The *Value Line Investment Survey Expanded* ($249.00/yr.) covers 1,800 additional stocks. The *Expanded* edition features about 140 new stock reports weekly, each report including a brief company business description, recent corporate developments, and the relative price performance rank for the next six to 12 months.

Evaluation: *Value Line Investment Survey* is a very popular investment advisory tool among the business and academic communities actively engaged in stock market issues. *Value Line Investment Survey* is recommended for all libraries. Large public and academic libraries should include the *Expanded* edition to provide a wider range of stock coverage for their business communities.

*1.193. The Wall Street Journal. New York: Dow Jones & Co., 1889–. Daily except Saturday, Sunday, and major holidays. $175.00. Web site: http://www.wsj.com/.

Authority and scope: The *Wall Street Journal* (WSJ), the primary business newspaper in the United States, includes top news stories, company news and information on business trends, industry, finance, the economy, and international commerce. It provides extensive price and securities data, and information on commodities, options, futures, foreign exchange, and money markets. The *Journal* is divided into three sections. Section one covers general business, political, and economic news; Section two, known as the "The Marketplace," includes articles on marketing, media, technology, and law; Section three, "Money and Investing," deals with investment-related articles and other financial markets. The *Journal* provides daily exchange rates in both United States dollars and the national currency for 50 countries. Breaking from a time-honored black and white format, the Dow Jones and Company switched the *Journal's* front page to a color format in April of 2002.

Evaluation: The *WSJ*, as the foremost newspaper for financial news and information, is recommended for all public and academic libraries as a key business tool.

1.194. The Wall Street Journal Index. Ann Arbor, MI: UMI, 1958–. Annual. 2 vols. $880.00 year. Available on CD-ROM. Web site: http://www.umi.com/.

Authority and scope: The *Wall Street Journal Index*, based on the final eastern edition of *The Wall Street Journal*, provides access to articles, columns, feature articles, editorials, letters to the editor, obituaries, some tabular information, earnings reports, dividend reports, and arts reviews. The index is divided into two parts: Corporate News (arranged alphabetically by company name), and General News (a combined list of subject headings, personal names, organization names, product names, and geographic names). Since 1997, entry information includes the headline, author, article type (feature or editorial), and subject terms under which the article is indexed. Prior to 1997, each entry included a brief abstract of the article followed by the date, page, and column of the article. The index also includes a subject headings category, which is subdivided by topic and geography. The Barron's index is included in the annual volumes.

Evaluation: Large academic and public libraries may want to access the *WSJ Index* via *Dow Jones Interactive*. Smaller libraries with limited budgets should consider purchasing either the CD-ROM or the annual volumes.

*1.195. **Ward's Business Directory of U.S. Private and Public Companies [2002].** Detroit, MI, Gale Group, 1961–. Annual. 8 vols. $2850.00 set; Vol. 5 only (Ranked by SIC) $1,025.00; Vol. 8 only (Ranked by NAICS) $695.00. Web site: www.galegroup.com/.

Authority and scope: *Ward's Business Directory* lists more than 110,000 public and private companies. Volumes one to three provide company information arranged alphabetically, with each profile including complete contact information, plus the names and titles of executive officers, number of employees, financial figures, stock exchange and ticker symbol for publicly traded companies, year founded, SIC and NAICS codes, and parent company name. Volume four lists the companies geographically by zip code within each state, and contains lists such as the top 1,000 public and privately held companies, 1,000 largest employers, and private and public companies by state and by revenue. Companies are ranked by sales within industry SIC codes in volume five and by NAICS codes in volume eight. Both volumes include information on the total number of companies, sales figures, and employees, with an alphabetical company name index following either the SIC or NAICS listings. Volumes six and seven provide company listings, first by state, then by SIC code. Employee and financial figures are included, along with a listing for the 100 largest private and public companies for each state, plus the 100 largest employers for each state. A company index appears in the back of volume seven.

Evaluation: *Ward's Business Directory* is an excellent tool for industry analysis. It is one of the few directories to rank private and public companies together by industry codes (SIC and NAICS), using financial data, which allows a researcher to learn who the "biggest" players are in that market. Some of the volumes can be purchased individually or as a smaller set; however, if only one or two volumes are affordable, volumes five and eight (SIC and NAICS, respectively) are recommended for those libraries whose business community is actively engaged in industry research. Both volumes are useful, not only for the 2002 edition, but also while the transition from the SIC system to the NAICS system for industry classification takes place. If cost is prohibitive for both volumes then the volume of choice is volume eight, sales ranked by NAICS.

*1.196. **Ward's Motor Vehicle Facts and Figures: Documenting the Performance and Impact of the U.S. Auto Industry [2001].** Southfield, MI: Ward's Communications, © 2001. $55.00. Web site: http://www.wardsauto.com/.

Authority and scope: Gathered from a variety of sources, this publication presents statistics useful for researchers and analysts in understanding the "big picture" of a major industry in the United States economy. Examples of tables included are total United States production and factory sales of passenger cars, trucks, and buses (five year increments from 1900 to 2000); world motor vehicle production by country and by manufacturer; U.S. retail sales of passenger cars by model (1996–2000); top selling vehicles and automotive paint color popularity (2000); state taxes on motor vehicles; personal consumption expenditures for transportation; federal exhaust emission standards for cars and light trucks (1991–2004); and motor vehicle deaths by type of accident and death rates

(1919–2000). An overview highlighting the previous year's trends for the industry is presented at the beginning of the book and an index to the tables is provided at the end.

Evaluation: This publication packs a punch with its data for the motor vehicle industry. Sources are credited at the bottom of tables and include various authoritative authors. Because the sources are varied, years of coverage also vary for the different tables of data. This handy publication gives a snapshot of the industry from a variety of angles, although no analysis of the data is presented other than the introductory overview. Public libraries, academic libraries, and libraries serving users in the transportation field should have this title in their collection.

*1.197. Weiss Ratings Guide to Common Stocks: A Quarterly Compilation of Ratings and Analysis Covering Common Stocks Traded on the NYSE, AMEX, and NASDAQ. Palm Beach Gardens, FL: Weiss Ratings, Inc., 2001–. $219.00, single edition. $438.00, for quarterly subscription. Web site: http://www.weissratings.com.

Authority and scope: As a rating agency for more than 30 years, Weiss has developed a reputation for objectivity and independence from the banks, brokerage, and insurance companies they rate. With a foray into rating common stocks, Weiss now offers individual investors a new tool to help monitor existing investments and to identify potential investments. Weiss uses a system that incorporates a range of fundamental and technical data and turns it into an overall performance rating of each stock's risk-adjusted performance. It does so with the simple letter grade (A-E) that the Weiss rating system has become known for. Novice investors can use the letter grade to screen companies for further research. Other investment data is also provided for each company, which gives sophisticated investors more information to analyze for decision-making. In addition to the featured section, Weiss provides lists of companies with the best and worst scores.

Evaluation: Whether new to investing or well seasoned, the individual investor should welcome the addition of this publication to the Weiss offerings. It has something for everyone, regardless of investment savvy. An additional strength is the large number of companies covered (nearly 9,000) compared to other investment advisory sources. Not under any contractual relationship with the stocks it rates, Weiss is free to rate the poorest performing companies with its worst rating (an "E") or to list them prominently as "high risk" if the data justify it. An objective source is especially important for individual investors, when trust in Wall Street has been damaged by scandals. This investment guide is recommended for public and academic libraries.

*1.198. Weiss Ratings Guide to HMOs and Health Insurers: A Quarterly Compilation of Health Insurance Company Ratings and Analysis [Fall 2001–2002]. Palm Beach Gardens, FL: Weiss Ratings, Inc., © 2001. $219.00, single edition. $438.00, for quarterly subscription. $495 with internet access. Web site: http://www.weissratings.com/.

Authority and scope: In this volume, Weiss Ratings, Inc. publishes information useful for policyholders and prospective policy purchasers evaluating health insurers, including for-profit insurers, mutual insurers, Blue Cross/Blue Shield plans, and for-profit and not-for-profit Health Maintenance Organizations (HMOs). The rating system uses a simple A-F grade, with very few companies receiving an A (excellent) rating, although there are many within the B (good) category. An even larger group falls into the broad average range, which receives C (fair) ratings. Companies that demonstrate serious vulnerabilities receive either D (weak) or E (very weak) ratings. Failed companies are designated with the letter F. To determine the ratings, annual and quarterly financial statements are obtained from state insurance commissioners and are supplemented by information requested directly from the insurance companies. Weiss analysts utilize hundreds of factors that are synthesized into a series of indexes, which are then used to arrive at a letter grade rating. A good rating requires consistency across all indexes. A weak score on any one index can result in a low rating, since insolvency could be caused by any one of a number of factors, such as inadequate capital, unpredictable claims experience, poor liquidity, speculative investments, or operating losses.

Evaluation: Weiss differentiates itself from other rating agencies by using a system that is fairly easy to understand, being the only company currently monitoring the financial condition of the majority of HMOs in the United States, and using a standard for measuring that identifies with the consumer. In another consumer-friendly gesture, the publisher listened to requests by librarians to offer their publications as "one-time" purchases, making them affordable to smaller libraries that can't afford the quarterly subscription. Other consumer-oriented ratings guides offered by Weiss should be acquired, if at all possible. All are available as single editions or on subscription: *Guide to Life, Health & Annuity Insurers; Guide to Property & Casualty Insurers; Guide to Banks and Thrifts; Guide to Brokerage Firms; Guide to Stock Mutual Funds;* and *Guide to Bond & Money Market Funds.*

*1.199. What Color is Your Parachute? A Practical Manual for Job-Hunters and Career-Changers [2002]. Richard Nelson Bolles. Annual. Berkeley, CA: Ten Speed Press, © 2001. $16.95. Web site: http://www.tenspeedpress.com/.

    Authority and scope: This guide, probably the best-known book related to job searching and changing careers, is full of "tell it like it is" information for those who have the challenge of "hiring a new employer," which is the way Bolles views the process. Facts and statistics are presented about the job-hunt game, along with advice on how best to play the game. The latest edition of *What Color is Your Parachute?* includes a chapter entitled "But What If That Doesn't Work?" dealing with alternative job-hunting methods.

    Evaluation: Published annually since 1975, this title continues to provide much practical advice and information, for which there is always a demand on this subject. Libraries that prefer sampling other titles or have the need to economize, might purchase the title in alternating years. Because it is so well-known, however, users would expect to find the latest edition in larger public and academic libraries.

*1.200. Who's Who in Finance and Industry [2001–2002]. 32nd ed. Chicago: Marquis Who's Who, 1936–. $295.00. Web site: www.marquiswhoswho.com/.

    Authority and scope: *Who's Who in Finance and Industry* provides authoritative biographical sketches of more than 22,000 business executives, selected government officials, heads of stock exchanges, business educators and researchers, directors of professional and trade associations, labor union officers, and selected small business professionals. This edition also includes the presidents, chairpersons, and CEOs of the largest minority-owned businesses and the largest Mexican and Canadian industrial firms. Top business school administrators and professors from Mexico, Canada, and the United States are also listed. Individuals are listed alphabetically by last name. Entry information includes the individual's name, position, birth date, parents, children, education, marital status, career history, civic and political activities, military service, professional certifications, memberships, political affiliation, religion, and home and office address. The "Standards of Admissions" statement indicates that the individuals were selected because of conspicuous achievements that distinguish them from the majority of their business contemporaries or because they are principals in firms or organizations of a certain size or type. A comprehensive professional index for fast, easy research by broad industry category or type of profession is provided at the end of the volume.

    Evaluation: The Marquis' *Who's Who* directory provides comprehensive biographical information in a regrettably small font. Marquis' *Who's Who in Finance and Industry* is recommended for all business-oriented academic and public libraries.

*1.201. Working Americans, 1880–1999. 3 volume set. Scott Derks. Lakeville, CT: Grey House Pub., 2000–. Volume I: working class; Volume II: middle class; Volume III is set to examine the upper class. $145.00 per volume. Web site: http://www.greyhouse.com/.

    Authority and scope: The working class volume examines the social and economic life of 34 families, while the middle class volume examines 32 families. Each family profile details the family earnings, spending habits, and how they spend their time at work and at home. *Working Americans* takes a decade-by-decade approach to illustrate the growth and development of the working and middle classes. Each chapter (decade) provides an overview of important events, a brief family profile, a historical snapshot, and an economic profile. The family profile description includes annual income and budget information, work, home, and community life. The historical snapshot section lists major events that occurred in a particular year. The economic profile provides salaries for routine working class jobs, selected prices (e.g., groceries, clothes, medical), key events, and inventions of the time. A bibliography of sources by decade completes each volume. Photographs and advertisements of the period are scattered throughout, making the book a delightful reference source to use.

Evaluation: Students and researchers alike should enjoy discovering the cost of a pair of shoes in 1919 ($3.75), or the price for a bottle of Pepsi in 1945 ($0.05). *Working Americans: 1880–1999* is recommended for all public and academic libraries.

*1.202. **World Almanac and Book of Facts [2002].** New York: St. Martins Press, 1868–. Annual. $29.95. Web site: http://www.facts.com/fdcrs/.

Authority and scope: The *World Almanac*, a compilation of facts, figures, and statistics that cover a vast array of subjects, contains important events of the previous year, election results, economic and employment statistics, scientific achievements of the year, and educational statistics. It includes the addresses of U.S. colleges and universities; astronomy, weather, and calendar topics; awards (books, broadcasting, movies, Nobel Prizes, etc.); prominent personalities; U.S. cities and states; flags of the world nations; and sports and vital statistics information. In addition, it contains consumer information, nutritional food values. societies and associations, biographies of U.S. presidents, the Constitution, and obituaries of famous people. Original statistical sources are cited at the base of the tables or column. The almanac has a very good general index in the front of the volume.

Evaluation: *World Almanac* is an excellent, long-established ready reference tool that belongs in all public and academic libraries.

*1.203. **World Bank Atlas [2001].** Washington, DC: The World Bank. 1967–. Annual. $20.00. Web site: http://www.worldbank.org/.

Authority and scope: *World Bank Atlas* provides a quick look at the state of life around the globe in more than 60 charts and over 20 maps that illustrate major world trends. The World View sections discuss the development goals for the 21st century. People, Environment and Economy sections chart life expectancy, infancy deaths, undernourished children, girls in school, water data, personal spending, forest and energy issues, income per person, growth, and agricultural and investment data. The States & Markets sections illustrate military spending, paved roads, telephone lines, and personal computers information. Global Links section chart private capital flow and the net aid to various countries. The *Atlas* is written in English, French, and Spanish.

Evaluation: *World Bank Atlas* is a worthwhile candidate for the ready reference collection as it provides a broad overview of world economies at a reasonable price. It is recommended for all academic and public libraries.

*1.204. **World Business Resources.com/: A Directory of 8,000+ Business Resources on the Internet.** Garrett Wasny. New York: McGraw-Hill, © 2000. $27.95. Web site: http://www.worldbusinessresources.com/.

Authority and scope: Global in scope, this annotated directory provides Web sites covering 230 countries and territories, and profiles of the leading trade applications and services on the Web in each of the 50 American states and 10 Canadian provinces. Tips for global businesspeople are also presented, as well as reviews of the leading Web-trade tools in 20 functional areas, including train-

ing, sales, purchasing, banking, accounting, law, customs brokerage, and shipping.

Evaluation: As with any directory packed with URLs (Web addresses), there
is a greater potential for out-of-date material. Nevertheless, the book has valuable information and leads to Web sites, especially useful to a small business
owner who wants to expand to the international marketplace. It is recommended
for public and academic libraries with small business clientele, especially because of the affordable price.

*1.205. **World Chamber of Commerce Directory [2001].** Loveland, CO: World
Chamber of Commerce directory, 1967–. $40.00. Web site: http://
www.chamberofcommerce.com/.

Authority and scope: The *World Chamber of Commerce Directory* provides
an alphabetical listing of all United States chambers of commerce by state, then
by town, with entry information including the president or manager of the chamber, address, telephone, fax numbers, and e-mail or Web address. State tourism
boards, convention, and visitor bureaus and economic development organizations are also included. Other listings cover the American chambers of commerce abroad, U.S. foreign and ethnic chambers, Canadian and foreign chambers,
and foreign tourist information bureaus. The U.S. government information section presents state capitol addresses and telephone numbers, governors, and U.S.
senators and representatives. Ambassadors, fax numbers, and in some cases e-
mail addresses, are included for the foreign embassies in the United States and
abroad.

Evaluation: Public and academic libraries should find the *World Chamber
of Commerce Directory* a useful ready reference resource with broader information coverage than implied by its title.

*1.206. **World Cost of Living Survey.** Robert S. Lazich. 2nd ed. Detroit: Gale
Group, 1997–. Biennial. $265.00. Web site: http://www.galegroup.com/.

Authority and scope: This resource is a compilation of price information
from 30,000 reports covering over 3,900 goods and services from around the
world. The information was derived from over 514 sources, including country
statistical reports, government publications, associations, and online services,
and has been designed to assist researchers, analysts, planners, relocators, and
travelers with data on cost-of-living standards in over 200 countries. The book
is divided into five sections, including cities by country, items covered, abbreviations, cost of living data, and the list of sources. The country and list of resources are the main sections. The country section is set in a table format with
the cities, provinces, and districts alphabetically arranged below the country
name, and major subjects alphabetically arranged below the city name. Some of
the subjects included are energy costs, family expenses, housing, and transportation prices. The country, city, and subject are listed in column one; measurement information such as dozen, hour, week is listed in the "per" column; the
"value" column contains average prices represented in U.S. dollars and some
foreign currency; the "date" column indicates the cost of an item at a particular

time from the consulted resource; the last column, "ref," contains a number that can be used to locate the item listed in the resource section.

Evaluation: The *World Cost of Living Survey* is recommended for public and academic libraries whose budget and clientele would indicate interest. Vacationers should find the book useful for estimating vacation expenses. Companies and employees planning to relocate to a foreign country can get valuable cost of living standards for possible salary adjustments or compensations.

*1.207. The World Economic Factbook [2001–2002]. 9th ed. London: Euromonitor, 1993–. $520.00. Web site: http://www.euromonitor.com/.

Authority and scope: The *World Economic Factbook* presents hard-to-find political and economic information on 205 countries of the world, laid out in a concise and consistent format. The main section of the book is arranged in alphabetical order by country, with each country presented as a two-page entry. The first page is a textual summary and the second contains statistical information for the years 1998–2000. The following are provided for most countries: inflation (percent change), exchange rate (per US$), interest rate (percent per annum, lending rate), GDP (percent real growth), GDP (million units of national currency), GDP (US$ million), GDP per capita (US$), consumption (US$ million), consumption per capita (US$), population, birth rate, death rate, number of households, total exports (US$ million), total imports (US$ million), tourism receipts (US$ million), and tourist spending (US$ million). Also covered are: urban population (percent), age analysis (percent), population by sex, life expectancy, infant mortality, and adult literacy. Finally, major export destinations and import sources of origin are given as a percent share per country. Other features include numerous tables ranking countries on the above criteria, and maps showing the different continents with the location of each country and a few major cities. On the textual information page, categories of information include area, currency, location, head of state, head of government, ruling party, political structure, last elections, political risk, international disputes, economy, main industries, and energy.

Evaluation: The information presented and consistency of presentation allows not only ease of access, but also the maximum degree of comparability, in this valuable resource. Whenever possible, data have been drawn from national sources, such as national statistical agencies, and supplemented where necessary from multilateral sources such as the International Monetary Fund, United Nations, or the International Labour Organization. In some cases, Euromonitor provided estimates, based on the best available external data. The information provided is of interest to wider audiences beyond business and is recommended for all libraries whose budget allows for purchase.

1.208. World Market Share Reporter 2001–2002. Detroit, MI: Gale Group, 1995–. $340.00. Web site: http://www.galegroup.com/.

Authority and scope: *World Market Share Reporter* (WMSR) is a companion volume to *Market Share Reporter*, with market share data gathered from published brokerage reports and periodical literature. The categories covered include corporate, institutional, brand, product, commodity, service, and facility shares. Share data is presented from more than 3,400 companies, 850 brands and 1,265 product, commodity, service, and facility categories. Miscellaneous areas such as environmental issues and governmental expenditure are dealt with in a category known as "other shares." Pie charts and bar graphs frequently appear in various entries, with sources cited at the base of each entry. An index section allows access by source, place names, products, services, names and issues, company, and brands. Two appendices deal with 1) the Standard Industrial Classification (SIC) code, the International Standard Industrial Classification (ISIC) code, and the Harmonized Code Classification (HC) and 2) an Annotated Source List.

Evaluation: *World Market Share Reporter* data is slightly dated because of the publication process difficulties, especially when the content is derived from other published sources. However, the business world's interest in market share data makes this unique resource important. Since *WMSR* is a companion to the *Market Share Reporter*, it is recommended that libraries consider purchasing both volumes. If budget considerations argue against that, the international volume would be more essential for academic and large public libraries, especially if the business community is oriented to global market share data.

*1.209. Worldwide Petroleum Industry Outlook: 2001–2005 Projection to 2010. Robert J. Beck. 17th ed. Tulsa, OK: PenWell, © 2000. $195.00. Web site: http://www.pennwell.com/.

Authority and scope: Produced by the publisher of the *Oil & Gas Journal*, this book is organized into 10 sections: worldwide outlook-demand; worldwide outlook-supply; U.S. outlook-demand; U.S. outlook-supply; capital expenditures; exploration, drilling, and production; refining and petrochemicals; transportation; natural gas; and other energy sources. The pattern of coverage includes a review, outlook, keys to the future, outlook table 2000–2005, growth rates table 2000–2010, and long-range outlook table, 2007–2011. In addition, each section also provides some unique data. The book concludes with a chapter on the Organization of Petroleum Exporting Countries (OPEC) and a chapter highlighting information from other forecasts, such as the United States Energy Information Administration (EIA).

Evaluation: This book presents information on the petroleum industry in narrative and statistical formats, a combination that enhances its value to the user. The author is a respected analyst in the energy industry, having established the largest private energy statistics database in the world at the *Oil & Gas Journal*, where he is the economics editor. The book is generously illustrated with tables and charts, and provides historical analysis as well as explanations of political and economic conditions affecting the energy industry today. The volume is recommended for public and academic libraries, as well as business libraries in the energy industry.

*1.210. **Writing a Convincing Business Plan.** Arthur R. Dethomas and Lin Grensing. 2nd ed. Hauppauge, NY: Barron's Educational Series, © 2001. $14.95. Web site: http://www.barronseduc.com/.

Authority and scope: *Writing a Convincing Business Plan* is a practical how-to book. Dethomas and Grensing guide the budding entrepreneur through the planning, research, and plan writing processes. The book is divided into two sections. Section one discusses the financing proposal and business description requirements; section two reviews elements need to prepare the operational portion of the business plan. The various chapters deal with how to conduct an industry or market analysis, sales forecasting, creating marketing and operating plans, a description of organizational and financial plans, and how to obtain financial assistance from primary and secondary sources. The latter part of the book contains a glossary, Web sites, and a list of business and library resources especially useful for small business owners.

Evaluation: *Writing a Convincing Business Plan* is an excellent reasonably priced guide for developing a top-notch business plan. It is written for those individuals planning to start or currently managing a small to medium-sized business. The book is recommended for academic and public libraries, and the small business entrepreneur.

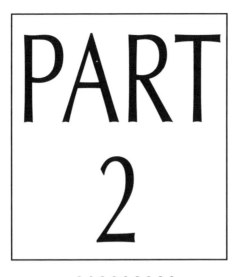

PART 2

Business Reference Sources and Services: Essays

Business Libraries:
Changing Collections, Services, and Roles

Jane Moore McGinn

INTRODUCTION

The early historical development of business libraries and services has been chronicled in a number of notable works, including Lapp, Cleland, Hyde, Perron, Handy, Johnston, and Blakely,[1] since John Cotton Dana created the first business branch of a public library in 1904.[2] In these works, a pattern emerges—business library services and collections have been in a continuous state of evolution. The evolution has been prompted by transitions in business operations, changes in the economy, rapid increases in the rate of technological changes, and related changes in business information needs, and in the production and delivery of business information. The business-related literature of the last decade continues to document this evolution of business libraries and their collections.

In the previous edition of this book, Hryciw-Wing[3] noted that "the literature related to business libraries, despite noting the importance of organizing business materials, has over the years concentrated on the retrieval of information for users and the 'servicing of users,' rather than on collections." Since 1995, the literature related to business libraries has continued to focus on retrieval, but much of the recent literature has not only addressed retrieval of business materials but also focused on the changing nature of the business environment, especially the impact of technological changes on collections and services in business libraries. Evolving roles for business or corporate librarians, the growing prevalence of "virtual business collections," and the call for new methods of organizing and accessing business resources have been predominant themes in business library literature since the mid 1990s. In the

---

Jane Moore McGinn is President of Library Management Solutions and Associate Professor, School of Communication, Information and Library Science, Department of Library Science, Southern Connecticut State University.

literature, one can follow the transformation of business library collections from primarily print (with access to few electronic databases) to what is now frequently referred to as the "digital" or "virtual" library. Almost invisible in the recent literature of business libraries is discussion of traditional library methods for organizing, classifying, indexing, retrieving and storing business information.

In its discussion of the changes in collections, services and roles within business libraries, the recent literature about business libraries primarily focuses on:

- Reengineering of business libraries;
- Changes in the information seeking behaviors of users;
- Changes in the format of business information; and
- Changes in collection development and collections access.

REENGINEERING THE BUSINESS LIBRARY

In 1995, Piggott[4] outlined the need for corporate librarians to reengineer business libraries, citing expectations of the corporate world to have products delivered faster to all parts of the world. She stressed that in addition to delivering information faster, while using the most cost-effective electronic resources available, information needed to be distributed via "a borderless service" through which information could "be sought wherever it exists and used immediately by local or remote customers."[5] Piggot cautioned that reengineering business libraries to meet the changing business environment would change the roles of business librarians. She advised that trained information professionals of the future would be "selecting, evaluating, and acquiring information required to do business and providing the training necessary to access and filter the information to achieve precision retrieval in a fast, accurate, and effective manner."[6]

Outsourcing

One side effect of corporate library reengineering, at least since the 1980s, has been the corporate trend toward downsizing. For example, Bank of America closed its corporate library and Chevron and Time-Life downsized their libraries.[7] Quint[8] warned librarians about the dangers of complacency during times of change by emphasizing that if librarians continued to emphasize "traditional services, e.g., collection over client service, in an environment driven by client concerns, the process of decline" would accelerate. Helfer[9] also wrote about the consequences of complacency when he described the trend toward outsourcing "many positions and services traditionally performed by permanent library employees." As an example, Apple Corporation's library was one of many libraries that were eliminated in favor of using outside library consultants to get information.[10] Similarly, Lemons[11] chronicled Ohio-based Owens Corning Library's transition from "Library" to "Knowledge Resource Services," including the decision to outsource specific library services and concentrate on developing, implementing, and managing expanded access to and use of knowledge resources and tools.

It should be noted, in contrast, that Sun Microsystems is unique in that it reversed the trend of "outsourcing" library services. Sun's library had its beginnings in 1982 as an outsourced operation; however, in 1991, some library services were brought in-house and "SunLibrary" was born. The new in-house library was reorganized, streamlining services such as photocopying materials available on their intranet and reducing the amount of data previously kept on the receipt and tracking of periodicals. Materials were identified and evaluated by library staff while their actual handling was outsourced. A contract staff person checked in and shelved periodicals, created the electronic table of contents, and claimed missing or damaged issues. The company's technical and market researchers performed SunLibrary's research, while outsourced vendors provided document delivery services.[12]

Changes in Job Priorities

Studies of special and research libraries, conducted by James Matarazzo[13] in 1997 and 2000 pointed to more innovation in the business libraries of the future. Business librarians who participated in Matarazzo's surveys indicated that in the future they would most likely "concentrate more on synthesizing, organizing, and filtering information and less on traditional practices such as cataloging, procurement, and routine searches. Electronic database publishing, Web pages, more powerful and effective search engines, and networks were frequently cited as important elements of the IT [Information Technology] landscape that . . . enabled corporate librarians to 'off-load' traditional activities to end-users."[14]

Changes in Organizational Alignments and Services

In part because of the trends noted above, corporate, research, and public business libraries have experienced many changes in their placement within management hierarchies. For example, corporate libraries are now often aligned with individual strategic business units, a centralized research and development service, or corporate-wide activities such as information technology or information systems. [15] And, the librarians in these corporations are often part of corporate teams, using their research skills to work more directly with marketing and other departments, tracking outsourcing efforts, and documenting what works or doesn't work for the best interests of the company.[16]

Business school libraries, while generally supervised by the dean or director of the university's library, often provide separate services within their own facilities, and often follow processes and procedures that are unique to the business school library (examples include the state-of-the-art electronic business information center at the University of California at Berkeley in its Haas School of Business Complex;[17] the Web-based Virtual Business Information Center business information portal developed collaboratively by University of Maryland libraries, College of Information Studies and the R.H. Smith School of Business;[18] and the University of Pennsylvania Wharton School's Lippincott Library's 1990 creation of an electronic library with free end-user access available on a local area network[19]).

Business departments of public libraries have followed patterns of transformation similar to those in corporate libraries. In her 1998 review of public library services to businesses, Beverly Lynch,[20] quoting Fenner,[21] identified two business library organizational patterns during the first half of the twentieth century. The first pattern was to open a separate business branch of the main library (for example, Newark Public Library); the second was to create a department within the main library building (for example, the Los Angeles Public Library). Fenner lamented that only a few libraries were promoting extensive service to businesses and corporations. The approach taken by most had been to serve individuals, not groups. The library collections and the kinds of information provided reflected the needs and interests of individual users.[22] By the end of the twentieth century, this situation had changed dramatically. In her review of recent changes in the business services provided by public libraries, Lynch[23] identified the availability of information resources over the Internet as the major catalyst for changing the ways in which public libraries provided business information services. Lynch predicted that as business information and economic data on the Web continued to increase, public librarians would have "to identify appropriate, accurate, and organized data sources and . . . assist patrons in accessing and interpreting the information."[24] Lynch's prediction was accurate, and Fenner's admonition to librarians that they needed to focus on business groups as well as business individuals was heeded. Some public libraries approached the tasks identified by Lynch through the creation of databases specifically designed to serve their local business communities (Georgia's Business Dateline full-text database and Kalamazoo County's Business Directory are two such models[25]). Other public libraries approached innovation differently, especially in the ways that they served small business owners. Deady[26] described the need for renovating or building new public library structures and work spaces to accommodate the computer workstations required for accessing the vast amounts of electronic business information. Hoffman[27] and Field[28] too, in their descriptions of the 1997 opening of New York Public Library's Science, Industry, and Business Branch, paid particular attention to the long list of CD-ROM and online services being offered to the business community. The installation of over 70 workstations in the new "Electronic Information Center," along with 50 new online public access catalog terminals, were touted as the "high-tech" model of the public library business department of the future. Similarly, Price, Whitney-Leigh, and Tripp[29] discussed Ontario's London Public Library's development of a unique business service designed to specifically meet the information needs of "homepreneurs," defined as "knowledge workers whose homes are their workplaces." Services included organizing support groups and networking sessions for homepreneurs, along with developing special collections of business books, videos, and information services.

Zarsky,[30] Erbes,[31] Trapp,[32] Hicks,[33] and Persic[34] summarized the types of new business information services that arose during the 1990s:

- Increased offerings of new online business information databases;
- Training in the use of online resources for researching business information;
- Home and office access to public library business materials, including document delivery via the internet or email; and
- Expanded collections of books and current periodicals focusing on business issues in the information age.

CHANGES IN INFORMATION SEEKING BEHAVIORS OF USERS

The business literature of the late 1990s suggested that changes had occurred in the ways in which employees of small businesses searched and used business information resources, as well as the implications for librarians assisting them. Ren[35] examined how small-business executives searched for government information, and stressed that public information specialists needed to inform small-business executives about their libraries' onsite assistance as well as the librarians' willingness to provide information assistance via phone, fax or e-mail. Baker[36] described focus group interviews by Iowa City Public Library, through which the librarians discovered that members of the business communities "were eager for services to help them access the library's collections without spending too much time waiting in line at the information or circulation desk" and that they wanted some form of information delivery to save time.[37] Similar findings were reported in the British Library Research and Innovation Centre's 1998 study of *Business Information and the Internet*,[38] which examined how small companies in Glasgow and London used the Internet for business information.

In general, studies of the information seeking behaviors of business users led to various innovations:

- Organization of business collections for easy off-site access;
- Creation of electronic information, searchable with simple language queries or industry specific terminology;
- Provision of professional search services to save end-user time in locating certain kinds of information (even if remote access to information was available); and
- Continuing purchase of print resources.

CHANGES IN THE FORMAT OF BUSINESS INFORMATION

The development of new formats and methods of delivery for business information is a primary focus of the business library literature. In her vision of the future, Eugenia Prime[39] foresaw changes in the collection, organization, and delivery of business information as she observed that "requesters" of information had become "accessors" of information.[40] Prime's 1993 observations keenly forecast the "virtual library" of today. Ghilardi[41] similarly predicted, in 1994, that future information centers would change dramatically, with few print resources remaining and more information being available at staff members' desktops, allowing them to do most of their own research. Surveys conducted by Forrester Research Projects[42] and Outsell, Inc.[43] documented growth patterns in the use of the Internet for accessing business information or for business-to-business services and products. And, in the third annual "Information Professional Study" from Outsell, Inc., Stratigos[44] reported that two-thirds of the respondents indicated a move "toward fully or nearly digital libraries."

In relation to the move toward virtual libraries, numerous articles, from a broad spectrum of disciplines, focused on the addition of new Web sites for business information or the entry of new Web-based versions of well-known proprietary business databases into the marketplace. Mick O'Leary [45] described the 1996–1997 introduction of Web-based versions of some familiar commercial databases and explained why so many companies moved to the Web. He outlined the key features of the first Web-based editions of *Profound*, *NewsNet*, UMI's *ProQuest Direct*, Dow Jones *Wall Street Journal Interactive* (*WSJIE*), Lexis Nexis' *reQUESTer*, and *DIALOG Web*.

Further reflecting the interest noted above, one of the oldest publishing companies of business information products, Thomas Publishing Company, began moving access to its products to the Internet in 1995. Thomas' first Internet product, the free *Thomas Register on the Internet*, offered brief company descriptions, while the CD-ROM, print, and other online versions offered the more extensive profiles. This Web site has undergone a number of revisions since its introduction. Thomas Publishers now provides a menu of free Web sites for different markets and has joined with other companies such as Dialog, EBSCO Publishing, and GE Information Services to produce new fee-based or subscription services via CD-ROM, Internet, or IntraNets.[46]

Another notable introduction along these lines was *Dow Jones Interactive (DJI)*, an updated, Web-based version of Dow Jones News/Retrieval.[47] *Bizsuite*, which combines three individual subscription databases, *Business & Industry*, *Business and Management Practice*, and *TableBase*, introduced a Web-based version of its CD-ROM product in 1999.[48]

There has also been a proliferation of business information Web sites hosted by colleges and universities, as noted by Brody[49] in 1999. These new ".edu" sites contain various types of information that serve a variety of business information needs. Generally, the .edu sites contain information such as course notes, supplemental sources, or teaching aids; samples or examples of the research output of the business faculty; information to fulfill the university's mission of disseminating information or knowledge to the public or to a particular community resulting from school research efforts; descriptions of collaborative efforts with government entities and nonprofit organizations concerning business interests; or business information to promote the school's public relations efforts.[50]

The rapid growth in the number of free business information Web sites, coupled with the introduction of revised CD-ROM or Web-based proprietary databases has generated frequent discussions in the library-related media on the benefits of accessing business information using these new delivery systems. Berman's[51] discussion of some of the virtues of these products, especially the appeal to small business owners because of the ease in searching for information and the availability of many free or rather inexpensive electronic resources, is particularly noteworthy.

CHANGES IN COLLECTION DEVELOPMENT AND COLLECTIONS ACCESS

Changes in format of standard business information resources have necessitated changes in the ways that librarians facilitate end users' access to business information.

New Cataloging and Classification Systems

In Marlene Manoff's[52] review of the literature related to "reconceptualization of collection development and bibliographic access," she cautioned librarians that "[as] online catalogs and library Web pages . . . merge[d] with [the] electronic journals and full-text databases to which they connect[ed]. . . . Patrons [would] find it difficult to distinguish catalogs from indexes, from full-text databases, from document delivery, from interlibrary loan, and even online reference."[53] In light of this observation, Manoff questioned the continuing wisdom of using traditional cataloging and classification systems such as Library of Congress Classification, Library of Congress Subject Headings, and Dewey Decimal Classification. She urged that these time-honored access tools might not be relevant any more because there no longer existed "a widely sustained belief that there is single nature and order to things, logically organized and structured as a hierarchy, ready to be embodied in a single classification scheme."[54] Manoff addressed the need for new access skills for business librarians and described some alternative methods for classifying electronic resources mentioned in recent literature. Access options noted by Manoff included use of MYLibrary[55] software (developed by Eric Morgan at North Carolina State University),[56] for the creation of in-house Web pages that utilized discipline specific subject thesauri, and implementation of *Dublin Core*,[57] "a metadata set established to provide simplified cataloging of electronic materials."[58]

New Indexing Methods

Boeri and Hensel[59] stressed the importance of new methods for indexing business information, due to the increased use of the Internet, intranets, and databases for storing and retrieving information. They noted that business librarians were turning to customized search software that allowed them to use a combination of traditional subject headings and natural language to access business information. New skills that were required to use or create customized access software for electronic resources required librarians to learn new indexing skills such as the ability to create customized thesauri, specify preferred "lexical character sets" for searching, and make decisions on whether electronic indexes would permit case-sensitive searches, number searches, or searches using combinations of numbers, letters, and characters. Other decisions to make included whether or not patrons would be able to search and retrieve information by keyword, keyword/title, company name, concepts (e.g., "strategic planning"), department name, industry name or SIC code, document type, geographic area, or source.[60]

Industry Portals

Another new access tool, introduced in the literature of the last few years, is the use of "industry portals." Ojala[61] explained a *portal* as a single Web page that served as a gateway to Web sites and other resources. For business librarians searching the Internet, Ojala noted that industry portals could "substitute for the checklist of the experienced searcher and . . . give a needed nudge to online veterans who suddenly . . . [ran] out of ideas when running into industry research brick walls."[62] Prior to Web sources becoming an integral part of online research, Ojala pointed out, most business researchers automatically started the search for industry information in subscription databases such as PROMT, Business and Industry, Investext, ABI/Inform, etc. Another notable observation by Ojala is that "…you won't find, on a non-library Web industry portal site, any indication that there is valuable industry information in the subscription databases information professionals know and love…" (e.g., Dialog, LexisNexis, PROMT and others).[63]

Transforming Library Space from "Physical" to "Virtual"

In his discussion of library facilities, Stratigos[64] noted the need for business libraries to transition from a "physical" to a "virtual" model in terms of space planning. He described the physical model as a library with a traditional reference desk and services, and a collection of print, microfilm, and media materials in browsable stacks or archives. As noted earlier, cataloging in the traditional physical model usually relies on the use of "Library of Congress/Dewey Decimal/UDC classification schemes, a physical card catalog, local electronic catalogs, and Union Lists."[65] Stratigos defined a virtual model as a library, which "acquires, stores, organizes, and distributes its information content primarily in electronic form."[66] In Stratigos' "virtual model" library, physical space would be designed to accommodate a central call center, desktop computers, self-serve information resources, and centralized systems for client e-mail and Web inquiries. The virtual model library would include printed books and journals in browsable stacks. But, the library would also include digital formats that would be made accessible through business information Web portals designed for specific end users, and providing both global access and access to the in-house resources of the company. Cataloging activities would include "networked online catalogs, the use of metadata/metatagging, text search engines, and dynamic business specific taxonomies for classification and retrieval."[67] An example of such a library is the Packer Engineering, Inc.'s[68] corporate library, where library and computer staff collaborated on the creation of an in-house customized online catalog accessible from every employee's desktop. The catalog, Library Services Database (LSDB), incorporated books and audiovisuals with call numbers, and digitalized versions of automotive manuals, vertical files, and company standards, as well as password-protected library tips sheets and index cards of login information to subscription services.[69]

Commercial Indexing Software

The massive migration of business databases to the Internet has been accompanied by changes in search and retrieval options that have, in many cases, eliminated the need for complicated search commands. For example, databases like *Dow Jones Interactive* no longer require "dot-dot" commands, knowledge of source codes for specific journals, or the syntax previously required to limit the time frame of a search,[70] and Web publishing software, such as DB/Text WebPublisher from Inmagic,[71] has been used by some libraries for managing Web/intranet site information because it combines the precision of a database system with the flexibility of a text retrieval system. Web publishing software has the advantage of allowing library staff to format information for specific groups of business information users by simply changing descriptor fields to key words.[72]

Use of Intranets

Business libraries are increasingly using intranet technology to disseminate information throughout their companies. For example, Mallinckrodt, Inc., a manufacturer of medical products and pharmaceuticals, added a variety of information resources to its Intranet in 1999. The first application launched was the resource catalog of its Information Resource Center (IRC), which included books, annual reports, and videos. Later, Mallinckrodt's databases of competitive files were added, along with summaries of pertinent news items that were delivered to staff via email around the world.[73] Similarly, the American Heart Association (AHA) National Center in Dallas, Texas has used an intranet-based library and help desk to disseminate information to AHA staff across the country. The Center also used DB/Text WebPublisher from Inmagic, Inc.[74] software to develop a news release database in which librarians indexed a journal's name, the article's authors, the page numbers, and key words for searching. On the library's intranet site, users were able to choose from a book catalog database, journal catalog, or the news release database, and use a search form designed by library staff to query the databases and access help pages.[75]

Owens Corning Library, after outsourcing its commodity services such as cataloging, document delivery, current awareness, and online services, focused its energies on creating "knowledge" navigational tools such as InfoMap, which allowed users to access the company's intranet without really knowing what a resource they might find there was used for or where it was located.[76] In another example, Kellogg's Information Center was redesigned to incorporate an intranet for dissemination of in-house research and commercial database information. A document management project to create an electronic depository for research documentation previously available only on microfilm involved scanning old print documents (performed by contract workers), to which the Kellogg Information Center librarians added indexing and tagging.[77] In still another example, the Digital Equipment Corporation (DEC) library launched its Web library in 1996 to distribute the company's research information to its employees around the world. DEC library organized and distributed its corporate information on its own global Intranet—using LiveLink content management software that aided in organizing huge volumes of intranet information.[78]

Not every business library digitalizes archival information and internal documents; some still use traditional classification and storage methods. Patricia Fernberg[79] described how SmithKline and French Laboratories Library reorganized their information services departments to gain better control over reams of documentation which supported the pharmaceutical company's computerized business systems. The librarians used a system of mixed media library shelving units with interchangeable filing components, including stationary and roll-out reference shelves and hanger-bars for storing computer system documentation and reference materials in Documate cartridges. Individual locking cabinets were used to store confidential materials. The library was organized by application areas, with technical reference volumes, publications, and storage cartridges arranged by numerical and color codes. A quick reference index was maintained to help users locate information. These traditional collection organization methods best suited the plans of the staff members restructuring the library in 1991, even with the variety of technological aids available at that time.

Another somewhat traditional approach for an insurance agency office was described by Gail Buchholz,[80] Director of the InfoCenter Life Insurance Marketing Research Association. She noted, in 1995, that "An elaborate classification system and card catalog are not necessary. Physical space, shelves, and a file cabinet are all that are needed to get started."[81] Books and videotapes were arranged on shelves by subject, with the business and insurance collection first, followed by each subject grouping of books alphabetized by title. The recommended periodical collection for a small insurance agency library included newspapers and business and trade press publications, *New York Times* and *Wall Street Journal* subscriptions, and weekly or biweekly news magazines, along with industry association publications. Establishing a clippings or vertical file collection of articles, pamphlets and booklets was also suggested. Buchholz[82] recommended using a Rolodex to inventory the library. She also suggested arranging vertical file materials according to an information retrieval index system published by Million Dollar Round Table (MDRT), an association for top sales professionals in the life insurance-based financial services business.[83]

Designing Access Systems for Specific Audiences

Some of the literature related to accessing business information has noted variations in the information needs of specific businesses and how these individual needs dictated the use of print or electronic resources. One such case, presented by Stinson,[84] described the Forbes Magazine Information Center, in which, Stinson explains, a well-organized print collection was essential to provide for fact-checking of information for news stories, an important part of employees' jobs in the media/publishing industry. Stinson described the 1999 organization of the Forbes library. Resources, recognized as reliable for fact-checking by both librarians and editions, were marked with a bright orange dot and grouped together on the shelves for quick access. At that time it was the information center's policy to use print resources for fact-checking and staff rarely used online databases for information. Stinson's work described the issues surrounding accuracy of sources and the reliability of information at that time. However, Stinson noted that some other newspaper libraries did not share the point of view expressed by Forbes employees, and related how some librarians and editorial researchers in the *Washington Post* and *Los Angeles Times* newspaper libraries preferred the use of databases such as LexisNexis, Dow Jones, Dialog, or the Internet to verify information. Librarians in those institutions noted the benefit of more newspapers making their archives available on the internet with keyword search functions.

The literature notes that business libraries in the United Kingdom (UK) and Canada vary in the degree to which the Web is used for accessing business information. CD-ROMs are still more widely used than Internet-based databases. Headland's Business Information Survey,[85] which tracked changes in the use of business information in the United Kingdom (UK) for several years, revealed that "company information" ranked as the most important information requested in business libraries. Pam Foster[86] reported in her work that United Kingdom companies were classified differently than in the United States, so that accessing information about United Kingdom businesses often required different information sources and different search strategies. United Kingdom companies were classified by three types of organizational structure: sole traders, partnerships, and companies, which were then subdivided into private limited (Ltd.) and public limited company (PLC) classifications. Foster advised business information seekers using Internet search engines to locate United Kingdom companies, that the inclusion of "PLC" in the company's name or adding ".co.uk" to the companies' URL might be important in retrieving the appropriate information.

Other important differences in locating UK business information were delineated by Foster. For example, in the United States, government information about companies is free through Web-based databases such as EDGAR. However, in the United Kingdom, company information filed with Companies House, a division of the United Kingdom's Department of Trade & Industry, may be part of the fee-based products and services offered on the Companies House Web page. Foster also cited examples of popular UK CD-ROM and internet-based business information resources, including some free Web sites.[87]

Finally, Wright[88] described some Canadian Corporate libraries' moves toward becoming "virtual libraries." He noted that Canadian banks had library-like departments, although by 1994 very few of them were actually called "libraries." Similarly, collections in these facilities consisted of very few books and relied more on online computer databases and CD-ROMs to access information requested by corporations and bank departments.[89] Stinson[90] presented an overview of corporate libraries in the Bank of Montreal, and noted that by 1995, the Bank of Montreal's Business Information Centers were using internal networks to distribute access to real-time news sources, and had installed research workstations where users could access CD-ROM services, the Internet, the library electronic catalog, and other resources.[91]

CONCLUSION

The literature since 1995 demonstrates that the world of business libraries has changed. Business librarians have had to reevaluate how business information is collected, stored, accessed, retrieved, and delivered to an ever-changing group of business information users. Literature on business libraries has steadily shifted from focusing on acquisitions, cataloging and appropriate search strategies, to how to best digitalize, organize, and facilitate access. Business libraries are restructuring and refocusing to accommodate vast amounts of electronic information from a variety of information sources and for an increasingly diverse set of information seeking behaviors among end users.

Although business librarians must understand the core classification systems and organization methods of the library profession, the migration of more and more business resources to electronic formats, especially Web-based, has created a need for new skills in using metadata for the organization and retrieval of information. Discussions about preserving and storing print archives of corporations are less prevalent than discussions about the latest scanning and computerizing software/hardware for creating electronic archives.

Corporate, academic, and public libraries all continue to develop better ways of providing access to print and electronic collections for employees, parent companies, business students, and local community businesses. Additionally, business library services are being redesigned and expanded to meet the growing business information needs of independent information-seeking public citizens and new groups of business information users such as the homepreneurs described by Gordon Price, et al.[92] As the predictions of Prime,[93] Stratigos,[94] Wright,[95] and others regarding the transformation of traditional business libraries to "virtual libraries" continue to materialize, one can expect that changes in the collections and services offered by business libraries, as well as the skills required of business information specialists will continue to be dramatic. The ability to deliver business information in an efficient, reliable, customized, and user-friendly manner has always been a goal of business libraries; the changes brought about by twenty-first century technology have made this goal more attainable, at the same time as the array of choices has become more complex.

NOTES

1. John A. Lapp, "Organized Information in the Use of Business," *Special Libraries* 6, no. 4 (April 1915): 57–61; Five *Hundred Business Books*, comp. Ethel Cleland, (Washington, DC: American Library Association. Library War Service, 1919); Dorsey W. Hyde, Jr., *Workshops for Assembling Business Facts* (Chicago: American Library Association, 1921); Lillian C. Perron, "Special Libraries: Twenty-Five Years Old," *Special Libraries* 26, no. 1 (January 1935): 6–7; Daniel N. Handy, "The Library as a Business Asset—When and How," *Special Libraries* 3, no. 8 (October 1912): 162–165; W. Dawson Johnston, "The Use of Books in Business," Special Libraries 8, no. 3 (March 1917): 44; and Margaret Blakely, "Business and Technology Section," Bulletin of the American Library Association 31, no. 11 (15 October 1937): 720–730, quoted in *Managing Business Collections in Libraries*, ed. Carolyn A. Sheehy, The Greenwood Library Management Collection (Westport, CT: Greenwood Press, 1996), 2.

2. *Managing Business Collections in Libraries*, ed. Carolyn A. Sheehy, The Greenwood Library Management Collection (Westport, CT: Greenwood Press, 1996), 2.

3. Carol A. Hryciw-Wing, "Organization of Materials in Business Libraries," in *The Basic Business Library: Core Resources*, ed. Bernard Schlessinger and Rashelle S. Karp. 3rd ed. (Westport, CT: Oryx Press, 1995), 283.

4. Sylvia A. Piggott, "Why Corporate Librarians Must Reengineer the Library for the New Information Age," *Special Libraries* 86, no. 1 (Winter 1995): 11. [Database online]. Available from: InfoTrac OneFile; Article no. 16512737.

5. Ibid.

6. Piggott, 11.

7. Barbara Quint, "Write If You Get Work," *Searcher* 2, no. 1 (Jan–Feb 1994): 4. [Database online]. Available from: InfoTrac OneFile; Article no. 14908584.

8. Ibid.

9. Doris Small Helfer, "Outsourcing, Teaming, and Special Libraries: Threats and Opportunities," *Information Outlook* 12, no. 2 (Dec 1998): 26. [Database online]. Available from: InfoTrac Business and Companies Resource Center; Article no. 52480035.

10. Ibid.

11. Nancy Lemon, "Climbing the Value Chain: A Case Study in Rethinking the Corporate Library Function," *Online* 20, no. 6 (Nov–Dec 1996): 50. [Database online]. Available from: LexisNexis Academic Universe; Article no. 00791503 or InfoTrac OneFile; Article no. 18848842.

12. Cynthia Hill, "Insourcing the Outsourced Library: The Sun Story," *Library Journal* 123, no. 4 (1 Mar 1998): 46. [Database online]. Available from: InfoTrac Professional Collection; Article no. 20400599.

13. James M. Matarazzo, "Bites, Bits, and Videao Games: The Changes Ahead," *Journal of Academic Librarianship* 27, no. 3 (May 2001): 171. [Database online]. Available from: Academic Search Elite; Article no. 4498372.

14. Ibid.

15. Matarazzo, 171.

16. Helfer, 26

17. "Thomas J. Long Foundation to Give $3.5 million for Library at UC Berkeley's New Haas School of Business Complex," *Business Wire*, Dec. 19, 1994, p.12190115. [Database online]. Available from: InfoTrac OneFile; Article A15942131.

18. Marydee Ojala, "Industry Portals," *Online* 25, no. 2 (March 2001): 63. [Database online]. Available from: InfoTrac, Professional Collection; Article no. 70910888.

19. Mick O'Leary, "Charting the Course for Online Innovation," *Online* 14, no. 4 (July 1990): 49. [Database online]. Available from: InfoTrac; Article no. 9065729.

20. Beverly P. Lynch, "Public Library Service to Business," *Public Libraries* 37, no. 6 (Nov–Dec 1998): 382–6. [Database online]. Available from: WebSpirs; Article no. 199900008800.

21. Edward H. Fenner, "Business Services in Public Libraries," *Special Libraries* 44 (1953): 224, *quoted* in Beverly P. Lynch, "Public Library Service to Business." *Public Libraries* 37, no. 6 (Nov–Dec 1998): 382–6. [Database online]. Available from: WebSpirs; Article no. 199900008800.

22. Lynch, 386.

23. Ibid.

24. Lynch, 385.

25. Lynch, 382.

26. Tim Deady, "Intelligence Lurks in the Home of the Business Tome," *Los Angeles Business Journal* 14, no. 21 (25 May 1992): 1. [Database online]. Available from: InfoTrac OneFile; Article no. 12274274.

27. David Hoffman, "NYPL Opens Science, Industry and Business Branch," *Computers in Libraries* 16, no. 6 (Jun 1996): 25. [Database online]. Available from: InfoTrac OneFile; Article no. 18383271.

28. Anne Field, "Biblio-tech," *Inc.* 19, no. 13 (16 Sep 1997): 21. Special Issue. [Database online]. Available from : LexisNexis Academic Universe or InfoTrac General Reference Center Gold; Article no. 19765799.

29. Gordon Price, Beth Whitney-Leigh, and Pat Tripp, "Homepreneur Support Groups: From the Water Cooler to the Branch Library," *Public Libraries* 37, no. 4 (Jul–Aug 1998): 229. [Database online]. Available from: WebSpirs; Article no. 199801293300.

30. Terry Zarsky, "Instruction for the Business Community at Pikes Peak Library District," *Colorado Libraries* 26, no.4 (Winter 2000): 38. [Database online]. Available from: WebSpirs; Article no. 200100260300.

31. William C. Erbes, "Reaching Out with Business-Related Information at the Bensenville Community Public Library," *Illinois Libraries* 82, no. 1 (Winter 2000): 40–2. [Database online]. Available from: WebSpirs; Article no. 200001072500.

32. Janice Trapp, "Networking Information Services to Support Local Business," *Rural Libra*ries 19, no. 1 (1999): 37–44. [Database online]. Available from: WebSpirs; Article no. 199900375600.

33. Jim Hicks, "Give Us the Business! St. Charles City-County Library District Provides Opportunities for Starting and Growing a Business," *Missouri Library World* 3, no. 4 (Fall 1998): 14–15. [Database online]. Available from: WebSpirs; Article no. 199900170300.

34. Peter V. Persic, "Businesses Find the Answer at the Central Library's Business Economics Department," *Los Angeles Business Journal* 16, no. 2 (17 Jan 1994): 2B. [Database online]. Available from: InfoTrac OneFile; Article no. 15216762.

35. Wen-Hua Ren, "Self-Efficacy and the Search for Government Information: A Study of Small-Business Executives," *Reference and User Services Quarterly* 38, no. 3 (Spring 1999): 283-91. [Database online]. Available from: Webspirs; Article no. 1999901051800.

36. Sharon L. Baker, "Improving Business Services Through the Use of Focus Groups," *RQ* 30, no. 3 (Spring 1991): 377. [Database online]. Available from: InfoTrac OneFile; Article no. 10641419.

37. Ibid.

38. Sue Allcock, Annette Plenty, Sheila Webber, and Robin Yeates, *Business Information and the Internet: Use of the Internet as an Information Resource for Small and Medium-sized Enterprises: Final Report.* London: The British Library, 1999. (British Library Research and Innovation Report; 136). Available from: http://business.dis.strath.ac.uk/project/final/.

39. Eugenie Prime, "The Virtual Library: A Corporate Imperative," *Information Technology and Libraries* 12, no. 2 (Jun 1993): 248. [Database online]. Available from: InfoTrac OneFile; Article no. 13188147.

40. Ibid.

41. J. Mellor Ghilardi, "The Information Center of the Future: The Professional's Role," *Online* 18, no. 6 (Nov–Dec 1994): 8. [Database online]. Available from: InfoTrac OneFile.

42. Wallys W. Conhaim, "Thomas Publishing: This 'Old-Line' Publisher is Leading Industry into the Emerging Electronic Marketplace," *Link-Up* (Jul–Aug 1998): 12. [Database online]. Available from: InfoTrac Business and Companies Resource Center; Article no. 20949204.

43. Jeff Pemberton, "An Industry Analysis with Outsell, Inc." (Interview with Outsell founders Greg Chagaris and Anthea Stratigos.) Originally published in *Online* (Jul 1999): pp. 40–46. Available from World Wide Web: http://www.onlineinc.com/articles/onlinemag/pemberton997.html.

44. Anthea Stratigos, "Going Virtual with the Corporate Library," *Online* 25, no. 2 (March 2001): 66. [Database online]. Available from: InfoTrac Professional Collection Article no. 70910889 or LexisNexis Academic Universe.

45. Mick O'Leary, "The Business Information Services: Old-Line Online Moves to the Web," *Computers in Libraries* 17, no. 6 (Jun 1997): 30. [Database online]. Available from: InfoTrac, Professional Collection, Article no. A19512549.
46. Conhaim, 12.
47. Mary Ellen Bates, "Interactive," *Online* 22, no. 5 (Sep–Oct 1998): 56. [Database online]. Available from: InfoTrac Professional Collection; Article no. 21086854.
48. Ed Tallent, "BIZSUITE." *Library Journal* 124, no. 14 (1 Sep 1999): 214. [Database online]. Available from: InfoTrac Professional Collection; Article no. 56183888.
49. Roberta Brody, "Doing Business with .edu," *Econtent* (Aug–Sep 1999): 1. [Database online]. Available from: InfoTrac Expanded Academic ASP.
50. Ibid.
51. Dennis Berman, "Mind Your Own Business," *Business Week*, 3650 (11 Oct 1999): F16. [Database online]. Available from: InfoTrac Professional Collection; Article no. 56001151.
52. Marlene Manoff, "Hybridity, Mutability, Multiplicity: Theorizing Electronic Library Collections," *Library Trends* 48, no. 4 (Spring 2000): 857. [Database online]. Available from: InfoTrac Professional Collection; Article no. 65806161.
53. Ibid.
54. Manoff, 857.
55. *My Library@NC State*, "About MyLibrary." Available from: http://my.lib.ncsu.edu/?cmd=about&id=39. Accessed 10 September 2001.
56. Manoff, 857.
57. *Dublin Core Metadata Initiative*, "An Overview of the Dublin Core Metadata Initiative." Available from: http://dublincore.org/about/overview/. Accessed 10 September 2001.
58. Manoff, 857.
59. Robert J. Boeri and Martin Hensel, "Special Libraries and Enterprise Knowledge Management," *EMedia Professional* 11, no. 4 (April 1998): 36. [Database online]. Available from: InfoTrac Professional Collection; Article no. 20406112.
60. Tallent, 214.
61. Ojala, 63.
62. Ibid.
63. Ojala, 63.
64. Stratigos, 66.
65. Ibid.
66. Stratigos, 66.
67. Ibid.
68. Sara R. Tompson, George L. Goehring, Patrick Farrell, Karen Crothers and Gwen Barber, "Engineering Our Own Library Catalog," *Computers in Libraries* 21, no. 2 (Feb 2001): 36. [Database online]. Available from: EbscoHost; Article no. 4078314.
69. Ibid.
70. Bates, 56.

71. *Inmagic Software Solutions*, "Inmagic DB/Text WebPublisher," Available from: http://www.inmagic.com/prod_data_webpub.htm. Accessed 10 September 2001.
72. "American Heart Association and Mallinckrodt, Inc: Healthcare Libraries Find Remedy in Corporate Intranets," *PRNewswire* (Woburn, MA) 21 Jan 1999, p. 8731. [Database online]. Available: InfoTrac OneFile; Article no. 53613995.
73. Ibid.
74. Inmagic Software Solutions.
75. "American Heart," 8730.
76. Lemon, 50.
77. Doris Small Helfer, "They're G-G-R-R-R-E-A-T! Kellogg's Librarians," *Searcher* 5, no. 7 (Jul–Aug 1997): 38. [Database online]. Available from: InfoTrac OneFile; Article no. 19638742.
78. Erin Callaway, "Online Corporate Libraries Stack Up," *PC Week* 15, no. 4 (26 Jan 1998): 80. [Database online]. Available from: InfoTrac OneFile; Article no. 20187547.
79. Patricia M. Fernberg, "Rx for a Rash of Documentation," *Modern Office Technology* 30 (Dec 1985): 70. [Database online]. Available from: InfoTrac OneFile; Article no. 4043388.
80. Gail W. Buchholz, "Get Organized: How to Set Up an Agency Library." *Managers Magazine* 70, no. 2 (Feb 1995): 8. [Database online]. Available from: InfoTrac OneFile; Article no. 16678638.
81. Ibid.
82. Buchholz, 8.
83. "Million Dollar Round Table," 2001. Available from: http://www.mdrt.org/whatsmdrt.html. Accessed 8 August 2001.
84. Stinson, 60.
85. "Annual Business Information Resources Survey," *Business Information Review* 17, no.1 (March 2000): 5, quoted in Pam Foster, "Tracking Down U.K. Company Information," *Online* 25, no. 2 (March 2001): 33. [Database online]. Available from: InfoTrac Professional Collection. Article no. 70910883.
86. Pam Foster, "Tracking Down U.K. Company Information," *Online* 25, no.2 (Mar 2001): 33. [Database online]. Available from: InfoTrac Professional Collection; Article no. 70910883.
87. Ibid.
88. Richard Wright, "Inside the Lenders' Libraries," *Canadian Banker* 101, no. 3 (May–Jun 1994): 18. [Database online]. Available from: InfoTrac OneFile; Article no. 15426005.
89. Ibid.
90. Stinson, 60.
91. Piggott, 11.
92. Price, 229.
93. Prime, 248.
94. Stratigos, 66.
95. Wright, 18.

3

Online in the Information Age—Access to Business Databases

Lucy Heckman

Since the last edition of this book, there have been rapid and dramatic changes in the world of electronic business information due especially to the expansion of databases and business information available through the World Wide Web and on the Internet. This may be shown by the fact that, in 1983, there were approximately 1,360 online databases that were provided through approximately 244 vendors. In 2001, the numbers had increased to 6,657 databases from 1,600 vendors. Of these, business databases comprised 24 percent of the total (*Gale Directory of Databases*. Volume 1: Online Databases. Erin Nagel, ed. Farmington, Hills, MI: The Gale Group, 2002). The availability of effective and fast electronic delivery systems has allowed and encouraged tremendous diversity in the types of electronic business information that are made available as well as in the packaging of this information. Business information sources have increased enormously, in part because new technologies provide abilities to unbundle previously printed publications into separately sold databases, tailor pricing platforms to a specific institution or a specific market, and market information directly to end-users. These changes, in turn, have led to increased end-user searching and a new generation of end users searching online. Even as recently as 1995 (the last edition of this book), patrons still

Lucy Heckman is Head of Reference and Associate Professor at St. John's University Library, Jamaica, New York.

    Consultants for this chapter were Basil Martin (Business Reference Librarian, Clarion University of Pennsylvania), who provided a perspective from the smaller academic library; Peggy Lynn Teich (adjunct librarian at CUNY Baruch College's Newman Library; former Vice President of Manager-Citicorp Research Library; and reference librarian, First Boston Corporation, Walter Thompson Company), who provided a perspective from special/corporate libraries; and Marilyn Harhai, Professor of Library Science, Clarion University of Pennsylvania, and former faculty member at Barry University School of Law, Orlando, Florida, who provided a legal perspective.

relied on librarians and other information professionals to conduct online searches for them. Today, instead of primarily conducting online searches for patrons, librarians must teach effective online search strategies to an increasing number of end-users.

Increased end-user searching has also led to increasing demands by end-users for more information in varying formats and through increasingly more convenient delivery systems. All of this has created tremendous opportunities for business librarians as they work in major areas such as collection development, library instruction and research training, and information policy. Of particular note is the role of librarians as selectors of databases and negotiators of contracts for end-users, bearing in mind cost, data accessibility, and training as key considerations. Selecting databases and negotiating information contracts places librarians in a far more central role as key developers of information policy for organizations. These proactive activities have caused librarians to devote greater attention to copyright compliance issues since increased end-user searching removes the librarian from personal interactions with patrons, during which copyright compliance problems were detected in the past. Librarians are spending more time and efforts training, assessing information needs, negotiating enterprise-wide contracts for information, working in partnership with constituencies to develop and coordinate information policy, serving as an organization's knowledge manager, and providing appropriate instruction.

The expansion of materials available electronically has moved a myriad of legal issues to prominence for subscribers. The move in format from paper to digital has changed how information is produced, procured, accessed, and stored. Each of these changes has legal implications for the purchaser or user. While complete coverage of these issues is beyond the scope of this chapter, the issues are raised in the text as appropriate. Most relevant are the legal rights of an author, not only to the content, but also the format of their writings. Database producers must secure the rights to produce an author's work in an online database, and this ultimately impacts the content of the database. As noted in this chapter, licensing agreements (contracts to use someone else's content), now need to be negotiated and must be considered when evaluating a database.

The explosive growth of proliferating online business information has made it even more critical that librarians "keep up." Journal articles are still helpful (for example, articles in periodicals such as *Business Information Alert*, Find/ SVP newsletters, *Information Today*, *Journal of Business and Finance Librarianship*, and *Online*), but keeping up with the literature must now be enhanced by librarians through various other venues, including electronic discussion groups (e.g., BusLib-L). Also helpful is attendance at the meetings of appropriate professional organizations (e.g., the Special Libraries Association and the

American Library Association's Business Reference and Services Section), because these venues allow librarians to speak with vendors and colleagues around the world. Keeping up with the field of electronic business information is especially critical in the area of database selection, where the proliferation and cost of full text databases often force librarians to decide between electronic and print subscriptions. Finally, noncompliance with legal requirements can be costly, so vigilance is required to keep abreast of changes with these and other issues.

ADVANTAGES OF SEARCHING ONLINE

Online searching, because of its ability to use technology to develop sophisticated search statements, requires more skill than searching traditional printed publications. Retrieval of online documents also adds complexities to the processes of reference citing, avoiding plagiarism, and complying with copyright laws. However, despite the added complexity, patrons often prefer online resources because they have become increasingly more familiar with the benefits of using online resources. These benefits include:

- Quick retrieval of data through keywords, company names, subjects, types of statistical data, and other business particulars
- One-stop access to full-text journal articles, saving the time required to locate the journal and photocopy
- Ability to download statistical data to local spreadsheets and to manipulate data over the Web
- Currency of information (for example, the ability to obtain real-time news and stock price information)
- Ability to e-mail search results and download to local files
- Ability to receive current awareness services such as "alerts"
- Increased range of retrospective coverage in databases
- Remote access features that allow patrons to access data from anywhere
- Availability of information that cannot be found in print (e.g., ABI/INFORM is an electronic database that does not have a print counterpart)
- Ability to obtain hard-to-find data and resources
- Ability to compare companies and industries by specifying specific parameters (e.g., locating the top 10 companies, ranked by sales revenue, in the automobile industry)
- Capacity to search and browse the full text of many journals and databases at once using one search strategy and/or platform

TYPES OF BUSINESS INFORMATION

The expansion of business information available online has correspondingly expanded the selection of subjects covered and types of databases. One of the largest areas of expansion is in the availability of full-text and full image (pdf) documents ranging from annual reports, balance sheets, and market research reports, to newspaper articles and articles in scholarly journals. For larger libraries, the move into online products has brought sophisticated data capabilities such as the ability to run statistical analysis software without having to download the data at a Web site into a local file. This may be applied, for example, to Wharton Research Data Services (WRDS—http://wrds.upenn.edu), an Internet-based business data service from The Wharton School, that offers access to financial, accounting, economic, management, marketing, banking, and insurance datasets from well known business information producers such as Standard and Poor's, Dow Jones, the stock exchanges, The Center for Research in Security Prices (CSRP—providing comprehensive daily and historical data files on the securities markets), and Thomson Financial. The same holds true for similar services and a wider range of resources vended to financial institutions and special libraries by FACTSET Research Systems Inc., which combines more than 200 databases into a single online information system (www.factset.com).

Many business-related subjects and areas, both domestic and international, are also now covered; these include general business information (e.g., from full-text journal aggregators), economics, statistics, accounting and taxation, the law, industry and market research reports and studies, securities information, portfolio tracking, demographic information, real-time stock quotes, real-time wire services, biographies of corporate executives, and detailed company information. The amount of information available online, and in some cases, *only* available online, makes it critical that librarians carefully evaluate online resources.

EVALUATING ONLINE RESOURCES

In addition to evaluating databases that must be purchased, librarians must also be careful to evaluate free business and financial data available through the Web, especially since some free information may be of questionable authority, may be presented in a less than user-friendly format, and may disappear without notice. Authoritative free sites such as those produced by government agencies (e.g., the United States Securities and Exchange Commission), the stock exchanges, public and private companies, and financial Web sites such as Bloomberg and CNNMoney provide vital, up to date information that is used frequently. Among resources obtainable through free Web sites are the full text of working papers produced by researchers at the National Association of Securities Dealers (NASD), at universities, and at other agencies; annual reports and quarterly statements of companies; economic indicators; stock indexes; and stock prices. Additionally, long-standing publishers of business data (e.g., the government, the exchanges, and organizations such as the International Monetary Fund) contain a wealth of reputable and authoritative data. To assist users in locating authoritative free business information on the Web, many librarians place annotated listings of recommended business information Web sites on their libraries' Web pages. Librarians have also substantially altered library and research instruction to include sessions on effective searching on the Web as well as techniques for evaluating business information and research resources that can be found on the Web. Major criteria for evaluating free Web resources are provided in the appendix at the end of this chapter. The criteria listed below apply to online databases from recognized publishers and producers of business information whose online products have been available long enough to be considered stable and reliable.

Usability

A myriad of minute details about a database, in aggregate, make a database easier or more difficult to use. Questions that one might ask include:

- Is the use of the database intuitive for the intended audience, or does effective use require training?
- How does the database "feel," given the organization's information literacy level?
- Is the database Windows-based or is it command-based?
- Is the library's clientele accustomed to Windows-based platforms, or command-based platforms?
- Is the database available with Web-based interfaces?
- Does the database use frames, style sheets, or some other type of Web format?
- If the "feel" of the database is not a good fit, can the look and feel of the interface be customized for the particular library clientele?

Coverage

In relation to coverage, the selector or user might ask:

- Which journal titles are included in full text, abstracting/indexing only, pdf format, html format, XML format, or other? Are the full text titles the ones that are most important for the library's clientele?
- What percentage of the database journals are provided in full text? How far back does the full text go? How quickly are full-text articles

added to the database? What is the lag time between appearance in the printed publication (if there is one) and appearance in the database?

- Is indexing for multiple databases available through one platform? For example, can a user retrieve documents from several databases with one search?
- Does the vendor provide access to other vendors' products on one platform? Some vendors have contracts with a limited number of competitors to allow the primary vendor to direct users from an index entry in the database being searched to a full text entry in another database. Although the technology doesn't always work as well as it should (the user is sometimes sent to the homepage for the competitor's database rather than the actual entry), the ability to access multiple databases from competing services is very convenient.
- What major business services and resources are included in the database that can be searched using the same platform?
- What is the domestic and international coverage?
- What is the archive policy of the database? How long are documents, data, and data sets archived? Are the archived materials automatically available with a current subscription? Does the library still have access to archived materials if the library opts to terminate its current subscription?
- Does the database provide full coverage of all articles in a journal, or are some articles deleted? What is the editorial policy regarding coverage of articles in a journal?
- Are bibliographic citations within the database linked to the source documents within the database, in other databases, or on the Internet?
- Can the library insert these links?
- Who is the intended audience for the database (e.g., consumers of general business information, statisticians, insurance brokers, business school faculty and students, personal investors)?

Accessibility

Again, the questions that might be asked that relate to accessibility include:

- Does the database's value-added indexing and abstracting meet the needs of the library's clientele?
- Are the abstracts informative (i.e., do they provide a summary of the document's major content) or are they merely indicative (i.e., do they provide an indication of the document's subject)?
- Is everything indexed and abstracted, or is some information not included? Does editorial policy index all articles, or only articles that are

longer than one page? Are advertisements and cartoons indexed? Are editorials indexed?

- What licensing rights has the database vendor acquired for the resources and business information that it provides? Can users print and download everything that they access or are some documents "read only," or "fax only?" Are there charges for documents from certain sources that must be paid for by the end-user as a credit card charge, or is everything available through a comprehensive subscription? Is everything in a source made available, or are certain documents and articles deleted from the database because the vendor could not negotiate a license with the author? For example, was the database affected by the Tasini decision, which required newspaper and magazine publishers that publish works by freelance writers in their hardcopy editions to obtain separate permission to include such works in electronic versions of those editions? Are pictures deleted from the database because the vendor couldn't negotiate a license to reproduce them?

- In addition to keyword indexing, does the database provide an effective hierarchical indexing system, online thesaurus, or other value-added indexing system? Does the vendor provide suggestions of related subjects when a user types in his/her search? Does the database provide hyperlinked suggestions of additional subjects or Web sites related to the user's search? Does the database provide the ability to search by business related codes (e.g., SIC) and index terms?

- What types of access are provided in addition to traditional keyword or hierarchical indexing (e.g., sophisticated Boolean searching, chronological or geographic searches, searches by dataset)? Which Boolean operators are able to be used in the database? For example, can a user limit his/her search to financial data from a company with sales of more than a certain dollar amount?

- What kinds of limits can users place on a search? Can users limit a search by peer reviewed or refereed sources, full-text articles, or type of content (e.g., statistical, company information, research report)? Can users limit a search to resources that the library holds locally? Can searches be limited by date, geography, or statistical category? Do the available limiting options meet the needs of the library's clientele? How easy is it to use the database's limit features?

- Does the database allow integrated searches where one search yields results from all of the database services at one time?

- What is the level of indexing? For example, can users access charts and graphs by keywords in the captions, column headings, or types of data presented? For a numeric database, which data elements are searchable?

- How are source citations indicated in the database? Is there enough information to allow a user to access the source? Are citations correct? Some databases provide very complete citations that include all of the pages for an original printed journal article. Other databases, however, merely provide the number of pages for a journal article (not the original page numbers), thus necessitating a footnote style that refers to the database entry rather than the printed article. This can cause problems for others who may wish to read the article, but don't have access to the database.
- Does the database provide hyperlinks to other related resources on the Internet? For example, if a user pulls up information on a company through an article in a journal database, does the database provide a link to the company's Web page on the Internet?
- Does the database provide hyperlinks to other related resources within the database (e.g., the ability to go from a citation in the footnotes to the actual document)?
- Can users download numeric information into local databases for data analysis? Does the database provide the ability to manipulate numeric data within the database's value added applications?

Quality Control

Questions that might be asked about quality control include:

- If documents are scanned, are stray letters and other scanning errors fixed?
- Are graphics in a format that is readable, printable, or downloadable (e.g., into a local spreadsheet)?
- Are parts of a document or resource missing from the database for no apparent reason?
- How are errors corrected?
- How current is the database? Librarians should know how frequently a database is updated (e.g., real time, hourly, daily, weekly, bi-monthly), and the amount of updating that occurs each time.

Support

In regard to support questions:

- Does the database vendor provide electronic bibliographic records that can be imported into a library's online catalog? For example, can the titles of full text journals or government documents in the database be imported electronically into a library's online catalog to allow for hypertext connectivity to the database or to cataloging and location information for printed versions that the library might hold?

- Can users reformat what appears on the computer screen for printing, so that icons and other extraneous materials do not print?
- Does the vendor support multiple access modes, including on-site access (e.g., from a registered IP address) and remote access (e.g., from someone's home).
- Does the vendor provide both print and online documentation and "how to" guides that are user-friendly? For example, are instructions for e-mailing or saving a document to a local file easy to use? Do the instructions work? Are there online help screens?
- Is the vendor representative willing to provide demonstrations or live sessions explaining the use of the database?
- Can users e-mail or save documents to local files in various formats (e.g., text only, html, or pdf)?
- How responsive is customer service? Is it available 24 hours? Is it available through an 800 number? Are the customer service representatives able to answer questions promptly?
- When major changes are made to the database (e.g., the user interface, massive changes in coverage), are users notified in a timely manner and is appropriate documentation provided in a timely manner? How are users notified of the changes?
- What kinds of statistics does the vendor provide regarding database use? Can statistics be downloaded into a local spreadsheet for local manipulation and reports? Do the statistics provided by the vendor match the library's needs for accountability? Are the statistics sent in a timely and consistent manner? Can the library customize the types of reports sent by the database vendor? How much control does the library have over the database's administrative modules?

Cost

Cost questions include:

- Is the database subscription-based, or do charges accrue as various parts of the database are used? Subscription-based databases are advantageous because they allow the library to plan its budget ahead of time. However, for databases that will not be used heavily, "pay as you go" can be a more cost effective option.
- Are subscriptions for unlimited use, or are there restrictions on the number of simultaneous users? For example, does the database only allow 10 people to be logged on at the same time, or can an unlimited number of people log on at the same time? Although it seems that

unlimited use subscriptions might be the preferred mode, it is often the case that simultaneous use subscriptions are more cost effective. For example, some databases count simultaneous users in terms of the number of people who literally "push the button" to print or download at the same time. Other databases track the number of people who are logged on at the same time. Depending upon the type of anticipated use for a database, as well as the way in which simultaneous users are counted, librarians may wish to consider options other than unlimited use subscriptions.

- Will a library consortium provide access to the database, possibly at a lower cost? In some cases, especially for public and academic libraries, library vendors may negotiate state-wide contracts that include all of the public and/or academic libraries within the state or within a specific state system. These types of consortium contracts can be much less costly than individual subscriptions.
- For subscription-based databases, is there enough flexibility for the library to purchase "bundled" services that will meet the needs of its clientele? It would be desirable to deal with a database vendor that can provide packages of services that are tailored for specific types of libraries or specific clientele. An academic library might purchase a business database that includes journal articles and SEC filings, but not market research reports, while a corporate library might purchase a business database that includes SEC filings and market research reports, but not journal articles. Some libraries might even want to purchase a specific set of online journals that the librarians have identified as most important. It is important that a database vendor provide options in terms of the pieces and types of information that can be purchased.
- If value-added features cost extra, are the value-added features absolutely necessary for the library's clientele? Does the library's clientele need to be able to download statistical data into local spreadsheets? Does the library's clientele need to be able to limit a search of journal articles to peer reviewed journal articles? Are informative abstracts necessary because the database is being used as a current awareness service, or are less costly indicative abstracts sufficient?
- Will the anticipated use of the database merit the cost of the database? One way to anticipate use of a database is to track use of specific print journals or documents that are included in the online databases. If the resources are used heavily in print, they will probably be used even more heavily once they are online. Another way to track use is to check with other libraries serving similar clientele to see if their use of the database has been high enough. Yet another method to track anticipated use is to analyze interlibrary loan requests for specific docu-

ments and within specific information categories. Regardless of how anticipated use is determined, it is critical that librarians track actual use of a database so that future contract decisions can be made on the basis of use data.

- How much of the database is found in other competing resources? Databases from competing journal aggregators often comprise the same core of journals in full text. Similarly, aggregators of financial data services compete with the vendors of each unique data service, many of whom vend their own products. It is important to determine whether the titles held uniquely by each database merit individual purchases, purchases of multiple aggregated databases, or purchase of just one aggregated database.

- Does the unique nature of the database's platform merit its purchase in spite of content duplication with other competing databases? For example, the sophisticated search capabilities of Dialog often merit its purchase in libraries where precise searches for small bits of information are required.

Output

The selector or user might ask:

- Can search results be printed, downloaded, and e-mailed? Can search results in numeric databases be downloaded into local spreadsheets? Can data be manipulated at the Web site, or does it have to be downloaded to a local computer? How easy is it for end users to perform these functions?

- Can the order of search results be specified (e.g., chronological, statistical, geographic, alphabetical)?

- How many search results does the database provide at a time? Is there a limit (e.g., 200 results, only back to certain date), or can users opt to review all of the search results? Can users set the results to a specific number?

- If the database provides images (e.g., jpeg, pdf, or tif files), are the images clear? Do users who do not wish to view images (which take a longer time to load) have the option to view thumbnails (small versions of an image) or plain graphics, both of which take less time to load? If the database provides pdf files, are these manageable as downloadable files, or are they too big to fit on traditional storage media such as external discs? Is there a long wait to print and/or download articles in pdf format?

- Is there a default search time (e.g., number of seconds per search)? A default search time of 10 seconds can result in different numbers of retrievals for the identical search performed at different times of the day. The idea that yield is dependent on network congestion is problematic and should be addressed when a library is configuring the database for use.

Reliability

Questions that might be asked about reliability include:

- How reliable are the database servers? What is the percentage of down time? How quickly does the vendor respond to local problems with access? Are the database servers able to handle the load of multiple users at one time, or are there long waits to access the database?
- How can librarians find out about the reliability of the database? Will the vendor provide a complete list of its customers so librarians can randomly check on the vendor's performance in various locations? Does the vendor keep a record of downtime and response time? Is this record available for review?

Pricing for Online Access

Libraries with limited budgets must be judicious in selecting online databases for their collections. Business information databases are costly, with some costing tens of thousands of dollars per year. And, the array of pricing structures can be overwhelming. For some libraries, an attractive pricing structure might be a multi-year subscription that allows unlimited use by patrons in the library and at remote locations (e.g., from home or another country). For other libraries, an annual or multi-year subscription for a limited number of simultaneous users (e.g., only 10 people logged on to the database at the same time) might be attractive. Some databases allow libraries to purchase a defined number of searches at a time, and other databases sell their services on a per use basis, charging for a combination of access time, type of information that is accessed, platform used, amount of information accessed, and types of applications that may be used (e.g., running statistical analyses).

Pricing may also be based on the number of patrons that the library supports. Some databases base their pricing on the number of print resources within the database to which the library subscribes, while others provide subscriptions to print resources at deep discount if the library subscribes to the online database through which the resources can be accessed. Subscription databases that allow unlimited use for an annual fee paid by the library are often the databases of choice when unlimited, unmediated end-user searching is the preferred research mode. However, the sophisticated search capabilities of some pay-as-you-go databases (e.g., Dialog databases) can sometimes merit their use.

Although pay as you go searches may, on the surface, seem less expensive, they can be more expensive on a unit cost basis. In many libraries, extended searches in these types of databases are charged back to the end-users.

Most databases "bundle" their resources and applications services into base packages that are attractive to larger groups of library constituencies. In addition to the core bundles, libraries usually also have options to add specific databases, resources, or services, depending upon the more unique constituencies that a library may serve. Competition among database vendors is fierce, and many times, competing databases offer similar, or even the same, products. For example, the same product might be offered by two competing databases that use different platforms. Although specific holdings information for databases is available, holdings are often not available in easily comparable ways. Sometimes, when comparing journal databases, the only way to differentiate the exact holdings of several databases is to download title lists from the internet into a spreadsheet that will allow sophisticated comparisons of a database's holdings by title, format (pdf, full-text, or abstract only), date (retrospective, current, or discontinued holdings), or other criteria that are important to a library's clientele.

Library consortia can often obtain the best prices for their member libraries, and, they can sometimes provide management information regarding overlaps and unique holdings. Librarians should not, however, assume that their consortium offers the best price. Sometimes individual negotiations will yield a better price, and sometimes a group of libraries can creatively join with each other to make a group purchase that yields a competitive price.

Before making a financial commitment to purchase a database, librarians should request vendor training and a free trial of at least six weeks so librarians and patrons can use and react to the database. It is important to solicit the positive and negative evaluations of patrons who use a database during the trial period. Large financial commitments should be based on a projection of extensive use by patrons. And, once there is a subscription, use must be monitored so that renewal decisions can be based on use and utility.

Finally, librarians should be aware that purchases of online databases require licensing agreements and contracts that can be problematic to a parent institution's legal or purchasing departments. Advance work with an institution's legal and/or purchasing department can avoid frustrating delays when a license agreement must be signed.

THE DATABASES

The choices in online databases are overwhelming. Much business information and many specific business information sources can be obtained from multiple vendors and on multiple platforms. To make things even more confusing, many database vendors repackage bits and pieces of unique business information sources to make a new resource that is renamed so it is vaguely recognizable, but not well enough described to let the potential purchaser know how much of the original resource has been licensed by the third party vendor. And, the range of repackaged information bundles, third party vendors, and even producers of business information changes almost on a daily basis.

The above factors make it impossible, in a short chapter, to adequately cover the field of business information and specific business information sources that are available from whom, on which platform, and in what type of repackaging. In fact, Gale publishes a 1,000+ page resource, twice a year, called the *Gale Directory of Databases* to try and keep up with the market. *Fulltext Sources Online* (ed. Donald T. Hawkins and Mary B. Glose), also published twice a year, provides information about periodicals that are accessible online in full text through journal aggregators (Needham, MA: Bibliodata).

In recognition of the difficulties noted, the list below deviates from the format and structure used in previous editions. Instead of listing specific business information resources that are available online over the Internet, the database list instead focuses on major database vendors that have been shown to be reliable and authoritative, and whose information content includes core business information for use in small to medium-sized public, special, and academic libraries.

The main entries below are listed alphabetically by the name of the database vendor. Annotations include a brief description of the major content areas for the databases provided as well as an indication of major databases that are provided, dates of coverage, the sources of information for specific databases mentioned in the annotation, and the vendor or vendors from whom the majority of the mentioned databases can be obtained. Because of the variability in pricing, prices are not included. Also, because of the variability in terms of databases and specific business information resources that are provided by major vendors, specific titles of business information resources and journals are generally not provided. Librarians are urged to contact the vendors in this list to determine which specific products they offer (either as their own products or as third party vendors). The core lists of resources that comprise much of this book indicate core resources that are, or may become, available online. Librarians might want to start with this list as they explore the products available from the core vendors in the paragraphs that follow.

American Stock Exchange. Securities information is provided, including stock market statistics, news reports, glossary of terms, and IPO filings, in addition to a history and timeline for Amex, and information on how to list on Amex. Portfolio tracking services are also provided. Coverage: current, with hourly updates. Source and Vendor: American Stock Exchange.

Bloomberg. Coverage is provided of the world's financial markets, including equity indexes; stock, bond, and commodity prices; currency exchanges; interest rates, and mutual funds. Substantial information is also included on personal finance, including the ability to track one's own financial portfolio. News coverage is updated throughout the day. Source: Bloomberg L.P. Vendor: Bloomberg L.P.; LexisNexis.

CCH Internet Tax Research Network. This site contains full-text coverage of federal tax information, including tax legislation, the Tax Code, cases, news reports and a federal tax archives, as well as state tax information including state tax reporters and a state tax archives. Coverage: Current, with updates as necessary. Source and Vendor: CCH.

Census Bureau. All census bureau publications released since 1996 in pdf format, including the *Statistical Abstract*, are provided. Information includes news briefs, population statistics, current economic census data, economic indicators, foreign trade data, and related statistics. Coverage: Census documents from 1996; data coverage depends upon report. Source and Vendor: U.S. Census Bureau.

CNNMoney. Formed through a collaboration between *Money* magazine and CNN, this site (some will remember it as cnnfn.com) includes coverage of the financial markets, including stocks, bonds, commodities, currencies, IPOs (Initial Public Offerings), technology stocks, mutual funds, and retirement investments. Also provided are business news, company information, and substantial information on personal finance, including the ability to track one's own financial portfolio. Coverage: current, with hourly updates. Source and Vendor: CNN America, Inc. An AOL Time Warner Company. Can also be obtained through LexisNexis.

Dialog. Dialog is a worldwide provider of online information services to organizations seeking strategic competitive advantages in fields such as business, science, engineering, finance, medicine and law. With over 1,200 databases, Dialog contains a range of sources in various formats. Its services include:

- Dialog®. Marketed to academic and larger public libraries. With particular emphasis on news, business, science, and technology, includes complete text articles from more than 7,000 journals, magazines, and newsletters; the complete text of over 100 leading U.S. and international newspapers, plus wire service stories from Knight-Ridder/Tribune Business News, PR Newswire, Business Wire; references to and abstracts of articles from more than 100,000 international publications on science and technology, social sciences, and humanities; financial profiles and background information on more than 12 million

U.S. and one million international companies; details on over 15 million patents from 56 patent-issuing authorities worldwide; and data on more than 10 million chemical substances.

- DataStar™. Marketed to special and corporate libraries. Includes scientific and business information; European company information; news on East and West Europe; biomedical, pharmaceutical and health care information.
- Profound®. Marketed to corporate and special libraries. Includes market research reports from leading publishers such as Frost & Sullivan, Datamonitor, EIU and Euromonitor; newspapers, magazines and trade journals; analyst reports from *Investext*; international economic analyses and forecasts around the globe; financial reports on public and private companies; specialist research journals across a broad range of industries; statistical data from key publishers; mergers and acquisitions; and patents and trademarks.
- NewsEdge. Marketed to special/corporate libraries and directly to knowledge and content managers at organizations worldwide. Provides tools to manage and deploy real-time news and other content and thousands of authoritative relevant news sources. Serves end-users through enterprise sites, portals, publisher Web sites and distribution channels.
- IntraScope. Developed to meet the enterprise-wide information needs of the corporate market, delivers (daily, weekly, or monthly) a customized collection of in-depth company or industry research that contains indexing to allow the information to be integrated into the customer's corporate intranet.
- InSite2℠. Developed for corporate end-users and libraries, features an extensive collection of trade sources and news from leading trade journals and business publications, a wide variety of newswires, and profiles of public and private companies worldwide.
- Intelliscope℠. Designed to meet the needs of the corporate market, provides access to industry analysis and coverage of breaking news and important events. Customers can search for information online via an intuitive user interface, or they can opt to use e-mail alerts that will deliver search results directly to the desktop or into an existing corporate intranet.

Dialog search features allow users to precisely retrieve key data from more than 800 million unique records, accessible via the Internet or deliverable to enterprise intranets. With direct operations in 30 countries, Dialog offers searching to more than 25,000 corporate customers libraries in over 100 countries. Coverage: Daily, with archives. Dates of coverage vary according to source and type of information. Source: Varies by database and type of information. Vendor: Dialog, A Thomson Company.

Dun and Bradstreet. Through its *Million Dollar Database* (and the North America edition), Dun and Bradstreet provides brief directory and company profile information for Canadian and U.S. public and private companies. Its *International Business Locator* service provides information on public and private companies in over 200 countries. Coverage: current year. Source and Vendor: Dun and Bradstreet Corporation.

EBSCOhost. This journal and document aggregator provides access to full text business periodicals covering management, economics, finance, accounting, and international business. Included in its coverage are databases such as *EconLit* (from the American Economic Association), which provides citations and abstracts to economic research books, journal articles and working papers dating back to 1969. Through its Business Source Premier product, subscribers can access over 2,000 full text scholarly journals and business periodicals. Subscribers can also access country economic reports from the EIU (Economist Intelligence Unit), DRI-WEFA, ICON Group, and Country Watch. EBSCO's Business Source Premier and Business Source Elite database bundles are marketed to academic and public libraries; Corporate ResourceNet is marketed to corporate and special libraries. Coverage: Full text and pdf from 1965, indexing from 1965; varies for each journal title. Source: varies, depending on journal. Vendor: EBSCO Publishing.

Economist Intelligence Unit (EIU), a division of the Economist Group. The EIU provides detailed, authoritative monthly country reports (200 countries in early 2002). The reports cover a nation's politics, economy, demographics, finance, risk prospects, and outlook. The EIU also publishes reports and forecasts on general management trends and selected industries, especially in trade and transportation. Also provided are daily country analyses and a full range of data services (e.g., macroeconomic and market size indicators). Source: The Economist. Vendor: Economist Intelligence Unit.

EDGAR. The SEC requires all public companies (except foreign companies and companies with less than $10 million in assets and 500 shareholders) to file registration statements, periodic reports, and other forms electronically through EDGAR. Anyone can access and download this information for free. This site provides free access to full-text of U.S. public corporation documents filed with the SEC, including 10K and 10Q reports. Coverage: varies, but much of the content goes back to 1993. Source and Vendor: U.S. Securities and Exchange Commission.

SEC filings can also be obtained from many of the databases listed in this chapter, including LexisNexis, Factiva, and Dialog. Pay-per-use services that are designed to facilitate more sophisticated access to and manipulation of

SEC filings can also be helpful, especially in corporate libraries. Two of these services are listed below.

- *EDGAR Online*. Marketed to brokerages, corporations, institutional and individual investors, journalists, investment banks, auditing and accounting firms, and other business organizations, the service provides access to documents filed with the SEC, as well as customizable portfolios, current awareness services, downloading of data to word processing documents and spreadsheets, office delivery of complete printed and bound copies of SEC filings, historical filings back to 1994, an IPO (Initial Public Offerings) current awareness service, and real time access. Basic free searches for SEC filings can obtained from EDGAR Online through their service, FreeEDGAR (http://www.freeedgar.com). Source: U.S. Securities Exchange Commission. Vendor: Edgar Online, Inc.
- *LIVEDGAR*. Marketed especially to law and accounting firms, investment banks, corporations, and the business press, this database provides comprehensive full-text searches of all EDGAR and paper filings, a No-Action Letter database (full-text searchable, with direct links to an original pdf image and a text version of each No-Action letter dating back to dating back to 1971; the most recent No-Action letters are available the same day they are released by the SEC); a registration and prospectus database; a mergers and acquisitions database; transaction data searching and downloading capability; 144A & Reg S database, including copies of the offerings; and SEC Foreign & Paper Filings. Source: U.S. Securities and Exchange Commission. Vendor: Global Securities Information, Inc.

Elsevier Science. For academic libraries that serve a science clientele as well as business clientele, this database might be considered. Two options are provided for obtaining full text of business-related journals from various publishers: 1) "web editions" provides Web access to journals within the Elsevier family to which the library subscribes in print; 2) "Science Direct" is a subscription database to the complete Elsevier family of full text journals, including coverage of business, management, and accounting. Coverage: varies according to the journal. Source: varies by the journal. Vendor: Elsevier Science.

Factiva. This site combines Dow Jones Interactive and Reuters Business Briefing to provide business information, including Dow Jones and Reuters Newswires, the *Wall Street Journal*, other business information sources from around the world, and business-related Web sites. These sources provide current news, historical articles, local-language articles, market research and investment analyst reports, and stock quotes. Factiva provides access to more than 900 non-English sources and provides access to key content in 22 languages from 118 countries. This database is especially used in special/corporate libraries. Coverage: current, updated in real time; archives of up to 25 years. Source: Dow Jones Reuters Business Interactive LLC (trading as Factiva). Vendor: Dow Jones Reuters Business Interactive LLC; Proquest Information and Learning provides access to Factiva.com for the library and academic marketplace.

FISonline. *FISonline*, the electronic version of Moody's, provides information from the Moody's manuals, including business and financial research information on over 12,000 U.S. public companies, 18,000 non-U.S. public companies, and 17,500 municipal entities; corporate and municipal bond information; UIT (unit investment trust) data; dividend information; and company histories. Also included is information from FIS Insider Trading and FIS Institutional Holdings. FISonline provides a real-time business newswire from the News Alert service, a real-time feed of SEC EDGAR documents going back to 1993, annual reports in pdf format, and an online archives (roughly corresponding to the Moody's microfiche collection). Coverage: Daily, with substantial retrospective information. Source and Vendor: Mergent, Inc. (Formerly Moody's Investor Services Financial Information Services).

Gale Group. The Gale Group produces and/or vends a host of services for business libraries and business clientele. Major resources are listed below.

- The Gale Group Business and Company Resource Center integrates several Gale Group products with other Thomson databases to provide information about large and medium-sized companies and industry sectors. Coverage includes full text periodicals reporting on industries, companies, markets, and technologies; company histories; research reports from investment banks, brokerage houses, and research firms; stock, balance-sheet, and insider trading information; company rankings; suits and claims information; product information; and the *Gale Encyclopedia of Associations.*
- Gale's Infotrac Web product provides access to full-text journals and reference sources, as well as *Investext* (investment research reports on publicly traded companies in a wide variety of industries), and *PROMT* (Predicasts Overview of Markets and Technology), including abstracts and full text from business and trade journals, industry newsletters, market research studies, news releases, and investement and brokerage firm reports.
- Responsive Data Services, Inc. Business Reference Suite. This service combines the information provided by three services: *Business and Industry* (company, product and industry information covering manufacturing and service industries), *Business and Management Practices* (articles in core professional and trade journals dealing with manage-

ment issues such as benchmarking and best practices, as well as functional areas such as human resources and information technology), and *Tablebase* (full text of tabular data in Gale Group databases; privately published statistical annuals; data from trade associations, nonprofit research groups, government agencies, and international organizations; and industry reports from investment research groups).

Hoover's Online. Reports for U.S. and international private, public, and subsidiary companies are provided. Special features include sections on careers, corporate news releases, and selected economic statistics. Coverage: Current year, with some retrospective information about company history. Source and Vendor: Hoover's, Inc.

Internal Revenue Service. The site contains full-text of current tax regulations, news reports, forms and instructions, and tax statistics. Public librarians will often refer individuals to this site to download tax forms. Coverage: most current information available. Source and Vendor: U.S. Internal Revenue Service.

ISI Emerging Markets. Included in this site are news, company and financial data, macro-economic analysis, and information about legal and current affairs from emerging markets in Asia, Latin America, and central and eastern Europe. Coverage: Daily updates, with archives. Source: Varies according to information. Languages also vary. Vendor: Internet Securities, Inc.

JSTOR (Journal Storage). For large academic libraries with scholarly clientele who are doing research in the social sciences and therefore require an archive of scholarly journals, this resource provides cover-to-cover, full-image archives of approximately 46 journals related to business. Although pricing goes down according to the size of the library, the prices are still high enough that larger libraries are the most likely to subscribe. Coverage: from volume one of each journal, excluding the latest 3–5 years. Source: JSTOR produces the images; source of journal depends upon journal publisher. Vendor: JSTOR.

LexisNexis Academic Universe and **Nexis.com.** The *Academic Universe* product is marketed to academic libraries and contains numerous business-related sections (including the *Advertising Red Books*), all in full-text format, and including: business news; articles from newspapers, wire services, and magazines; transcripts; company financials; biographical records; SEC filings and reports; industry and market news; accounting articles from journals; and trade show information. Full-text of law reviews and U.S. and state laws is included, as well as *CIS Statistical Universe*, providing access to selected statistical data. Nexis.com, a subscription which provides more depth and greater search capability than Academic Universe is especially helpful for special/corporate libraries and large public libraries in major metropolitan areas. Particularly important in this database are market research reports. Coverage: Daily updates, with archives. Dates of coverage vary by source and type of information. Source: Varies by database and type of information. Vendor: LexisNexis, a Division of Reed Elsevier, Inc.

MarketResearch.com. This site provides access to the full text of 50,000+ publications from over 350 leading research firms and includes what was formerly Kalorama Academic. Coverage: Updated daily, with an archives back to 1994. Source: varies, according to market research report. Vendor: MarketResearch.com.

Morningstar. The resource provides mutual fund, stock, and variable-annuity investment information for over 9,000 mutal funds, closed-end funds, and variable stock annuitities. Coverage: Current, with historical information for over 1,500 funds. Source and Vendor: Morningstar, Inc.

Multex.com, Inc. Investment information is presented for the financial services industry. Among the services offered are MultexNET, which provides real time investment research, morning notes, earnings estimates, and stock screening applications for professional investors. Market Guide provides investment-grade financial and business data, including detailed financial statements, ratios and comparisons, and extensive company descriptive information for over 15,000 publicly traded companies. Multex Global Estimates includes real-time consensus and detailed forecasts of earnings, sales, profitability, cash flow, and other key metrics for public companies worldwide. Source: Varies according to information. Vendor: Multex.com, Inc.

Nasdaq Stock Market. Coverage in the site includes current and retrospective market statistics, history and timeline, listing information, company news, and links to related Nasdaq sites, as well as portfolio tracking. Coverage: Current with hourly updates. Source and Vendor: Nasdaq Stock Market.

New York Stock Exchange. Current trading data, retrospective stock statistics, listed companies, history and timeline, news releases, and portfolio tracking are included here. Coverage: current with hourly updates. Source and Vendor: New York Stock Exchange.

OCLC First Search. The OCLC FirstSearch service delivers electronic journals from OCLC FirstSearch and OCLC Electronic Collections Online. OCLC FirstSearch is a third party provider for business information content in more than 70 databases including business databases from leading information providers such as Gale Group, Proquest Information and Learning, and Thomson Financial. Coverage: varies according to journal and database. Source: varies according to journal and database. Vendor: OCLC Online Computer Library Center, Inc.

Ovid Technologies. Traditionally used in academic libraries, this service provides indexing, abstracting and full text for business journals and reports, and provides online access to resources such as *Wilson Business Abstracts* (produced by H.W. Wilson Company, a bibliographic and full text database of articles from 400 English-language periodicals published in the United States and elsewhere, including the leading business magazines and trade and research journals), and *PAIS International* (Public Affairs Information Service), which indexes journals, books, yearbooks, directories, conference proceedings, research reports and documents published worldwide and covering public and social policy, economics, finance, law, international relations, public administration, and social sciences. Consumers can access information through two platforms: Ovid (which includes more full text), or Silverplatter (mostly indexing and abstracting, but with links to Ovid's full text). Coverage: varies according to database. Source: varies according to database. Vendor: Ovid Technologies.

Proquest. Through its journal and document aggregator databases, Proquest Information and Learning provides full-text journals and newspapers covering a broad range of subject areas and a broad range of standard business information sources, including *ABI/INFORM* (citations, abstracts and/or full text of business and economics articles appearing in professional, trade, and academic journals covering management, accounting, marketing, economics, finance, health care, and insurance); *Accounting and Tax Database*, which provides cover-to-cover abstracting and indexing of key publications in accounting and auditing and financial management, including official releases from the AICPA (American Institute of Certified Public Accountants) and FASB (Financial Accounting Standards Board), and selective indexing of tax-related information in business journals (1971 to present); and *Banking Information Source* (full text of publications that provide information on the financial services industry). Coverage: 1971 to present, with archives (*Proquest Digital Vault*) dating back to the 1400s. Included in the archives are full runs of journals including *New York Times* and *Wall Street Journal*, as well as full runs of scholarly business, social science and humanities periodicals. Source: varies, depending upon journal and/or database. Vendor: Proquest Information and Learning.

ReferenceUSA. Directory and other information on U.S. and Canadian businesses and residents are provided. Coverage: Current, information is updated on a six-month cycle. Source: Sources include telephone directories, annual reports and SEC filings, government agencies, and postal service. Vendor: infoUSA.

Standard and Poor's Net Advantage. Access is included to online editions of S&P Register, Corporation Records, Industry Reports, the Outlook, Stock Reports, Mutual Funds Report, Stock Guide, Dividend Record, Earnings Guide, and Bond Guide. Coverage: most recent month or quarterly, depending on the publication. Archives (two years) of Industry Surveys can also be accessed. Source and Vendor: Standard & Poor's.

STAT-USA. STAT-USA, an agency within the Commerce Department's Economics and Statistics Administration, provides economic, business, and international trade information. *State of the Nation* provides data on the U.S. economy; *Global Business* provides information from the Defense Logistics Agency, United Nations and *Commerce Business Daily*; *National Trade Data Bank* provides market research reports, U.S. trade statistics, and country commercial guides; and *International Trade Library* provides full text of over 40,000 documents related to international trade Coverage: daily updates, archives vary by service. Source: U.S. Government and private sources. Vendor: STAT-USA.

Thomas Register Online. This site provides product information for over 137,000 U.S. and Canadian manufacturing companies and the industrial, service and retail segments of the food industry. Data can be accessed by Product/Service, Company Name, or Brand Name. Coverage: Current year. Source and Vendor: Thomas Online.

Thomson Analytics™ (formerly called PirhanaWeb). Especially used by corporate and academic libraries whose users require the ability to manipulate data and produce locally tailored reports, Thomson Analytics provides company financials, annual reports, company research, business descriptions, market statistics, earnings estimates, equity prices, real-time news, and market quotes. Also provided is access to company filings, research reports, and spreadsheet-ready financials via Thomson Research (formerly Global Access™). Over 2,000 distinct search fields can be used, and over 200 pre-formatted presentation ready reports and charts containing financials, earnings ratios, and stock data are provided. Coverage: Current with real-time updates. Source: Varies according to information. Source: Thomson Financial.

Thomson Research (formerly called Global Access). Thomson Research tracks all SEC filings and provides market and company research reports, annual reports of domestic and international public companies, as well as company financials, earnings estimates, market pricing, and news. Within the database, customers can screen, report, and chart data in tailored sets, as well as download data into local Excel files. Investext® contains investment research reports written by top analysts at over 600 top investment banks, brokerage houses, and consulting firms worldwide. MarkIntel® contains market research from international consulting and market research sources which report in-depth primary research and statistics, market trends, forecasts, and segment analysis. MarkIntel contributors include *Euromonitor*, GartnerGroup's DATAQUEST, IDC, and The Yankee Group. Industry Insider™ provides trade association research from chief economists at over 200 trade associations worldwide. Morning Meeting Notes provides insights and recommendations from international research firms, with more than 2,200 notes added weekly. Contributors include Credit Suisse First Boston, Merrill Lynch, Morgan Stanley Dean Witter, and Salomon Smith Barney. Source: Varies, according to the information (e.g., EDGAR, Compustat, Worldscope, IBIS, DataStream). Coverage: 1969 to present for SEC filings; 20 years of data for database contents. Vendor: Thomson Financial.

Value Line Investment Survey. Provides information and advice on 1,700 stocks, 90 industries, the stock market, and the economy. Coverage: Updated on a thirteen week cycle, with historical coverage of 10 years. Source and Vendor: Value Line Investment Survey.

DIRECTORY OF DATABASE VENDORS

American Stock Exchange
86 Trinity Place
New York, NY 10006
http://www.amex.com

Bloomberg, L.P.
The best way to contact Bloomberg is to go to their Web site, and click on feedback. At this page, users can contact Bloomberg electronically.
http://www.bloomberg.com/

CCH Headquarters, CCH Incorporated
2700 Lake Cook Road
Riverwoods, IL 60015
http://www.cch.com

CNN America, Inc. An AOL Time Warner Company
The easiest way to contact this company is via e-mail through their Web site at http://money.cnn.com. Users can click on "contact us."

Dialog, A Thomson Company
Corporate Headquarters
11000 Regency Parkway
Suite 10
Cary, North Carolina 27511
http://www.dialog.com; http://www.newsedge.com; http://intelligencedata.com

Dow Jones Reuters Business Interactive LLC (trading as Factiva)
3495 Piedmont Road, NE
Suite 302, 11 Piedmont Center
Atlanta, GA 30305
http://www.dowjones.com

Dun and Bradstreet Corporation
One Diamond Hill Road
Murray Hill, NJ 07974–1218
http://www.dmb.com

EBSCO
10 Estes Street
Ipswich, MA 01938
http://www.epnet.com

Economist Intelligence Unit
The Economist Building
111 West 57th Street
New York, NY 10019
http://www.eiu.com

Edgar Online, Inc.
50 Washington Street, 9th Floor
Norwalk, CT 06854
http://www.edgar-online.com

Elsevier Science, a Reed Elsevier Company
Sales Office Customer Support Department
P.O. Box 945
New York, NY 10159–0945
http://www.elsevier.com; http://www.sciencedirect.com; http://www.sciencedirect.com/web-editions

Gale Group
27500 Drake Rd.
Farmington Hills, MI 48331–3535
http://www.galegroup.com

Global Securities Information, Inc.
419 Seventh St. NW, Suite 300
Washington, DC 20004
http://www.gsionline.com

Hoover's Online
5800 Airport Blvd.
Austin, TX 78752–3812
http://www.hoovers.com

infoUSA
5711 South 86th Circle
P.O. Box 27347
Omaha, NE 68127
http://www.referenceUSA.com

Internet Securities, Inc.
Corporate Headquarters
488 Madison Avenue
New York, NY 10022
http://site.securities.com

JSTOR
120 Fifth Avenue, 5th Floor
New York, NY 10011
http://www.jstor.org

LexisNexis™
P.O. Box 933
Dayton, OH 45401–0933
http://www.lexis-nexis.com

MarketResearch.com
641 Avenue of the Americas, 4th floor
New York, NY 10011
http://www.marketresearch.com

Mergent, Inc. (Formerly Moody's Investor Services Financial Information Services)
60 Madison Avenue, 6th floor
New York, NY 10010
http://www.fisonline.com

Morningstar, Inc.
225 W. Wacker Dr.
Chicago, IL 60606
http://www.morningstar.com

Multex.com, Inc.
Corporate Offices
100 William Street, 7th Floor
New York, NY 10038
The Web site for library information services is http://www.multexusa.com/solutions_cicbip.asp. The general Web site for Multex.com is http://www.multexusa.com/

Nasdaq Stock Market
There are many physical addresses for NASDAQ, depending on the type of information the user is seeking. The best way to identify the most appropriate office is to visit the Web site, and click on "contact us."
http://www.nasdaq.com

OCLC FirstSearch
OCLC Online Computer Library Center, Inc.
6565 Frantz Road
Dublin, OH 43017–3395
http://oclc@oclc.org/home

Ovid Technologies (including SilverPlatter)
100 River Ridge Drive
Norwood, MA 02062
http://www.ovid.com; http://www.silverplatter.com

ProQuest Information and Learning
300 North Zeeb Road
P.O. Box 1346
Ann Arbor, MI 48106–1346
http://www.umi.com

Standard and Poor's
ATTN: John Quealy
55 Water Street
New York, NY 10041
http://www.standardandpoors.com

STAT-USA
Room 4885
1401 Constitution Ave
Washington, DC 20230
http://www.stat-usa.gov

Thomas Register
Five Penn Plaza, 12th Floor
New York, NY 10001
http://www93.thomasregister.com/

Thomson Financial
Client Services
195 Broadway
New York, New York 10007
Thomson Financial home page is: http://www.thomsonfinancial.com
The Web pages for Thomson Analytics and Thomson Research seem to be
in flux at the time of printing for this edition *of Basic Business Library*.
Potential users might want to try contacting the vendor via e-mail at
tfsd.cs@tfn.com, or by phone at 1-800-843-7747. At the time of printing for
this edition of *Basic Business Library*, the Web site for information about
Thomson Research is http://research.thomsonib.com/; the Web site for
information about Thomson Analytics is http://analytics.thomsonib.com.

U.S. Census Bureau
Postal Address:
U.S. Census Bureau
Washington, DC 20233

Physical Address:
4700 Silver Hill Road
Suitland, MD 20746
http://www.census.gov

United States Internal Revenue Service
To find the appropriate address, users should go to the Web address below, click on "contact us," and then click on the state for which tax information is required.
http://www.irs.gov

United States Securities and Exchange Commission
To find the address and other contact information for the appropriate regional branch, users should go to the Web address, http://www.sec/gov/contact/addresses.htm. A list of regional offices will appear, along with contact information. The Web site for EDGAR is http://www.sec.gov/edgar

Value Line Investment Survey
220 East 42nd Street
New York, NY 10017
http://www.valueline.com

APPENDIX

CRITERIA FOR EVALUATING FREE WEB RESOURCES

Free Web resources can offer "hidden treasures" of research material that are not available elsewhere. However, because anyone can publish on the Web, users must choose Web sites wisely. Search engines often include annotations of sites, and trade/subject journals frequently have reviews (e.g., *Choice* regularly reviews and evaluates Web sites in specific disciplines). Users can also consult articles that provide Web site evaluation criteria (e.g., Kim Kapoun's "Teaching Undergrads Web Evaluation," from *College and Research Libraries NewsNet*, available at the Web site http://www.ala.org/acrl/undwebev.html). Below are some basic criteria, in addition to those provided earlier in this chapter, for determining the credibility of free Web sites and the information they provide.

- Determine if the Web site is sponsored by a reputable agency. It is usually safer to select Web sites from state, local, and federal agencies such as the IRS and Census Bureaus; company Web sites; trade associations; established publishing houses; news agencies; universities; stock exchanges; and "think tanks."

- Avoid Web sites that contain biased statements and suspect data. One way to check the accuracy of data on a suspect site is to compare the data with those presented on government sites.
- If the Web site is sponsored by an association, check to see if the association is still in existence and if its focus might indicate biased information at the Web site. Users can check the *Encyclopedia of Associations* for an address and a description of the agency. This will provide users with information about the focus of the association as well as any potential biases that might be present in the Web site information. If Web information is being used to provide directory information about an association, users might want to phone the association to see if it is still in existence.
- Check to see that the individual responsible for the Web site has the credentials or experience to produce the information on the Web site. Users can check a Web author's credentials through faculty directories, biographical sources, citation resources, and bibliographical resources; these sources provide information about an author's background and current publishing activities. Users might also want to check if the author of the Web site has provided a contact address. Remember, anyone can publish on the Web.
- Check the date on which the site was last updated. In order to confirm that a Web site has been updated, users can check to see if the links in the Web site still work. Users can also check to see if information on the site is out of date. Preference should be given to frequently updated sites.
- Regularly check trade, professional, and scholarly journals for profiles of Web sites. Some journals have annual issues that profile and evaluate Web sites in a specific field.
- Bookmark and/or keep a log of sites consulted. Check these sites over time to see if they are still there. Since many sites can literally disappear overnight, keeping a list of sites with longevity can be handy.

4

Access to U.S. Government Information:
Recommended Guides, Directories, Indexes, Bibliographies, and Catalogs

Eric Forte and Michael R. Oppenheim

In the realm of collection and dissemination of business information, the U.S. government is unrivaled. As it strives to protect and promote a fair and vital marketplace, ensure the rights of businesses, workers, and consumers, and measure various social and economic factors related to the nation's business climate, the Federal government produces a prodigious amount of information, both about business, and for the benefit of business, workers, and consumers. In addition, much of this information forms the basis for many business publications and products of the private sector. Examples of government information related to business include: the EDGAR database of corporate information, an outgrowth of the government's role in safeguarding a fair and honest securities marketplace; the Federal Reserve's *Beige Book*, a periodic analysis of the nation's economic situation that plays a key role in informing Federal monetary policy; STAT-USA, a trade information library intended to help U.S. businesses compete overseas; and various official statistics related to economic performance, such as GDP, unemployment, and consumer spending, and consumer tips from the Federal Trade Commission. Many laws and regulations govern the business climate generally, covering such topics as occupational health, banking, antitrust and other unfair business practices, and environmental protection.

This essay reviews the major indexes, guides, and directories that the user of government-produced business information can consult when trying to locate a specific document or piece of information. The following essay will

Eric Forte is Economics Librarian at the University of California, Santa Barbara. Michael R. Oppenheim is Reference/Instructional Services Librarian at the Rosenfeld Library, The Anderson School at UCLA.

cover the most essential and frequently consulted specific business information sources from the Federal government.

The sources in this and the next chapter will answer such questions as: "Where can I find the GDP for the last 40 years?"; "What is the U.S. trade deficit with Japan?"; "Where can I find government contract opportunities for my business?"; "What's the telecommunications market like in Bulgaria?"; "Can I register this trademark?"; "What does the average worker make per hour in Chicago?"; "What kinds of skills and training does this occupation require?"; "Has my child's car seat been recalled?"; "What does my employer have to do to help me with ergonomics?"; "How do I get a small business loan?"; and "How do I write a business plan?"

BACKGROUND: GOVERNMENT PUBLISHING

The Government Printing Office (GPO) is the printer for the Federal government. It also manages the Federal Depository Library Program, through which the Federal government distributes documents, free of charge, to approximately 1,350 Federal Depository Libraries throughout the United States and its territories, at least one in almost every Congressional District. In practice, when an agency has a publication that needs to be printed, GPO will also make enough copies to distribute an extra to each depository library. Federal Depository Libraries receive materials free of charge, and in return must house them and make them available to the public. This arrangement accomplishes two key goals: it sustains the ongoing creation of a catalog (*Catalog of United States Government Publications*) of Federal government documents; and it insures that copies of important government documents are located in potentially hundreds of sites, leaving most of the nation's populace quite close to government information they may be seeking. It should be noted that depository libraries come in many different sizes and shapes, so that although all might reasonably be expected to have, for instance, current laws passed by Congress, not all may have each of the thousands of technical reports on physics and aeronautics issued by NASA.

Although this system of distributing materials to depository libraries has existed for over 100 years, recent developments in information technology have had a profound and quickly evolving effect on how government information is disseminated. For business information users in particular, electronic dissemination has made for greater timeliness than ever, "instant" access to longtime series, and the ability to extract and manipulate data with an ease heretofore unimagined (from the desktop convenience of cutting, pasting, and exporting, to the wonders of the interactive online data extraction tools discussed below, such as those provided by the Census Bureau and Bureau of Labor Statistics).

Information technology—and especially Web publishing of government information—has affected GPO in several ways. While still distributing thousands of documents per year in print format, GPO now makes a considerable effort to manage Federal government information on the Web. Much of this energy goes into managing the countless documents housed as part of GPO databases and initiatives, such as those in *GPO Access*. But GPO also strives to find and catalog Federal government information which evades the traditional printing process, and which is posted (and often removed) directly by agencies on their own Web sites.[1] Because of this effort, the *Catalog of United States Government Publications* remains an excellent catalog of the information of the Federal government, regardless of format.

Inevitably, however, much publicly accessible government information exists which eludes GPO's notice all together. To find this information efficiently requires the government information specialist's Web skills combined with a fairly in-depth knowledge of the Federal government. In short, if an item can't be located in the *Catalog of United States Government Publications*, the next approach should be to look at the appropriate agency's Web site. So, while GPO remains the primary clearinghouse for government information, a role that also applies to its work with Web-based information, successful retrieval of government information requires familiarity with government structure and responsibilities, as well as an ability to exploit the resources and tools of the World Wide Web to their fullest advantage.

In addition, several more issues currently exist regarding Federal government information. These issues include security issues related to the events of September 11, 2001, the role of the private sector in repackaging and retailing tax-supported government information, the responsibility for archiving electronic sources and Web sites, and even the constitutional authority of requiring the dissemination of government information. All of these issues have left the traditional methods of government information dissemination to the public on very uncertain terms; major changes can happen any time. Indeed, no recent session of Congress has passed without some significant proposed change in government information policy or practice.

In the entries for sources in this essay, it should be noted that items available free to depository libraries will include a SuDoc (short for Superintendent of Documents) number. A SuDoc number is a classification number assigned to items by GPO; the system is based on, and reflects, the structure of the government. SuDocs numbers are usually used in various ways by depository libraries in which Federal documents are shelved or housed separately from other collections, and act as an access point in electronic cataloging records of documents. Most depository items will also include a "Stock Number" (S/N), which is used for items available for purchase from GPO's U.S. Government Online Bookstore, http://bookstore.gpo.gov/. Each entry below begins with a full citation, followed by price information (if pricing was available), SuDoc number (if it was available), and electronic access information (if available). If an item was available from the GPO bookstore, the price and SuDoc number from the bookstore were used, and availability of paper or cloth editions is noted. For regularly published subscription items, prices are for an annual subscription; for less frequent serials and annuals, the price and SuDoc number from the latest available edition is provided. For commercially produced regularly published subscription items, prices are for an annual subscription; the International Standard Serials Number (ISSN) is also provided. Less regularly published annuals and serials include the price and International Standard Book Number (ISBN) of the most recent available edition. Monograph entries include the price and ISBN for the most recent edition.

GENERAL GUIDES AND DIRECTORIES

The following general guides and directories to government information include key textbooks on government information, and several general directories, including directories of U.S. government organization and Federal Depository Libraries, whose professional staffs are expert in locating Federal government information. All resources here cover the entire realm of government information, and therefore include (but are not limited to) business information.

Federal Agency Internet Sites. Washington, DC: GPO and Baton Rouge, LA: Louisiana State University Libraries. Available online: http://www.access.gpo.gov/su_docs/locators/agency/index.html.

This directory, a partnership between GPO and the Louisiana State University Libraries, provides a comprehensive listing of Federal government Web sites. Many sites have obvious links to bibliographies, catalogs, or publication lists for the agency listed. The directory should be used in conjunction with the U.S. Government Manual (see this section, below).

Federal Depository Library Directory. Washington, DC: GPO. Irregular (SuDoc: GP 3.36/2:).

Federal depository libraries are listed here, by state and city. Each library included houses at least the most important and basic government documents (for instance laws, local census information, presidential documents, Statistical Abstract of the United States, etc.) and all should have staff well-versed in government information, regardless of format. A related resource is Locate Federal Depository Libraries, where one may search for depository libraries by state, area code, and U.S. Congressional District, http://www.access.gpo.gov/su_docs/locators/findlibs/index.html.

Hoffmann, Frank W. and Richard J. Wood. Guide to Popular U.S. Government Publications, 5th ed. Englewood, CO: Libraries Unlimited, 1998. 300p. $38.50 (ISBN 1–56308–607–7).

Annotated guides to many of the most essential publications of the Federal government are included in the *Guide*. Chapters such as Business and International Trade, Consumer Information and Protection, Labor and Employment, and Taxes and Taxation are of particular interest.

Morehead, Joe. *Introduction to United States Government Information Sources*. 6th ed. Englewood, CO: Libraries Unlimited, 1999. 491p. $47.50 (ISBN 1–56308–735–9, paper).

This long-standing and well-known textbook is now in its sixth edition. Extended treatment is given to electronic sources and issues, and coverage of both current and historical reference sources is comprehensive. Special attention is given to the Government Printing Office and the Federal Depository Library Program, knowledge of which is fundamental to understanding document sources and how documents are acquired and organized. Highlights for the business user include the detailed surveys of legislative branch publications, regulations, statistical sources, and intellectual property.

Official Congressional Directory. Washington, DC: GPO, 1887– . Biennial. $32.00. (S/N 052–070–07229–6, paper). SuDoc Y 4. P. 93/1:1/.

This is *the* directory of members of Congress. For each member of Congress, it includes brief biographical information, Washington, DC and local office addresses and phone numbers, and district information. Also included are committee assignments, directories of other legislative branch personnel, major executive branch officers, foreign diplomats, international organizations, and district maps.

O'Hara, Frederick M. Jr. and Frederick M. O'Hara III. *Handbook of United States Economic and Financial Indicators*. Westport, CT: Greenwood Press, 2000. 395p. $89.50 (ISBN 0–313–27450–9).

The O'Haras provide a welcome overview of economic and financial data collected by the Federal government. For some 284 frequently cited indicators, the book describes what they are, how they are calculated, and how and where they are published.

Robinson, Judith Schiek. *Tapping the Government Grapevine: The User-Friendly Guide to U.S. Government Information Sources*, 3d ed. Westport, CT: Oryx Press, 1998. 286p. $45.50 (ISBN 1–57356–026–3).

The subtitle is correct: This highly readable volume is an excellent field manual for newcomers to the territory of government information. Seasoned users will also appreciate its well-organized format, clear prose, and humorous style.

Sears, Jean L., and Marilyn K. Moody. *Using Government Information Sources*. 3d ed. Westport, CT: Oryx Press, 2000. 536p. $125.00 (ISBN 1–57356–288–2).

Perhaps the single most comprehensive guide to Federal government information, and a great ready reference source for anyone dealing with government information, this tool offers actual, detailed search strategies for locating over 50 different categories of government-produced information. For business information seekers, it features such chapters as Business Aids, Selling to the Government, Occupations and Jobs, and Business and Industry Statistics.

United States Government Manual. Washington, DC: Office of the Federal Register, 1935-. Annual. $36.00 (S/N 069–000–00134–3). SuDoc: AE 2.108/2: Available online: http://www.access.gpo.gov/nara/nara001.html.

Published annually since 1935, the *Manual* provides descriptions, missions, and, in some cases, organizational charts for legislative, judicial, and executive agencies and offices, as well as for independent boards, commissions, committees, and quasi-official agencies. Entries include dates of establishment, key personnel, major sub-agencies, programs and services, and Web addresses.

University of Michigan Documents Center. Ann Arbor, MI: University of Michigan Libraries. Available online: http://www.lib.umich.edu/govdocs/.

One of a number of excellent Web sites created by librarians that provide both guide and directory to government information, *Government Information by Type of Business Information Need* (under "Specialized Business-related Guides and Directories," below) is the standard bearer for government-produced business information on the World Wide Web. However, Grace York's multi-award–winning site at the University of Michigan is another leader among depository library Web sites. Arranged by hundreds of categories, it is an access point for what's on the Web for a number of business topics. Among the categories included on this site are Business and Industry, Cost of Living, Economics, Finance and Currency, and Foreign Trade.

Worldwide Government Directory, with International Organizations. Bethesda, MD: National Standards Association, 1981–. Annual. $315.00 (ISSN 0894–1521).

The businessperson exporting or working abroad often operates in an environment completely different from that of the United States. This directory provides names, addresses, and telephone numbers for foreign governments and their primary agencies, as well as major international intergovernmental organizations, such as the United Nations and the North Atlantic Treaty Organization (NATO).

SPECIALIZED BUSINESS-RELATED GUIDES AND DIRECTORIES

The following are general texts, guides, and directories to government information—but each focuses only on either business or some other specialized class of government information relevant to business.

BLS Handbook of Methods. Washington, DC: U.S. Bureau of Labor Statistics. 1966–. Irregular. $25.00 (S/N 029–001–03265–0). SuDoc: L 2.3: 2490 *[latest edition]*. Available online: http://www.bls.gov/opub/hom/.

The Bureau of Labor Statistics collects data related to employment/unemployment and prices. This publication details the major statistical programs of the BLS, covering methodology and definitions.

Fed in Print. Philadelphia, PA: U.S. Federal Reserve Bank of Philadelphia. 1973–. Semiannual. (ISSN 0891–2769). Recent issues also available online: http://www.frbsf.org/publications/fedinprint/index.html.

Fed in Print is a subject index to periodicals and research reports issued by the Federal Reserve Board and the 12 regional Federal Reserve Banks. The Web version is searchable by keyword (title, subject, and abstract), title words, author, Fed Bank, and publication name or year (including publication dates from 1965 on). For publications from 1996 on, links to the full text (in HTML or PDF formats) are provided, wherever available.

Government Information by Type of Business Information Need. Los Angeles, CA: Rosenfeld Library, Anderson School at UCLA. Available online: http://www.anderson.ucla.edu/resources/library/govinfo_bytype.htm.

For those looking for government business information on the Web, this is an excellent access site, divided into 11 categories, such as Demographics, Industry Trends, Real Estate, and Taxation. Within each category are links to virtually all the essential government information on that topic that is available online.

Guide to the 1997 Economic Census. Washington, DC: U.S. Bureau of the Census. Available online: http://www.census.gov/epcd/www/g97toc.htm.

The guide to the *Economic Census* is a key resource discussed in detail in the next essay.

Harmonized Tariff Schedule of the United States: Annotated for Statistical Reporting Purposes. Washington, DC: U.S. International Trade Commission. Annual, with midyear update. $62.00 (S/N 949–016–00000–5). SuDoc: ITC 1:10: *year*. Available online: http://purl.access.gpo.gov/GPO/LPS2145.

This product classification manual, featuring an alphabetical index by product, is a "must-have" aid when searching for import and export statistics. The Web site contains the most recent edition, and is fully searchable.

North American Industry Classification System. Washington, DC: U.S. Office of Management and Budget, 1998. 1247p. $30.00 (S/N 041–001–00509–9, paper). SuDoc: PrEx 2.6/2: IN 27/997. Available online: http://www.census.gov/epcd/www/naics.html.

NAICS categorizes businesses by type, and forms the basis of many statistical publications of both the Federal government and the private sector. The successor to Standard Industrial Classification (SIC) codes, NAICS includes categories for many new types of businesses, such as those engaged in activities based on various emerging technologies (e.g., Internet service providers). The Census Bureau offers a fine home page explaining and fully detailing NAICS: http://www.census.gov/epcd/www/naics.html. The changeover from SIC to NAICS will take quite a few years to be fully reflected in both government and commercial publications, and for the foreseeable future it is necessary to be familiar with both. The Web page, noted above, contains a section on "Implementation" at the NAICS site, for the projected implementation dates for agencies throughout the Federal government. Especially valuable are the *1997 NAICS* and *1987 SIC Correspondence Tables*, available at <http://www.census.gov/epcd/www/naicstab.htm>.

Standard Industrial Classification Manual. Washington, DC: U.S. Office of Management and Budget, 1987. 705p. $36.00 (S/N 041–001–00314–2) SuDoc: PrEx 2.6/2:In 27/987. Available online: http://www.osha.gov/oshstats/sicser.html.

The *SIC Manual* defines U.S. industries and services with a four-digit code number—the SIC code number, reflecting the composition and structure of the

U.S. economy. This standard identification system, originally developed in the late 1930s to promote the comparability of economic statistics, is very widely used in commercially published directories and reports, as well—and will continue to be, for some years to come. SIC codes are slowly being replaced by NAICS (North American Industry Classification System, see above).

Stratford, Jean Slemmons, and Juri Stratford. *Major U.S. Statistical Series: Definitions, Publications, Limitations.* Chicago: American Library Association, 1992. 147p. $35.00 (ISBN 0–8389–0600–1).

An in-depth discussion of Federal statistics programs focusing on the nature and methodology of their collection is provided in this tool. The authors, University of California at Davis government information librarians with extensive backgrounds in social sciences research and publication, review and analyze statistical data concepts, publications, problems, and anomalies.

User's Guide to BEA Information. Washington, DC: U.S. Bureau of Economic Analysis. Irregular. $65.00 (S/N 721–041–00000–0). (SuDoc: C 59.8: B 89/994).

The BEA is one of the most important publishers of economic information, as it tracks and reports on national accounts, including Gross Domestic Product, personal income, and certain international transactions. In recent years, the *User's Guide* has appeared periodically in the monthly *Survey of Current Business* (described in Chapter 5).

GENERAL INDEXES, CATALOGS, AND DATABASES OF GOVERNMENT INFORMATION

Catalog of United States Government Publications. Washington, DC: GPO, 1994–. Available online: http://www.access.gpo.gov/su_docs/locators/cgp/index.html. Print equivalent: *Monthly Catalog of United States Government Publications.* Washington, DC: GPO, 1895–. Monthly. (SuDoc: GP 3.8:) Supplemented by *Serials* (formerly *"Periodicals"*) *Supplement* and *Serial Set Catalog.* $65.00 (S/N 721–041–00000–0).

This is *the* catalog of U.S. government publications—the most complete bibliography of government publications available. The Web version, known as the *Catalog of United States Government Publications,* has coverage dating from January 1994. The print version, the *Monthly Catalog of United States Government Publications* (also called MOCAT), began publication with the 1895 Printing Act that established GPO. The catalog contains all publications that come through the depository system, selected non-depository items (items which are produced by the government but, for various reasons, do not have copies sent to all of the Federal Depository Libraries, or bypass GPO dissemination entirely), and selected Web sites and documents. Commercial versions of the *Catalog* are available through various vendors (e.g., Marcive, OCLC FirstSearch, Ovid, Silverplatter).

FirstGov. Washington, DC: General Services Administration. Available: http://firstgov.gov/.

FirstGov is a recent public-private partnership that aims to be "your first click to U.S. government." In addition to a browsable directory of government information, it includes a search engine that aims to index all Federal (and state) government Web sites. *Google Uncle Sam*, http://www.google.com/unclesam also indexes and searches for information on Federal government Web sites.

SPECIALIZED INDEXES, CATALOGS, AND DATABASES OF GOVERNMENT INFORMATION

Although the *Catalog of United States Government Publications* discussed above is the single standard catalog of U.S. government publications, a number of specialized indexes and databases exist which index some particular type or class of information. Those that focus on business information, or otherwise have applications to business research, are discussed below.

American Statistics Index (ASI). See *Statistical Universe*, below.

CQ.com on Congress. Washington, DC: Congressional Quarterly, Inc. Available online (fee-based): http://www.cq.com/.

Like *Congressional Universe* below, *CQ.com on Congress* is a major commercial service for research on congressional activity, laws, and regulations. The free government sites GPO Access and THOMAS (see below) perform many of the same functions.

Congressional Universe. Bethesda, MD: Congressional Information Service. Available online: http://web.lexis-nexis.com/congcomp (via subscription only; for more information, see http://www.lexisnexis.com/academic/1univ/cong/default.htm). Compiles numerous print products, most notably: *CIS/Index.* Washington, DC: Congressional Information Service, Inc., 1970–. Annual, (*CIS Annual, Legislative Histories of U.S. Public Laws*), with monthly supplements.

Along with *CQ.com on Congress* above, this is a major commercial source for research on congressional activity, laws, and regulations. While the free government sites GPO Access and THOMAS (see below) perform many of the same functions, *Congressional Universe* adds a number of features and components, including indexes of Congressional hearings, prints, the *United States Serial Set*, and regulatory materials.

FedStats. Washington, DC: Federal Interagency Council on Statistical Policy. Available online: http://www.fedstats.gov.

Introduced in the Spring of 1997 and greatly redesigned and enhanced in 2001, this excellent site provides quick and easy "one-stop-shopping" access to the complete range of publicly available statistics on the Web from more than 100 U.S. government agencies. Multiple searching "gateways" are offered, including by topic (guided, A–Z), statistical agency, and agency by statistical subject.

GPO Access Databases. Washington, DC: GPO. Available online: http://www.access.gpo.gov/su_docs/index.html.

There are many specialized databases available through the GPO Access service. These include indexes and full-text of many legislative materials, such as current bills and their status; the U.S. Code of laws currently in force; an index and full-text of regulations and regulatory materials, via the *Federal Register* and *Code of Federal Regulations*; and many other materials, such as the Federal budget and the *Economic Report of the President* (discussed in Chapter 5).

NTIS Database. Springfield, VA: National Technical Information Service. Available online: http://www.ntis.gov/search. Continues *Government Reports Announcements and Index (GRAI)*. Springfield, VA: National Technical Information Service, 1946–1994.

This specialized index provides access to scientific and technical reports prepared as a result of government-funded or contract research, and includes citations for reports and products produced from 1990 to the present. The traditional, most comprehensive source was NTIS's *Government Reports Announcements and Index (GRAI)*, which ceased publication in 1994. A subset of the NTIS electronic catalog, the NTIS *Business and International Trade Online Bookstore*, is available at http://tradecenter.ntis.gov/.

Statistical Universe. Bethesda, MD: Congressional Information Service. Available online: http://web.lexis-nexis.com/statuniv (via subscription only; for more information, see http://www.lexisnexis.com/academic/1univ/stat/default.htm). Also available in print as: *American Statistics Index (ASI)*. Washington DC: Congressional Information Service, 1973–. Monthly; quarterly cumulative index; annual; *Index to International Statistics*. Bethesda, MD: Congressional Information Service. 1983–. Monthly; quarterly cumulative index; annual; and *Statistical Reference Index (SRI)*. Bethesda, MD: Congressional Information Service, 1980–. Monthly; quarterly cumulative index; annual.

Statistical Universe is the online compilation of the *American Statistics Index*, *Index to International Statistics*, and *Statistical Reference Index*. The *American Statistics Index* is an indispensable comprehensive index with abstracts to all Federal government publications (depository and non-depository) containing statistics. It includes Superintendent of Documents (SuDocs) classification numbers, Item Numbers, and Internet URLs and provides selective retrospective coverage of publications dating back at least as far as 1960. It also features full-text of many of these U.S. government sources. Additionally, *Statistical Universe* also includes the *Index to International Statistics*, which provides the same excellent indexing and abstracting service for international statistics (from foreign government, intergovernmental, and non-governmental sources), and the *Statistical Reference Index*, which does the same for statistics published by state governments, trade and professional associations, research organizations, and commercial publishers. The *American Statistics Index*, *Index to International Statistics*, and *Statistical Reference Index* are also available in print editions.

THOMAS. Washington, DC: Library of Congress. Available online: http://thomas.loc.gov.

The Library of Congress' THOMAS covers much of the same territory as the legislative materials on GPO Access, featuring indexes, full-text (for the *Congressional Record*, for example), and status of legislation in the U.S. Congress.

NOTE

1. Neither the laws regarding federal printing and the Federal Depository Library Program (found in title 44 of the *United States Code*), nor the policies put forth by the Office of Management and Budget are currently clear about posting and retention of Federal government information on the Web. As such, documents and Web pages often disappear, leaving no permanent archive. The University of North Texas maintains a *Cybercemetery,* http://govinfo.library.unt.edu, of the Web site contents of defunct agencies and offices of the Federal government. However, there is currently no uniform effort to archive all Federal information that appears or disappears on the Web.

5

Access to U.S. Government Information:
Essential Sources for Business

Eric Forte and Michael R. Oppenheim

The previous essay introduced government-produced business information and resources, and discussed the guides, directories, and catalogs relevant to their use. This essay focuses on specific and essential government publications (in any format) relevant for business use. Arrangement is by the following broad topics:

- Statistical Compendia
- General Economic Conditions
- Business and Industrial Conditions
- Fiscal and Monetary Conditions
- Foreign Trade and International Business
- Labor
- Government Procurement and Assistance
- Government Oversight: Corporate Finance, Taxation, Consumer Information, and Intellectual Property
- Government Oversight: Laws and Regulations

In the entries for sources in this chapter, it should be noted that items available free to depository libraries will include a SuDoc (short for Superintendent of Documents) number, a classification number assigned to items by GPO in a system based on, and reflecting, the structure of the government. SuDoc numbers are usually used by depository libraries in which Federal documents are shelved or housed separately from other collections, as an access point in electronic cataloging records of documents. Most depository items will also include a "Stock Number" (S/N), which is used for items available for pur-

Eric Forte is Economics Librarian at the University of California, Santa Barbara. Michael R. Oppenheim is Reference/Instructional Services Librarian at the Rosenfeld Library, The Anderson School at UCLA.

chase from GPO's U.S. Government Online Bookstore, http://bookstore.gpo.gov/.

STATISTICAL COMPENDIA

The following compendia all provide statistical data from a variety of (mostly) government sources. For instance, the *Statistical Abstract of the United States* pulls out selected popular data from thousands of other statistical resources (primarily, but not exclusively, those of the Federal government); likewise, the *American FactFinder*—although offered as the interface to data from the *2000 Census of Population and Housing*—actually includes data from a number of additional major Census Bureau statistical programs and publications, including the *American Community Survey*, the 1990 *Census of Population and Housing*, and the 1997 Economic Census. Most of the tables in these compendia cite the original source publication—and in so doing, act as an index to more detailed statistical publications and data.

    American FactFinder. Washington, DC: U.S. Bureau of the Census. Available online: http://factfinder.census.gov/.

        Introduced in 1999, *American FactFinder* is the Census Bureau's chief dissemination vehicle for its population and economic data. It is designed to be *the* place to access data from, among other items, the 2000 Census (see *United States Census of Population and Housing*, this section) and the 1997 *Economic Census* (discussed below under "Business and Industrial Conditions"). In addition to the data, the page also features a concise summary of the Decennial Census, the ability to create thematic maps based on Census data, a tool for generating 2000 Census data by street address, and rankings and 1990–2000 comparisons of population change for the United States, states, counties, metropolitan areas, and large places.

    CenStats®. Washington, DC: U.S. Bureau of the Census. Available online: http://tier2.census.gov/dbappweb.htm.

        Originally a fee-based Web subscription service (for which Federal Depository Libraries received one free password), in 1999 *CenStats* became free to all on the Web. It offers "more sophisticated" and value-added "interactive search-and-display" access to such Census Bureau databases as *County Business Patterns*; *USA Counties 1998*; the *Annual Survey of Manufacturers*; *ZIP Business Patterns*; the *Census Tract/Street Index*; *Building Permits*; *U.S. International Trade Data*; and *Detailed Occupation by Race, Hispanic Origin & Sex*. (It should be noted that many of these specific publications are treated independently under the appropriate category within this chapter.)

    County and City Data Book. Washington, DC: U.S. Bureau of the Census, 2000. Quinquennial. $60.00 (S/N 003–024–08862–2, cloth). SuDoc: C 3.134/2:C 83/2/. Also available on CD-ROM. 1062p.

        Published every five years (although updated annually by private publisher Bernan's *County and City Extra: Annual Metro, City and County Data Book*.

Lanham, MD: Bernan Press, 1992–.), this "supplement" to the *Statistical Abstract of the United States* (see this section, below) is the best place to find quick statistics for specific places in the United States. For each state, county, and city of over 25,000 in population, the source provides data on population and demographics, socioeconomic indicators, business climate, and a number of other factors. Data is also available for cities between 2,500 and 25,000 in population, although in less detail.

Historical Statistics of the United States: Colonial Times to 1970. 2 vols. Washington, DC: U.S. Bureau of the Census, 1975. $79.00 (S/N 003–024–00120–9). SuDoc: C3.134/2:H62/789-970/.

This two-volume set compiles popular statistical data from the earliest time it was available until 1970. It includes an index, and presents comprehensive source notes from which the user can often track data to their earliest published sources. Because statistics were gathered on a much smaller scale in the past, *Historical Statistics* is unable to provide older data for many items treated in sources such as the *Statistical Abstract* (see below).

STAT-USA. Washington, DC: U.S. Department of Commerce. Available online: http://www.stat-usa.gov.

STAT-USA is a clearinghouse of international trade information and domestic economic data. Although a Federal government site, *STAT-USA* is required by law to be self-funding; therefore, it must recoup its costs via subscriptions or pay-per-use. Accordingly, it requires a fee to use *unless* it is accessed from within depository libraries, which are allowed free access. More than 50 Federal agencies provide economic data and the full-text of thousands of reports, including many key statistical titles. Highlights include current and archival market research reports, *Country Commercial Guides* (discussed individually under "Foreign Trade and International Business" below), and current popular economic statistics.

State and Metropolitan Area Data Book. Washington, DC: U.S. Bureau of the Census, 1997–1998. 177p. $31.00 (S/N 003–024–08827–4). SuDoc: C3.134/5:. Latest edition available online: http://www.census.gov/statab/www/smadb.html.

Like the *County and City Data Book* (see above, this section), this "supplement" to the *Statistical Abstract of the United States* has been published at irregular intervals starting in 1979, and is an excellent compendium of statistics for states and cities of the United States.

Statistical Abstract of the United States. Washington, DC: U.S. Bureau of the Census, 1878–. Annual. $39.00 (S/N 003–024–08857–6, paper). SuDoc: C3.134:. Available on CD-ROM and online: http://www.census.gov/statab/www/.

The number-one annual compilation of economic, industrial, demographic, social, and political statistics, the *Statistical Abstract* is the single place to begin any statistical search. The data—covering most topics of interest—comes from thousands of different sources (including some nongovernment sources). Most tables provide statistics for a recent range of years ("time series"). Footnotes for every table cite the original source(s) of the information, thus making the *Statistical Abstract* an indispensable guide to further research. The Web site currently contains the editions from 1995 forward (although copyright restrictions exclude several tables from the Web version).

United States Census of Population and Housing. Washington, DC: GPO, 1790–. Decennial. 1990– also available on CD-ROM, DVD, and online: http://www.census.gov.

"Census 2000" is the latest decennial Census of Population and Housing, of great interest to businesses and marketers. It offers comprehensive demographic data for geographic areas as small as "Census blocks"—roughly the equivalent to a city block—all at no cost to the user. Historically, each Census has produced hundreds of print volumes of statistics. Most data from 1990—and nearly all from 2000—are also available via CD-ROMs (or DVDs, in the case of 2000), and via the Census Web site. The key interface to Census 2000 data on the Web is *American FactFinder* (http://factfinder.census.gov/, discussed above in this section). Although access via *American FactFinder* should prove easier than using the hundreds of print volumes from previous censuses, Census 2000 remains an undertaking of such scale that understanding all of what's available—and how to find it—is nearly a full-time job in itself. In addition to background and instructional materials available via the Census Web site, the materials produced by Census watcher Grace York at the University of Michigan—her *Census 2000* Web page (http://www.lib.umich.edu/govdocs/cen2000.html) and her *American Factfinder Tutorial* (http://www.lib.umich.edu/govdocs/amfact/slide1.htm)—should prove helpful.

USA Counties. [CD-ROM]. Washington, DC: U.S. Bureau of the Census, Economics and Statistics Administration, 1992–. Biennial. $150.00, available from the Census Bureau. SuDoc: C 3.134/6:.

Another of the Census Bureau's handy compilations of statistics, this CD-ROM compiles just about every piece of statistical data that the government collects at the county level. Recent versions of *USA Counties* are also available via *CenStats* (see above) and the excellent *Government Information Sharing Project* at Oregon State University http://govinfo.kerr.orst.edu/.

GENERAL ECONOMIC CONDITIONS

Beige Book—see *Summary of Commentary on Current Economic Conditions*, below.

Business Statistics of the United States. Lanham, MD: Bernan Press, 1996–. Annual. $147.00 (ISBN 0–89059–282–9). Continues *Business Statistics*. Washington, DC: U.S. Bureau of Economic Analysis, 1951–1992. Biennial.

Bernan, a private publisher with a long history of working with government information, publishes this continuation of the now defunct *Business Statistics*, which was a periodic supplement to the *Survey of Current Business*. The work contains a vast range of chiefly domestic economic data, with explanatory notes, definitions of terms, and methods of calculation. Many of the same BEA editors who produced the government publication now work on the Bernan edition.

Consumer Expenditure Survey. Washington, DC: U.S. Bureau of Labor Statistics. Annual. 1972–. SuDoc: L 2.3: *report number*). Recent issues available online: http://www.bls.gov/cex/.

A detailed analysis of household expenditure patterns, by region and type of household is provided. The Web site offers current and historical *CE Survey* data products in a variety of forms.

CPI Detailed Report. Washington, DC: U.S. Bureau of Labor Statistics, 1953–. Monthly. $45.00/yr. (S/N 729–002–00000–3). SuDoc: L 2.38/3:.

The CPI (Consumer Price Index) is often used as one method of measuring inflation (inflation itself is a concept, and not an official statistic). This source provides measures of price increases at the consumer level. Data are presented for individual goods and services for the United States, regions, and major Metropolitan Areas. Consumer Price Indexes, http://www.bls.gov/cpi/, while not containing the full-text of the *CPI Detailed Report*, is nonetheless a great source of the most recent consumer price data.

Economic Indicators. Washington, DC: U.S. Congress, Joint Economic Committee, 1948–. Monthly. $55.00/yr. (S/N 752–004–00000–5). SuDoc: Y4.EC7:EC7/. Recent issues available online: http://www.access.gpo.gov/congress/cong002.html.

This is a key source of convenient, easy-to-use charts and tables documenting the current and historical condition of the U.S. economy, prepared officially for use of the Joint Economic Committee (and the American public). The full-text back to 1995 may be searched via the Web site; more usefully, perhaps, issues from 1998 forward may be browsed at the same Web site.

Economic Report of the President. Washington, DC: Executive Office of the President, Council of Economic Advisors, 1947–. Annual. $29.00 (S/N 040–000–00740–7). SuDoc: PR [# *of president*].9: Recent issues available online: http://w3.access.gpo.gov/eop/.

For time series of popular economic data, the *Economic Report of the President* may be the most useful general volume the Federal government produces. Issued by the Council of Economic Advisers, this annual report includes a long discussion of current economic policy and trends, followed by a detailed appendix of time-series tables of U.S. economic data on topics ranging from GDP to employment to interest rates. Much of the data in the *Economic Report of the President* is collected from historical Bureau of Labor Statistics data and the monthly *Economic Indicators*. The Web site features recent issues. Users may download the entire reports from previous years, or access the statistical tables as spreadsheet files (1997–forward).

Economic Statistics Briefing Room. Washington, DC: White House. Updates are primarily monthly. Available online: http://www.whitehouse.gov/fsbr/esbr.html.

This convenient, "ready-reference" Web site provides fast and easy access to current, popular Federal economic indicators in the following areas: production, sales, orders, and inventories; output; income, expenditures, and wealth; employment, unemployment, and earnings; prices; money, credit, and interest rates; transportation; and international statistics.

U.S. Economy at a Glance. Washington, DC: U.S. Bureau of Labor Statistics. Available online: http://www.bls.gov/eag/.

 U.S. Economy at a Glance is a useful summary of employment, price, and productivity statistics from Bureau of Labor Statistics publications. Data is available for the United States, states, and major metropolitan areas, and often dates back to the early 1990s. The site also links to *Industry at a Glance,* http://www.bls.gov/iag/iaghome.htm, which has profiles of the nine major industry groups as defined by SIC codes.

National Income and Product Accounts of the United States, 1929–1997. Washington, DC: U.S. Bureau of Economic Analysis. 2001. $70.00 (S/N 003–010–00288–3). SuDoc: C 59.11/5: 929-97/V. 1–2.

 A supplement to the *Survey of Current Business* (see below, this category), this periodically updated historical compilation provides the latest revised national estimates for national outputs and receipts for a 65+–year period. Data are presented in annual, quarterly, and monthly time series. *GDP and Other Major NIPA Series, 1959–99* (http://www.bea.doc.gov/bea/dn/1299nip2/maintext.htm) provides time series of 1959–1999 GDP and other major NIP data in HTML format, from the December 1999 *Survey of Current Business,* while more data is available via *Interactive Access to National Income and Product Accounts Tables,* available at http://www.bea.doc.gov/bea/dn/nipaweb/. Further, the April 2000 *Survey of Current Business* has "Improved Estimates of the National Income and Product Accounts for 1929–1999" (http://www.bea.doc.gov/bea/an/0400niw2/maintext.htm).

PPI Detailed Report. Washington, DC: U.S. Bureau of Labor Statistics. 1996–. Monthly. $55.00/yr. (S/N 729–009–00000–8). SuDoc: L 2.61: year/month.

 PPI Detailed Report provides highly detailed measures of inflation from the seller's (producer's) perspective, over time, at the wholesale level, by specific commodity. The Consumer Price Index (CPI), by contrast, measures price change from the buyer's perspective. Prior to 1985, this was known as *Producer Prices and Price Indexes* (1978–1984); *Wholesale Prices and Price Indexes* (1956–1978); and *Wholesale Price Index: Prices and Price Relatives for Individual Commodities* (1952–1955). Producer Price Indexes (http://www.bls.gov/ppi/) offers links to news releases, the "Most Requested Series" of data, historic charts, and information about the nature of the PPI.

Regional Economic Information System. [CD-ROM]. Washington, DC: U.S. Bureau of Economic Analysis, 1991–. Annual. $35.00, available from the Bureau of Economic Analysis. SuDoc: C 59.24:.

 REIS, with over 30 years of various economic data at the national, state, and county levels, is especially useful. This CD-ROM resource provides regional economic profiles and projections, Gross State Product, personal income data, commuter flows, and farm income. The *REIS* data is also available via the University of Virginia Library's Geospatial and Statistical (GeoStat) Data Center (http://fisher.lib.virginia.edu/reis/), and from the Oregon State's *Government Information Sharing Project* (http://govinfo.kerr.orst.edu/reis-stateis.html).

Summary of Commentary on Current Economic Conditions [The "Beige Book"]. Washington, DC: U.S. Board of Governors of the Federal Reserve System. 1983–. (Non-depository). Recent issues available online: http://www.Federalreserve.gov/policy.htm.

Each Federal Reserve Bank collects reports on the latest economic conditions in its district from bank and branch directors, interviews with leading members of the business community, economists, market experts, and others. This information, summarized by district and sector, is issued eight times per year. Known as the "Red Book," starting with its 1970 inception, it changed cover color to tan, or "Beige," when the publication became available to the general public around 1983. The Web site currently includes the complete texts of reports back to 1996. A complete (1970 to current) *Beige Book* archive, searchable by year and quarter, is available at the Federal Reserve Bank of Minneapolis site: http://minneapolisfed.org/bb/.

Survey of Current Business. Washington, DC: U.S. Bureau of Economic Analysis, 1921–. Monthly. $49.00/yr. (S/N 703–036–00000–7). SuDoc: C 59.11:. Recent issues available online: http://www.bea.doc.gov/bea/pubs.htm.

The *Survey* is a primary, "first-stop" source for a vast range of domestic and international economic data, including the Gross Domestic Product and its components, and balance of payments. Each issue also includes a few scholarly articles analyzing business conditions. The Web site currently contains issues back to January of 1994.

BUSINESS AND INDUSTRIAL CONDITIONS

Agricultural Statistics. Washington, DC: U.S. Department of Agriculture. 1936–. Annual. $38.00 (S/N 001–000–04694–2). SuDoc: A 1.47: *year*). Recent issues available online: http://www.usda.gov/nass/pubs/agstats.htm.

This extensive almanac of agricultural production figures, prices, and other related data is the number-one source for agricultural statistics. The Web site currently contains issues back to 1994. Additional important Web sites for economic statistics for agriculture include Cornell University's Mann Library's *USDA Economics and Statistics System* (http://usda.mannlib.cornell.edu/usda/), and the U.S. Department of Agriculture's Economic Research Service (http://www.ers.usda.gov/).

County Business Patterns. Washington, DC: U.S. Bureau of the Census, 1964–. Annual. $8.00/paper volume; $50.00/CD-ROM, available from the Census Bureau. SuDoc: C 3.204/3–). Recent years available on CD-ROM and online: http://www.census.gov/epcd/cbp/view/cbpview.html.

County Business Patterns presents annual statistics on the number and size of establishments, employees, and payroll by SIC classification at the county level, but does not cover government employees, domestic workers, farm workers, and the self-employed. The 1998 *CBP* is the first to use NAICS. The Web site features most of the data from 1993 forward, while the University of Virginia Library's Geospatial and Statistical (GeoStat) Data Center offers an interactive *CPB* database (among others), covering 1977–1997 data by SIC code, and 1998 data by NAICS, searchable at the national, state, and county levels (http://fisher.lib.virginia.edu/cbp/).

Current Industrial Reports. Washington, DC: U.S. Bureau of the Census. 1959–. Publication schedules varies. SuDoc: C 3.158: *[report number]*). Available online: http://www.census.gov/cir/www/.

These reports provide statistics on commodity production, inventories, and shipments for some 4,400 products, representing 30 percent of all U.S. manufacturing. As of 1993, the *Current Industrial Reports* began to be issued largely in electronic form, although some were still being issued in paper as well as late as 1998. The electronic versions on the Web are available in pdf, ASCII text, and spreadsheet formats, with many reports archived as far back as 1991 or 1992.

Economic Census. Washington, DC: U.S. Bureau of the Census, 1954–. Quinquennial. Much recent data is also available on CD-ROM and online: http://www.census.gov/epcd/www/econ97.html.

The *Economic Census* is somewhat similar to the more famous *Census of Population and Housing.* While the latter counts people every 10 years, the former counts business every five years, thereby presenting a statistical portrait of the U.S. business climate. Businesses ("establishments") are counted and categorized by type, and data such as number of employees and net sales are collected. Data are available by type of business and for states and counties, so that the *Economic Census* provides a statistical portrait of thousands of industries for the nation, or within a state, county, or metropolitan area. Like the *Census of Population and Housing,* no names are revealed in the *Economic Census*; data is aggregated for all the businesses of a type within the nation, state, and smaller geographic areas. This results in certain data being "suppressed" to insure confidentiality. The 1997 *Economic Census* marked the first time businesses were categorized using the North American Industry Classification System (NAICS) codes; previously, the Standard Industrial Classification (SIC) codes were used. Generally speaking, the reports and data for the *Economic Census* are broken down into 18 major industries, taken from the major breakdowns in NAICS. The result for each of these industries is referred to as its own Census; i.e., *Census of Manufacturers,* or *Census of Finance and Insurance* (it should be noted that as of the 1997 *Economic Census,* agriculture is no longer part of the *Economic Census,* and is conducted by the Department of Agriculture as the *Census of Agriculture* (http://www.nass.usda.gov/census/); similarly, government is also treated outside of the Economic Census, although it is still covered by the Census Bureau and called the *Census of Governments* (http://www.census.gov/govs/www/). The results of the *Economic Census* are published in print, CD-ROM, and online formats, but the trend is clearly towards the Web.

Housing Statistics of the United States. Lanham, MD: Bernan Press. 1997–. Irregular. $89.00 (ISBN 0–89059–214–4).

This private publication, based largely on statistics gathered by the Federal government, provides a good starting point and compilation of housing data. The U.S. Census Bureau compiles much of the original housing data; *Census*

Bureau Housing Topics (http://www.census.gov/hhes/www/housing.html) provides an interface to many of their publications and statistics on housing and construction, including the data collected in the *United States Census of Population and Housing.*

U.S. Industry and Trade Outlook. Washington, DC: U.S. Department of Commerce and the McGraw-Hill Companies. 1997–2000. Annual. $76.00 (S/N 003–009–00717–8). SuDoc: C 61.48: *year.* Quasi-commercial product, with a currently uncertain future. See http://www.ita.doc.gov/td/industry/otea/outlook/webnotice.html for more information).

The *U.S. Industry and Trade Outlook* traces back to the *U.S. Industrial Outlook* (C 61.34: *year*), a standard reference guide to American industry that the Commerce Department published annually from 1960 onward, until it ceased in 1994. Its renaissance as a "commercial government publication" (hence the description above as "quasi-commercial") has represented an unusual public–private collaboration. Although the book is sold commercially, Commerce and the National Technical Information Service publicly vowed in July 1997 to provide each Federal Depository Library with a free depository copy. Depository Libraries have continued to receive one free copy of the text. However, as noted in the bibliographic information, it appears that there will be another publishing change, which again appears to place its status as a "free" depository item in jeopardy, despite the fact that it remains a project produced at taxpayer expense. Regardless of how it is published, this remains an excellent overview of the U.S. business climate. Each chapter covers a different industry, reviewing the current state and trends of that industry in text and data.

ZIP Code Business Patterns. [CD-ROM]. Washington, DC: United States Census Bureau. 1994–. Annual. $50.00, available from the Census Bureau. SuDoc: C 3.294:. Available online: http://tier2.census.gov/cbp_naics/index.html (1998–, NAICS based) and http://tier2.census.gov/zbp (1993–1997, SIC-based).

One of the datasets available via *CenStats* (see "Statistical Compendia" above), *ZIP Code Business Patterns* is based on *County Business Patterns*, with the data sorted by ZIP code. Data for 1997 and earlier are arranged by SIC code; data for 1998+ are arranged by NAICS code.

FISCAL AND MONETARY CONDITIONS

Annual Statistical Digest. Washington, DC: U.S. Board of Governors of the Federal Reserve System. 1971/75–1994, Annual. 1995–, Quinquennial. (ISSN 0148–4338). SuDoc: FR 1.59: *years*). Non-depository.

This is a convenient compilation of economic and financial "time-series" statistical data, as originally published in the *Federal Reserve Bulletin* (see below). Economic indicators, the money supply, interest rates, flow of funds, and credit are only a few of the categories included. At this writing, the publication itself— reproducing its print format—has yet to appear free of charge on the Web, and the 1990–1995 compilation remains the most recent available. Some current data *is* available at http://www.Federalreserve.gov/releases/.

Annual Report to Congress—Board of Governors of the Federal Reserve System. Washington, DC: Board of Governors of the Federal Reserve System. 1914–. Annual. SuDoc: FR 1.1: *year*. Recent reports available online: http:// www.Federalreserve.gov/boarddocs/RptCongress/.

In addition to providing exhaustively detailed narrative and statistical coverage of the year's operations of the Federal Reserve System, this report also includes an excellent overview and analysis of the national and international economy for the past year. The Web site links to the full texts of reports back to 1995.

Budget of the United States Government. Washington, DC: Office of Management and Budget. 1922/23–. Annual. $44.00, not including appendices. (S/N 041–001–00552–8). SuDoc: PrEx 2.8: *year*. Recent years available online: http:// w3.access.gpo.gov/usbudget/index.html.

This major source of current, historical, and projected government spending has also been available on CD-ROM for several years SuDocs PrEx 2.8/1:. The Web site currently provides links to the full texts from fiscal year 1996 forward, along with the year's *Economic Report of the President.*

The Economic and Budget Outlook. Washington, DC: Congressional Budget Office. 1985–. Annual. $18.00 (S/N 052–070–07247–4). SuDoc: Y 10.17: *years.* Recent years available online: http://www.cbo.gov/byclasscat.cfm?class=0&cat=0.

Every year, the CBO issues this analysis—with four-year projections—of the U.S. economy as a whole, and Federal government spending policies and trends. Each edition looks at the 10-year period beginning with the current fiscal year.

FDIC Quarterly Banking Profile. Washington, DC: Federal Deposit Insurance Corporation. 1988–. Quarterly. SuDoc: Y 3.F 31/8:29/*issue number.* Recent issues available online: http://www2.fdic.gov/qbp/.

The *Profile's* statistical tables, graphs, and written analyses provide the earliest available "financial report card" for the banking industry—all insured commercial banks and savings institutions—within 75 days after the end of each quarter (March 31, June 30, September 30, and December 31).

Federal Reserve Bulletin. Washington, DC: Board of Governors of the Federal Reserve. 1915–. Monthly. (ISSN 0014–9209). SuDoc: FR 1.3: *volume/number* (Nondepository, but libraries may subscribe at no cost). Recent issues available online: http://www.Federalreserve.gov/pubs/bulletin/.

This is a key source of summary economic and financial statistics, such as Gross National Product, the Consumer and Producer Price Indexes, flow of funds, the money supply, interest rates, dollar value, consumer credit, and industrial production indexes. The statistical series are compiled annually in the Board's *Annual Statistical Digest* (see description above). Federal Reserve Board research articles are also published. Although the Web site does not reproduce the full text of the *Bulletin,* it does contain many articles from 1997 to current.

FRED: Federal Reserve Economic Database. St. Louis, MO: U.S. Federal Reserve Bank of St. Louis. Available online: http://www.stls.frb.org/fred/.

Exceptionally useful, this is an easily searchable repository of historical U.S. economic and financial data, including daily U.S. interest rates, monetary and business indicators, exchange rates, and regional economic data for Arkansas,

Illinois, Indiana, Kentucky, Mississippi, Missouri, and Tennessee. Also included are the full texts of recent Federal Reserve Board statistical releases.

Treasury Bulletin. Washington, DC: U.S. Treasury Department. 1939–. Quarterly. $41.00/yr. (S/N 748–007–00000–8). SuDoc: T 63.103/2: *year/month.* Recent issues available online: http://www.fms.treas.gov/bulletin/index.html.

The *Treasury Bulletin* publishes summary data on the national debt and other topics relating to the finances of the Federal government. The Web site provides the 1996 to current issues of the *Bulletin.*

U.S. Government Annual Report. Washington, DC: U.S. Treasury Department. 1894–. Annual. $5.00 (S/N 048–000–00537–3). SuDoc: T 63.101/2: *year.* Recent years available online: http://www.fms.treas.gov/annualreport/index.html.

This is the concise, illustrated overview of *the* officially recognized receipts and outlays of the Federal government. A few hundred pages of much greater detail, including some comparative historical statistics, are published in the companion *Annual Report Appendix* (T 63.101/2-2: *year*). The Web site includes the full texts from fiscal year 1995 forward, as well as the *Appendix* for fiscal year 1998 forward.

FOREIGN TRADE AND INTERNATIONAL BUSINESS

Basic Guide to Exporting. Washington, DC: U.S. International Trade Administration. Irregular. $18.00 (S/N 003–009–00708–9). SuDoc: C 61.8: EX7/3/*year.* Available online: http://www.unzco.com/basicguide/index.html.

What a potential exporter could possibly need to know is contained in this latest edition (1998), "Prepared by the U.S. Department of Commerce with the assistance of Unz & Co., Inc." The Web URL links to the 1998 edition. A similar guide is the Small Business Administration's *SBA Guide to Exporting* (http://www.sba.gov/OIT/info/Guide-To-Exporting/). Also useful is the U.S. Customs Service Web site for "Importing and Exporting," <http://www.customs.ustreas.gov/imp-exp/rulings/rulelist.htm, which includes current and archival issues of *Customs Bulletin and Decisions*, a compendium of U.S. customs laws, and other resources.

Country Commercial Guides. Washington, DC: U.S. Department of State. Updates are approximately yearly. Available online: http://www.state.gov/e/eb/rls/rpts/ccg/.

U.S. embassies prepare these comprehensive "doing business in" type reports, with the assistance of other Federal government agencies. Each country guide provides extensive facts and analyses covering the economic, market, and political topics of greatest concern to potential importers and exporters. These information-rich reports have succeeded the Commerce Department's *Overseas Business Reports* ("OBRs"), which ceased publication in 1993–94. At the above Web site, reports are available from fiscal year 1996 forward.

Country Reports on Economic Policy and Trade Practices. Washington, DC: U.S. Department of State. 1989–. Annual (since 1994). SuDoc: Y 4.IN 8/16: C 83/997 *[latest edition; earlier SuDocs numbers vary]*). Recent issues available online: http://www.state.gov/e/eb/rls/rpts/eptp/.

Detailed reports and analysis of the economic conditions, policies, and trade practices of each country with which the United States has an economic or trade relationship are provided in this resource. Coverage includes key economic indicators, debt management policies, and general macroeconomic trends. The Web site contains the issues since 1993.

Department of Commerce Export Portal. Washington, DC: U.S. Department of Commerce. Available online: http://www.export.gov/.

This is a new collection of information and statistics about foreign trade, geared towards the U.S. businessperson looking to export or operate abroad. It contains much of the same data as *STAT-USA* (see "Statistical Compendia," above), without the need to be in a depository library for no-cost access. Included are *Country Commercial Guides*, a variety of market research reports, trade opportunities and leads, statistics, advice on exporting, and information on government assistance for the exporter.

Foreign Trade of the United States: Including Exports by State and Metro Area Export Data. Lanham, MD: Bernan Press. 1999–. Irregular. $147.00 ISBN 0–89059–249–7).

Another of Bernan Press' compilations of data from the Federal government, this statistical publication collects in one place foreign trade data from the U.S. Census Bureau, Bureau of Economic Analysis, and International Trade Administration.

Foreign Trade Statistics: Your Key to Trade. Washington, DC: U.S. Bureau of the Census. Updates are continuous. Available online: http://www.census.gov/ftp/pub/foreign-trade/www/.

Foreign Trade Statistics offers a most impressive array of information resources, including the Bureau's *Guide to Foreign Trade Statistics*, its *Schedule B: Export Commodity Classification Guide*, data tables showing U.S. trade with all partners, the most recent trade data from the FT900 press release, trade balances, and other links to current and historical trade and country data.

Handbook of International Economic Statistics. Washington, DC: U.S. Central Intelligence Agency. 1975–. Annual. $20.00 (S/N 041–015–00185–0). SuDoc: PrEx 3.16: *year*). Recent years available online: http://www.odci.gov/cia/di/products/hies/index.html.

This handbook provides comparative economic statistics for most countries of the world.

STAT-USA—see "Statistical Compendia," above.

U.S. Exports of Merchandise [CD-ROM] SuDoc: C 3.278/3: *year/month* and *U.S. Imports of Merchandise* [CD-ROM] SuDoc: C 3.278/2: *year/month*. Washington, DC: U.S. Bureau of the Census. 1991–. Monthly, with annual cumulations. $1200/yr, available from the Census Bureau.

Two complementary statistical files provide year-to-date (YTD) data on U.S. exports and imports by detailed commodity classification, as well as data broken down by port district, and country of origin or destination. Each title also includes an annual historical disk. The latest historical CD-ROM compilations (covering 1994–1998) are searchable on the Web via Oregon State's *Government Information Sharing Project* (http://govinfo.kerr.orst.edu/).

U.S. Foreign Trade Highlights. Washington, DC: U.S. International Trade Administration. 1984–. Annual. $19.00 (S/N 003–009–00670–8). SuDoc: C 3.278/3: *year/ month.* Available online: http://www.ita.doc.gov/td/industry/otea/usfth/.

Summary data on U.S. imports and exports by country and by broad commodity groups are presented. The Web site offers vast amounts of current and historical data.

LABOR

BLS Create Customized Tables. Washington, DC: U.S. Bureau of Labor Statistics. Available online: http://www.bls.gov/data/sa.html.

At this interactive site users can create their own tables of labor statistics data from those provided by the Bureau of Labor Statistics.

Dictionary of Occupational Titles. Washington, DC: U.S. Employment Service. 1939–[1991]. Irregular, issued approximately every 15 years. $61.00 (S/N 029–013–00094–2). SuDoc: L 37.2: Oc 1/2/*year.*

Concise, standardized job descriptions for more than 20,000 occupations are detailed here, arranged according to the *DOT*'s special classification categories. The latest edition, issued in 1991, is the last; a searchable version is mounted at the site of the Department of Labor's Office of Administrative Law Judges: http://www.oalj.dol.gov/libdot.htm. The Department announced in 1997 that the "outmoded" *DOT* would be replaced by O*NET (L37.25: OC1/CD), the Occupational Information Network, "a comprehensive database system for collection, organizing, describing and disseminating data on job characteristics and worker attributes." O*NET provides cross-references to the DOT. It is available as a CD-ROM or diskette (called O*NET 98), and through the Web, at http://www.doleta.gov/programs/onet (alternate URL: http://online.onetcenter.org/).

Employment and Earnings. Washington, DC: U.S. Bureau of Labor Statistics. 1954–. Monthly. $50.00/yr. (S/N 729–004–00000–6). SuDoc: L 2.41/2: *volume/issue number.*

Employment and Earnings is the source for employment and unemployment statistics. Its separate *Annual Supplement* (L 2.41/2-2:) covers "Establishment"-level data only. Although the actual publication is not available online, news releases and most of the data for recent years is available via the *Employment, Hours, and Earnings from the Current Employment Statistics:* http://www.bls.gov/ces/.

Handbook of U.S. Labor Statistics. Lanham, MD: Bernan Press, 1997–. Irregular. Commercial product. Continues *Handbook of Labor Statistics.* Washington, DC: U.S. Bureau of Labor Statistics, 1924–1989. Irregular. $147.00 (ISBN 0–89059–281–0).

This prime source of time-series data for a broad range of labor statistics, encompassing most of the major series tabulated by the BLS was discontinued after the 1989 edition. In Spring 1997, Bernan Press brought the publication back to life, employing many of the BLS personnel who last produced it, as *Handbook of U.S. Labor Statistics.*

Monthly Labor Review. Washington, DC: U.S. Bureau of Labor Statistics. 1915–.
Monthly. $43.00/yr. (S/N 729–007–00000–5). SuDoc: L 2.6: *volume/issue no.*
Recent issues also available: http://stats.bls.gov/opub/mlr/mlrhome.htm.

This core resource offers outstanding articles on current labor trends, as well
as summary statistics taken from other BLS publications. Among the special features in the January issue are articles on the collective bargaining outlook for the
year ahead, summaries of changes in state labor laws, and a labor relations "year-
in-review." A review article on "Wage Adjustments in Contracts Negotiated in
Private Industry" appears in May, and a corresponding article for the public sector appears in the June or August issue. The Web version mirrors the print publication, and provides a decade's-worth of archives, back to 1989.

Occupational Outlook Handbook. Washington, DC: U.S. Bureau of Labor Statistics.
1949–. Biennial. $49.00 (S/N/ 029–001–03331–1, paper). SuDoc: L 2.3/4: *years.*
Recent issues available online: http://stats.bls.gov/ocohome.htm.

This all but "universal" core reference source provides brief overviews and
employment outlook data for several hundred of the most common occupations
in the United States. The Web site features the most current edition.

O*Net—see *Dictionary of Occupational Titles*, above.

OSHA Handbook for Small Businesses. Washington, DC: U.S. Department of Labor.
Occupational Safety and Health Administration. 1996. $8.50 (S/N 029–016–
00176–0). SuDoc: L 35.19: B96/996). Available online: http://www.osha-slc.gov/
Publications/Osha2209.pdf.

Although sources for laws and regulations in general are covered in a separate section below, this guide is seen as a convenient handbook that helps businesses comply with occupational safety and health standards and regulations.
The OSHA home page (http://www.osha.gov/) actually provides full-text of the
regulations themselves, as well as numerous other publications designed to help
business with OSHA.

GOVERNMENT PROCUREMENT AND ASSISTANCE

Catalog of Federal Domestic Assistance. Washington, DC: U.S. Office of Management and Budget. 1965–. Annual, with mid-year updates. $60.00 (S/N 922–025–
00000–2). SuDoc: PrEx 2.20: *year.* Most recent issue available online: http://
www.cfda.gov/.

"What money does the Government have to give away?" This reference
department mainstay is *the* guide to Federal grants and assistance available to
state and local governments, small businesses and other organizations, and individuals. It covers 1,450 domestic assistance programs sponsored by 57 Federal
departments and agencies, and includes qualification requirements and suggestions for writing grant proposals. The Web site provides the latest available information, fully searchable by keyword, or browsable by section (e.g., sponsoring
agency, program title, or application deadline). Introduced in 2000, *The Federal
Commons* (http://www.cfda.gov/Federalcommons/index.html), functions as a portal to Federal agencies' grant sites (by May 2001, all Federal agencies were required to develop plans for the online processing of grants).

Commerce Business Daily. See *Federal Business Opportunities* below.

Federal Acquisition Regulation[s] (FAR). Washington, DC: U.S. General Services Administration. 1984– Available online: http://www.arnet.gov/far/. Also available as Title 48 of the *Code of Federal Regulations* SuDoc: AE 2.106/3: 48/.

"What regulations do I need to know to do business with the government?" The Web site provides the full-text (in HTML and PDF), fully searchable. *FAR Circulars* are also available at the site, in looseleaf and *Federal Register* format.

Federal Business Opportunities. Washington, DC: U.S. General Services administration 2002–. Available online: http://www.fedbizopps.gov/. Continues: *Commerce Business Daily.* Washington, DC: U.S. Department of Commerce. 1954–2002. Daily. SuDoc: C 1.76: *date.* Available online: http://cbdnet.access.gpo.gov/.

"What does the government want to buy?" The answer is here, in this daily detailing of U.S. government procurements sought, sales and contract awards, surplus property sales, and research and development sources "gone out for bid."

SBA: Small Business Administration Home Page. Washington, DC: U.S. Small Business Administration. Available online: http://www.sba.gov/.

The Small Business Administration's Web site is a clearinghouse of information of use to small business. Among its resources are guides to starting and running a business, resources for finding funding for a business, and information on the various SBA programs designed to aid the small business.

U.S. Business Advisor. Washington, DC: U.S. Small Business Administration. Available online: http://www.business.gov/.

Maintained by the Small Business Administration, this Web site collects information helpful to business that has been produced by any of the Federal agencies that aid and/or regulate business. It's a good starting point for finding out how the Federal government can help the businessperson.

GOVERNMENT OVERSIGHT: CORPORATE FINANCE, TAXATION, CONSUMER INFORMATION, AND INTELLECTUAL PROPERTY

Basic Facts about Trademarks. Washington, DC: U.S. Patent and Trademark Office. Irregular. $3.25 (S/N 003–004–00694–3). SuDoc : C 21.2:T 67/4. Also available online: http://www.uspto.gov/web/offices/tac/doc/basic/.

Basic Facts describes trademarks, and details registration procedures. Although this publication is the best introduction to trademarks, the Trademark section of the *U.S. Patent & Trademark Office's home page* (http://www.uspto.gov/main/trademarks.htm) provides many more trademark resources, and the *Patent and Trademark Depository Library Program* (http://www.uspto.gov/go/ptdl/) lists and links to these special libraries designed to provide access and aid with patent and trademark information needs.

Business Taxpayer Information Publications. Washington, DC: Internal Revenue Service. 1996–. Annual. $71.00 (S/N 648–200–00003–0). SuDoc: T 22.44/2: 1194-B/.

The IRS annually collects and updates its publications related to tax on businesses. These publications walk the businessperson through the tax landscape, summarizing the law and identifying necessary tax and filing requirements, for a number of business situations. Users can retrieve current and historical IRS tax publications and notices, full-text and in multiple file formats, at http:// www.irs.ustreas.gov/forms_pubs/pubs.html.

Consumer Product Safety Commission Home Page. Washington, DC: Consumer Product Safety Commission. Available online: http://www.cpsc.gov/.

The Consumer Product Safety Commission Web site lists product recalls and features hundreds of publications about safety relating to various products and activities.

Directory of Companies Required to File Annual Reports with the Securities and Exchange Commission. Washington, DC: U.S. Securities and Exchange Commission. 1973–. Annual. SuDoc: SE 1.27: *year.*

This directory lists the more than 13,000 (public) companies required to file annual reports with the Securities and Exchange Commission under the Securities Exchange Act of 1934, alphabetically and by SIC industry classifications. It is one of the few government publications that actually names company names, and may be used in conjunction with EDGAR, below.

EDGAR Database of Corporate Information. Washington, DC: U.S. Securities and Exchange Commission. 1994–. Daily updates. Available online: http:// www.sec.gov/edgar.shtml.

EDGAR provides free, full-text reports on U.S. public companies which are *all* now required (as of March 1997) to file data electronically with the SEC. Coverage begins, incompletely, with 1994 filings, and *is* complete starting with 1997 (and many 1996) filings. As of 2001 filings, the SEC is not yet requiring the use of the North American Industry Classification System (NAICS).

Federal Trade Commission Home Page. Washington, DC: Federal Trade Commission. Available online: http://www.ftc.gov/.

The FTC performs a variety of duties related to ensuring a fair and open marketplace. In so doing, the Commission produces many valuable brochures and factsheets that inform both businesses and consumers about potentially confusing and/or deceptive business practices (covering such topics as buying a used car, applying for credit, and identity theft). The FTC also regulates and approves mergers and works to enforce antitrust laws. All of the information produced is identified on this Web site.

General Information Concerning Patents. Washington, DC: U.S. Patent and Trademark Office. Irregular. $4.75 (S/N 003–004–00683–8). SuDoc: C 21.26/2: *year.* Most of the text is available online: http://www.uspto.gov/web/offices/pac/doc/ general/.

This source provides a concise guide to patents: what they are, how to file for one, etc. See also the *Patent and Trademark Depository Library Program* (http:// www.uspto.gov/go/ptdl/), featuring a listing and links to these special libraries designed to provide access and aid with patent and trademark information needs.

Statistics of Income: Corporation Income Tax Returns. Washington, DC: U.S. Internal Revenue Service. 1954–. Annual. $26.00 (S/N 048–004–02436–5). SuDoc: T 22.35/5: *year.*

Aggregate income statements and balance sheets for major industry group-
ings, based on corporate tax filings, are provided in this publication. The companion publication, *Statistics of Income Source Book* (T 22.35/5-2: *year*) provides
more detailed information, including more specific breakdowns by SIC code number. The Web site, *Corporation Tax Statistics* (http://www.irs.ustreas.gov/tax_stats/
corp.html), provides links to articles and taxation data files, both recent and
historical, downloadable in both Excel and pdf formats.

Tax Guide for Small Business. Washington, DC: Internal Revenue Service. 1996–.
Annual. $5.00 (S/N 048-200-00032-0). SuDoc: T 22.44/2: 1194-B/. Available
online: http://www.irs.gov/pub/irs-pdf/p334.pdf.

Similar to *Business Taxpayer Information Publications* (see above), this document ("Publication 334") summarizes what the small business owner needs to
know about taxes.

United States Patent and Trademark Office Home Page. Washington, DC: Available
online: http://www.uspto.gov/.

This Web site features information about patents and trademarks, as well as
a searchable database of patents and pending patents (including detailed patent
entries back to 1976, and patent images only back to 1790), and a searchable
database of trademarks and pending trademarks. Also included is information
about Patent and Trademark Depository Libraries (http://www.uspto.gov/web/of-
fices/ac/ido/ptdl/index.html).

GOVERNMENT OVERSIGHT: LAWS AND REGULATIONS

Several of the sources already discussed cover legal and regulatory issues on
certain topics (taxes, occupational safety and health, intellectual property);
numerous other laws and regulations exist that relate to business. The search
for laws and regulations can be complicated, and it is recommended that one
at least be familiar with the legislative and regulatory processes and publications by reading the relevant chapter in any of the textbook-type sources listed
under "General Guides and Directories" in Chapter 4.

Code of Federal Regulations. Washington, DC: National Archives and Records Administration, 1949–. Revised annually. $1049/yr. (S/N 869-044-00000-8).
SuDoc: AE 2.106/3: Available online: http://www.access.gpo.gov/nara/cfr/
index.html (and from various commercial vendors).

The *CFR* is the codification, by "Titles," of regulations currently in force.
New regulations first appear in the *Federal Register* (see below), but will appear in
the CFR within a year. Both the print and Web versions feature an index. Volumes are arranged by topic, making browsing a useful approach as well. To keep
up-to-date between the rolling annual revisions of CFR "Titles," one should consult the monthly *LSA, List of CFR Sections Affected* SuDoc: AE 2.106/2:. The
current year and four years back are searchable via GPO Access, at http://
www.access.gpo.gov/nara/lsa/srchlsa.html.

Environmental Protection Agency Business and Industry. Washington, DC: Environmental Protection Agency. Available online: http://www.epa.gov/epahome/
business.htm.

   This Web site offers information about compliance with environmental laws
   and regulations, aimed at the businessperson.

Federal Register. Washington, DC: National Archives and Records Administration,
1936–. Daily. $697.00/yr. (S/N 769–004–00000–9). SuDoc: AE 2.106: Available
online: http://www.access.gpo.gov/su_docs/aces/aces140.html and from various
commercial sources.

   Regulations are first published in this source, in draft form, for public comment. Final Regulations are likewise first published in the *Federal Register*, before
   they are inserted, by subject(s), into the CFR.

United States Code. 1994 ed. with supplements. Washington, DC: GPO, 1994–.
SuDoc: Y 1.2/5: Also available on CD-ROM; via GPO Access at http://
www.access.gpo.gov/congress/cong013.html; and from various commercial vendors.

   The U.S. Code contains all laws currently in force, arranged by subject.
   New laws, changes to laws, and repealed laws are all covered. When laws are first
   enacted, they are published individually as *Slip Laws* SuDoc: AE 2.110:), with a
   "P.L." designation indicating the Congress and the law number. GPO Access
   provides a searchable Public Laws database (http://www.access.gpo.gov/nara/
   nara005.html), covering legislation enacted since the 104th Congress (1995–
   1996).

6

Business Periodicals:
A Core Collection for the Smaller Business Library

Elizabeth C. Clarage

Since the business periodicals list in the previous edition was compiled, the U.S. economy continued on the longest economic expansion in its history. In Spring 2000, the U.S. financial markets led by the technology heavy NASDAQ went through a correction. Even so, the Internet and technology in general have revolutionized the way companies do business; a company's stock can now be traded after market hours and nearly 24 hours a day, and the markets worldwide affect one another's economies. Because of the changes in the world and because business and business changes seem to move at a faster and faster pace, keeping track of current news and trends is even more important to the individual consumer, the individual investor, the small business owner, and top executives. Magazines and journals continue to provide the current up-to-date information needed by the business community.

Subject matter and cost are important issues when selecting titles, but access to the content of the titles is equally important. Indexing and abstracting resources aid in identifying business articles, and electronic versions of the key indexing and abstracting sources have become increasingly important in this regard because of the changes in how people do research. Over 96 percent of the titles on this list are indexed, abstracted and, in some cases, have full-text available in either *ABI/Inform, Business Periodicals Index / Business Abstracts, LexisNexis,* or *PAIS International.*

Besides the paper or electronic databases used to identify the content of magazines and journals, the Internet now plays a greater role in all libraries. In September 2000, the U.S. National Commission on Libraries and Information Science released selected findings of a study on public libraries and connectivity entitled *Public Libraries and the Internet 2000.* The Commission found that 95.7 percent of all public libraries are connected to the Internet and 94.5

Elizabeth C. Clarage is Consortium Director for the Illinois Cooperative Collection Management Program.

percent provide public access to the Internet. Many of the titles on this core list have some Internet identity. Some provide free access to all or selected portions of their content. Some include electronic access with a paid paper subscription, while others only provide access when the title is subscribed to electronically. Some titles are available through the publication's Web site, while others only have electronic access through a vendor or aggregator. If the information was available, the Uniform Resource Locator (URL) for Internet access is given after the publication information for the title. The Web site addresses were checked for accuracy in April 2002.

The core list of basic periodicals useful to any business collection contained herein should serve as a starting point for selection decisions, with the decisions themselves based on the needs of the specific library and its clientele. Sixty titles comprise this list. The prices for the titles on the list reflect the trend of rising prices of journals in business and economics. According to the May 2000 issue of *American Libraries*, the average price of business and economic titles in 2000 was $142.08, a 50.5 percent increase from the average price in 1995 when the previous edition was published. The total cost of the titles on this year's list at current prices for institutional subscribers is $7,199.09, 67.5 percent more than the total for the previous list. The average cost for a title on this list is $119.98, up from the previous average of $76.64, with the percent increase for the average title cost from the previous list to this one standing at 56.6 percent, in line with the price increase for business titles in general.

The titles on this list were checked against the serial holdings at the University of Illinois at Urbana-Champaign and at Milner Library at Illinois State University, as well as the owning library information in WorldCat, the OCLC database. The publication and pricing information was confirmed by checking the collection at the University of Illinois at Urbana-Champaign, WorldCat (the OCLC database), UlrichsWeb.com (the electronic form of *Ulrich's International Periodicals Directory*), and if available, the publication's Web site.

The reader may note that the list in previous editions has been changed to include additional titles published by the United States government, international titles that reflect the globalization of business, and more titles in the areas of real estate and Internet business. Business subject areas retained from previous editions include accounting, construction, economics, finance, information technology, insurance, marketing, and management. Titles that have been excluded are those trade publications specific to a particular city, region, or country, such as *Crain's Chicago Business*, the *South Florida Business Journal*, or *Business Africa*. However, since libraries have differing needs depending on their location, specialized titles such as these should be considered for collections depending on the needs of the library's clientele.

THE LIST

The Accounting Review. American Accounting Association. 1926–. Quarterly. ISSN: 0001-4826. $125.00. Available online: http://www.rutgers.edu/Accounting/raw/aaa/pubs/acctrev.htm.

This peer-reviewed journal is aimed at those interested in accounting research "including but not limited to academicians." The primary criterion for publication is the significance of the contribution an article makes to the literature. All aspects of accounting are covered. Typical articles include the results of accounting research and explanations and illustrations related to research methodology. Book reviews are also included.

Across the Board. The Conference Board Inc. 1976–. 10/yr. ISSN: 0147-1554. $40.00. Available online: http://www.conference-board.org/atb/ATBindex.cfm.

The Conference Board, the publisher of *Across the Board*, has a two-fold mission: "to improve the business enterprise system and to enhance the contribution of business to society." This publication aimed at the general business manager is one way the organization tries to accomplish that mission. Articles focus on ideas and opinion and explore serious issues in an understandable manner. The January issue contains an annual economic forecast.

Advertising Age. Crain Communications, Inc. 1930–. Weekly. ISSN: 0001-8899. $119.00. Available online: http://www.adage.com/.

Aimed at executives in the advertising industry, this weekly trade journal covers all aspects of advertising, including current news, events and promotions, media and marketing, and people. Typical articles include information on advertising campaigns and advertising agencies, as well as reviews of current advertisements. One section of the publication, Interactive, contains information about advertising and the Internet. Several annual features are anticipated every year, including the 100 Leading National Advertisers, Agencies Reviews, and Top Brands.

American Demographics. Cowles Business Media. 1979–. Monthly. ISSN: 0163-4089. $69.00. Available online: http://www.inside.com/default.asp?entity=AmericanDemo.

American Demographics contains articles that discuss the trends in consumer behavior and provide written analysis as well as statistics on a variety of consumer groups, products, and brands. Each issue is divided into how the reader will use the information, *now* (which includes current news and snapshots of consumers), *soon* (which includes information about consumer trends that will endure or be current for approximately 6 months), and *future* (which includes more in-depth pieces about long-term trends).

The American Economic Review. American Economic Association. 1911–. 5/yr. ISSN: 0002-8282. Free to members; $140.00, institutions. Available online: http://www.aeaweb.org/aer/.

A peer-reviewed journal of the American Economic Association, this publication covers all aspects of economics. Longer articles as well as shorter papers are included. The May issue contains papers and proceedings of the annual association meeting. Every fourth year, a sixth issue is published which is a directory of AEA members.

B to B: The Magazine for Marketing and E-Commerce Strategists (formerly *Advertising Age's Business Marketing*). Crain Communications, Inc. 2000–. Biweekly. ISSN: 1530–2369. $59.00. Available online: http://netb2b.com/.

"B to B" is business jargon for a business-to-business relationship. This biweekly trade journal is aimed at the marketing professional and contains practical and insightful news on traditional and electronic marketing, technology trends, case studies, statistics, real world tips, and reviews of marketing campaigns.

Barron's: The Dow Jones Business and Financial Weekly (formerly *Barron's National Business and Financial Weekly*). Dow Jones & Co., Inc. 1994–. Weekly. ISSN: 1077–8039. $145.00. Available online: http://www.barrons.com/.

Aimed at the knowledgeable investor, *Barron's*, which has a publishing history dating back to 1921, publishes news and analysis on the economy, companies, and industries. A good portion of the publication contains statistics about stocks, bonds, options, mutual funds, commodities, indices, and economic indicators.

Best's Review: Insurance Issues and Analysis (formerly *Best's Review: Life/Health Insurance* and *Best's Review: Property/Casualty Insurance*). A.M. Best Co. 2000–. Monthly. ISSN: 1527–5914. $25.00. Available online: http://www.bestreview. com/.

Published under various titles since 1899, this title now covers all aspects of the insurance business for the practitioner, including agents, brokers, and insurance company management. Each issue is divided into four sections: life/health, property/casualty, industry trends, and technology. The January issue has an annual "year in review" feature and the July issue includes ratings and rankings on the top firms in both life/health and property/casualty industries.

Black Enterprise. Earl G. Graves Publishing Co., Inc., 1970–. Monthly. ISSN: 0006–4165. $21.95. Available online: http://www.blackenterprise.com/.

Aimed at "business leaders, corporate executives, professionals, and entrepreneurs" in the African American community, the mission of *Black Enterprise* is to promote black business as well as report on it. Several special features are published each year including the B.E. 100s, which are lists of the top businesses that are majority-owned by blacks, and an annual investment guide.

Brandweek. BPI Communications, Inc. 1980–. Weekly. ISSN: 1064–4318. $145.00. Available online: http://www.brandweek.com/.

This weekly touts itself as the newsweekly of marketing. It contains a mix of short articles for current awareness on brands and people, and longer articles that explore marketing issues such as consumers, forecasts, and licensing.

Business and Society Review. Blackwell Publishers, Inc. 1972–. Quarterly. ISSN: 0045–3609. $71.00, individuals; $131.00, institutions. Available online: http:// www.blackwellpublishers.co.uk/asp/journal.asp?ref=0045-3609&src=ind.

The articles in this peer-reviewed journal, published for the Center for Business Ethics at Bentley College by Blackwell Publishers, Inc., are written by experts in the field, both academics and practitioners, and address "a wide range of ethical issues concerning the relationships between business, society, and the public good."

Business Cycle Indicators. The Conference Board. 1996–. Monthly. ISSN: 1088–7857. $120.00. Available online: http://www.tcb-indicators.org/.

In 1995, the U.S. Department of Commerce decided to outsource the collection and publication of several economic indicators. The Conference Board became the official source for the composite indexes of leading, lagging, and co-incident indicators and publishes them in this title. Also included are the underlying components used to construct the series, alternative indices of business conditions, and a brief analysis of the U.S. economy. Some international data is provided for comparison purposes.

Business Horizons. Elsevier Science. 1957–. Bimonthly. ISSN: 0007–6813. $96.00, individuals ; $252.00, institutions. Available online: http://www.elsevier.com/locate/bushor/.

Published for the Indiana University Kelly School of Business by Elsevier Science, this journal's audience is academics and practitioners of business. The journal aims to publish articles written in a readable, nontechnical manner, balanced between the practical and the theoretical. Special features of the publication include, "On the Horizon," brief reports of original projects initiated at companies that may be relevant to other organizations; "Executive Briefing," summaries of trends from the business and professional literature; and book reviews.

Business Week. McGraw-Hill Companies. 1929–. Weekly. ISSN: 0007–7135. $54.95. Available online: http://www.businessweek.com/.

Described as the U.S. business newsweekly, *Business Week* covers all areas of business, as well as news that affects business, including politics, science, and social issues. This publication aims to keep all business people up to date on business, economic, and corporate developments. Several in-depth articles are published each week and several company pieces are covered briefly. Annual features include an industrial outlook, a ranking of business schools, and the Global 1,000, the top 1,000 companies worldwide.

California Management Review. University of California, Berkeley. 1958–. Quarterly. ISSN: 0008–1256. $65.00, individuals; $90.00, institutions. Available online: http://www.haas.berkeley.edu/News/cmr/index_.html.

Aimed at both practicing business managers and academicians, this title's contributors include consultants, policy makers, executives, and business school faculty. The publication emphasizes three areas, "strategy and organization; global competition and competitiveness; and business and public policy." Regularly included are articles on knowledge management, strategies for innovation, corporate culture, and business ethics. The editorial board consists of scholars from seven of California's business schools.

The CPA Journal. New York State Society of Certified Public Accountants. 1930–. Monthly. ISSN: 0732–8435. $42.00. Available online: http://www.cpajournal.com/.

This trade journal's audience includes those interested in accounting issues in public practice, industry, education, and government. The articles published are peer-reviewed and have been considered for relevancy, contribution to the literature, and benefit to the practicing accountant. Brief articles of accounting news, as well as book reviews, are also published.

The Economist. Economist Newspaper Ltd. 1843–. Weekly. ISSN: 0013–0613. $59.00, online subscription; $125.00, print subscription. Available online: http://www.economist.com/.

> *The Economist* describes itself as a newspaper because it is interested in "views as well as news." International and nonpartisan, all articles are written anonymously "because it is a paper whose collective voice and personality matter more than the identities of individual journalists." The publication offers "reporting, commentary and analysis on world politics, business, finance, science and technology" along with cultural features and a regular review of books. It is known for its surveys, which are either subject- or country-oriented, and cover the topic thoroughly. Brief economic and financial indicators are included in each issue. Its main audience is senior decision-makers; however, it is an extremely readable publication that would give the general reader a sound overview on the issues covered.

ENR (formerly *Engineering News Record*). McGraw-Hill Companies. 1987–. Weekly. ISSN: 0891–9526. $74.00. Available online: http://www.enr.com/.

> A trade journal with a publishing history that dates back to 1874, *ENR* includes business and technical news on all sectors of the construction industry. Information about construction costs, relevant legislation and the publication's calculated Construction Cost Index and Building Cost Index are included in each issue. Significant worldwide events that have an impact on the industry are covered.

Euromoney. Euromoney Publications plc. 1969–. Monthly. ISSN: 0014–2433. $296.00. Available online: http://www.euromoney.com/.

> *Euromoney* covers all topics that deal with the international capital markets, including international financial institutions, corporate finance, foreign exchange, financial instruments, and banking. Its goal is to promote capitalism and free markets. Several supplements are published each year that range in topic from currencies to specific country overviews.

Export America (formerly *Business America*). U.S. Department of Commerce. International Trade Administration. 1999–. Monthly. $61.00. Available online: http://www.trade.gov/exportamerica.

> Aimed at people interested in exporting goods from the United States, this monthly publication includes general news of interest to U.S. exporters, information from the U.S. Department of Commerce, technical advice, new opportunities for foreign trade, and information on upcoming trade events and shows. Current statistical charts on U.S. exports are also included.

Far Eastern Economic Review. Review Publishing Co. Ltd. 1946–. Weekly. ISSN: 0014–7591. $125.00. Available online: http://www.feer.com/.

> This weekly publication seeks to keep business people informed on all aspects of Asian business by providing news and analysis on the region. Each issue

has a section devoted to regional developments and innovations, money, local and global business opportunities, and current events.

Federal Reserve Bulletin. U.S. Board of Governors of the Federal Reserve System. 1915–. Monthly. ISSN: 0014–9209. $25.00. Available online: http://www.federalreserve.gov/pubs/bulletin/.

Regular articles on the U.S. economic and banking systems are contained in this monthly publication from the Board of Governors of the Federal Reserve System. Minutes of the Federal Open Market Committee are also included. A good portion of the title contains financial and economic statistics, with topics covered including money stock and bank credit, policy instruments (including interest rates), the financial markets, federal finance, real estate, consumer credit, flow of funds, and some selected international statistics (including exchange rates).

The Financial Analysts Journal. Association for Investment Management and Research. 1945–. Bimonthly. ISSN: 0015–198X. $175.00. Available online: http://www.aimr.org/publications/faj/.

Published by the Association for Investment Management and Research (AIMR), the journal is "devoted to the advancement of investment management and security analysis." Each article undergoes a double blind referee process. In 1999, the publication added author digests which summarize each article and its practical significance. In-depth book reviews are also published.

Financial Times. Financial Times. 1888–. 6/wk. ISSN: 0307–1766 (UK edition); 0884–6782 (U.S. edition). GBP 480.00 (UK edition); $298.00 (U.S. edition). Available online: http://www.ft.com/.

The *Financial Times*, which places "business and economic news into a global context," is a London newspaper that contains daily news and analysis on current events, business topics, companies and markets, currencies, commodities, global equity markets, international capital markets, and international affairs. Statistics from international markets are also included. Special supplements of the newspaper, called Surveys, are published over 200 times each year. A Survey contains comprehensive coverage of a topic such as geographic regions, countries, industries, investments, or technology.

Forbes. Forbes, Inc. 1917–. Biweekly. ISSN: 0015–6914. $59.95. Available online: http://www.forbes.com/.

Aimed at the affluent investor and business leaders, *Forbes* contains current news and analysis on companies, people, ideas, marketing, entrepreneurs, technology, money and investing, and products. Several annual features that are anticipated include the 400 Best Big Companies in America (the Platinum List), the World's Richest People, the Richest People in America, the Forbes 500: Annual Directory of America's Leading Companies, Up & Comers: The Best Small Companies in America, and Mutual Fund Ratings.

Fortune. Time, Inc. 1930–. Biweekly. ISSN: 0015–8259. $59.95. Available online: http://www.fortune.com/.

This general business magazine includes news and analysis on all aspects of business including the economy, companies, industries, executives, investments, management, and global markets. The *Fortune* 500, now part of the American lexicon, is one of several annual features. Other annual articles include the 100 Best Companies to Work For, 100 Fastest Growing Companies, and the World's Most Admired Companies.

Harvard Business Review. Harvard Business School Publishing. 1922–. 10/yr. ISSN: 0017–8012. $118.00. Available online: http://www.hbsp.harvard.edu/products/ hbr/index.html.

Aimed at the "people leading business around the world" with the goal "to improve the practice of management" articles in *Harvard Business Review* are written by practitioners and academics who "explore new business ideas." Each issue includes an *HBR* Interview; an *HBR* case study, a fictional account of a business problem; book reviews; and executive summaries of articles in the issue.

H R Focus. Institute of Management and Administration, Inc. 1991–. Monthly. ISSN: 1059–6038. $259.00. Available online: http://www.ioma.com/products/ prod_detail.php?prodid=3.

This monthly newsletter contains short articles for the human resources professional. Summaries of current news on human resources are included. Topics recently covered include compensation, legal issues, training, benefits, technology, and retention.

Inc. Goldhirsh Group, Inc. 1979–. 18/yr. ISSN: 0162–8968. $19.00. Available online: http://inc.com/incmagazine/.

Inc. is aimed at the small business entrepreneur and includes case studies on companies, management ideas and techniques, and technology issues. Two annual features include the State of Small Business, an overview of the business climate, and the *Inc.* 500, a ranking of the fastest growing private companies in America.

Industrial and Labor Relations Review. Cornell University, New York State School of Industrial and Labor Relations. 1947–. Quarterly. ISSN: 0019–7939. $26.00, individuals; $43.00, institutions. Available online: http://www.ilr.cornell.edu/depts/ ilrrev/.

A peer-reviewed journal aimed at practitioners and academicians, this publication covers all aspects of labor relations, and includes articles on education and employment, industry studies, wages, unions, and union impact on employment. In-depth book reviews are also published.

IndustryWeek. Penton Media, Inc. 1970–. 22/yr. ISSN: 0039–0895. $65.00. Available online: http://www.industryweek.com.

With a publishing history that dates back to the latter part of the 19th century, *IndustryWeek* is aimed at senior executives in manufacturing, and managers that work in manufacturing industries. Articles include "trends, technologies, and management strategies that drive continuous improvement enterprise-wide." Special annual features include a census of manufacturers, the World's 100 Best-Managed Companies, and the IW 1000, a report on the world's 1,000 largest publicly held manufacturing companies.

International Labour Review. ILO Publications. 1921–. Quarterly. ISSN: 0020–7780. $80.00. Available online: http://www.ilo.org/public/english/support/publ/revue/ index.htm.

Published by the International Labour Office, a specialized agency of the United Nations, this title is aimed at an audience of economists, labor lawyers, and other experts. Its goal is to contribute "to a wider understanding of labour and employment issues," by publishing articles of original research, short articles on emerging issues, and reviews of recent publications.

Internet World: The Voice of E-Business and Internet Technology (formerly *Web Week*). Penton Media, Inc. 1997–. 22/yr. ISSN: 1081–3071. $160.00. Available online: http://www.internetworld.com/.

This trade journal provides information and "expert insights to make informed and effective strategic management and purchasing decisions to drive business Internet initiatives."

Journal of Accountancy. American Institute of Certified Public Accountants. 1905–. Monthly. ISSN: 0021–8448. Free to members; $59.00, nonmembers. Available online: http://www.aicpa.org/pubs/jofa/joaiss.htm.

Published by the American Institute of Certified Public Accountants (AICPA), the *Journal of Accountancy* covers all issues within the discipline for the practicing accountant, including articles on technology, practice management, professional issues, auditing, and financial reporting. Every issue includes information on the AICPA, letters, and official literature such as exposure drafts and outstanding and official releases of standards.

The Journal of Finance. Blackwell Publishers, Inc. 1946–. Bimonthly. ISSN: 0022–1082. Free to members; $207.00, nonmembers. Available online: http://www.blackwellpublishers.co.uk/asp/journal.asp?ref=0022-1082.

Published by Blackwell Publishers for the American Finance Association, this peer-reviewed journal contains accounts of original research in all areas of finance. Specific disciplines included are corporate finance, investment banking, international finance, emerging markets, banking, and real estate.

Journal of International Business Studies. Journal of International Business Studies. 1970–. Quarterly. ISSN: 0047–2506. $65.00. Available online: http://www.jibs.net/.

A joint publication of the Academy of International Business, the Copenhagen Business School, and the McDonough School of Business at Georgetown University, the title reflects the mission of the Academy of International Business "to foster education and advance professional standards in the field of international business." Interested in publishing interdisciplinary research, the journal contains articles on a variety of social science topics that impact and advance business research. Topics such as multinational firms, "managerial processes that cross national boundaries," and interactions of firms with economic, political or cultural environments are included.

Journal of Marketing. American Marketing Association. 1936–. Quarterly. ISSN: 0022–2429. $45.00, members; $80.00, nonmembers; $200.00, institutions. Available online: http://www.marketingpower.com/live/jump.php?Item_ID=1054.

This peer-reviewed quarterly publication of the American Marketing Association includes articles that have undergone a blind review process, unless they are noted as exceptions to that process. All aspects of marketing are covered, including pricing, advertising, ethics, and distribution. The title is aimed at academics and practitioners, with the goal of bridging theory and practice. It contains book reviews and a review of the marketing literature from other periodical publications.

JMR, Journal of Marketing Research. American Marketing Association. 1964–. Quarterly. ISSN: 0022–2437. $45.00, members; $80.00, nonmembers; $200.00, institutions. Available online: http://www.ama.org/pubs/jmr/index.asp.

JMR, a second peer-reviewed quarterly publication from the American Marketing Association, contains articles that explain and illustrate all aspects of marketing research, from the philosophical to the practical techniques.

Journal of Retailing. Elsevier Science. 1925–. Quarterly. ISSN: 0022–4359. $112.00, individuals; $287.00, institutions. Available online: http://www.elsevier.com/locate/jretai.

The Leonard N. Stern School of Business at New York University issues this title that is published by Elsevier Science. It is aimed at "academicians, economists, geographers, researchers, top business executives, and consultants," and includes articles on theoretical and empirical research in retail marketing. The goal of the publication is to produce new literature that provides "critical new understanding about the management and technology of retailing and retail/service systems, as well as the environment and history in which retail institutions operate and evolve."

Journal of World Business (formerly *The Columbia Journal of World Business*). Elsevier Science. 1997–. Quarterly. ISSN: 1090–9516. $112.00, individuals; $258.00, institutions. Available online: http://www.elsevier.com/inca/publications/store/6/2/0/4/0/1/index.htt.

Now published by Elsevier Science, this title has a history that dates back to 1965 when it was published by the Graduate School of Business at Columbia University. A peer-reviewed journal that seeks to publish on all aspects of business, this quarterly publication has an international scope and publishes articles from academics worldwide. Recent topics covered include marketing in emerging and transition economies, strategic alliance management, international acquisitions, intellectual property protection, international global staffing, and trade promotion policies.

Kiplinger's Personal Finance. Kiplinger Washington Editors, Inc. 1947–. Monthly. ISSN: 1056–697X. $23.95. Available online: http://www.kiplinger.com/magazine/.

Aimed at the average consumer, the title covers all aspects of personal finance. Three separate sections cover information on money management, investing, and a monthly "best buy" topic that ranges from automobiles to education.

Management Science. Institute for Operations Research and Management Sciences. 1954–. Monthly. ISSN: 0025–1909. $136.00, nonmember print; $80.00, nonmember online; $177.00, nonmember print and online; $68.00, member print; $40.00, member online; $88.00 member print and online; $425.00, institutions print and online. Available online: http://mansci.pubs.informs.org.

A reference journal of the Institute for Operations Research and Management Sciences (INFORMS), *Management Science* is aimed at both academics and practitioners. Articles included cover theory and innovation that "scientifically address the problems, interests, and concerns of organizational decision-makers." The title encompasses a variety of disciplines, including operations research, mathematics, statistics, political science, psychology and sociology, and cross-disciplinary research.

Mergers & Acquisitions: The Dealermaker's Journal. Securities Data Publishing. 1965–. 10/yr. ISSN: 0026–0010. $550.00.

This complete overview of U.S. mergers and acquisitions discusses industry news and trends and contains information on proposed mergers. Half the publication, The M & A Roster, reports on merger, acquisition, and divestiture activities of U.S. firms in a brief summary format. Mergers and acquisitions must be greater than $25 million to be included in the M & A Roster.

MIT Sloan Management Review (formerly *Sloan Management Review*). Massachusetts Institute of Technology. 2001–. Quarterly. ISSN: 1532–9194. $89.00, individuals; $148.00, institutions. Available online: http://www.mit=smr.com/.

With a history that dates back to 1960, the *MIT Sloan Management Review*'s mission is to "bridge the gap between management research and practice." The publication reports on new research to help "identify and understand significant trends in management," and contains peer-reviewed articles on all management disciplines with an "emphasis on corporate strategy, leadership, and management of technology and innovation." Article summaries, book reviews, opinion columns, roundtable discussions, and interviews are also included. A recently added Intelligence section reports on "business implications of recent research from academia, consulting firms and industry."

Money. Time, Inc. 1972–. 13/yr. ISSN: 0149–4953. $39.89. Available online: http://money.cnn.com/.

Money is aimed at the individual consumer, with a mission to provide investment advice to help "consumers make wise investing and spending choices." Topics covered include stocks, mutual funds, real estate, insurance, retirement, taxes, and personal finance. Special annual features include a forecast issue and The Money 100: The Nation's Best Mutual Funds.

Monthly Labor Review. U.S. Bureau of Labor Statistics. 1915–. Monthly. ISSN: 0098–1818. $31.00. Available online: http://stats.bls.gov/opub/mlr/mlrhome.htm.

Published by a section of the U.S. Department of Labor, this title includes articles on "the labor force, labor-management relations, business conditions, industry productivity, compensation, occupational safety and health, demographic trends, and other economic developments." Many articles are written by government economists. The second half of the publication contains current labor statistics, which includes data on the U.S. labor force, compensation, consumer and producer prices, productivity, injuries and illnesses, and some international comparisons.

National Real Estate Investor. Intertec Publishing. 1959–. 16/yr. ISSN: 0027–9994. $105.00. Available online: http://industryclick.com/magazine.asp?mazazineid= 126&site ID=23.

This trade journal contains news and analysis on all aspects of commercial real estate including hotel, industrial, multifamily, office, retail, and senior housing. Industry news, trends, and reviews are included. Annually, several reviews of the real estate market in major metropolitan areas are published. Other special features include a forecast issue, published in the fall, and a year in review issue, published in the spring. The *NREI* Sourcebook, a directory of people and firms in the commercial real estate business from architects to real estate investment trusts, is published at the end of each year.

OOQ: Occupational Outlook Quarterly. U.S. Bureau of Labor Statistics. 1957–. Quarterly. ISSN: 0199–4786. $9.50. Available online: http://stats.bls.gov/opub/ooq/ ooqhome.htm.

In-depth articles on a variety of careers are contained in this quarterly publication, published by a section of the U.S. Department of Labor. Information on the employment market, occupations, and trends in employment and earnings are also included, as is information on other publications from the Bureau of Labor Statistics.

Operations Research. Institute for Operations Research and Management Sciences. 1961–. Bimonthly. ISSN: 0030–364X. $120.00, nonmember print; $80.00, nonmember online; $156.00, nonmember print and online; $60.00, member print; $40.00, member online; $78.00, member print and online; $295.00, institutions print and online. Available online: http://or.pubs.informs.org/.

Published by the Institute for Operations Research and Management Sciences, this peer-reviewed journal is for practitioners, researchers, educators, and students. The journal aims to "provide a balance of well-written articles that span the wide array of creative activities in OR." Each issue has an article that chronicles a successful application of operations research. Areas covered include computing and decision technology; decision analysis; environment, energy, and natural resources; financial engineering; manufacturing, service, and supply chain operations; military; optimization; policy making and public sector OR; simulation; stochastic models; telecommunications; and transportation. Executive summaries and abstracts of all articles are included.

The Practical Accountant. Faulkner & Gray, Inc. 1967–. Monthly. ISSN: 0032–6321. $69.95.

This monthly magazine, aimed at the practicing accountant, contains a mix of short summaries of current news relevant to accountants and longer articles of professional interest.

Public Administration Review. American Society for Public Administration. 1940–. Bimonthly. ISSN: 0033–3352. free to members; $135.00, nonmembers second class mail; $150.00, nonmembers first class mail. Available online: http:// www.aspanet.org/publications/par/indexz.html.

A scholarly peer-reviewed journal written by experts in the field, *Public Administration Review* publishes articles which combine practice and theory, for a wide range of topics in public sector management. Book reviews and columns on the law are included in each issue. Some guest editorials or invited articles may not be peer reviewed.

The Public Interest. National Affairs, Inc. 1965–. Quarterly. ISSN: 0033–3557. $25.00. Available online: http://www.thepublicinterest.com/.

Original essays and excerpts from books on a variety of topics such as capitalism, conservatism, public policy, politics, and culture are contained in this title. Contributors include academics as well as specialists in their field. Book review essays are included in each issue.

Public Personnel Management. International Personnel Management Association. 1973–. Quarterly. ISSN: 0091–0260. Free to members; $50.00, print or online; $75.00 print and online.

Public Personnel Management, formed by the merger of *Personnel Administration* and *Public Personnel Review*, is a peer-reviewed journal aimed at both practitioners and academics. All aspects of personnel management in the public sector are covered. Included are articles from a practitioner's perspective and articles on emerging national and international trends. Recent articles covered such topics as the workplace environment, diversity, appraisal systems, recruiting and retention.

Sales and Marketing Management. Bill Communications, Inc. 1918–. Monthly. ISSN: 0163–7517. $48.00. Available online: http://www.salesandmarketing.com/salesandmarketing/index.jsp.

Aimed at executives "involved in the management of a company's sales and marketing effort," the title includes in-depth articles on current topics, monthly columns, and several short articles about good company practices. The publisher is also known for its annual publications on buying and purchasing power, with excerpts from these larger publications appearing as a special issue of *Sales and Marketing Management*.

Social Security Bulletin. U.S. Social Security Administration. 1937–. Quarterly. ISSN: 0037–7910. $16.00. Available online: http://199.173.224.108/policy/pubs/SSB/index.html.

Various aspects of social insurance and public policy are included in this title, with most articles written by experts within the Social Security Administration. In 2000, the publication launched a new section, Perspectives, which contains peer-reviewed articles. The second half of the *Bulletin* contains current operating statistics on programs administered by the Social Security Administration, as well as other government statistics that affect the programs.

Survey of Current Business. U.S. Department of Commerce. Bureau of Economic Analysis. 1921–. Monthly. ISSN: 0039–6222. $48.00, second class mail; $120.00, first class mail. Available online: http://www.bea.doc.gov/bea/pubs.htm.

The *Survey of Current Business* is divided into two sections. The first section contains articles on different aspects of the U.S. economy. Many of the articles are updated annually and contain government analysis and the most current statistics on the subject. The second section contains national, international, and U.S. regional data on a variety of economic topics. In 1996, the U.S. Department of Commerce outsourced the collection and the publication of the leading, lagging, and coincident indicators to the Conference Board. Those statistics can now be found in the publication *Business Cycle Indicators* which is described earlier in this list.

T&D Magazine (formerly *Training and Development*). American Society for Training and Development. 2001–. Monthly. ISSN: 1553–7740. $85.00. Available online: http://www.astd.org/virtual_community/td_magazine/.

Currently published by the American Society for Training and Development, this title, with a history that dates back to 1947, covers all aspects of employer-sponsored learning, including information on learning styles, trends, technology, and media reviews. An annual feature is a human resources salary survey.

Treasury Bulletin. U.S. Department of the Treasury. 1939–. Quarterly. 0041–2155. $33.00. Available online: http://www.fms.treas.gov/bulletin/index.html.

This quarterly publication from the U.S. Financial Management Services, a bureau of the Department of the Treasury, contains statistics on "treasury issues, federal financial operations and international statistics." Current information on the federal debt and the U.S. currency in circulation is included.

The Wall Street Journal. Dow Jones & Co., Inc. 1889–. 5/wk. ISSN: 0099–9660. $175.00, paper; $59.00, online. Available online: http://online.wsj.com/public/us/.

Designed to be the only newspaper needed by the business professional, *The Wall Street Journal* includes in-depth coverage of business, as well as news and analysis of current national and world events. Its strength is its domestic U.S. coverage, but it has expanded its international coverage as the world has developed into a global marketplace. The economy, companies, industries, management, marketing, and consumers are covered topics. A third of the paper is devoted to "Money and Investing," containing articles on these topics, as well as a vast array of current statistics, all from the previous trading day. A newer section of the paper, Weekend Journal, published on Fridays, contains lifestyle and culturally related articles, including current reviews, travel, and shopping information. This title is not published on the days that the U.S. stock markets are closed.

Workforce (formerly *Personnel Journal*). A C C Communications, Inc. 1997–. Monthly. ISSN: 1092–8332. $59.00. Available online: http://www.workforce.com/.

Aimed at human resource professionals, this publication, dating back to 1922, contains information on all aspects of personnel issues including interviews, orientations, retention, unions, and retirement plans. Articles delve into theory as well as practice.

7

The Best Investment Sources

Barbara A. Huett

INVESTMENT ADVISORY SERVICES

Since the previous edition of this book, the World Wide Web was launched and has impacted the publishing world so strongly that electronic versions have become a close competitor of the paper format. These days, print and online publications—even of the same title—are rivals. Many advisory services and charting newsletters have gone online, with several hundred in the investment field. It remains a challenge for even the most astute investors or information specialists to be able to select the best publication.

Selection of an advisory newsletter may be facilitated by first identifying the investing methods that are most appropriate for the individual, and then determining a suitable newsletter with a record of successful investment advice. Many newsletter publishers offer free or inexpensive trial periods, thereby enabling investors or librarians to examine and test the advice given before making a final choice. Publishers of online versions of newsletter titles often provide a seamless and easy way to subscribe to these demonstration trials.

Guides to investment newsletters can be used as selection aids. However, many guides, such as Michael Thomsett's *Investor Factline: Finding and Using the Best Investment Information* have not been updated, so users may find that many of the recommended titles are no longer available or up-to-date.

The following representative sampling of services is based on performance ratings and current business collections' holdings in several academic and public libraries of varying size.

Bob Brinker's Marketimer—http://www.bobbrinker.com/
  Bob Brinker has more than 25 years of investment management experience and is currently host to the weekend financial management talk show, *Money Talk*. This newsletter covers stock market timing, federal reserve policy, specific mutual fund recommendations, individual stock selections, and selection of model portfolios. It is designed for investors with aggressive growth objectives.

Barbara A. Huett is Director of Library Services at Franklin College—an American University—in Lugano, Switzerland.

Dick Davis Digest—http://www.dickdavis.com

Publishing for 20 years, a subscription to the *Digest* includes the standard bi-weekly newsletter digest and separate "Income," "Technology," and "Untapped Opportunities" digests. Included in these digests are recommendations for technology stocks and mutual funds with the most potential; market forecasts from technology insiders; industry-specific articles explaining the latest technologies in telecommunications, medical and computer businesses; and up-to-the-minute charts and graphs of sizzling technology stocks and market segments. The *Digest* is recommended for investors who are seeking in-depth, researched technology recommendations.

Dow Theory Letters—http://www.dowtheoryletters.com/dtlol.nsf

Richard Russell began publishing *Dow Theory Letters* in 1958, and he has been writing the *Letters* himself, ever since, making *Dow Theory Letters* the oldest service continuously written by one person in the business. Russell gained wide recognition via a series of over 30 Dow theory and technical articles that he wrote for *Barron's* during the late-1950s through the 1990s. Russell was the first (in 1960) to recommend gold stocks. He called the top of the 1949–1966 bull market. And almost to the day, he called the bottom of the great 1972–1974 bear market, and the beginning of the great bull market which started in December 1974. The *Letters*, published every three weeks, cover the U.S. stock market, foreign markets, bonds, precious metals, commodities, economics—plus Russell's widely-followed comments, observations, and stock market philosophy.

Hulbert Financial Digest—http://www.hulbertdigest.com

A highly regarded monitoring service, this digest analyzes returns for approximately 500 model portfolios in over 160 newsletters. It contains a monthly scoreboard, topical articles, and editorial comments, and it offers trial issues.

DRIP Investor—http://www.dripinvestor.com

"Dividend Re-Investment Plans" service provides information, recommendations and forecasts on how to reinvest dividends. DRIPs, offered by about 1,000 companies and closed-end funds, are programs which allow current shareholders to purchase stock directly from the company, thus bypassing the broker and brokerage commissions. This monthly newsletter service is published by Horizons Publishing Company and is written by Charles B. Carlson.

Individual Investor—http://www.individualinvestor.com/

Subtitled "the newsletter for undiscovered stocks," this service provides comprehensive investment tools for individual investors. Tools include news and analysis, commentaries, recommendations, and daily stock activity.

Insiders' Chronicle—http://www1.firstcall.com/index.shtml

Securities and Exchange Commission reports of corporate officers' stock transactions are monitored in this publication on a weekly basis, summarized quarterly, and indexed. It also includes corporation profiles and a "Wall Street Summary." Considered a leading newsletter dedicated to analysis of insider trading activity, *Insider's Chronicle* is written by the industry's leading expert on the subject, Bob Gabele of FIRST CALL Insider Research Services. In addition to special commentary and analysis, the *Chronicle* regularly features tables listing major insider trades for NYSE, NASDAQ, and AMEX stocks for the previous week; industry rankings for insider accumulation, disposition, and calculation of the weekly buy/sell ratio; and 13D filings (when an individual or institution goes over 5 percent ownership).

Institutional Investor—http://www.institutioninvestoronline.com/index.htm

Having served the professional finance community for over 30 years, this service provides comprehensive coverage of the issues, personalities, trends, and analyses shaping market industries, as well as rankings of equity, and fixed-income derivatives sectors, among others.

Jay Schabacker's Mutual Fund Investing—Potomac, MD

For the past 20 years, Schabacker, who is editor of this newsletter and is also a well-known author and commentator on the mutual fund industry, has focused on his system of "safety-first, high-performance" investing in mutual funds. To date, there is no online version of this monthly newsletter.

Kiplinger's Personal Finance—http://www.kiplinger.com/

Kiplinger.com is the Web site for the *Personal Finance* newsletter, as well as a gateway to all Kiplinger publications. Since 1947 it has been considered a reliable source of information on saving and investing, taxes, credit, homeownership, paying for college, retirement planning, car buying, and many other personal finance topics.

Moneyletter—http://www.moneyletter.com

A recipient of the Newsletter Publisher's Association's "Best Financial Advisory Newsletter" Award, this advisory service has provided comprehensive coverage of mutual funds on a bimonthly basis since 1980. Advice on what to buy and what to sell for different portfolios, as well as news, trends, and analyses are included. More than 2,000 funds are covered.

Morningstar—http://www.morningstar.com

This service profiles performances of stocks and funds, providing key statistics, historical background, and risk analyses. A monthly subscription includes commentaries on current topics in the industry, performance indexes for all funds being followed, average total returns within fund/stock categories, and industry news.

Mutual Funds Forecaster—http://www.kiplinger.com/investing/funds/

Approximately 4,000 funds can be searched by fund name, category, returns, down-market, performance, and other attributes. Included are the top 101 U.S. funds, international funds, as well as short-/long-term forecasts. Daily news and analyses are provided on this Web site.

No Load Fund Investor—http://www.sheldonjacobs.com/

Designed for different risk preferences, this newsletter recommends portfolios of "higher-quality growth" funds that are selected by a system based on the previous year's record. Its investment system and performance data include all NoLoad and LowLoad funds.

The Outlook—http://www.spoutlookonline.com/

This traditional Standard & Poor's publication includes forecasts, how-to-invest recommendations, economic statistics, and follow-ups on previous recommendations. Features include model portfolios such as long-term gain, promising growth, cyclical/speculative, and income with inflation protection.

Smart Money—http://www.smartmoney.com/

    This diversified advisory service provides online newsletters covering stocks, bonds, mutual funds, and personal finance. Included are news and analyses, economic trends, and other relevant information for individual investors.

Value Line Investment Survey—http://www.valueline.com/

    One of the leading investment publications, this service reviews over 2,000 stocks and 100 industries. Information on each company and industry is updated quarterly on a rotating basis. Included are multiyear statistical histories, growth projections on key investment factors, and coverage of current developments. During a 35-year period Value Line's "Timeliness Ranking System" has accurately anticipated stocks' subsequent relative price performance.

Value Line Mutual Fund Survey—http://www.valueline.com/topfunds.html

    Following the same format as the *Value Line Investment Survey*, this service follows over 2,000 mutual funds, providing risk analyses and rankings, 16 years of performance data, portfolio analyses, and industry news.

Weisenberger Investment Companies Service: Investment Companies—http://www.wiesenberger.com/resources/links.shtml

    An authoritative source on mutual funds and investment companies, this annual publication explains the different types of funds and gives advice on how to select them and monitor performance. One of the most comprehensive of such sources, it profiles over 2,000 investment companies and tracks performance of individual funds over 10-year intervals (back to 25 years).

INVESTMENT NEWSLETTER SELECTION

Given current economic and budget considerations, a conservative approach for smaller libraries or collections might be to subscribe to Standard & Poor's *The Outlook*, and/or one of the newsletter digests, such as the Hulbert *Financial Digest* or Davis *Digest*. Two other services which would be very useful are *Value Line* and *Wiesenberger Investment Companies Service*. If the budget permits, an added Standard & Poor's advisory service would be valuable.

For a more comprehensive collection, librarians should consult periodic reviews and ratings of advisory services in *Barron's*, *Forbes*, *Fortune*, and *The Wall Street Journal*, in addition to other business publications [see following "Periodicals" section]. Sources that abstract financial newsletters include:

Hulbert Guide to Financial Newsletters. New York: New York Institute of Finance (Simon and Schuster).

Newsletter Sourcebook. Irving, TX: Future World.

Newsletters in Print. Farmington Hill, MI: Gale Group.

Oxbridge Directory of Newsletters. New York: Oxbridge Communications, Inc.

INVESTMENT PERIODICALS AND STATISTICAL SOURCES

For this area of the collection, the following titles are suggested for consideration. General business publications, such as *Business Week*, are included on the basis of special features of interest to investors. Most of these titles are either abstracted and/or available full-text online.

AAII Journal. American Association of Individual Investors, Chicago. Monthly.
    Published by the American Association of Individual Investors, this publication features articles on investment instruments and strategies enabling investors to become effective managers of their assets. It also covers technical analysis, tax information, investment news and forecasts, book reviews, association news, and editorial commentary.

Bank and Quotation Record. National News Service, Inc., Daytona Beach, FL. Monthly.
    Provided here are monthly summaries of price ranges for stocks and bonds listed on the American, New York, Boston, Midwest, Pacific, Philadelphia, and Toronto exchanges, as well as NASDAQ OTC securities. Data are also provided on U.S. government securities, municipal bonds, foreign government and corporate bonds, mutual funds, commercial paper, stock market indexes, and foreign exchange rates.

Barron's National Business and Financial Weekly. Dow Jones, New York. Weekly.
    Published since 1921, this well-respected publication is written solely for investors. Consulted heavily for its detailed financial tables, it also features articles on various topics. Its easy-to-read format has weekly (rather than daily) stock prices (high, low, closing), as well as coverage for bonds, NASDAQ stocks, regional and Canadian exchanges, and stock options. Also useful are its Week's Market Transactions which cover securities quotations, its Market Laboratory offering financial statistics reports, and its data from various proprietary sources such as the Lipper Mutual Fund Performance Averages.

Better Investing. NAIC (National Association of Investment Clubs). Royal Oak, Michigan. Monthly.
    Designed for the individual investor, this periodical provides up-to-date investment information. Features include articles and analyses of issues pertaining to individual investors.

Business Week. McGraw-Hill, New York. Weekly.
    In addition to its excellent articles, this publication has many special lists of interest to investors, including "Bank Scoreboard," "Corporate Scoreboard," "International Corporate Scoreboard," and "Investment Outlook Scoreboard."

Capital Changes Report. Commerce Clearing House, Chicago. Weekly updates.
    This loose-leaf service traces the capital histories of corporations, utilizing a thorough index. In alphabetical arrangement, it provides chronological information on each company, including date of incorporation, stock rights, stock splits, dividends, recapitalization, reorganization, mergers, and consolidation. A separate income tax rate section—New Matters—covers the most recent changes.

Although designed for income tax purposes, it also aids investors in assessing taxable income and capital gains of stock transactions. Other features of the service include a listing of worthless securities (as designated by the U.S. Treasury Department), historical tables on dividend taxability, and a tax guide.

Forbes, Inc. New York. Bi-weekly.

This well-known and acclaimed general business publication's Annual Directory issue ranks the 500 largest corporations (industrial or service) by sales, profits, assets, stock market value, and employees; the Annual Report on American Industry ranks within industry groups according to profitability and growth. There is also a Special Report on International Business, an Annual Mutual Funds Survey, and the Annual Forbes 400 list of the wealthiest Americans. The publication includes reports on accounting trends affecting investment.

Fortune. Time, Inc., New York. Bi-weekly.

Best known for the Fortune 500 (a ranking of the largest U.S. industrial corporations), *Fortune* compiles many other lists. The Service 500 comprises separate rankings in the areas of diversified service, banking, diversified financial, life insurance, retailing, transportation, and utility companies. Companies on both lists are ranked by sales, assets, net income/stockholders' equity, earnings per share, and total return to investors. The World Business Directory covers both industry and banking.

Futures. Futures Magazine, Inc., Chicago. Monthly.

Futures compiles dozens of articles and columns on topics ranging from paper trading to brokerage issues to the best markets for small traders. Included are tips and strategies regarding day-trading futures and options. This publication's readership comprises active participants in the futures, options, and derivatives markets, including asset, money, and risk managers; fund managers and sponsors; brokers; and high net worth individual speculators.

Investext. Thomson Financial Networks, New York. Weekly.

An electronic database available from various services, Investext is undoubtedly one of the most comprehensive guides to investment reports. It offers full-text of more than 2.3 million Wall Street broker and investment bank reports since 1982, including Asian, Canadian, and European brokers. The database includes "The Market Guide," which covers smaller OTC companies.

Investor's Business Daily. Investor's Daily Inc., New York. Daily.

Concentrating on investment information, this attractive publication attempts to rival the venerable *Wall Street Journal.* Subtitled "America's Business Newspaper," its brief articles analyze company and industry activity, with the majority of the publication devoted to financial tables. Its coverage of business, economic, national, and world events is excellent, while its definitive advantages include quotation tables, bond rating tables, and statistical summaries. This publication should be viewed as a companion to the *Wall Street Journal*, not as a replacement. Full-text of *Investor's Business Daily* is available online through Lexis Nexis, and retrospective access is offered on BRS. *Investor's Business Daily Almanac*, published annually, reviews the previous year's activities in the market and the overall economy. Included are a stock symbol guide, guide to the newspaper, and a calendar of events.

Money. Time, Inc., New York. Monthly.

This popular magazine is geared to the middle-class individual or family. It provides general money-management advice, case histories, mutual fund surveys, and occasional product reviews. Regular features of interest to investors include "Wall Street Letter," "Stock of the Month," "Investor's Scorecard" (interest rates), and "Fund Watch."

Moody's Bond Record, Moody's Investors Service, New York. Monthly.

Moody's provides summary data on corporate bonds listed on the New York and American exchanges, and assigns ratings to bonds. This and other Moody's publications may be acquired as a part of a customized package based on the type of library.

Moody's Dividend Record. Moody's Investors Service, New York. Bi-weekly.

Almost identical to Standard & Poor's *Dividend Record,* this publication provides current information on stock and mutual fund dividends, indicating the amount and the date paid. Both services cover almost all public companies and mutual funds in the United States and Canada. There are periodic and annual cumulations.

National OTC Stock Journal. OTC Stock Journal, Inc., Denver, CO. Bi-weekly.

Gathering the stock information directly from market-makers by telephone, the publishers provide price data from the complete NASDAQ list and non-NASDAQ companies. This leading financial journal offers a complete list of new stock registrations and a guide to insider trading activities. Also included are news items, editorial coverage, and feature articles.

Official Summary of Security Transactions and Holdings. U.S. Securities and Exchange Commission. Washington, DC. Monthly.

This publication is made up of securities holdings figures showing owners, relationships to issues, amounts of securities bought or sold by each owner, their individual holdings at the end of the reported month, and types of securities.

Standard and Poor's Bond Guide, Standard & Poor's Corp., New York. Monthly.

Similar to Moody's *Bond Record Service,* this publication provides summary data on corporate bonds listed on the New York and American exchanges, and assigns ratings to bonds. Standard & Poor's service provides more information, however.

Standard and Poor's Stock Guide, Standard & Poor's Corp., New York. Weekly.

This guide covers every company listed on the New York, American, and Over the Counter (OTC) stock exchanges. It provides 10-year summaries, shareholder information, and general data on many of the companies. Its breakdown of sales by industry is similar in format to *Value Line Investment Survey.* Data from this guide are available online through commercial online services, including Standard & Poor's.

The Wall Street Journal, Dow Jones, New York. Daily.

Considered the nation's leading business newspaper, this publication would also appeal to the general reader. For investors, its coverage of financial activities is unsurpassed. It provides detailed financial tables on stocks, bonds, mutual funds, FOREX (foreign exchange rates), selected foreign stocks, commodities, futures, money rates, and economic indicators. Dow Jones publishes its own index, but it can also be accessed electronically through other indexing services such as Dow Jones/News Retrieval.

COMMERCIAL ONLINE INFORMATION SOURCES OF INVESTMENT INFORMATION

The following list provides contact details for commercial online information services that offer access to investment information. A variety of databases are offered through these services, providing extensive data on stocks, bonds, commodities, and other investment instruments. Many of the services include discussion forums which allow the exchange of information and ideas with fellow investors. Some services also provide gateway access to competitor services.

Bloomberg Professional Service—http://www.bloomberg.com/corp/profservice/professional.html. New York, NY 10022, (212) 318-2000

Burrelle's Broadcast Database—http://www.burrelles.com/. Livingston, NJ 07039, (800) 631-1160

Dialog: A Thomson Company—http://products.dialog.com/products/dialogweb/. Cary, NC 27511, (919) 462-8600

Dow Jones Interactive—http://bis.dowjones.com/. Libraries may contact Bell & Howell: (800) 521-0600

LexisNexis—http://www.lexis-nexis.com/academic/solutions/. Bethesda, MD 20814-3389 (800) 638-8380

NewsEdge—http://www.newsedge.com/flash.asp. Burlington, MA 01803 (800) 255-3343

Reuters—http://www.about.reuters.com/products. 85 Fleet St., London, UK EC4P4AJ (44-20) 7250 1122; New York, NY 10036 (646) 223-4000

MOODY'S AND STANDARD & POOR'S INVESTMENT SERVICES

In keeping with their long-held reputation as highly respected business and investment publishers, these two companies offer investment guides that are useful for all investment collections. Both offer "library packages" of certain publications, which are significantly more economical—in general—than purchasing the titles on an individual basis. Online Internet access of their materials is also available by subscription.

Due to pricing and the packages' content changes, collection development specialists/librarians should contact both publishers in order to examine the package suitable to the type and size of the library collection, as well as make comparisons of both services.

Mergent, Inc.—formerly known as Moody's Financial Information Services—publishes detailed business descriptions, corporate histories, and financial information on over 10,000 U.S. public companies, 17,000 non-U.S. public companies, and 18,000 municipal entities. Their publications include historical stock price and volume data, detailed annual and quarterly financial data, industry and segment analysis, as well as a firm's investment potential.

Another global leader in investment information services—Standard & Poor's—is also acknowledged as an international leader in the provision of fund information, covering nearly 60,000 institutional, pension, insurance, and mutual funds worldwide, with 400 research professionals in 13 countries who track and analyze funds. Standard & Poor's offers small and medium libraries two types of packages entitled *Library Reference Shelf 1 and 2*. These include varying combinations of the *Bond Guide, Corporation Records, Statistical Service* and *Stock Guide*, among others. Pricing depends on the selected inclusion of these titles in either *Reference Shelf* package.

REFERENCE BOOKSHELF FOR INVESTMENT SOURCES

The following are recommended sources for a reference bookshelf. Larger libraries and information centers should use the list below as a collection checklist. Smaller libraries might consider including at least a general business or investment dictionary and one of the basic investment handbooks, as well as specific items based on the needs of their clientele. Budget restraints on acquisitions may often be circumvented through the use of electronic sources such as commercial online database services.

Almanac of Online Trading: The Indispensable Reference Guide for Trading Stocks, Bonds, and Futures Online. Terry Wooten. McGraw-Hill, 2000.
  This guidebook for individual investors covers the basics of online trading and provides information such as steps in opening an account, how to get started, a complete reference of symbols of traded securities, the names and addresses of state regulators, a listing of online brokers, and a glossary of terms for those new to online trading.
Angel Investor's Handbook: How to Profit from Early-Stage Investing. Gerald A. Benjamin and Joel Margulis. Bloomberg Press, 2001.
  In this groundbreaking work, Benjamin and Margulis offer angel investors a hands-on manual for profiting from early-stage, private equity deals with attention to early-stage investing in emerging companies. The term "angel" originates from the practice in the early 1900s of wealthy businessmen investing in Broadway productions. Today "angels" typically offer expertise, experience and contacts, in addition to funding, and are generally individuals who invest in businesses looking for a higher return than they would see from more traditional investments. Coverage includes developing investment criteria and overall game plans, locating viable investment opportunities, assessing and managing risks, negotiating the most favorable deal terms, conducting thorough due diligence, and planning the all-important exit strategy. Included in the guide is information the

angel investor needs to profit in a fragmented market, comprehensive examples of actual documents used in completed transactions, guidelines for separating fact from fiction in the pre-IPO market, and authoritative, proprietary research from recognized angel-investing experts. Also included is an extensive directory of top venture forums, angel organizations, publications, and Web sites.

Annual Guide to Stocks: 2001 Directory of Obsolete Securities (Directory of Obsolete Securities, 2001). Financial Information Inc., annual.

Published since 1927, this is a cumulative list of companies whose identities have been lost due to name changes, mergers, acquisitions, dissolutions, reorganizations, bankruptcies, charter cancellations, or related capital changes. Listings indicate the manner in which the change occurred, the name of the new company (if any), and the year in which the action took place.

Barron's Finance and Investment Handbook, 5th ed. John Downes and Jordan Elliot Goodman, eds. New York: Barron's, 1998.

This reasonably priced compendium covers 30 investment vehicles, defines more than 5,000 terms, discusses 30 key investment opportunities available to the public, and explains financial news and corporate reports. Appendixes list world currencies, abbreviations, acronyms, and related titles for further reading.

CRB Commodity Yearbook (2001). Commodity Research Bureau. Bridge Information Systems Inc (Editor), Inc. John Wiley & Sons. Annual.

An invaluable and essential commodity reference for analysts, traders, and portfolio managers, *Commodity Yearbook* has been recognized as the "bible" by market analysts and traders since 1939. The Yearbook provides financial professionals with indispensable information on 105 domestic and international commodities, from alcohol to zinc. It includes seasonal patterns and historical data from the past 10 years, as well as pricing and trading patterns on a monthly and annual basis. It also features more than 1,000 charts, tables, and graphs covering crucial data on production/consumption, supply and demand patterns, and trading highlights, and presents three articles on the most popular commodities-oriented topics each year. The included information is available online, on CD-ROM, and through newsletters, charting services, and wire reports. The *Yearbook* is closely associated with the Chicago Mercantile Exchange and the Chicago Board of Trade, and gathers its authoritative data from government reports, private industry, and trade and industry associations

Encyclopedia of Chart Patterns. Thomas N. Bulkowski. John Wiley & Sons, 2000.

This one-volume encyclopedia details over 50 chart patterns that signal whether a stock is in bullish, bearish, or neutral mode. It identifies each pattern, explains how and why each chart was formed, and predicts where it will go next. Included in its chapters are at-a-glance data indicating average market rises or declines, failure rates, price prediction accuracy, failure patterns, statistics, trading tactics, and sample charts with hypothetical trades using real data.

Fitzroy Dearborn Encyclopedia of Banking and Finance. Charles J. Woelfel, ed. Fitzroy Dearborn Publishers, 1998.

Previously entitled *Encyclopedia of Banking and Finance*, this has been the standard authority in the field since 1924. The present edition contains some

4,000 entries. In addition to definitions of basic banking, business, and financial terms, in-depth entries provide information such as historical background, analysis of recent trends, illustrative examples, statistical data, and citations of applicable laws and regulations. The entries have been updated and expanded as necessary, and new terms have been added to reflect developments in the field.

Gale Directory of Databases. Marc Faerber, ed. Gale. annual.

The most current information is provided on more than 15,300 databases and database products of all types in all subject areas produced worldwide in English and other languages. The databases covered are offered by some 2,000 online services and database vendors and distributors. Three indexes are included, by subject, by geography, and a master index. The source is available by direct lease, license, or purchase as a CD-ROM, diskette, magnetic tape, or handheld product.

Handbook for No-Load Fund Investors (2000 Edition). Sheldon Jacobs and Layne Aurand. The No-Load Fund Investor, Inc. Annual.

Written for mutual fund investors, this source includes performance tables, a directory, and industry statistics. Abundant advice is given on methods of selection and the mechanics of buying and selling.

Handbook of Credit Derivatives (Irwin Library of Investment and Finance). Jack Clark Francis, ed. McGraw-Hill, 1999.

This is considered to be the first encyclopedic reference—for both financial managers and investors—in the developing world of credit derivatives. From an operational perspective, credit derivatives (securities that permit financial managers and investors to shield themselves from the risk of issuer default) are still developing. But from the perspectives of utility and value, these instruments have become a vital insurance policy in today's risk-sensitive financial environment

Handbook of Key Economic Indicators. R. Mark Rogers. McGraw-Hill, 1998.

Geared to analysts, traders, and investors who need quick access to data relating to key U.S. economic indicators, this handbook identifies the primary non-financial indicators most closely followed by financial markets, especially those that move financial markets on a regular basis. Among the indicators covered are employment, personal income, consumer spending, international trade, and the Commerce Department's composite indicators.

Handbook of World Stock, Derivative and Commodity Exchanges. Financial Publications. Annual.

Covering hundreds of stock, derivative, and commodity exchanges globally, this handbook is divided into two parts: essays on particular stock exchanges by leaders in the field, and descriptions of international securities markets arranged in alphabetical order by country name. Information is provided on contact details, office locations, a brief history, hours of operation, indexes, trading systems, and contract developments. A glossary defining terms, an index of exchanges by commodity, and a listing of persons cited in both parts are also included.

Indexing for Maximum Investment Results. Albert S. Neubert, ed. Glenlake Publishing Company/Fitzroy Dearborn, 1999.

Based on the fact that almost 10 percent of the total market value of all stocks traded in the U.S. is indexed to the S&P 500, this guide includes most aspects of indexing, including choosing a benchmark, using derivatives to index, performance track record versus active management, index methodology, index price effects on constituent securities, and indexing other asset classes.

International Business Information: How to Find It, How to Use It. 2nd ed. Ruth A. Pagell and Michael Halperin. AMACOM, 2000.

This highly useful reference source facilitates learning about new sources for international business information by librarians and business researchers in the emerging global economy about new sources of information, as it expands their understanding of international business subjects. Covering more than 600 sources, there are 16 chapters arranged into five major areas such as company information, marketing, and international transactions.

International Encyclopedia of the Stock Market. Michael Sheimo, ed. Fitzroy Dearborn, 1998. 2 vols.

This encyclopedia defines 2,000 terms about practices, economies, people, and the history of world stock markets.

Investment Management. Peter L. Bernstein and Aswath Damodaran, eds. Wiley, 1998.

This do-it-yourself reference book on the subject of investing includes insights from leading Wall Street figures such as Charles Ellis and Robert Arnott, as well as from respected academics to guide readers through the investment process. Similar to *The Portable MBA in Investment,* it attempts to provide everything one needs to know about investing, without doing MBA coursework. Included are chapter questions and a teacher's manual.

Investment Statistics Locator. Jennifer J. Kiesl, et al., eds. Oryx Press, 1995.

Investment Statistics Locator contains more than 50 investment and economic statistical source listings. The sources are indexed alphabetically and cover mutual funds and variable annuity/life accounts, overseas investment data, and worldwide economic statistics. The new edition includes several new investment publications and expanded coverage of electronic sources and government documents.

The Irwin Guide to Stocks, Bonds, Futures, and Options. K. Thomas Liaw and Ronald L. Moy. McGraw-Hill, 2000.

A contemporary, comprehensive guide to investing and investment markets, the *Irwin Guide* also covers key topics, including risk management and portfolio rebalancing; evaluating Internet stocks; and buying and selling mutual funds, futures and options, and fixed income securities.

Morningstar Mutual Fund 500: 2001–2002 Edition. Mary Casey, et al., eds. McGraw-Hill. Annual.

Morningstar has been evaluating and ranking funds within the mutual fund industry since 1984. Each year the Morningstar editors list the best 500 funds, presenting data on performance, risk, and portfolio analysis, as well as commentary about the fund and its management. The guide is prefaced with advice on evaluating funds and includes a useful glossary of financial terms.

Mutual Fund Fact Book (2001): A Guide to the Trends and Statistics Observed and Recorded in the Mutual Fund Industry. Investment Company Institute. Annual.

This basic guide to trends and statistics of the mutual funds industry is divided into two parts. Part one covers the general history and developments of the industry, including the key benefits and features of the listed mutual funds; part two provides a table of contents designed to locate specific information in each data table, labeled by classification, industry totals, long-term funds, and short-term funds.

NASDAQ-100 Investor's Guide 2001–2002. Michael P. Byrum (commentary) and Editors of the New York Institute of Finance. New York Institute of Finance, 2001.

Devoted exclusively to the companies and stocks in the world's best-performing market index, this guide contains 100 of the largest non-financial companies traded on the NASDAQ exchange and provides readers with an overview of this popular index. Profiles of each stock are presented with graphs and charts from Baseline. (Baseline is a comprehensive service reporting key fundamental information on more than 7,000 companies. Graphics provide a window on company vital signs, and the service includes earnings estimates). NASDAQ-100 also includes an in-depth analysis of 25 favorite stocks for the year ahead, and advice for the coming year's market are also included.

Nelson's Directory of Investment Managers. Nelson Information, 2000.

This comprehensive directory lists several thousand money management firms. Each entry in the alphabetical arrangement includes over 15 categories of data (e.g., investment specialties, decision-making process, and fees) in addition to standard directory information. There are separate sections listing firms geographically, by total assets managed, by organization type, and by area of specialization. Another useful section lists the most successful firms in descending order, based on previous year(s) results.

Plunkett's On-Line Trading, Finance and Investment Web Sites Almanac, Jack W. Plunkett, ed. Plunkett, Inc., 2000.

Profiles are presented of the 500 most vital Web sites in researching data on investments, stocks, bonds, commodities, banking, mortgages, economics, and trends.

Pratt's Guide to Venture Capital Sources. Stanley E. Pratt, ed. Venture Economics. Annual.

Generally referred to as the "Money-Seeker's Bible," this directory provides detailed profiles of nearly 1,000 U.S. and Canadian venture capital firms, in addition to articles authored by leading venture capitalists and industry analysts. Each profile includes contact details, investment amounts, investment priorities, company financing, and various categorical preferences. Three indexes provide access.

Wall Street Dictionary. Robert J. Shook. Career Press, 1999.

Written by the best-selling author of *Turnaround: The New Ford Motor Company* and other business guides, this dictionary provides concise definitions of more than 5,000 financial, investment, and economic terms. Concise explanations for many unfamiliar and complex terms, including specialized items, current slang, and related jargon, are given.

INVESTMENT BOOKSHELF

The following titles are suggested for inclusion in a comprehensive investment bookshelf. Book reviews of current investment titles, as well as forthcoming ones, may be located in paper and electronic business indexes, in *Books in Print*, and in the various financial newspapers.

Amram, Martha. *Real Options: Managing Strategic Investment in an Uncertain World*. Boston: Harvard Business School Press, 1999.

Benjamin, Gerald, et al. *Finding Your Wings: How to Locate Private Investors to Fund Your Venture*. New York: John Wiley, 1996.

Berlin, Howard M. *The Informed Investor's Guide to Financial Quotation: Evaluating Stocks, Bonds, Mutual Funds, Futures and Options*. Burr Ridge, IL: Irwin, 1994.

Bernstein, Jacob, and Jake Bernstein. *The Compleat Guide to Day Trading Stocks*. New York: McGraw-Hill, 2000.

Buffett, Warren. *Thoughts of Chairman Buffett: Thirty Years of Unconventional Wisdom from the Sage of Omaha*. New York: HarperBusiness, 1998.

Case, Samuel. *Socially Responsible Guide to Smart Investing: Improve Your Portfolio As You Improve the Environment*. Rocklin, CA: Prima Publishing, 1996.

Coker, Daniel P., and Marc Robins. *Mastering Microcaps: Strategies, Trends, and Stock Selection*. Bloomberg Professional Library. Princeton, NJ: Bloomberg Press, 1999.

Ellinger, A.G., and John Cunningham. *The Art of Investment*. New York: John Wiley & Sons, 2000.

Fridson, Martin S. *It Was a Very Good Year: Extraordinary Moments in Stock Market History*. New York: John Wiley, 1998.

Graham, Benjamin, and Warren E. Buffett (Preface). *The Intelligent Investor: A Book of Practical Counsel*. New York: HarperCollins, 1985.

Hagstrom, Robert G. *The Warren Buffett Portfolio: Mastering the Power of the Focus Investment Strategy*. New York: Wiley, 1999.

Judd, Elizabeth. *Investing with a Social Conscience*. New York: Pharos Books. 1990.

Lehmann, Michael B. *The Irwin Guide to Using The Wall Street Journal*. 6th ed. New York: McGraw-Hill, 2000.

Miller, Alan J. *Socially Responsible Investing: How to Invest with Your Conscience*. New York: Institute of Finance, 1991.

Morton, James, ed. *The Financial Times Global Guide to Investing: The Secrets of the World's Leading Investment Gurus*. London: Pitman Publishing, 1995.

O'Shaughnessy, James P. *What Works on Wall Street: A Guide to the Best-Performing Investment Strategies of All Time*. New York: McGraw-Hill, 1997.

Rachlin, Robert. *Return on Investment Manual: Tools and Applications for Managing Financial Results*. Armonk, NY: Sharpe Professional, 1997.

Seyhun, H. Nejat. *Investment Intelligence from Insider Trading*. Cambridge, MA: MIT, 1998.

Siegel, Jeremy J. *Stocks for the Long Run: The Definitive Guide to Financial Market Returns and Long-Term Investment Strategies*. 2nd ed. New York: McGraw-Hill, 1998.

Simmons, Richard. *Buffett Step-by-Step*. Upper Saddle River, NJ: Prentice-Hall, 1999.

Slutsky, Scott, et al. *Complete Guide to Electronic Trading Futures: Everything You Need to Know to Start Trading Online*. New York: McGraw-Hill Professional Publishing, 1999.

Stern, Kenneth A. *Secrets of the Investment All-Stars*. New York: AMACOM, 1999.

Stigum, Marcia, et al. *Money Market and Bond Calculations*. Chicago: Irwin Professional Publications, 1996.

Taulli, Tom. *Investing in IPOs*. Princeton, NJ: Bloomberg Press, 1999.

Williams, Larry. *Day Trade Futures Online (Wiley Online Trading for a Living)*. New York: John Wiley and Sons, 2000.

Acquisitions and Collection Development in Business Libraries

Stephen S. Crandall and Toni P. Olshan

The material used to prepare this chapter was derived from the literature and from a survey of 24 business librarians. The survey asked them to detail their current practices, favorite selection tools, and impressions of the process of acquisitions and collection development of business materials in their libraries. Ten of the respondents worked in academic libraries, eight in special or corporate libraries, and six in public libraries. Their budgets for business materials ranged from a low of $9,000 to a high of $750,000. Half of the librarians focused exclusively on business in their collection development work, the other half ordered in other subject areas in addition to business.

TODAY'S OPERATING ENVIRONMENT

Although the primary mission of the business librarian in collection development remains getting the resources the patron needs in the format he/she prefers, as indicated in the survey conducted to prepare for this essay, the changing world of today's librarianship has markedly affected that mission in a number of ways.

1. The Web has significantly altered the process of acquisitions and collection development and it continues to impact the process in ever-increasing ways, as the mechanisms for both acquiring materials and providing them to patrons have become more and more Web-based.

2. The trend toward delivering resources on the Web has made significant impacts on the relationship between libraries and publishers. As publishers simultaneously attempt to protect their existing revenues while

Stephen S. Crandall is Library Director and Liaison to the College of Business at Herrick Memorial Library, Alfred University, Alfred, NY. Toni P. Olshan is Collection Management Coordinator at Herrick Memorial Library, Alfred University, Alfred, NY.

adding revenue from new electronic products, librarians must then deal with rapid changes in the publishing business.

3. One response to the attempts of publishers grappling with the changing environment has been for libraries to band together in consortia to ensure more favorable pricing than they can obtain on their own. Savings from consortial arrangements have been used to invest in enhanced resources. At the same time, the responsibility for reviewing the terms of these services' complex contracts has become a major component of the collection development librarian's job. In some libraries a person whose title might be "collection management librarian" carries out these responsibilities.

4. Questions have arisen in the field that never existed before. Which contract with which consortium offers the best price? What rights to distribution of the content does the library retain (i.e., will the contract allow a library to fill an interlibrary request from a particular full-text periodical database)? Will the contract provide for stable, long-term access to the product being considered, or will the library lose all access when the subscription lapses?

5. Publishing houses have been bought and merged together, which has made communication with vendors more difficult, as publishers lay off staff and their remaining staff members take on responsibility for additional product lines.

SELECTING BUSINESS MATERIALS

The survey showed that collection development for business collections is still patron-driven. In the academic library, the patrons are the faculty who design the curriculum, and their students who request specific materials. In the public library, the patrons are most often members of the local business community. In corporate libraries, the patrons are both the corporate staff and clients of the corporation.

Responsibility for Selection

The responsibility for selecting seems to vary more by the size of the library than by the type. In small libraries the library director is generally the final selector of materials. Very large academic and public libraries are apt to have subject bibliographers/specialists who do all the selecting and acquiring of the materials for that subject area. Mid-size libraries may assign collection development responsibilities to staff members, each of whom covers a different subject area. In all cases, the selectors try to keep in touch with the patrons they serve to ensure the best possible selection.

Determining Need

The selectors, the survey indicates, decide what to purchase by surveying patrons directly and indirectly. In smaller libraries, the selectors talk directly to patrons to find out what they need. Most often this exchange happens at the reference desk—an excellent reason to have all library selectors spend time on duty at the reference desk, or if this is not possible, for the selectors to consult the reference librarians when making collection decisions, especially for very expensive materials. Online and in-house suggestion boards can also help in identifying important patron needs. For academic libraries, course syllabi should be reviewed each term to determine what kinds of resources are necessary for students to do their coursework. Many academic libraries also share *CHOICE* reviews with appropriate faculty and ask them to recommend items for the collection based on those reviews. All types of libraries can design formal patron surveys that can be issued at the circulation desk or put online from the library's homepage.

Further, library management system (LMS) software has report functions which can generate reports on the use of the collection, thereby showing a selector which parts of the collection are popular, and which are neglected by patrons. As examples, it is possible to generate a report that gives total circulation within a business-related call number range, or to generate reports on particular subtopics, like accounting or marketing. Usage reports on the circulation of individual titles can help a selector to decide whether or not to purchase a new edition of that title. Additionally, interlibrary loan requests should be reviewed regularly to see if demand among targeted areas is changing, and to determine whether additional titles should be added to the collection. LMS software tracks and generates reports on interlibrary loan activity by call number range and individual titles, information which allows selectors to recognize a collection's unique strengths by looking at requests from other libraries to borrow items, and to note weak areas in a library's collection by examining titles borrowed from other libraries. For example, if many articles were requested from the *Journal of Marketing* over the course of one year for many different patrons, the selector should consider subscribing to that journal. On the other hand, if the requests were from just one patron, a subscription might not be necessary, since only a special project might be triggering the requests.

Aggregators

As the missions of publishers, jobbers, and library support organizations have changed, so has the proliferation of both free and fee-based Web sites and "portals" related to the world of business. A *portal* is an Internet site that gives personalized, broad access to the Web in a particular subject area. Portals aggregate content, including original material and third-party information. As they provide search capabilities and links to external Web site resources, they employ advertising and sponsorships to provide revenue streams. They also offer e-commerce opportunities for users, as well as free services to users, including e-mail, chat forums, and personalization features.[1] *Portal B*, created by Data Downlink Corporation, is a fee-based business portal described by a review in *Library Journal* "as part data aggregator and part searchable directory for the business researcher."[2] *Northern Lights* fits the description of a free portal which would be very useful to the business researcher, particularly an investor. The collection development librarian needs to understand the changing environment very well to make sensible buying decisions for the library. For example, company information is available in print, in microform, on CD-ROM, and online at free and fee-based Web sites and portals. Because the gathering of business data is a costly process, very often the site-licensing fee for a good database can be thousands of dollars a year. On the other hand, a free site like EDGAR (the Electronic Data Gathering, Analysis, and Retrieval system) which collects, validates, and indexes the forms that public companies are required to file with the U.S. Securities and Exchange Commission (http://www.sec.gov/edgar/) might be able to provide 75 percent of the information required by most of the library's business patrons. The other 25 percent might be obtained from other established channels.

In addition to strictly business databases, databases of full-text articles are also becoming more integral to a business library's core resources. They provide easy, inexpensive access to a larger pool of information than most libraries could afford to buy as individual subscriptions. However, a countervailing trend is the erratic removal of titles from these aggregates by publishers who are concerned about diminishing revenues. This action forces libraries to start new subscriptions on very short notice or be suddenly left without access to the title. Products like JSTOR (Journal Storage) provide stable, complete back runs for periodical titles, but newer issues are not available. For example, most journals only allow volumes older than three to five years to be included in JSTOR. Products like JSTOR provide online access to back runs of classic periodical titles, thus allowing libraries to withdraw physical volumes from their collections to gain shelf space, and also allowing library users to search older materials more easily and more conveniently. These opposing trends continue to make decision-making difficult, and add considerable ambiguity to collection development strategies.

To stretch resources, some libraries will be tempted to substitute free sites, such as business.com, for some of their paid database subscriptions. Without exception, our survey responses indicated that none of the current free sites is able to meet their patrons' needs for business information.

The collection development librarian must work with the acquisitions person (often one in the same) to look at the overlap in the proliferation of new aggregated electronic products being developed and the overlap of these new products with traditional print sources and with each other. This is becoming a very time consuming responsibility in the business library especially, because of the slicing and dicing of data to make many different products which all have parts of each other included. Overlap studies address the fact that many journals are represented in multiple aggregations by vendors. Without studying the coverage of each database's collection of journals and comparing them, it is impossible to determine whether one collection can be substituted for another. Librarians can initiate their own overlap studies of products they are considering and/or they can research the library literature to see if someone else has done the study. Either way much more time needs to be spent in this area.

Other Selection Strategies

Other important selection strategies in use by business librarians include the following:

- Slip approval plans allow a library to set up an interest profile with a vendor who then sends notification of newly published titles in an area.
- Checking the catalogs of libraries known for their strength and excellence in a specific area identifies important new materials.
- Analyses of the bibliographies of faculty and student research papers identify often-used materials as well as unique titles that might be considered for purchase.
- Review of standard general selection tools, like Katz's *Magazines for Libraries*,[3] especially by very small libraries, provides references to the most important materials in all subject areas.

Format Decisions

The question of which formats to support is now a large issue in business libraries, especially whether or not materials will be purchased in print and/or Web-accessible format. The well-funded library may be able to purchase both formats, but libraries with smaller budgets generally are forced to choose one or the other, keeping in mind the use habits of the majority of their patrons. It should also be remembered that a decision to drop paper subscriptions in favor of access through online databases raises concerns about the completeness of the online edition as well as the long-term availability of resources. For instance, a library that supports marketing research may not want to substitute an online, full-text version of those periodical titles that are important to patrons, because front and back covers, advertisements, the placement and order of advertisements, and images within the text of the articles will be lost. This issue is similar to concerns regarding the substitution of microform for periodicals whose graphics (in their original formats), are of value to the user. Some publishers are switching entirely to online products, thus eliminating the ability to choose with regard to the print products. For example, the Government Printing Office (GPO) makes some of its information available on CD-ROM and the Web, but not in print. In addition to knowing current publisher policies regarding publication formats, librarians need to be alert to changes in policy, especially so that they can provide alternative access for their patrons to important publications, or to the important content of specific publications.

Books are also problematic in terms of format decisions, as they have become easily accessible in electronic versions over the Internet (e-books) using a variety of methods. E-books are particularly appropriate and appealing for both far-flung business enterprises and colleges providing resources for students taking coursework through distance learning projects. NetLibrary (http://www.netlibrary.com) uses a model that replicates a conventional library. Institutional subscribers pay for a selection of titles which will be available to their users. The users "check out" a book for a specific time period. During that period no one else can check out the same book, unless the library pays for access to a second copy. NetLibrary has restrictions built in that limit the number of pages that can be printed (one can't just sit down and print out the whole book). Books 24x7 (http://www.books24x7.com) uses an Amazon.com–type model, users can buy access to individual books online or pay for a yearly subscription (either individual or multiuser) to the entire collection. Users can personalize the books by adding notes and other study or learning aids.

Libraries will be operating in a hybrid environment, acquiring materials in multiple formats (print, microform, CD, video, DVD, Web, electronic) and, as discussed later in this chapter, using multiple methods to order those materials for the foreseeable future.

Location of the Librarians

Some large universities are experimenting with scheduling library subject specialists to spend time in the departments that they serve.[4] Even if this is not possible, most campuses have Internet and e-mail access throughout the institution which facilitate librarians' interactions with faculty and students in the department's own location by using the library's online collections and services at a computer workstation to answer research questions. This is also an excellent way to get information on selection directly from patrons, and to promote the library's collections, services, and librarians. As an example, a faculty member developing a new course, without making a trip across campus, could conveniently meet with the librarian to look at the online catalog, the library's research databases, appropriate Internet Web sites, research guides, and online reference and interlibrary loan services that might help in the design of the course. Similarly, students can also easily meet with a librarian between classes, thus saving them time when they are at the library. Being available to faculty and students in this routine way is a chance to learn directly what kinds of materials and services would be useful to this particular patron group.

SELECTION TOOLS FOR BUILDING A BASIC BUSINESS COLLECTION

Identification of patron needs, as noted above, is the first step in selection. Once patron need is determined, the next step is to identify and evaluate available materials. To accomplish identification and evaluation, the business collection selector may use networking through listservs, conferences, and local and regional library and business organizations; review of targeted ads by publishers known to produce quality products; reading of reviews in both the library and business literature; approval plans, which allow either the responsible librarian and/or the faculty/patron to examine the materials and make recommendations; and screening of online products that offer free trials for potential customers. As new materials are evaluated, a collection development librarian will always review the balance of materials already in the collection, as well as standing orders of annual reviews, publisher's packages, and serials. In this process, out-of-date materials, little-used materials, and orders no longer necessary can be eliminated.

The librarians who responded to our survey indicated the use of a wide variety of tools to identify materials for their collections. It should be noted that many librarians in the survey identified a surprising new selection (and acquisitions) tool, Amazon.com (http://www.amazon.com), usually thought of as an online bookstore. The customer reviews and publisher reviews found in Amazon, theoretically of limited value due to a lack of objectivity and/or a broad knowledge of the subject area of the books, are now considered a value-added feature because of the Web site's ease of use. Although Amazon does not help the selector distinguish between titles that might be important seminal works and those that will be of limited interest for a short time, it is judged valuable by librarians because the bibliographic information is easy to retrieve and enhanced with some reviews, pictures of the covers, referrals to other books on the same topic, or referrals to other books by the same author. Some librarians have cancelled their *Books in Print* subscription in favor of free and easy access to Amazon.com. It is difficult to judge how effective a tool Amazon will be for appropriate long-term development of the collection, but it is certainly a significant part of the picture.

More traditional resources identified by the survey respondents include the following resources:

Harvard Business School Core Collection (Boston, Harvard University, 1999) published annually, and kept up to date by *Recent Additions to the Baker Library* (Boston, Harvard University), published monthly. Both of these are based on the collection of the Baker Library of the Harvard University Business School, the most comprehensive and well-regarded source for information on business books.

Lorna Daniell's *Business Information Sources* (Berkeley: University of California Press, 1993).

Michael R. Lavin's *Business Information: How to Find It, How to Use It.* (2nd edition. Westport, CT: Oryx Press, 2001).

James Woy's *Encyclopedia of Business Information Sources* (15th ed. Farmington Hill, MI: Gale Group, 1992; 3rd edition expected fall 2003).

Association of College and Research Libraries' *Books for College Libraries* (4th ed. Chicago, IL: American Library Association, 1988; new edition expected in 2001).

The following titles, based on the survey and on the opinions of the authors, are recommended for regular review.

American Libraries. Chicago, IL: American Library Association, 1970–.

American Reference Books Annual. Englewood, CO: Libraries Unlimited, 1970–.

Book Review Digest. New York: H.W. Wilson, 1905–.

Book Review Index. Farmington, MI: Gale, 1965–.

Booklist. Chicago, IL: American Library Association, 1905–.

Business Week. New York: McGraw-Hill, 1929–.

Choice. Middleton, CT: Choice, 1964–.

College and Research Libraries. Chicago: Association of College and Research Libraries, 1934–.

Encyclopedia of Business Information Sources. Farmington, MI: Gale. Irregular.

Forbes. New York: Forbes, Inc., 1917–.

Fortune. New York: Time, Inc., 1930–.

Harvard Business Review. Boston: Harvard University, 1922–.

Library Journal. New York: Cahner's Business Information, 1876–.

Management Review. New York: American Management Association, 1923–.

New York Times Book Review. New York: New York Times, 1896–.

Publisher's Weekly. New York: Cahner's Business Information, 1873–.

Recent Additions to the Baker Library. Boston: Harvard University. Monthly.

RSR (Reference Services Review). Bradford, W. York, UK: MCB University Press Ltd., 1972–.

Wall Street Journal. New York: Dow Jones, 1889-.

Several of the above publications offer "best books" lists periodically. *Library Journal* publishes its best business books list on March 15th; *Business Week* listed best-sellers in their December 25, 2000 issue; and the *Wall Street Journal* publishes a list of best-selling books weekly.

Specific subject areas within business are covered by the following journals:

Academy of Management Review. Briarcliff Manor, NY: Academy of Management, 1976–.

Accounting Review. Sarasota, FL: American Accounting Association, 1926–.

Financial Analysts Journal. Charlottesville, VA: Association for Investment Management and Research, 1945–.

Journal of Banking and Finance. Amsterdam: North-Holland, 1977–.

Journal of Business Ethics. Dordrect, Netherlands: Kluwer Academic Publishers, 1982–.

Journal of Economic Literature. Nashville: American Economic Association, 1963–.

Journal of Finance. Malden, MA: American Finance Association, 1946–.

Journal of International Business Studies. London, ON: University of Western Ontario, 1970–.

Journal of Macromarketing. Thousand Oaks, CA: Sage Publications, 1981–.

Journal of Marketing. Chicago, IL: American Marketing Association, 1934–.

Journal of Marketing Research. Chicago, IL: American Marketing Association, 1964–.

Journal of the Academy of Marketing Science. Thousand Oaks, CA: Sage Publications, 1973–.

Many survey respondents mentioned their reliance on publisher's brochures and catalogs for information on the availability of new business resources. Recommended publishers and their Web sites include:

American Association of Individual Investors. 625 N. Michigan Ave., Suite 1900, Chicago, IL 60611. URL: http://www.aaii.com

American Enterprise Institute for Public Policy Research. 1150 17th St., NW, Washington, DC 20036. URL: http://www.aei.org

American Institute of Certified Public Accountants. 1211 Avenue of the Americas, New York, NY 10036-8775 URL: http://www.aicpa.org

American Management Association. 1601 Broadway, New York, NY 10020. URL: http://www.amanet.org

Barron's Educational Services, Inc. 250 Wireless Blvd., Hauppage, NY 11788. URL: http://www.barronseduc.com

Brookings Institution. 1775 Massachusetts Ave., NW, Washington, DC 20036. URL: http://www.brook.edu

Bureau of National Affairs, Inc. 1231 25th St., NW, Washington, DC 20037. URL: http://www.bna.com

Commerce Clearing House. 4125 W. Peterson, Ave., Chicago, IL 60646. URL: http://www.cch.com

Dow Jones-Irwin. 1818 Ridge Rd., Homewood, IL 60430. URL: http://www.factiva.com

Dun & Bradstreet, Inc. Dun's Marketing Services, 3 Century Dr., Parsippany, NJ 07054. URL: http://www.dnb.com

Gale Group. 27500 Drake Rd., Farmington, MI 48331. URL: http://www.galegroup.com

Investment Company Institute. 1401 H St., NW, 12th Fl., Washington, DC 20036–5503. URL: http://www.ici.org

Lexington Books. 4720 Boston Way, Lanham, MD 20706. URL: http://www.lexingtonbooks.com

Matthew Bender and Co., Inc. 11 Penn Plaza, New York, NY 10001. URL: http://www.bender.com

Moody's Investor Service. 99 Church St., New York, NY 10007. URL: http://www.moodys.com

National Retail Federation. 325 7th St. NW, Ste.1100, Washington, DC 20004. URL: http://www.nrf.com

Prentice-Hall, Inc. Englewood Cliffs, NJ 07632. URL: http://vig.prenhall.com

Standard and Poor's Corporation. 25 Broadway, New York, NY 10004. URL: http://www.standardandpoors.com

It should further be noted that today's librarians must evaluate both free and fee-based Web services for selection. An excellent article by Steven Bell, "Choosing Wisely from an Expanding Spectrum of Options: Business Information and the Internet" offers a comprehensive introduction to the process of selecting materials which "run the gamut from traditional print to CD-ROM to commercial online database to Internet Web site."[5] Bell specifically recommends the *Scout Report for Business & Economics* to "identify new and useful Web sites." (http://scout.cs.wisc.edu/report/bus-econ/current).

In addition to the Bell article, other useful tools in this regard include:

1. Listservs, which allow librarians to query other business librarians who can recommend excellent resources. The two most relevant listservs for business librarians are: BUSLIB-L (http://listserv.boisestate.edu/archives/buslib-l.html) with over 2,000 members, and SLABF-L (http://www.slabf.org/slabf-l.html). The ability to contact hundreds of practicing professionals simultaneously frequently results in surprisingly quick and useful responses.

2. *Library Journal* (*LJ*) and *College and Research Libraries News* (*C&RL News*), which have columns that evaluate and recommend Web sites. *LJ*'s column, Web Watch, offers topical guides to Web resources, featuring a different specific subject area each month. *C&RL News*' column, Internet Reviews, offers a collection of reviews in each issue. Also, *Choice's* An-

nual Special Supplement, which appears in August, includes all of the Web site reviews from the previous year.

3. *Information Today* (http://www.infotoday.com), which is very useful in keeping up-to-date with new services and the perpetual reconfigurations of service providers. Also valuable in staying current are *Online* (http:// www.onlinemag.net) and *Econtent* (http://www.econtentmag.com). *Online* provides evaluations and offers guidance for selecting and managing electronic information resources. *Econtent* covers trends and issues affecting the digital content industry.

The exponential growth of the Web makes searching for useful information increasingly difficult. There is continual experimentation with new methods and protocols for accessing Web sites which will match a searcher's parameters. Google (http://www.google.com) and AskJeeves (http://www.askjeeves.com) are two examples of effective software to enhance the appropriateness of Internet search results by allowing searchers to use natural language in formulating their questions. Oingo (http://www.oingo.com), a thesaurus-driven Web site, allows patrons to search for a topic through a variety of subjects interconnected to related topics.

ACQUIRING BUSINESS LIBRARY MATERIALS
Communication Modes

One librarian's survey reported that "The Web has made acquisitions easier and faster." Most libraries still use jobbers as their primary method of acquiring materials. And, most jobbers have designed Web interfaces that allow all ordering and follow-up transactions to be done online. Many libraries are finding it worthwhile to learn the protocols for their vendors' interactive databases that typically allow ordering, checking the status of an order, claiming, checking the library account and other specialized features such as "rush" or "out-of-print" ordering. Acquisitions departments fortunate enough to have in-house programming expertise and/or sophisticated integrated automated library systems might be able to order from vendors online and download that information into their own local acquisitions database, thus eliminating the need to input order data a second time. Additionally, many vendors provide cataloging information for the materials they sell, further reducing the need for labor-intensive processing of library materials.

Only three libraries indicated that they were using the mail as their primary method of ordering and claiming. In fact, 14 survey respondents indicated that they did most of this work online. Three libraries ordered by fax the most, and three used the mail. It should also be noted that many libraries still use the phone to order and claim when the vendor makes that possibility available.

However, regardless of the method used for ordering and claiming, phone support from the vendor or publisher is important.

Price Negotiations

Acquisitions librarians spend a great deal of time networking to find buying consortia that handle the online products their library wishes to buy. When a consortium does not exist for a product, it is often the acquisitions librarian who negotiates directly with the publisher. Therefore, the acquisitions librarian needs to understand licensing law and differential pricing, to insure that the contract he or she signs works well for the library. Trisha L. Davis's chapter "Licensing in Lieu of Acquiring" in *Understanding the Business of Library Acquisitions*, 2nd ed.[6] is an excellent overview of this relatively new and rapidly expanding responsibility.

Consortial agreements between libraries are critical in maximizing limited resources. Ohiolink and Galileo (Georgia) are prime examples of statewide resource sharing agreements that include consortial mechanisms to create larger discounts from vendors. Generally, the more FTEs (full-time equivalent students) represented by a consortium, the lower the per student cost. Librarians in this environment should not make assumptions about where they will obtain the lowest cost access to the resources they need. Some will find that their personal contacts with vendors yield the lowest cost option; others will find that consortial pricing is most beneficial. The pricing situation itself is very fluid. For example, Elsevier, which has a long-standing reputation for excellent but high-priced journals, made it possible for libraries to obtain access to a greater variety of its journals with a modest increase in cost by making each title subscribed to by consortial members available to every member in the consortia.

To add to the complexity, after many years of double-digit increases in the prices of many periodicals, librarians and researchers have begun to pursue alternative distribution methods for scholarly communication. A well-known organization is SPARC (The Scholarly Publishing & Academic Resources Coalition). One of SPARC's primary roles has been to draw attention to high costs and pricing policies, and inform faculty of alternative publishing options.[7] These initiatives have encouraged some publishers to mitigate their price increases, but whether totally new distribution mechanisms will be widely implemented is still unclear.

Verifying Orders

Acquisitions librarians still have to verify orders. This means they have to check their own catalogs to make sure they do not already own the desired material. They also need to be sure they have accurate ordering information before they order materials. *Books in Print* is still the primary tool for bibliographic verification. The CD-ROM or the online versions are much better for the acquisitions department than the print because they are faster, easier to read, and offer concurrent value-added information such as which vendors offer the title in question. Some libraries have experienced slower response time using the Web version. Therefore, they prefer to use the CD-ROM version for verifying large batch orders. Because Amazon.com provides critical bibliographic information, the site is also used by many libraries as an alternative verification tool. Additionally, patrons prefer using Amazon to *Books in Print*, and Amazon is free. This makes it tempting for libraries with small budgets to eliminate *Books in Print* entirely. However, to substitute a consumer catalog for a tool designed with libraries in mind may not serve larger or specialized libraries well.

In spite of the focus on currency of information in business collections, sometimes critical material has been identified, but it is old and out of print. Out-of-print vendors on the Web can help get these materials in a timely and efficient manner. *Bibliofind*, available through Amazon.com, and *Advanced Book Exchange* (http://www.abebooks.com) are two such out-of-print vendors.

Record Keeping

Keeping records of new acquisitions and generating reports that are appropriate for different audiences can be easily accomplished by taking advantage of software programs such as Microsoft Access. On some campuses acquisitions reports are customized by subject area, requestor, fund line, and other attributes. They are then sent as attachments to offices around campus, or they are mounted on the university's Web site. This has eliminated a lot of time at the copier machine, time spent folding reports to mail, and labeling envelopes. The more the acquisitions staff knows about exploiting the features of the software, the better.

Shipping and Handling

In the area of shipping and handling, most book jobbers discount or waive these fees entirely for a certain level of routine business with their company. Private shippers like U.P.S. offer tracking and pick-up services that make some acquisitions procedures logistically easier.

As the survey respondents have indicated, this is a transitional period in acquisition and collection management for all library materials. Although there are emerging trends, the whole process is undergoing tremendous change and a librarian must remain vigilant to stay informed about the tremendous number of new products and services. Along with the variety of products there are also many avenues through which to acquire them. Local circumstances often create situations where solutions will work for one institution but not every institution. Consortial agreements, statewide purchasing arrangements, and state-financed resources vary widely, and need to be investigated carefully to maximize each library's purchasing power.

There is an almost magical quality to the depth of resources available and the ease with which they can be acquired. It is a very exciting time to be a collection management librarian.

NOTES

1. Sistek-Chandler, Cynthia, "Portals: Creating Lifelong Campus Citizens" (© 2000). *Converge Magazine*. http://www.convergemag.com [2001, May 18].

2. Schulman, Andrea, "Portal B." *Library Journal* 125, no. 18 (November 1, 2000): 149.

3. Katz, William A., Berry G. Richards, and Linda Sternberg Katz, *Magazines for Libraries*. (New York: Bowker, irregular.)

4. Rahman, Shabiran, "Liaison with Faculty: Librarians in Academic Departments." Presented at the Western New York/Ontario Fall Conference, September 27, 1996. *Libraries Without Walls: Reaching out to Users and Colleagues*. East Aurora, New York.

5. Bell, Steven J., "Choosing Wisely from an Expanding Spectrum of Options: Business Information and the Internet." *Journal of Library Administration* 30, no. 1/2 (2000): 75–104.

6. Schmidt, Karen A., *Understanding the Business of Library Acquisitions*. 2nd ed. (Chicago: ALA, 1998).

7. Albanese, Andrew, "SPARC to Researchers, Faculty: Declare Independence" *Library Journal* 126, no. 2 (Feb. 1, 2001): 14.

9

The Practice of Organization in Business Libraries and Information Centers

David Miller

Previous editions of *The Basic Business Library* reported on surveys (1980/82, 1987, and 1992) of selected business libraries and information centers. This essay reports the results of the 2001 survey, which was mailed to the participants, via both postal mail and electronic mail, with follow-up contacts by telephone and electronic mail.

THE SURVEY

Most of the libraries surveyed in 1992 were recontacted in 2001. Two of the corporate libraries included in 1992 could not be located; one other of similar size and type, which did not participate in 1992 but had been included in the previous surveys, was included instead. One of the public libraries included in the 1992 survey did not respond in 2001. Additionally, one library counted as a corporate library in 1992 was reclassified as "other special," using Daniells' terminology.[1] The survey group of 10, therefore, comprised four company (or corporate), two academic/business school, two public, and two "other special" libraries. As in previous surveys, the public libraries included were those with separate business branches or departments. The corporate and special libraries included three insurance libraries, one professional association library, one newspaper library, and an economics library.

The discussion that follows is devoted primarily to comparing the 1992 and 2001 surveys. Between 1992 and 2001, the information environment changed radically, with the development of the Internet (at least in North America) being the driving force behind most of the pertinent changes. Additionally,

David Miller is Head of Technical Services at Levin Library, Curry College, Milton, MA.

online library catalogs became the norm, and as of this writing many are accessible via the World Wide Web. Corporate intranets have flourished, and full-text databases are widely available to end users, as compared with the specialized searchers of a decade ago. Electronic mail has not only transformed organizational communication but has proved to be another important tool for information centers, and in applications such as electronic reference service and personalized information services such as SDI (Selective Dissemination of Information). As a result, the most relevant discussion for the present edition of this book is one that "crosses the divide" of practices just before, and somewhat after, the rise of the Internet.

These circumstances also necessitated a revision of the questionnaire used for this edition of *The Basic Business Library*. While the same general format, including the sequence of questions, was followed, several questions had to be revised to accommodate the changed environment. Most important was the change in questioning for what is considered to be the library's own collection, as compared to other resources for which the library provides access. For example, where the 1992 survey asked for information on "Aids to Information Access," the current survey asked for information on "Aids to access information resources not managed by the library/information center." Similarly, the survey question asking for information about "Collections/Files Maintained" was rewritten to ask for information about "Collections and files maintained (including digital resources owned and/or managed by the library/information center, either alone or as part of a cooperative or consortium)." The distinction between the library's "local collection" and other materials was retained, but it was refocused to emphasize the point that local collections frequently include materials that are leased rather than owned, as well as materials that are not in physical form.

Two revisions in the survey reflect specific effects of the general move to online catalogs. The earlier survey question, asking for information about the library's "Type and Form of Catalog," was recast to ask for information about "Access to Catalog: Web/Telnet/Not online." If a library did not have an online catalog, the respondents were asked to describe the physical form of the library catalog. Reflecting the ubiquity of online catalogs, the earlier survey question about "Filing Rules" was dropped. Whether for good or ill, the debate over whether the dictionary, divided, or classified form of the card catalog is preferable have largely lost pertinence, to be replaced by a panoply of indexing means provided by different system vendors. Concerns about filing rules have also been largely superseded by vendors' default algorithms for the sorting and display of search results. While there is some debate over the effects of different normalization rules as applied to data entered in MAchine Readable Cataloging (MARC) format (to name the dominant standard), it is the author's observation that most libraries either have little control over these matters, or simply accept the vendor's basic recommendations. It is hoped that this will change, and that it will become the norm for online system vendors to allow their customers a wide variety of easy-to-implement choices regarding which data elements are indexed, which types of data are included in each index, and how search results are presented to patrons. To the extent that this comes to pass, survey questions similar to the earlier ones for "form of catalog" and "filing rules" will again be pertinent.

SURVEY RESULTS

Collections/Resources Maintained

All of the libraries surveyed maintain book collections, though the size of these collections ranges from 1,000 for one of the insurance company libraries, to over 600,000 volumes in the case of a business school library. The size of the former's book collection seems to have shrunk radically since 1987 (this library did not provide data in 1992), when 18,000 book volumes were reported. Every other collection, however, has at least maintained its approximate size (in the case of the company libraries) or shown healthy growth. The indication is that the "decline of the book" has proved to be a concept whose day is still far off, if indeed it ever arrives, for the majority of institutions.

As was the case in 1992, the collections managed by the libraries show great variety in types of materials. Pamphlet files, printed periodicals, looseleaf services, video and audiotapes, microform materials, rare books, archives and manuscripts, working papers, maps, vertical files, city directories and telephone books, and photograph and slide collections can be found in these collections in different combinations. The greatest variety of materials, including rare and archival materials, is found in the larger of the business school libraries, but three of the smaller company libraries include archives and nonprint materials as well. At least three libraries have developed digital archives. The newspaper library's archive, available to the public on its Web site for a fee and updated daily, includes materials dating from 1983. Since most of the newspaper's history obviously dates prior to then, and the archive does not include graphics, the library continues to maintain its physical archives of clippings, photographs, and slides for use by patrons. One public library has digitized its print and picture collection photographs, and made them available on its Web site. Similarly, the larger of the business school libraries has created online "exhibits" of visual material from its historical collections. The economics library participates in the development of a digital collection of publications made available to the public. This library has, as well, a collection of CD-ROM discs with materials on economics and finance. Although the general trend in database searching is away from the use of CD-ROMs and toward Web-based searching, one of the public libraries lists over a dozen CD-ROM databases on its Web site. Recent developments in information technology have evidently expanded the range of materials available, as well as increased the options for means of access. None of the libraries reported plans to do away in large measure with any of the physical collections.

Between the 1987 and 1992 surveys, the conversion from card to online catalogs was evidenced. In the earlier survey, four of the 11 libraries included had online catalogs; by 1992, that number had doubled. This trend has not continued, at least with the group of libraries under consideration. In 2001, three of the four company libraries still had card catalogs, with only one of these planning automation in the foreseeable future. Another of these three reported having a database system available for in-house use. The fourth company library has a "small home-grown system," essentially the same system as was reported in 1992, for serials check-in, creating catalog records, and tracking payment of bills. By contrast, all of the public and academic libraries, as well as the economics library, had online, Web-based catalogs. However, not all of these catalogs were available to the public. The economics library reported that its catalog was only available via the corporate intranet, for security purposes.

The "digital divide" between the company libraries and the others is softened to some extent by the extensive use in one case of a company intranet, described further below, and the newspaper library's digital archive. The development of these types of digital resources points up the convergence between different information discovery tools—in this case, library catalogs, intranet pages, and digital archives. It also raises the question of what the benefit is to a library of automating its catalog, if its "traditional" print collection is a relatively minor, and possibly declining, portion of its most-used resources? To ask this question is not to argue against automation under any circumstances, but rather to speculate on a possible cause of the seeming lag by company libraries in introducing online catalogs.

Materials Accessed through the Catalog

The summary of the 1992 survey reported that, in contrast to the previous decade, materials in all formats were generally available in the catalogs of these libraries. That general situation remains true, and in fact one could hardly expect fewer types of materials to become available over time, as increased complexity and diversity of services over time is the general rule. One new addition to the picture is that at least two of the libraries with Web-based catalogs include records for selected freely available Web resources, in addition to records for materials actually owned or leased.

There are a few exceptions to the rule of access to all formats. The one company library with plans to automate includes only books and periodicals in its card catalog "for now." In 1992, it responded that its audio and video-tapes were listed separately, uncataloged, in book format, and that it maintained looseleaf files of articles, listed alphabetically by subject. The association library, with a card catalog and in-house computer catalog, includes books, pamphlets, and treatises in its catalog. This library, however, also supports a separate database index to insurance journals, also available in-house at present. The newspaper library includes only books and pamphlets in its card catalog, though again this picture of access is complicated by the library's development of its digital archive, the material in which may not be available "through the catalog," but is nevertheless available in an organized fashion to a broader public than are the cataloged materials. It should be noted that in this case, though an online catalog would undoubtedly be a benefit for the library and its users, electronic access to materials is developing via a parallel effort. It will be of interest to see whether, if the libraries with card catalogs automate in the medium term, they will be able to merge their existing, separate electronic resources with "the catalog," or will require different sets of resources to be accessed separately.

Other Means of Access to Locally Managed Collections

Two questions were asked about means of access, beyond the library catalog, to information resources. As was stated in the introduction to this section, this question is complicated by the developing uncertainty, in an environment with burgeoning digital resources, as to what constitutes the local collection. In 1992, one could still speak of "information access" as something separate from access to the local collection. By "information access," one would have meant access to external databases, not available to the end user, not considered to be part of a library's own resources, and certainly not integrated with the library catalog. Currently availability of external resources to the end user, and convergence of such resources with an institution's catalog or Web site, are becoming ubiquitous. The survey questions therefore attempted to distinguish between resources not included in the catalog, which the library owns or manages (for example, via license agreements) and those to which it more simply points (for example, through "lists of links" for recommended Web sites).

The survey questions failed to make this intended distinction clear enough, and many of the respondents included databases, to which *access* is managed by the institution, in the subsequent question about resources managed externally. Although these resources are selected and licensed for end-user access, and are increasingly available seamlessly from the library's catalog or Web page, they are still considered external resources. The specific content of these databases is not generated, selected, or controlled by the library (at least for the most part), to the extent that the items in a physical collection are. This summary, therefore, attempts to follow the consensus expressed by the respondents, as to what belongs and does not belong to a local collection.

Two of the company libraries reported the use of corporate intranets to make information about uncataloged materials accessible to internal clients. These materials include periodical articles and audio- and videotapes. One of these libraries uses routing software internally to notify clients of new issues of periodicals. The economics library's intranet also enables access, for internal clients, to the publications and services of other corporate departments. Paper files, and simple physical arrangements of various materials, are still very much in use as well. The public libraries use paper files of continuation cards or index cards to keep track of periodical issues. The public libraries also provide uncataloged collections of material in microformats, particularly sets of corporate annual reports arranged alphabetically. Other alphabetically arranged materials include periodicals, specialized directories and telephone books. In general, it seems that the types of uncataloged physical materials made available are the same as or similar to those in 1992, and that the means of access within the libraries to these materials has also changed little. Clearly, these materials are still regarded as useful.

One public library notes that it retains a shelflist for materials added to the collection prior to 1984. This library's catalog first went online in 1986 and, as with many larger libraries, it appears that retrospective conversion of older holdings has not been completed. It also may not be regarded as much of a priority at this point in time, given the general public's demand for current materials. Still, one means of access outside the catalog proper is provided in this way for older items in the collection.

Access to External Information Resources

In her discussion of the 1992 survey, Hryciw-Wing observed that access to online information databases had become nearly ubiquitous, and that the likelihood was "remote" that any business library would be without such access in the future. What appears to be the case, with the libraries surveyed in 2001, is another symptom of an increasingly unbalanced distribution of resources. While most do provide access to multiple databases, two of the company libraries and the association library reported none whatever, either leaving the question blank or replying "n/a." At the other end of the spectrum, one business school library offers access to nearly 90 online databases, directly from its Web page, searchable alphabetically or by topic. The other business school library offers over 30 remote online databases. One public library, with access to about a half-dozen online databases in 2001, had no such access in 1992, while the other, which also provides over 30 databases, offered only one in the earlier survey. Two company libraries and the economics library provide a variety of databases via their intranets, serving as in-house gatekeepers for their clients.

Two other major categories of external resources, commonly available online, are the catalogs or Web sites of other libraries, and lists of evaluated but un-cataloged World Wide Web resources. In 1992, access to other library catalogs was not commonly provided, probably because few were easily available from other locations. Some libraries had begun to provide access (slow and expensive by current standards) via dialup or telnet connections, and if one were really determined, there were printed catalogs to consult in the larger libraries, generally in book form. The situation obviously changed in 2001. One of the public library branches provided easy access to other library catalogs via its parent library's home page, as did one of the business schools. These two libraries in fact belong to consortia, in which the collections of consortial partners may be regarded either as an extension of the local collection, or as easily available external resources, depending on one's perspective. One of the company libraries also included access to OCLC and the catalogs of area law libraries in its role as gatekeeper.

With regard to materials on the World Wide Web, practices varied among the public and business school libraries. One public library branch highlights "business bookmarks" and "selected business Web sites by subject" on its home page, while the home page for the other public library system did not appear to feature selected Web sites anywhere. Similarly, one of the business schools provides an annotated list of recommended "search engines and Web guides" (not listing specific Web resources), while the other school does not appear to include any such links on its site. As of this writing, it is still a matter of debate among librarians as to whether it is worth the time and trouble to attempt to provide controlled access to frequently elusive Web resources, so it is not surprising that there is no uniformity in practice here. The two "other special" libraries both have their own Web sites which provide general information to an external public, but do not see it as their business to interpret the larger world of the Internet to that public. Further, as noted already, three of the company libraries are not online; the newspaper library's home page is that of the newspaper itself, and that page is naturally devoted entirely to providing and selling the paper's own resources. The economics library uses its intranet, again, to provide links to pertinent external services and other online sources. It is interesting that this library is the only one that reported maintaining physical files, to aid access to external resources. These "source files" were described as "files in a file cabinet at the reference desk under various subject headings to aid us in reaching—referencing—remembering materials not managed by our library."

Classification Systems, Subject Headings, and Authority Files

With regard to the classification systems and subject heading lists used by the libraries, the picture is essentially unchanged since 1992. With the major developments of the past decade in the areas of digital provision of materials, the rapid spread of electronic networks, and the radical changes in the forms of library catalogs, there has been little time left to consider such issues as changes in classification or subject provision. Additionally, the days are gone when numerous libraries needed to consider switching to standard classifications to take advantage of the economics of shared cataloging. That phase of technical services management is largely a thing of the past.

Three of the company libraries and one of the public libraries reported the use of the Dewey Decimal System (DDC) for classification, while the economics library, the other public branch, and both business schools use the Library of Congress (LC) classification. The association library continues to use its own local classification system, developed early in the 1970s, which, as Hryciw-Wing noted, features "highly specific insurance categories and notations for these categories." The larger of the business school libraries discontinued its own in-house classification system in 1971, but still retains that system for materials acquired before that time. It also uses a 7-digit sequence number, rather than LC classification, to arrange post-1970 serials. One of the public libraries notes that, in addition to its use of DDC, it provides access to NAIC and SIC codes through various directories and databases. Most of the libraries use Library of Congress Subject Headings as their primary standard for cataloged materials. The newspaper library uses Sears Subject Headings, and the association library uses its own "proprietary" headings list, as it did in the past.

It seems reasonable to assume that the coming decade will see little abandonment of the current standards of classification and subject heading systems. In keeping with the picture of increasing diversification, however, it may very well be that these standards will be supplemented by a variety of metadata schemes. Many of these developing schemes are particularly well-suited for enabling access to individual items in a collection, at a finer level of granularity than a whole book or serial run, or vertical file drawer. As archival materials, photograph and slide collections, clipping files, and files of "gray literature" are digitized or otherwise placed online, the use of metadata will plausibly be seen as an important complement to traditional library classification systems and subject heading lists.

Authority files, which document the established forms of name, title, and/ or subject and genre headings and which provide references from other headings, are commonly found in online systems. All libraries surveyed that used online systems have authority files integrated with their catalogs. The libraries which still rely on card or other physical catalogs must make a management decision as to whether or not it is worthwhile to create and maintain separate authority files. One of the company libraries with a card catalog reports that it does maintain authority files. This is the one company library with plans to automate in the near future. It would seem that its parent company has provided this library with a comparatively generous level of support. In contrast, another company library, which reported in 1987 that it did have separate authority files, stated in 2001 that it did not have these files. This is the same library which reported a radical decline in numbers of holdings during this same period, and it might be surmised that this library may be a steadily diminishing priority for its parent company. With regard, then, to the subject of authority files in general, the question for the future is likely to be not whether a library maintains them, but rather whether or not the library system is automated. If so, whether or not the system makes use of authority files, and in what ways they are integrated with end-user searches and results displays, will depend mostly on the options available from the system vendor. The choice of vendor, in turn, will largely depend on the budget granted by the library's parent institution, leading to the conclusion that the sophistication of authority control will be an indirect consequence of the library's position within its institution.

Aids to and Codes for Cataloging

The primary aid available for obtaining cataloging copy is membership in a bibliographic utility, which provides catalog records from a great range of libraries, thereby minimizing the time and expense involved in original cataloging. As was the case in the previous section, this is an area which has stabilized and where practices have become standard. Seven of the libraries, the same number as in 1992, belong to OCLC and therefore presumably obtain the majority of their catalog data from that utility. Three of the libraries apparently do none of their own cataloging, either original or copy; one of the company libraries receives its catalog cards from a company office in another city, and the public library departments receive their catalog data from the main library. The association library, which maintains its in-house classification system and subject thesaurus, answered "n/a" to this question, which would seem natural, considering that its work is highly customized. Although the bibliographic utilities are an invaluable resource for most libraries, many still find that they still must perform original cataloging and/or edit some of the shared catalog data they obtain. In this connection, one of the business school libraries reports the use of "Cataloger's Desktop," a CD-ROM product from the Library of Congress which integrates the *Anglo-American Cataloging Rules*, second edition revised (*AACR2R*), with *Library of Congress Rule Interpretations* (*LCRI*), the current MARC21 formats, the Library's *Subject Cataloging Manual*, and a great many more specialized standards. The use of this product may replace the need for many shelves of paper products, and the ability to search and link between different standards within the same resource has the potential to save cataloger time and improve productivity.

The use of OCLC for cataloging copy essentially mandates *AACR2R* as the cataloging code to use, supplemented by *LCRI*, at least for the majority of items handled. This is another area where past debates have essentially been resolved, at least within the mainstream. The larger of the business school libraries, however, makes use of additional standards for descriptive cataloging of its extensive collection of archival and historical materials. These include *Descriptive Cataloging of Rare Books* (DCRB), *Archives, Personal Papers, and Manuscripts: A Cataloging Manual for Archival Repositories, Historical Societies, and Manuscript Libraries* (APPM), and Encoded Archival Description (EAD), the current standard for encoding archival finding aid data using Standard Generalized Markup Language (SGML). While the first two of these standards extend the provisions of *AACR2R* for description of rare books and archives in a traditional cataloging environment, EAD provides a means of online resource discovery. Similar to the increasing mix of physical and digital materials found in business library collections, it is almost certain that there will be an interlocking of cataloging standards: those which address the characteristics of physical collections and those more appropriate to intangible data.

Open-Ended Questions

The 1992 survey was the first in this series that included a set of questions designed to elicit responses on more general topics. The 2001 survey included the same questions as the previous survey, albeit somewhat reworded. The questions were:

1. Who is responsible (professional catalogers, paraprofessional staff, reference staff, etc.) for cataloging business materials or developing aids for accessing collections/files? How much time is spent on these activities?

2. Do you think more or less time should be spent by staff at your library/information center in organizing materials or developing aids for accessing materials? Please explain.

3. Are there better methods that you or your staff would like to develop for organizing or accessing materials, than those you currently employ? Please explain.

4. What events or activities have most affected your efforts to organize materials, or develop aids for accessing collections/files, at your library or information center in the last five years?

5. From your present perspective, what developments do you expect will affect your efforts to organize and provide access to materials in the near- to mid-term (2–5 years)? How would you compare these developments to those affecting similar libraries or information centers?

Apart from the three libraries, noted above, which receive all of their cataloging copy from elsewhere in their organizations, the extent of human resources devoted to cataloging materials and developing other access aids varies widely. The newspaper library's director devotes about one hour per month to cataloging activities, but the paper's online archive is updated daily by the staff. The association library's professional staff spends about 10 percent of its time on cataloging, and an additional 15 percent on in-house indexing of its journals and periodicals. The economics library utilizes one full-time professional, who catalogs part-time in addition to other duties, as well as two part-time paraprofessional staff. The public library departments, though not performing cataloging duties within their departments, use a mixture of professional and paraprofessional staff to develop indexes and other aids to locally-held materials, such as pamphlet files and directories. One of these departments reports that data for newly received volumes are attached to systemwide catalog records by paraprofessional staff, taking about 10 hours a week of time. The larger of the business school libraries, not surprisingly, has a proportionately larger staff available for these purposes; five professional staff and three paraprofessional staff spend approximately 140 hours per week on cataloging or developing aids for accessing collections. The other business school reports that, having recently lost a full-time professional cataloging position, it now operates with two part-time catalogers, one professional and one paraprofessional, for a total of 25 hours per week of time. The smaller libraries, regardless of type, are less likely to have a separate staff devoted entirely or primarily to technical services. Still, the majority of all libraries devote some proportion of professional staff time to organization of materials.

Regardless of the size of the library or the extent of its human resources, most libraries did not feel that the amount of time spent on organizing materials and developing access aids was appropriate. The economics library, and the smaller of the business school libraries, felt that the time spent on these activities was sufficient, and in fact both used the word "adequate" in their responses. The one company library with plans to automate expressed the hope that less staff time would need to be spent following automation, once the initial setup and profiling of the system was accomplished. One of the public library branches felt similarly, that as it developed an electronic database of its uncataloged materials, the time spent on these materials might be used more efficiently. The other respondents, though, expressed a need for more time to organize backlogs of material, including donations and historical materials that might be better used if represented in the catalog or other aids. Both business school libraries stated that they may turn to outsourcing to address some human resource needs. The smaller school, which said that it spent adequate time on organizing materials, still foresaw the "probable outsourcing of technical services functions." The larger school did not predict such a drastic change in its operations, but stated that outsourcing some of its backlog might be necessary if additional staff could not be obtained.

When it came to expressing ideas about possible better methods for serving patrons, the technological divide in this group of libraries reappeared. The one company library with plans to automate hopes that this will enable better service; another company library, with no such plans, stated simply, "We would like to be online." By contrast, the larger business school library stated, "We are beginning to explore ways in which to more completely integrate our Web site, online catalog, and the individual Web-based information products we develop so that users have more comprehensive access more easily. We are also participating in the selection of a School-wide content management system that will effect the ways in which we organize and provide access to information resources." These two statements are quoted in full, as they most clearly point out the contrast between the different ends of this spectrum. There is no basis for any assumptions about the relative professional vision, imaginative power, or leadership ability of the librarians working in either of these organizations. What is clear, however, is that different degrees of institutional support, relative to the size and mission of an organization, can either release the potential of its libraries and library staff, or starve it. Between these two extremes, there were a number of good ideas expressed for better service, including "one-stop shopping for locating materials in all formats," better signage for patrons, further development of departmental Web sites and online pathfinders, and replacement of card files with databases. Most of these suggestions point back to the convergence of physical with digital materials and aids that were noted throughout the survey. Finally, the economics library was the only one which reported support for staff development activities, such as attendance at workshops and professional conferences. However, to presume that none of the other libraries support staff development is probably not safe, since most survey responses concentrated on in-house issues.

Respondents reported two categories of recent developments as having the greatest impact on organization of materials in their libraries: the increase in digital information sources, and changes in staff. The first category includes library resources themselves, as well as the networking needed to provide them. Two company libraries and the economics library reported development of their intranets as being of great importance. The latter also cited development of corporate Internet resources and an upgraded online catalog as the other two major developments of the recent period. One of the business school libraries also referred to a change in their library system vendor, which "resulted in the need for several data conversion cleanup projects." As has been noted, the newspaper library listed the development of its electronic archive as having a major impact on its operations. One public library noted that the plethora of digital materials now available, while being of great benefit to patrons, brings with it at least one difficulty: "trying to catalog electronic databases is just impossible, so when you buy new ones, no one knows about them unless you tell people individually." This comment points to the connection between the acquisition of material in new formats and the impact on staffing. The second public library stated that there are now multiple Internet-access terminals installed, and that it is difficult, without additional staff, to assist patrons with good search strategies during busy periods. Some of the other libraries mentioned staff turnover, the loss of staff, increased hours without additional staff, and the need to balance multiple demands in allocating staff time as having a strong impact on the services they can provide.

The final question asked for a forecast of future developments which would likely impact their services in the medium term. Again, technology was prominent in the answers, with many (but not all) of the respondents projecting further enhancements to their existing capabilities. On the modest side, the company library with plans to automate was very much looking forward to the improvements that would bring; the company with a "home-grown" system was hoping to see its serials and catalog information made available to clients on a "read-only basis." The association library is intending to make its database index to insurance journals available via its Web site. The economics library, similarly, is looking toward Internet access to its catalog for the general public, once security issues have been addressed, and expects that participation in OCLC's CORC (Cooperative Online Resource Catalog) project will also prove significant. The larger business school library, by contrast, spoke of the "introduction of a School-wide content management system together with the continued implementation of other new or improved technologies to help manage and provide access to information resources." This library is looking toward the tighter integration of its own digital resources with that of its parent school, in addition to advanced technological development.

Not surprisingly, staffing issues were mentioned as an important influence on future services, as well. The second business school library predicted outsourcing of technical services functions, and one public library branch simply stated: "It just seems like it will get tougher and tougher to keep our patrons apprised of all of our services." The second public library department cited a number of major changes taking place in its parent institution, which will have impact on all departments, and for which no additional staffing is planned. A proposed addition to the central library would involve assessing and moving every part of the collection; seventh and eighth grade school groups will no longer be served in the central children's department; library hours will be increased; and there will be a major effort to enter retrospective periodicals data into the library catalog. With regard to business services specifically, this library significantly expects "increased use of the collection by Business students in local colleges and graduate schools."

CONCLUSION

There is no doubt that the staff of the business libraries surveyed are all dedicated to providing the best service to the widest range of pertinent materials possible, given their varied circumstances and clientele. The impact of digital technology has been extensive, so much so that a great gulf seems to separate the responses of the 1992 and 2001 surveys. And yet, what one observes is not an outright replacement of older, paper-based materials by digital materials. Even the most technologically sophisticated business libraries in this group are not really paperless, not entirely digital. Nor is this likely to be the case in the foreseeable future. As Walt Crawford observes, "The future is not what it used to be. Few sensible people still believe that we're on the verge of abandoning all existing media for the One Big Wire, the single digital source for all data and entertainment."[2] Libraries will be "complex institutions for the foreseeable future," with collections made of steadily more diverse combinations of media. It is probable, though, that *means of access* to those collections— library catalogs, finding aids, databases, even simple alphabetical lists—will continue to increase in usefulness and flexibility to the extent that they are network-based.

There is one caution that must be mentioned in conclusion. It has been noted repeatedly that the gap between the well-supported libraries in this group, and those that are poorly supported by their parent institutions, seems to have widened since 1992. It is not certain that all of these libraries will make it across the gulf, to achieve a position of basic technological competence for the twenty-first century. In this we can see the operation of the "Matthew Effect," so named by the sociologist Robert K. Merton.[3] The effect is named for a passage in the Christian Bible's Gospel of Matthew: "For unto every one that hath shall be given, and he shall have abundance: but from him that hath not shall be taken away even that which he hath." One wonders about how clients will fare, who work for businesses whose libraries are not only falling farther behind relative to other business libraries, but may be declining in absolute terms, such as extent of resources and staffing. "Doing more with less" should not be a permanent mandate in any situation, but must at most be a phase through which healthy organizations pass from time to time. How do businesspeople, who may have benefited from well-supported business school or public branch libraries, regard the neglect of coherent, professionally managed information resources in their own companies? Do they notice, or care? That may be a subject for further study.

NOTES

1. Lorna M. Daniells. *Business Information Sources*. Rev. ed. (Berkeley: University of California Press, 1985), 1–3.
2. Walt Crawford. *Being Analog: Creating Tomorrow's Libraries*. (Chicago: American Library Association, 1999), 13.
3. Robert K. Merton. The Matthew Effect in Science. *Science* 159 no. 3810 (January 5, 1968): 56–63.

10

Reference in the Business Area

Jerry Bornstein

THE CHANGING WORLD OF BUSINESS REFERENCE

The information revolution is totally transforming work at the reference desk across the country, whether in academic, public, or corporate libraries. So profound are these changes that some observers predict "the end of reference as we know it"[1] and warn that reference librarians may be an endangered species. The current reference upheaval in large part stems from: (1) a tendency for the displacement of traditional reference sources by electronic media, and (2) the transformation of virtually every information seeker into an end user online searcher by the proliferation of the World Wide Web. These developments impact many aspects of the library profession, but for this discussion of business reference services the focus will be: (1) the drastically changing types and formats of reference sources; (2) the consequent changes in the nature of the reference collection; and (3) the changing nature and frequency of reference interactions.

Reference desk inquiries have been declining throughout the late 1990s by as much as 6 percent to 15 percent per year.[2] This doesn't mean necessarily that patrons are actually finding good quality information on their own, but there has been a cultural shift in the behavior of information seekers that raises serious questions for the library profession, particularly for business reference service. The profit potential for business-related information has triggered an incredible growth in business-oriented Web sites and services, as well as a large scale migration of traditional online subscription databases to Web formats that no longer require mediated searches by professional librarians. Confronted with changes wrought by the digitalization of information, by the generalization of end-user searching, and by the ever-changing supply of information sources, reference service in the business area is confronted with great

Jerry Bornstein is Reference Librarian at Baruch College, City University of New York.

Special thanks are due to the author's colleagues, Stephen Francoeur and Lisa Ellis, who generously shared their research and insights on digital reference services as this chapter was being written.

challenges in the immediate and longer term future. While this turmoil may cause discomfort for some, for others it offers a sense of opportunity, professional revitalization, and innovation.

The traditional paradigm for business reference, as for general reference, is increasingly antiquated. The old paradigm conceived of the reference collection essentially as a closed entity with a finite quantity of books and body of information, greater or lesser depending on the specific library. Graduate library science students enrolled in reference courses that emphasized key reference books and their contents. In this model, business reference service focused on the confluence of three critical elements: (1) familiarity with business information and topics, (2) familiarity with the collection and especially the contents of key business reference books, and (3) skilled reference interviewing to determine the patron's information needs to match those needs to the information available in the collection. The limitations of a specific reference collection could be compensated for by referring to the library's general collection, by utilization of supplementary databases generally performed through mediated online searching or by referral to another library or information provider. This paradigm no longer corresponds to the reference desk reality in a world in which every information seeker is potentially an end user searcher, using subscription databases and the Internet, and to the related changes in library collection development. It is no longer enough for the business reference librarian to memorize key business concepts and the contents of key books, and to place the reference question in the right pigeon hole to match it to the best available information in the reference collection. The world has become much more complicated in the last decade, and that includes life at the reference desk.

The emerging paradigm, while far from settled, promises to be much more dynamic. Certainly business librarians will still need knowledge of basic business concepts and print resources, but, more importantly, business reference librarians must be cognizant of the rapidly changing information environment, and the implications this has for their service to library patrons. A centerpiece of the new paradigm will no doubt be a more dynamic conception of training for business reference, resting on the principle that the only thing that will remain constant in the world of business reference is the fact that things will constantly change. Instead of a one-time, definitive training process for business reference, the future will require commitment to a never-ending process of professional development. Reference librarians henceforth will require a constant alertness to the process by which print sources are disappearing and being replaced by electronic versions; a preoccupation for evaluating and acquiring new electronic resources as they come on the market, including the plethora of free Web sites springing up and disappearing seemingly overnight;

and a commitment to learning new technologies and new ways of transmitting research skills to patrons who increasingly do their own electronic searching on end-user databases and the World Wide Web. This means that the regular consultation of professional journals, attendance at conferences, enrollment in seminars, and other such activities will necessarily become an integral part of the job description, even for librarians at the smallest public or special library. In special library settings, parent company managers will have to be convinced that failure to permit, provide, and budget for such professional development will doom them to inadequate information services, and put firms at a competitive disadvantage in the world of the information age.

Some patrons will, of course, continue to approach the reference desk seeking a simple answer to their question from the librarian, especially in public libraries where there may be more one-shot interactions with information seekers. But in special library settings in corporations, or in academic libraries, where interaction with patrons may be more continuous over time, librarians are already increasingly taking on the responsibility for educating patrons in the use of the electronic resources, to develop their skills and competencies as end users. This is in marked contrast to the prevailing situation less than a decade ago. In the early 1990s, librarians performed mediated online searching for patrons on subscription databases that were very expensive and difficult to search, requiring arcane search protocols. Reference librarians played the role of gatekeeper in accessing online information. By the mid 1990s, the situation had begun to change. Sophisticated patrons were being trained to use CD-ROM database products. These were difficult to master and often user-unfriendly, but contained valuable information. Because they were not "live" online, there was no charge for the time spent searching these electronic databases, so the less experienced, less expert end users were permitted access to these databases. Use of more expensive online databases like LexisNexis, Dialog, BRS, and Dow Jones, where the meter was constantly running and every minute online cost money, was reserved for the professional librarians. Finally, the Internet, which previously had been largely limited to academics and government researchers, experienced an exponential growth rate since 1995, with the advent of the World Wide Web, creating the present near-universality of end user searching.

In less than a decade, business reference librarians have lost their monopoly on accessing online business information, print resources are declining in importance and quantity, and business librarians must adapt to the new information environment. While the situation is far from static today, it is worthwhile to examine where the field is headed and what this means for business reference service in the future.

INFORMATION COMPETENCIES AND THE REFERENCE PROCESS

Responding to the challenges posed by the prevalence of electronic information, the Association of College and Research Libraries (ACRL) adopted standards for information literacy in January 2000.[3] Drawing on an earlier American Library Association report on information literacy, the ACRL document addresses issues that impact reference work. ACRL cites an early American Library Association definition of information literacy as "a set of abilities requiring individuals to 'recognize when information is needed and have the ability to locate, evaluate and use effectively the needed information.' "[4] The new electronic information environment, characterized by a proliferation of information resources available on the Internet, a dramatic increase in public access to "unfiltered" information, and widespread availability of new formats of information, raises new problems for evaluating and understanding information. "The uncertain quality and expanding quantity of information pose large challenges for society. The sheer abundance of information will not in itself create a more informed citizenry without a complementary cluster of abilities necessary to use information effectively."[5] In this sense, information competencies are broader than simple computer or technology literacy. While fluency in the use of "computers, software applications, databases and other technologies" is often a precondition to effective utilization of online resources, information competency involves far more than simple "training" in the search protocols of specific databases, but focuses instead "on content, communication, analysis, information searching, and evaluation."[6] It involves understanding the production, organization, and distribution of information, sensitivity to the inherent biases and limitations of information sources, and critical thinking skills necessary to evaluate and manipulate information.

According to the ACRL objectives, individuals possessing information competencies would be able to exhibit the following performance behaviors:

- determine the extent of information needed
- access the needed information effectively and efficiently
- evaluate information and its sources critically
- incorporate selected information into one's knowledge base
- use information effectively to accomplish a specific purpose
- understand the economic, legal, and social issues surrounding the use of information, and access and use information ethically and legally.[7]

Though developed as guidelines primarily for instruction librarians in academic settings, the information competency standards have relevance for the reference desk as well. Any information seeker in today's world requires the indicated critical thinking abilities, particularly in a business reference environment, where the information sought is often the basis, at least in part, for significant economic decision-making. In this context the development of information competencies in library patrons cannot simply be an issue for instructional librarians alone, but must also be one for librarians at the reference desk as well. In a complex electronic information environment, in which end-user searching is the norm, not the exception, reference librarians increasingly must be ready to teach at the reference desk, not merely to answer questions. As much as is feasible, the reference librarian must take advantage of these teachable moments, when the need for specific information makes the patron most open to learning how to locate accurate data in the most effective manner. This not only satisfies the patron's immediate information need, but, by the development of transferable research skills in the utilization of electronically formatted materials and evaluation of information, prepares the patron for future information research.

The reference interview, which in the past served the primary function of enabling the reference librarian to understand more precisely what information the patron really needed to best answer the question, can in this sense be transformed into an important instructional vehicle. In the past, the underlying premises behind the questions asked by the reference librarian were not necessarily transparent to the patron. In the information literacy framework, the reference interview no longer simply provides the librarian with valuable data necessary to match the information need to the appropriate resource, but can be used to help patrons understand the thought processes used by information professionals in identifying the parameters of a reference question, the potential producers of required information, and the most appropriate sources to which to turn. The reference interaction can thereby transcend its traditional service provision character and take on a teaching or instructional aspect. This will not turn patrons into information professionals but it will help them to pose questions more clearly and to be alert to the authority of sources they consult in fulfilling their information needs on their own.

COPING WITH THE WEB

The problems inherent in widespread reliance on Web searching make it incumbent on librarians to foster increased patron sophistication in the use of this resource. Information literacy skills such as evaluation of information and recognition of the potential biases in information sources are particularly relevant for Web users. All too often the typical business library user turns either to a company home page or to a search engine for access to information.[8] Both approaches are problematic. While considerable information may be available on company home pages, patrons need to be mindful of the inherent bias of company-produced information, as compared to the material available at more unprejudiced sites.[9]

The limitations of Web search engines also require sophistication in using the Internet. No search engine claims to cover more than approximately one-third of the Web, and even that claim is disputable. In an exhaustive study reported in *Nature*, Lawrence and Giles found that "no engine indexes more than about 16 percent of the Web."[10] Their research also found that because search engine indexing is not based solely on Web page content, but also takes into account the "popularity" of links to a Web page (i.e., the number of Web pages linking to the site), search results are often biased against "new, unlinked pages [that] have an increasingly difficult time to become visible in search-engine listings. This may delay or even prevent the widespread visibility of new high-quality information."[11]

While the quantity of information accessible to end users increases dramatically, the role of librarians in promoting the ability to discern "the jewels in the garbage," as Katz puts it,[12] becomes an increasingly indispensable aspect of work at the reference desk, particularly business reference. Librarians need to help patrons understand that when they submit a query to a search engine, they are not really searching the World Wide Web, but rather a database of Web pages maintained by the search engine, and that none of the search engines approaches complete coverage of the Web. Even a metasearch engine, which sacrifices the use of advanced search features on most search engines, increases Web coverage to only 42 percent.[13] Furthermore, search engines vary greatly in how deeply they index a site, perhaps including only the first two or three levels, making valuable information buried deeper at the site unretrievable by the search engine. In addition, the extensive collection of articles available full-text from Web-based subscription databases maintained by vendors such as LexisNexis, Dialog, Dow Jones/Factiva, Infotrac, and Proquest are inaccessible via Web search engines. Librarians can help users compensate for the weakness of the Web by emphasizing the information producer model discussed earlier, an approach that enables patrons to identify agencies, associations, organizations, or publications that might have published on a specific research topic, and go directly to appropriate Web sites or online databases in search of information.

REFERENCE COLLECTION

Detailed recommendations for reference titles, both print and electronic, are beyond the scope of the present chapter. However, the intertwined relationship between collection development and business reference services makes a few observations necessary. It is no longer inappropriate to argue that the Internet has transformed the nature of the reference collection, that the ability to find answers to reference questions is no longer limited in any physical sense to the materials on premises, or that answers can be located at any source in the world accessible by electronic databases or the Internet. No one disputes that traditional print resources are still important, but increasingly these are appearing in electronic format. Reference librarians must therefore wrestle with difficult choices about discontinuing print titles and switching to electronic sources. The choices may involve whether to supplement the traditional print title with its electronic counterpart, discontinue the print copy and switch to the electronic version only, or replace a traditional print title with an electronic product that covers the same material but is not an electronic form of the old print title. These decisions are not easy, especially since faculty at a business school may still insist on their students using the same print sources that they themselves have used for years. This is true even though the cost savings in switching to a free Web product may seem to outweigh this consideration.

The array of electronic subscription databases on the market today is staggering, and decisions regarding subscriptions must be based on such considerations as the information needs of library patrons, the quality of the information provided by the database, searchability, user friendliness, and cost. While certain databases such as LexisNexis (end user version), ABI/Inform (Proquest), Business and Company ASAP (Infotrac), Dow Jones (Factiva), and Wilson Business Periodicals Index would appear to be core business periodical databases for any reference collection, there are no rigid guidelines applicable for all situations. A reference service in a large business college serving the needs of students and faculty in a range of business disciplines will have different requirements than a special library serving a banking institution or an advertising agency. Given budgetary constraints, cost issues will inevitably carry great weight, but subscription decisions should not be seen primarily as a financial question. These are critical collection development questions that should involve the input of all business reference staff to set priorities to insure that patrons' information needs will have paramount consideration.

Business reference collections are increasingly becoming virtual reference libraries, expanding to include Web subject guides or Web links pages on the library's reference Web site. These can provide library users an authoritative alternative to Web search engines, by facilitating access to information on the Web that has been analyzed, categorized, and annotated by professional librarians. Business reference librarians should use the same criteria in deciding what sites to link to, as they would in purchasing a new reference work for the traditional print collection, making certain that authority, purpose, scope, and intended audience of the sites is appropriate for library users. Links can be established to already existing sites that have gathered pertinent Web sites. For example, the New York–based College of Insurance has published an "Insurance on the Web" page, providing a gateway to a definitive collection of insurance information on the Web. Another option is to develop Web links independently. Often this involves exploring already existing links sites at other institutions, dissecting them, locating relevant materials for patrons, verifying their quality, and crafting annotations aimed at library users, as well as consulting such Web collection development tools as Scout Report for leads. Inclusion of annotations is critical. Failure to do so risks undercutting the patrons' ability to discern the utility of the Web link for their research purposes. Simply listing titles of Web links without annotation, as some libraries do, can be considered analogous to a book catalogue entry with title only, and no subject headings.

REFERENCE PROCESS

The reference interview continues as the cornerstone of the reference process, not only as a means of helping the librarian determine what the patron needs, but, as pointed out earlier, as an opportunity to help the patron develop information literacy, i.e., to understand the process of refining an information question to initiate the research process. More than ever the reference interview requires tremendous communication skills. The librarian must be resourceful in the interview process, especially in relaxing anxious patrons, and in getting them to talk about what they want and why they want it. Anthropologist Bonnie Nardi, who has studied patron-librarian interactions at the reference desk, has concluded "that a large part of what we do is what she calls 'information therapy,' helping [patrons] figure out what it is they really want to know. She regards this information therapy as an example of human intelligence, when applied to the search problem, that cannot be replaced by a computer but that doesn't get included in the measurements of what we do."[14]

So how do we practice information therapy at the reference desk? A frequently heard query at the reference desk is "I need to find out information about a company." The librarian must draw the information seeker out, asking questions that help refine and focus the research question:

- What kind of company, public or private? Domestic or international?
- What kind of information about the company—directory, contact financial, stock data, organizational, marketing strategies, research and development, etc.?
- Why is the information needed, how will it be used—to contact the company, to write an in depth analysis of the company, to make an investment decision, to prepare for a job interview?
- Is current information or retrospective information required?

Answers to these questions have direct bearing on the information search. By involving the patron in this process we can help educate him or her on how to think about future research questions in a more methodical manner.

All schema for describing or categorizing interactions at the reference desk are necessarily flawed and somewhat arbitrary; they can run the risk of over-simplifying a complex reality, but they can often be helpful in orienting discussion. For instance, it can sometimes be useful to conceive of business reference questions as generally falling into three broad categories: company information, industry information, and business topics (a rather broad umbrella rubric). In addition, it is often helpful to think about the information producers for different types of information, i.e., who are the organizations, professions, disciplines, agencies, institutions, and individuals that have an interest in, and produce information on, the particular topic. This approach can lead the researcher, especially with the assistance of a reference librarian, in a logical, methodical way to the appropriate indexes, sources and databases.

Within this framework, if a librarian asks the question, who produces information about companies, even an inexperienced undergraduate shouldn't have too much difficulty in developing a list that includes such information producers as the companies themselves, journalists, government agencies, scholars, financial analysts, consumer groups, associations and organizations, and professional or trade organizations.

With a little guidance from the librarian, it can become clear that companies produce information themselves in the form of required government filings (Annual Report to Stockholders, SEC documents, press releases, or other official statements). In addition to being available often in traditional print sources, these materials are available electronically. SEC documents, for example, can be located in such sources as EDGAR, LexisNexis, Dialog, Dow Jones (Factiva), Primark Global Access (Disclosure), or Standard and Poor's Net Advantage. Press releases, and company or executive statements are available in databases such as PR Newswire, LexisNexis, Factiva, and Web sources, as well as on company Web pages. Occasionally, 10-ks are also published on company Web pages.

Journalists produce company information in the form of reports and analyses available in the general press, in trade publications, newsletters, and wire services, and in all media (print, broadcast, online and Internet). Sometimes journalists even write book-length reports, as well, that might be listed in the library catalog.

Government agencies supervising a company's activity, including commissions, regulatory agencies, and legislative hearings, also publish information. This material is available in paper and increasingly online, on databases like LexisNexis, and on the Web at the agency's homepage or at the GAO site.

Consumer groups, associations, and organizations may publish reports, publications, testimony, and other documents, which generally advocate a particular point of view, and are often available at organizational Web sites.

Academics produce information on companies that may be available in books, academic journals, government testimony, or op-ed and letters-to-the-editor in news media. All of these are accessible through library catalogs, online databases and Web sites.

Investment analysts produce reports on companies that assess profitability and operations, and are available directly from Investext, or through online vendors, or through investment guides such as *Value Line*.

Directories such as *Standard & Poor's Corporate Records*, and *Mergent* (formerly *Moody's*), include not only basic directory information (names, addresses, etc.) but also limited company financial data. These are available both in print and electronic versions.

Similarly, industry information can also be sketched out using the information producer model. Journalists produce industry information in articles and reports in the media, accessible by databases and Web pages. Government agencies produce information in such sources as *US Industry and Trade Outlook*, market outlooks for foreign countries in the *National Trade Database (NTDB)*, regulatory commission reports and white papers, and legislative hearings. Investment analysts prepare industry reports available in *Standard & Poor's Industry Survey, Investext*, and *Value Line*. Information produced by academics can be found in journal articles, testimony, and books, and can be accessed through the appropriate research tool. Trade and professional associations may publish trade publications, often found in the library's periodical collection, or reports and data that are often available at organizational Web sites. Consumer groups that act as watchdogs on industry activities also publish written reports available in library collections or located on the Web.

The catch-all business topics category includes such disparate areas as product safety, job discrimination against women and minorities, environmental issues, ethics, management, marketing, human resources, and operations management, is covered in journalistic reporting, academic sources, and government documents, and can be supplemented with material from consumer groups, trade organizations, and sometimes companies.

ELECTRONIC REFERENCE

A direct consequence of the proliferation of the Internet and end-user searching is the emergence of electronic reference services that allow patrons at remote locations to seek research assistance. The practice of accepting remote reference queries predates the Web era. For instance, at NBC as early as the late 1980s, journalists and researchers from remote bureaus around the world would routinely send electronic messages requesting background research from librarians at NBC News headquarters in New York. The growing trend toward electronic reference services on a more general scale, corresponds to the changing information environment. As the librarians at Baruch College who have designed the library's new e-reference services put it, "digital reference services . . . are intended to provide an online base from which we can help those users in a newly evolved point of need: the digital library. It makes sense that if we have created a digital library environment that we also provide a way to assist patrons in this new place."[15] Newly emergent technologies now facilitate the library's ability "to provide reference in this asynchronous environment where you typically never see your customer face to face."[16] Queries may be e-mailed to the reference staff by library users from home, from dorms, or from offices whenever help is needed, even when the library is closed. Librarians can respond within 24 hours with research suggestions. Sometimes the librarian may find it necessary to conduct a modified reference interview, through an exchange of e-mails, to clarify the research question to better assist the patron.

Even more dynamic are the chat reference services now offered by more than fifty public and academic libraries across the country. These services, such as the "Ask a Librarian Live" service at Baruch College, allow "users to click on a link on the library Web site . . . that will open a chat program on their computers and let them exchange short, text messages back and forth with a librarian and let them have Web pages pushed onto their browser by the librarian assisting them."[17] These kinds of services can be particularly useful to special libraries servicing parent corporations whose patrons, scattered at different locations whether in another building, another city around the country, or even around the world, can receive online live assistance with research problems. The software products currently being used or experimented with in these applications include AOL Instant Messenger, Camden, ChatSpace.Com, Conference Room, eGain, Human Click Pro, Live Assistance, Live person, NetAgent, Netscape Chat, Virtual Reference Desk, Virtual Reference Librarian, and Webline.

NOTES

1. Jerry D. Campbell, "Clinging to Traditional Reference Services," *Reference & User Services Quarterly* 39 no. 3 (2000): 223.
2. Steve Coffman, "The Librarian and Mr. Jeeves," American Libraries (May 2000): 66–69; 66.
3. Association of College and Research Libraries (ACRL). Task Force On Information Literacy Standards, "Information Literacy Competency Standards for Higher Education," *College & Research Libraries* (March 2000): 207–215; 207.
4. American Library Association. *Presidential Committee on Information Literacy. Final Report* (Chicago: American Library Association, 1989) http://www.ala.org/acrl/nili/ilit1st.html.
5. ACRL, 207.

6. Ibid, 208.
7. Ibid, 207.
8. Steven J. Bell, "Weaning Them from the Web: Teaching Online to the MBA Internet Generation," *Database* (June/July 1998): 67–69; 67.
9. To illustrate this point, in the fall 2000 semester I gave students in a course on Information Research in Business a homework assignment requiring them to compare the information about the defective tires on Ford Explorers on the Ford Motor Company home page to that on Consumers Union's site.
10. Steve Lawrence and C. Lee Giles, "Accessibility of Information on the Web," *Nature* 400 (8 July 1999): 107–109; 107.
11. Ibid, 109.
12. William A. Katz, *Introduction to Reference Work, Volume I: Basic Information Sources* (New York: McGraw Hill, 1996), 33.
13. Lawrence and Giles, 108.
14. Anne G. Lipow, "Serving the Remote User: Reference Service in the Digital Environment," http://www.csu.edu.au/special/online99/proceedings99/200.htm.
15. Stephen Francoeur and Lisa Ellis, "Proposal for Digital Reference Services at the Newman Library," unpublished document. pp. 3, 8.
16. Campbell.
17. Francoeur and Ellis, 1.

11

Marketing the Business Library

Joseph P. Grunenwald

Many of today's public and academic libraries are engaged in a serious attempt to serve the business community as part of their basic operational mission. Development of new collections focused on business concerns, addition of information services related to business activities, and participation by librarians in the business community are all strategies employed to enhance business outreach. Given that the personal backgrounds and professional development of most librarians are found in areas other than business management, establishing and marketing a credible program targeted on business entities can be confusing and difficult. The following pages outline practical steps necessary in the business library marketing process.

BACKGROUND

For more than 20 years, librarians and other managers of nonprofit, service organizations have been urged to embrace marketing management techniques to expand the usership of libraries generally and grow their importance to their publics in the community.[1] Going further, there has also been encouragement for libraries to target professional groups such as the legal community with their marketing approaches.[2]

Considerable attention has been paid to the potential of applying marketing concepts to libraries. Moreover, a wide variety of conferences, workshops, and seminars have been offered across the county over the last two decades that focus upon general marketing of the library. Librarians have been urged to engage in service area research to identify potential market segments and the needs of individuals or organizations within those segments. Many surveys have revealed that business and industry could well utilize library services, and in fact seem willing to partner with libraries in their market areas. Despite significant efforts by some librarians in this regard, businesses and corpora-

Joseph P. Grunenwald is Provost and Academic Vice President of Clarion University of Pennsylvania, Clarion, PA.

tions remain largely underserved by small to medium-sized libraries and represent an important potential market segment yet to be tapped.

The reasons for the absence of usage of libraries by businesses are many. These vary from dissatisfaction with library collections, to the lack of available business services in most libraries, to the perception that libraries are simply not intended to provide service to businesses at all. Much of this may be attributed to the historic mission accepted by libraries and their hesitation to vary from it in significant ways. Libraries have generally organized themselves and their collections to serve the needs of recreation and reference patrons, researchers, children, and users of specialty materials related to regional interests, the library staff, or influential supporters. Businesses have not been seen as comprising a segment related to this mission.

Whether fueled by a belief that businesses represent a major part of every community or by recognition of the fact that businesses have financial resources that might be shared with those friendly to their operations, small and medium-sized libraries have recently demonstrated expanded interest in building relationships with companies. Although they may be tenuous at first, these relationships can grow into attractive partnerships that may greatly enhance both the library and the businesses they serve. However, this will happen only if librarians are willing to consider new approaches—new ways of doing business.

A STRATEGIC MARKETING PLAN FOR THE BUSINESS LIBRARY

Librarians are not strangers to effective planning. In well-managed libraries, careful thought about the mission of the library and the services that it will undertake to carry out the public portion of that mission have lead to the creation of effective plans for activities. This must equally be the case in the development of a business library. Careful attention to the needs of the "public" or "patron" being served, as well as the operational and financial concerns of the library, must be accommodated. The development of a cogent marketing strategy is the first step in accomplishing these outcomes.

Establishing a Rationale for Business Use of the Library

Businesses have very specific information needs. These are centered on their core activities and processes, and are often measured in importance by the profit potential of their satisfaction. Companies typically do not engage in activities that fail to contribute to the bottom line of profits; hence, business information must be clearly focused upon those things that aid businesses to achieve their objectives. These may include developing an understanding of issues in the business environment, increasing sales volume, enhancing productivity and efficiency, maximizing return on investment, expanding utilization of environmental management approaches, or other objectives. The first step in building a successful and lasting relationship with businesses is for the librarian to commit to satisfying business needs in a way that business can understand and use.

This commitment to satisfaction of business needs begins with a desire to build a library business collection and a set of business information services that are practical and have reasonable breadth and depth. Smaller libraries may shy away from the business market as a result of this requirement. Not only do librarians in these libraries often lack financial resources necessary to mount a "full-scale" business program, but they also typically believe that they do not have the business training necessary to support the business users as well. However, neither having a generous collections budget nor an MBA from a prestigious business school are required to effectively support the vast majority of American businesses. What is required first is that librarians make choices about the direction they will take in serving businesses. Just as it is impossible to serve the needs, wants, and desires of every general library patron, it is impossible to be everything for every business. Instead, libraries must narrow the field by serving well those special needs of the companies in their service areas. This will most probably take the form of establishing an efficient small business or entrepreneurial collection as opposed to a comprehensive corporate reference service, which will involve collecting materials that take a distinct "how to" approach as opposed to laying out theoretical or method-ological concerns. It may also require involvement with basic database re-search services rather than the more esoteric research services common in larger academic libraries.

To put it simply, the librarian must develop a reason for businesses to "need" the library. A company must come to understand that using library services, whether on-site or through electronic means, will help to lead to accomplish-ment of corporate objectives. A business must believe that turning to the li-brary will result in obtaining practical and relevant information—and perhaps as important, that librarians really want to provide it.

Establishing a Business Library Marketing Strategy

Librarians must think clearly about the way that the business community will be serviced within the library's overall service mission. This type of thinking is critical, since the vast majority of public and academic libraries are simply financially unable to assemble a business collection that is comprehensive, current, and contains both the underpinnings of business theory as well as the background for practical application required by business managers. Establish-ing a set of business marketing strategies emanates from a clear understanding of the business market being served and how the library can best serve that market.

As an example, a major research university serving a faculty dedicated to creation of new knowledge will attempt to mount a broad collection containing a wide array of current theoretical journals and periodicals that provide the latest possible research. On the other hand, a proprietary library serving the interests of a particular company or industry (e.g., steel, hospitality, agriculture, computer technology) will tend to assemble a collection specific to its own particular applications. But neither of these two types of specialized collections that serve the interests of specialized audiences is likely to be typical of the collections necessary in most small and medium-sized libraries to serve their business community.

Choosing the appropriate business library strategy begins with the identification of the business market to be served, followed by recognition of the information and service needs of that market that the library can reasonably expect to serve. Some examples of business market segments that libraries might choose and the nature of the collection and service strategies that might result can include the following:

Nature of Business Market Segment	Collection/Service Strategy
Small Businesses	Entrepreneurship, small business development, family business management, starting and managing the new business enterprise
Industry-Specific Businesses	Applied management, process management, technical reference, governmental regulations, industry legal issues
Large Corporations	Business conditions (e.g., economic, labor market, financial, etc.), functional management, competing markets

It should be clear that these sample business market segments are very general categorizations. For the majority of libraries, however, the choice of a segment, defined even as broadly as these, allows the planning of business library outreach to be effective and practical. The selection of a small business segment, for example, narrows the focus of collection development and service design to a scale that is "doable" for a small or medium-sized library. Materials acquisition, service implementation, personnel training, and library operations design approaches are much better understood, and the general direction of the business library program can become clear.

Conducting Market Research

Most librarians shy away from the market research needed to develop the effective marketing strategy discussed above because they believe that market research studies are difficult to design and contain statistical analyses that are difficult to interpret. While many market research projects contain these elements, the kind of research necessary to develop the business library marketing program does not.

Good market research is designed to gather, organize, and evaluate information directly relevant to the marketing task at hand. For the library, this means first that research must be designed to provide an understanding of the number and types of businesses in the service area. The study methodology for gathering this kind of information may be as simple as consulting secondary data sources such as Chamber of Commerce or Economic Development Authority listings of area businesses that contain a general description of the type of business being conducted. State governments maintain excellent regional descriptions of business and industry, often listed by Standard Industrial Classification Code (SIC), that can be extremely helpful in getting to know the flavor of business activity.

In terms of analysis, librarians should avoid the temptation of turning the market study into the definitive statement on local business operations. The intent instead is to know enough about the business community in the library service area to support the development of business surveys or focus group discussions of the information needs of business that fall into the "must have," "would be nice to have," and "not necessary" categories that practical library management requires.

This kind of approach is absolutely critical in that the development of the business library will be a long-term proposition. Having solid information on patron needs is a fundamental tenet of library management and so it is here as well. Focused collection development and implementation of only those services that are necessary will enhance business patron satisfaction and reduce costs—outcomes that are crucial to long-term success.

USING THE MARKETING MIX

The traditional marketing mix includes the elements of (1) establishing a solid product/service offering, (2) creating an attractive price/savings environment, (3) developing an attractive physical environment in which the product/service is "consumed," and (4) promoting the product/service using advertising, public relations, promotions, and personal selling. While these elements seem best suited to the sale of retail or industrial products, their application to the business library can be of enormous value.

Defining the Product

Surveys, suggestion boxes, sample collection lists from vendors, business focus groups, and company requests can all be good sources of information regarding the products of the business library. Books and periodicals are still a critical element of the product that the library offers, even in a high technology information environment. These materials play a key and irreplaceable role in the acquisition of business knowledge and the mastery of business techniques. The fact that the virtual library has had, at best, moderate success, implies that libraries will continue to need to have a reasonable physical collection as a basis from which to grow the business product/service offering.

This should not be taken to mean that the technologically enhanced business library is unimportant. To the contrary, the electronic library is very much in evidence and in most instances critical to providing business information services. Databases, online catalogs, CD-ROM information, and other media provide a welcome expansion to the library collection. Indeed, these forms of information storage may well be the only practical way to provide access to the technical or specialized information that many businesses need.

The current state of communications technology provides an important way for librarians to engage other library professionals in discussion about business collections, electronic services, and other issues by way of chat rooms or listservs. Identification of business librarians from various areas that target similar business interests in communities like the service area of the business library at hand can be essential to success. Information sharing with noncompeting libraries and librarians can be the most effective way to uncover "what's hot and what's not" in the ever-changing business world.

Providing Business Information Services

Establishing a product concept for the business library goes well beyond the physical or electronic collection. Providing services in addition to a good business collection is key to serving the information needs of the business community. It is important to note that showing a business patron to the stacks or bringing up a computer database is not service. The librarian must be willing and able to show the way, especially for small businesses and first-time business library users. The fact that companies recognize the need for information does not necessarily mean their people have any idea about how to get that information.

Satisfying information needs of businesses must necessarily begin with knowledge of library resources and how they might be employed. Unfortunately, many business people may have no recent experience with what a library can be, their experience having ended with work on a college term paper or even a high school writing project. This means that the relationship with businesses must be developmental in nature. Beginning with issues surrounding information literacy and moving toward efficient retrieval and analysis of data and information involves training and takes time. Librarians can and must begin at this elemental stage of partnership to build relationships.

The library must also consider introducing business programming that is quite different from programming in other aspects of library operation. This includes sponsorship of events intended for businesses in the service area. Examples include conducting workshops or seminars on business issues conducted by a local business consultant or university business development center; providing the setting for business meetings or planning sessions; offering "business after hours" social opportunities for business people in the service area; and other activities designed to cast the library in a central and prominent position of support for the business community.

The library will want to consider possibilities related to providing consultation services specifically for the business community. These need not necessarily be provided by librarians themselves, but may be offered by partnering with other community resources. For example, if the market area does not have a "retired executives program," the library may consider developing the service. Patterned after the Federal Service Core of Retired Executives (SCORE) program, the offerings may involve the use of experienced, retired individuals from the community who are willing to serve in an advisor or mentoring role for developing businesses in the community. These services can be particularly helpful to small businesses and provide a good opportunity for the library to partner with individuals who very likely are well known in the community. Another way of providing this same type of service is to become an outreach location for the consulting services available from a university business development center. In whatever way they are provided, effective consultation services greatly enhance the credibility of the business library in the perception of business people.

Another issue in service arises in that, with the advent of the electronic library, a bewildering volume of business information sources has become available. Given that the largest proportion of these sources have been developed in the last half decade or so, business personnel are unlikely to be aware of their existence and even less likely to be able to use them. The librarian, with solid skills in efficient information storage and retrieval honed by applications in other areas, can provide a real, direct service to business partners through training and assistance in using these resources. The library should, therefore, consider offering its own training sessions on available databases, electronic collections, and other assets and how the businessperson can use them.

Location of the Business Library

The traditional "place" for the library has been the physical space of the library building itself. Electronic technology and the preferences of the business user regarding the manner of use of library assets can blur the precise description of the library's actual location. In most public or academic libraries, however, the physical location of the library, a kind of "home base," remains an important part of the product/service package. The physical location is the starting point for building a "critical mass" of information for the business library user.

Another place issue arises from the fact that the library collection may be supplementary to other information resources in the business community. Companies themselves, vendors and suppliers, business consultants such as accountants and lawyers, and other business entities are likely to maintain their own small library collections in their fields of expertise. The public or academic library should seek to supplement, as opposed to duplicating, readily available resources in other accessible locations, by forming library/business collection partnerships that provide access to the assets of both organizations. This may be an opportunity for the library to provide an important business information service that the librarian is ideally suited by training to provide— cataloging of existing resources in the business community regardless of their ownership or physical location. This kind of service may help to cement the importance of the role of the library among the companies it serves because it greatly enhances ability of businesses to access necessary information.

Selling the Business Library

Librarians are generally not interested in taking positions in sales. Not only do they find the techniques of selling unattractive and uncomfortable, but the constant seeking of customers and the continual requirement to convince them of the value of the product or service is an unnatural act. Nonetheless, personal selling is precisely what the business librarian must do, since companies may have never heard of the library product/service concept, may have never used it, and may not understand it even if they are aware of it.

Further, although the "wire-rimmed shusher" librarian is a nearly extinct species, remnants of old-time librarianship are still relatively easy to find in small to medium-sized public and academic libraries. Librarians in these facilities may be products of educational experiences from 20 or 30 years earlier or may have no formal training at all and have simply worked their way through the various ranks of library service in their own library.

In addition to the dislike of selling, and the prejudice for traditional librarianship instilled in training, many librarians remain anti-business because of a distaste for a profit motivation, a belief that businesses intentionally engage in activities designed to damage the environment, a fear of "selling out" to business interests, or bad personal consumer experiences. If there is such an anti-business attitude, business people will quickly perceive it, and react negatively to using the facilities. It is very important, therefore, for the librarian to remember that, like it or not, he or she adds to the personality to the library. The librarian must demonstrate an appreciation for and understanding of the business context as a fundamental requisite of job performance. The librarian must be positive toward free enterprise and sympathetic to the stresses that businesses encounter in their business environments. This attitude must be genuine and consistently portrayed. Businesses must know that their information partner is dependable and supportive of their goals if there is to be any hope that companies will use the library.

Public Relations in a Business Library Context

Critical to implementing an effective business information outreach service is finding ways that the library and its professional staff can become a public part of the business community. This does not mean that librarians have to start up their own businesses or even have extended periods of business employment. But librarians must look for ways to interact with businesses and meet their people. Participation in the activities of chambers of commerce or merchants associations is one good way to achieve this. Being active in the economic development community provides an opportunity for librarians to show that they believe that supporting business activity is important. In such activities, the librarian must always seek to become a source of business information. This may be as simple as volunteering to produce a summary report of area business conditions or providing background information on a particular topic of importance.

Another way of interacting with the business community is to use media outlets to raise the visibility of the library information resources in the corporate arena. Writing, or even just sponsoring, a monthly column on business issues for a local newspaper or finding ways to get library information into company newsletters can go a long way toward establishing library credibility and educate library personnel at the same time.

Finally, it should be noted that, while many communities and academic institutions automatically think of librarians as their information sources, the library is not a "top of mind" option for most business people seeking business information. Gathering business data and seeking needed analysis is much more likely to be done by way of personal networks, material or equipment suppliers, or industry associations. This is primarily a function of awareness and the comfort level of the business user who has repeated contact with these sources. Librarians need to find ways to cause companies to think of them as part of the "solution set" for information provision.

MAKING IT HAPPEN

In summary, establishing an effective marketing program for the business library is a realistic strategic possibility for small and mid-sized libraries that accept three basic principles of marketing programs:

1. The library must identify and accommodate to the needs of the business community through the use of a well-defined product/service concept.

2. Marketing activities must be coordinated so that consistent service delivery is achieved and integrated approaches are implemented.

3. As a result, libraries will derive long-term profits (benefits) from long term satisfaction of customer (business) needs.

Some will recognize these three steps as being a paraphrase of venerable marketing concepts which have served widely and well in a vast array of marketing settings. These concepts can serve the librarian as well in the development of a business library program that is well-received in the business community, if properly applied and joined with the librarian's desires to "make it happen."

NOTES

1. Philip Kotler. *Marketing for Non-Profit Organizations* (Upper Saddle River, NJ: Prentice-Hall, 1982).
2. Joseph P. Grunenwald and Kenneth Traynor. "A Marketing Plan for the Law Library." *Law Library Journal* 1 (1987): 93–101.

Index

About the Authors

RASHELLE S. KARP is Professor in the Department of Library Science at Clarion University of Pennsylvania. She teaches primarily in the areas of collection development, business bibliography, services for differently abled patrons, indexing and abstracting, management, and special libraries.

BERNARD S. SCHLESSINGER is Professor Emeritus from the School of Library and Information Studies at Texas Woman's University in Denton. Recently retired after a 35-year career in information science, he is the author of 125 journal articles, many of them in the area of business, and several books, including the first, second, and third editions of *The Basic Business Library: Core Resources* and the first and second editions (with June H. Schlessinger) of *The Who's Who of Nobel Prize Winners*, both published by Oryx Press.